WAITING IS NOT AN OPTION

THE TRANSITION FROM UNLIMITED GROWTH TO LONG-TERM SURVIVAL

RESILIENCE REQUIRES PREPARATION BEFORE THE CRISIS

DICK RAUSCHER

WAITING IS NOT AN OPTION:
The Transition from Unlimited Growth to Long-Term Survival
RESILIENCE REQUIRES PREPARATION BEFORE THE CRISIS

print ISBN: 978-1-09835-133-5
ebook ISBN: 978-1-09835-134-2

CONTENTS

INTRODUCTION

The Future Isn't What It Used to Be

Like so many today, I have been feeling a sense of despair and a lack of hope as I've watched the climate crisis grow in severity. Storms are intensifying. Forests are burning. Droughts are increasing. Atmospheric rivers are increasing their water content. Rain-bomb flooding grows in severity. Despite the growing severity of these events, I found it difficult to understand why "somebody" wasn't doing "something" to address the growing crisis.

About two years ago, I accepted the sobering reality that *somebody* or *something* simply wasn't going to happen.

I don't like feeling hopeless, frustrated, or powerless. As a mental health therapist, those are not feelings I tolerate for long. So I decided to learn more and get more insight into why no one seemed overly concerned about the growing climate crisis. It felt insane to me that climate scientists were describing global warming as an *existential* crisis, and the rest of the world was essentially ignoring the problem. It reminded me of frogs sitting in a pot of water, ignoring the reality that the water in the pot was slowly warming. And we all know how that story ended!

Two years of research has convinced me that the "future" is not what it used to be, and that future will be far more dire than most people believe— even more alarming than the environmental scientists have been warning. I also learned that global warming is only one of the existential force-multiplier threats that will threaten our future. There are more, *a lot more*. And I realized that I could not remain silent. I had to share what I've learned.

This book is my warning to those who will struggle with the challenge of surviving the future that's coming. And that future is *not* the future that it used to be. Not even close.

But this book also offers a path to what I believe is a realistic hope for those who begin to prepare now for that future.

Change: The Reality That *Everything* Changes

The more I learned, the more it felt as if the whole world was ignoring the reality that *everything* in creation experiences never-ending change. My classes in physics while working for a degree in electrical engineering taught me that *everything* in the universe is continually changing, evolving, and *becoming* something new. And because some changes can be dangerous when they are ignored, we were also taught the simple logic that we need to pay careful attention to the reality of change.

One of my favorite reminders on the reality of change came from the book *Who Moved My Cheese*, by Spencer Johnson in 1998. This quote from his book has hung on the wall of my writing studio since 1998. It's titled "Change Happens."

> *Change Happens*
> *They Keep Moving the Cheese*
> *Anticipate Change*
> *Get Ready for the Cheese to Move*
> *Monitor Change*
> *The Cheese Is Getting Old*
> *Adapt to Change Quickly*
> *The Quicker You Let Go of Old Cheese,*
> *The Sooner You Can Enjoy New Cheese.*
> *Change*
> *Move with the Cheese*

create the resilience they will need to survive those changes and threats when they arrive and threaten the foundations of human culture.

I am under no illusion that the concepts and ideas in this book will save my life. But *I am* hopeful that they could help people in the younger generations survive the future challenges and massive existential changes that they are inheriting. For them, the future isn't going to be what it used to be, and their future survival *will require intentional preparation* to begin *now* for the life-altering changes that are coming. Only intentional preparation will create the resilience they will need to survive the future they are inheriting. And that future is coming far sooner than most people in the world are prepared to survive.

A Dark Future and Two Hopeful Paths

As my research continued, I realized that global warming and climate change was only one of the existential threats facing us as a species. In fact, it wasn't even the most urgent critical threat. As I dug in a bit deeper, I realized that the nine force-multiplier threats and economic triggers described in Part 2 chapters of this book each have the potential, *in the near future*, to create the social and civil collapse of human culture and human civilization as we know it. I also realized that waiting to begin preparing for the massive changes and existential threats that are coming was *not* an option.

To create the resilience that we will need to survive as a species, it became clear that not only do we need to begin preparing *now* for the massive existential changes that are coming, but *now* is already borderline *too late*. The massive life-altering changes are not only unavoidable but I now believe they are coming far sooner than most people think. Those realizations created in me an overwhelming feeling of despair and hopelessness.

The future I had researched in Part 2 was so overwhelmingly dark and unavoidable, I knew I couldn't drop the project unless I could find some realistic way to embrace a hopeful future. It took time and more research, but I eventually concluded that there are two paths that could offer humanity a realistically hopeful future. Those two paths toward a hopeful future were the incentive that led to the writing of this book. Both paths toward hope will be challenging, but both paths are realistic.

Path 1 is the *intentional* taming and evolution of the collective, immature, primitive ego-consciousness of humanity and its early childhood conditioning that we will explore in Chapters 1 and 2. The immature collective primitive ego-consciousness of humanity is directly responsible for creating each of the existential threats in Part 2. Unless, and until, we tame and evolve our collective primitive ego-consciousness; and our greed-based business-as-usual path toward profit and unlimited economic expansion, humanity *will* continue on the path to extinction.

Path 2 is Localization: creating self-reliant, sustainable local communities and local economies. In Chapter 10, we will explore local communities based on well-being, not greed and growth.

We will explore these two paths of hope in detail in the pages that follow. The concepts included in this book are meant to offer the younger generations insight into the severity of the problems they will face as they cope with the growing reality of a future that will grow darker every day as our global human society continues its business-as-usual quest for unlimited economic expansion and wealth accumulation. But more importantly, I wrote this book to offer them the two realistic, hopeful paths for their survival I described above.

The hopeful future, and the two paths I urge younger readers to embrace in this book, are both offered as a future created by science and data, not the "Tinker Bell thinking" that is so prevalent in the media today. Because the data is changing rapidly, and not for good, I urge all readers of this book to confirm the data I will include in the pages that follow to ensure that you are using the latest up-to-date information.

Also, as you do the challenging work that is required on the two paths of hope—and as those around you dismissively label you as "alarmist"—keep in mind that the complacency in the world around you *is not real*, it is unconscious *denial* and an intentional *lack of attention*. Data matters. Science matters.

Facts matter. Truth matters. If you stay grounded in those important realities, it will give you the information and courage you will need as you prepare for the future existential life-altering challenges and changes.

A Brief Overview of the Book

In Part 1, we will take a look at primitive ego; how it was formed, the dangerous reality distorting bent-nickel beliefs that unconsciously influence and continue to support primitive ego thinking. And we will learn what we will need to do to *intentionally* tame, evolve, awaken, and mature our immature collective childhood primitive ego consciousness.

We created the existential threats we will explore in Part 2, and only we can create the solution each of those threats require; and seeking those solutions must begin with the intentional taming, maturing, and evolution of our collective primitive ego human consciousness. As Einstein warned, attempting to solve a problem using the same consciousness and thinking process used to create that problem will rarely work.

We must become a more mature, awakened, self-aware species, or we will not survive. And that awakening and evolution of our collective human consciousness must begin *now*. We have set in motion the force-multipliers, existential threats, and economic triggers of Part 2 that are all but certain to create social collapse and end life as we know it on this planet. Surviving that social collapse will require aggressive and intentional action now. Waiting is no longer an option.

In Part 2, Chapters 3 to 9, we will focus on the primary and secondary force-multipliers that *will* have the ability to trigger social and civil collapse. They represent the triggers of collapse that are *inevitable* in the very near future, and each of them *will* eventually create massive disruptive change. We will look at the powerful existential force multiplier threats that are all but sure to create the social and civil collapse of human culture and human civilization in the near future, including why they are already irreversible and why they *will* lead to the social and civil collapse of human culture and human society as we know it. These seven chapters will illustrate clearly why the successful taming of our collective primitive ego human consciousness and the creation of the sustainable, self-reliant local communities of Chapter 10 are critically important and necessary.

In Part 3, Chapter 10, we will see that self-reliant local communities are a realistic hope, not Tinker Bell thinking.

I believe creating self-reliant, sustainable, self-sufficient local communities and local economies could be the best, and most realistic, hope for the future of humanity on our planet. We will look carefully at why these self-reliant local communities will require the insights, wisdom, and intentional taming of their collective community consciousness if their long-term goal is to become a viable, long-term, successful option for the future of humanity.

I wrote this book based on what I believe could be a source of "real" hope for the younger generations as they prepare for the sobering realities and massive changes I am convinced are coming. In Chapter 10, we will explore in-depth the creation of these viable, self-reliant, sustainable local communities and their local economies.

All ten chapters *are* the golden arch of this book. And each chapter will support the belief that the future of humanity on this planet will depend on how well we can embrace the concepts contained in this book. It's time humanity evolved and matured its collective consciousness. It's time we became a mature, self-aware, awakened species. In the words of Howard Thurman, "You can't stand in the midst of the world and struggle for fundamental change unless you are standing in your own space and looking for change within."

Embracing Change Within: A Helpful Metaphor

About five years ago, I read the book *Switch: How to Change Things When Change Is Hard*, by Chip and Dan Heath. The authors used the helpful metaphor of a rider on an elephant. The rider represented left-hemisphere logic. The elephant represented right-hemisphere emotions; what I have always assumed reflect the immature, unevolved emotional primitive ego and the unconscious conditioning of early childhood.

They pointed out that change requires clarity. Until the rider has crystal-clear clarity as to the exact goals or changes it wants to achieve, it will find itself hopelessly lost, caught in the morass of ambiguity and too many choices. When this happens, the rider becomes immobilized by *decision paralysis.*

Their point was simple. To create long-term change, we need *clarity about the critical moves that will be required to achieve the change* we want to achieve. Stated simply, until we have the courage to change ourselves, and until we have internal clarity on *precisely* the change we want to embrace, creative and sustainable external change *will never happen.* The rational rider of the elephant will be overcome by *decision paralysis,* and the emotional elephant (our immature primitive ego) will turn back to the same old, same old routines and habits. Change will die, stillborn. Business as usual and the march toward extinction will continue.

A Final Reminder Before You Begin Chapter 1: Do Your Research

As I mentioned earlier, the objective of this book is to prepare for change to create resilience. I did not write this book to prove to the reader that global climate change is real or human-caused. Or that the force-multipliers of Part 2 are valid or not. Those realities are well supported by rapidly growing scientific facts that support those realities. I will offer some statistics and facts to illustrate and support the concepts presented in this book, but my recommendation is, "Always do your own research." This admonition will become increasingly important as the spin, distortions, and misrepresentations inevitably increase in the coming years.

The greed and power of those profiting from the continued use of fossil fuels and neoliberal global capitalism will continue to grow. The distortions and spin they *will* create to protect their power and wealth *will also* increase. Do your own research. Follow the facts. Look at the research the climate scientists are doing. Truth matters! Embracing a truth that encourages you to prepare for the massive changes that *are* coming could save your life, the lives of your children, your grandchildren, and the children of future generations. Truth, facts, and data matter.

Change is inevitable, but *we* created this world, and perhaps *we* can create the next one more sustainably if we can admit that we need to change and mature the way we think. I wrote the book based on the need to evolve, mature, and tame our collective primitive ego-consciousness by becoming more self-aware.[1] Until we intentionally tame our collective primitive ego thinking, we will simply re-create another future based on greed, unlimited growth, the intentional ignorance of denial, immature *self*-focused thinking, and the dangerous illusion that we are separate from the rest of creation.

That is, of course, assuming we survive as a species as this world comes to an end.

I wrote this book to encourage all of us to begin the work of intentionally taming our immature collective primitive ego thinking and to begin building sustainable, self-reliant, local communities. To be successful, these local "seed" communities will need to fully embrace a taming of their immature collective primitive ego-consciousness. We are not separate from nature. We are interconnected and interdependent on the eco-systems and natural resources of the entire planet. The sustainable well-being of the local communities in Part 3 will need to be the primary social contract embraced by these local communities if their goal of survival and the survival of humanity itself is to be successful.

Any local community that retains even remnants of untamed primitive ego thinking will not survive.

I believe this moment in time is humanity's last opportunity to redefine hope and the viable future of the human species. If we fail to rebuild human civilization on the principles of a fully tamed, mature, and enlightened human consciousness, our future on this planet *will* come to an end. The future will *not* be what it used to be. The evidence surrounds us. We need to embrace

---

1   See Chapter 2.

the simple reality of that evidence. History is warning us that attempting to rebuild a successful human civilization using the current collective primitive ego thinking and its early childhood conditioning is impossible. It is too unevolved and immature.

That, in a nutshell, is the golden arch of the book.

I hope you have the courage to continue reading. Our collective future depends on it. And *your* future depends on it. We have time to prepare for the changes that are coming *if we begin that preparation now.*

The following quotation captures my thoughts about our future and the social, civil, and economic collapse that I believe is coming. In the words of the former leader of the Soviet Union, Vladimir Lenin, "There are decades where nothing happens, and there are weeks where decades happen" (David Stockman, 2020).

The big-picture scenarios of change presented in this book are the "weeks where decades happen" kind of events. The force-multipliers of Part 2 began at glacial speed with the seeds of collapse being sown over years, if not decades. The problem, of course, is we never know where the spark or black swan event will come from that triggers the avalanche. But the economic, social, and civil collapse avalanche *is* coming. I see no realistic way to avoid it.

I believe it is our moment, our destiny as a species, to awaken the collective consciousness of humanity and begin the creation of a more local, more evolved, more sustainable, more mature, more self-reliant, and wiser human culture on our planet.

And here is a quotation from the movie *Brave* based on a story written by Brenda Chapman that embraces the concept I tried to capture in this book:

There are those who say that our fate is something beyond our command.
That our destiny is not our own.
But I know better.

Our fate lives within us.
You only have to be brave enough to see it.

This quote captures the courage and motivation that will be needed to embrace our destiny; our future. I offer this quote hoping that it might encourage the younger generations of readers to embrace the courage to see their future and destiny and begin *now* to embrace the creation of their own small self-reliant communities. As they create the transition from unlimited growth to long-term survival, I believe that it could save not only *their* lives but the future of the human species on this planet.

Preparation is always required *before* a crisis in order to create the resilience that will be needed for survival *after* the crisis arrives.

Before You Begin: A Final Note for All Readers

I wrote this book to offer those in the younger generations a realistic and hopeful vision of a future that could help them survive the massive changes that are coming. Preparation for the future that is coming requires:

- The ability to *pay attention* to the realities happening in the world where we live; in other words, to stay focused on the big-picture existential force-multipliers. Don't get caught up in the day-to-day media news details.

- Understanding the *long-term impacts* and system interconnections of those big-picture existential force-multiplier realities,

- Assessing the primary and secondary force-multipliers in Part 2, and *their ability to impact the vulnerable systems* we have created as human civilization,

- Realistically *assessing what self-reliant skills and resources will be required* to survive a future that will be far more challenging and dangerous than few in the developed world have experienced in recent generations,

- Most importantly, *find ways to survive the massive changes* that are coming as human cultures and human civilization as we know it begins to collapse when the primary and secondary force-multipliers, and the existential threats they represent, begin to work together to systemically ensure that collapse.

When you have finished reading the book, my hope is you will have the foundational wisdom, encouragement, and knowledge to create the self-reliant, local "seed" communities that will pave the road to a human culture, and human civilization, that is sustainable, just, and compassionate. A world that protects our planet and sees all of creation as a "thou" to be protected, not an "it" to be consumed.

Evolving and maturing our collective human consciousness will never be finished. The threat that humanity could quickly revert back to immature, primitive, unevolved thinking will always require *attention* and the *intentional* taming of our human primitive ego-consciousness. We can never let down our guard and assume that ignorance has been removed from our human consciousness.

As I said above, any local community that retains even remnants of untamed primitive ego thinking will not survive long-term.

PART 1:
PRIMITIVE EGO: WE ARE THE PROBLEM

CHAPTER 1

Definition of Primitive Ego

This chapter will explore the fundamental beliefs and thinking process of the unconscious primitive ego and its early childhood conditioning listed below; the unconscious, immature, unevolved early childhood primitive ego-thinking process resides in humanity's collective consciousness. We will see how this collective unconsciousness thinking embedded in humanity's collective consciousness created the existential force-multiplier threats in Part 2 that threaten the future of humanity and our planet. The force-multiplier threats in Part 2 are not the problem. They are symptoms. We are the problem. We created the existential threats. *We* are responsible for the pain, suffering, aggression, conflict, and violence that our collective primitive, immature, unevolved thinking creates in the world.

This book's primary golden arch is the urgent need to *intentionally* tame, awaken, mature, and evolve humanity's collective primitive ego consciousness. And *waiting* to do this work is *not* an option.

We are the problem: fundamental beliefs and illusions embedded in the collective consciousness of humanity:

a. "What's in it for me" **greed**.

b. Need to be **"right"** (aggressive arrogance, extreme cognitive dissonance/confirmation bias).

c. Inability to replace **"me"** thinking with **"we"** thinking (compassion, mutuality, cooperation).

d. I want what I want **when I want it**.

e. **Blames** others for *our* feelings (inability to own our feelings).

f. Ignorance regarding the **danger of exponential growth** (e.g., COVID-19).

g. A lack of interconnected, interdependent **systemic thinking**.

h. Survival-of-the-fittest thinking.

i. Black versus white, **zero-sum thinking** (*You* can't have that, it's *mine!*) (I win, you lose).

j. An exaggerated aggressive, narcissistic self-focused sense of **entitlement**.

k. An inability to connect short-term choices with long-term consequences.

l. The **fear of change** (uncertainty, not knowing).

m. The unending, obsessive desire for **more.**

n. The need for power "over" rather than power "with."

o. The illusion of separateness from the rest of creation (I'm a unique *"me"*).

p. The inability to embrace long-term thinking.

This chapter, on the *definition of primitive ego,* and the next chapter, on *taming the primitive ego,* will provide the bedrock concepts that define two of the book's golden arch concepts. Primitive ego thinking created all of the existential force-multiplier threats, challenges, and economic triggers that threaten the likely future collapse of social and civil order in human culture and the growing potential extinction of our human species. Understanding humanity's collective primitive ego-consciousness is critically important in understanding and making sense of how we got to this dangerous and unstable time in human history. Chapter 2 will examine each of the existential force-multiplier threats and economic triggers created by our collective primitive ego human consciousness and its immature thinking process. We will discuss the fundamental beliefs and thinking process of the unconscious, immature, unevolved collective primitive ego-consciousness of humanity.

Golden Arch Reality #1: Every existential force-multiplier threat challenging the future of human culture that we will explore in Part 2, including the survival of the human species, *has been directly created by the collective human primitive ego-consciousness of our unconscious inner child.*

Golden Arch Reality #2: Until this primitive, early childhood ego of our inner child is intentionally tamed, matured, and evolved, it will continue to be one of the most potent and destructive existential forces threatening the human species' future on this planet.

What Is the Primitive Ego? Where Did It Come From? What is Our Inner Child?

The primitive ego of our inner child is understood best as the archive of *all* the experiences, beliefs, opinions, fears, expectations, assumptions, survival skills *(simplistic early childhood ways of keeping the world safe)*, habits, illusions, and defenses that our early childhood psyche learned and adopted by the time we reached seven to eight years old. This is the approximate age in childhood that our rapidly evolving human mind coalesces and morphs into that of an "internalized object," a *felt* sense of being a unique *me*. A *me* that is unique and separate from the rest of the universe *(the illusion of separateness).*

When our psyche's self-identity or sense of *self* slowly evolves into this feeling that we are a unique *me* separate from everything else in the universe; all of the beliefs, fears, survival skills, expectations, and assumptions that our primitive psyche has created, learned, or adapted to cope with our experience of early childhood, become the unconscious primitive ego of our inner child. The unconscious *inner child* that resides in each of us.

If we want to survive as a species on this planet, understanding the collective primitive ego of humanity and learning to *intentionally* tame, mature, and evolve that collective human primitive ego-consciousness is unquestionably the most primary, critical, and existential goal facing humanity. Waiting to *do* this work is not an option, nor is waiting to *begin* this work. We have wasted almost four decades ignoring climate scientists' dire warnings regarding the growing dangers of global warming and climate change. We are now out of time. And the climate crisis is only "one" of the black swan force-multiplier challenges, economic triggers, and existential threats in Part 2 that are currently threatening the future of our species on this planet! We urgently need to mature and evolve our collective human consciousness and begin *now* to prepare for the massive changes that *are* coming.

In this chapter, we will focus on the developmental *formation* of our inner-child and its primitive ego. Understanding the material in this chapter will be essential when we move to Chapter 2, where we will learn how to tame the collective primitive ego consciousness of humanity intentionally. The failure to successfully tame the collective primitive ego consciousness of humanity will, *more than any other existential threat or event,* lead to the all-but-certain collapse of social and civil order and compromise humanity's future survival as a viable species on this planet.

Formation of Our Inner-Child and Its Primitive Ego

Growing up as young children, we learn a lot about life. What's safe and fun, and what's dangerous and what's hurtful. We learn to *know* when we are good and when we are bad. Over time, we develop survival skills to take care of ourselves. We learn many survival skills as children that are in no small measure based on the home and family environment we experienced growing up. However, some survival skills are common to virtually everyone.

Splitting or Dualistic Thinking

For example, to keep the world simple and more understandable, we learn very early in childhood to split the world into the simple dualistic categories of either/or. This dualistic splitting skill of black and white, good or bad, right or wrong, either/or thinking is a typical early developmental stage of early childhood. It's often referred to as all-or-nothing, zero-sum thinking. The concept is that for someone to win, someone else has to lose.

Virtually all of the survival skills we develop in early childhood tend to be simplistic and primitive. However, we should not assume that primitive and simplistic are bad or wrong. Black-and-white splitting was extremely helpful for us in early childhood. It was *primitive* only in the sense that this survival skill was adopted by us before our minds had developed or matured. And it was *simplistic* only in the sense that we had to keep our survival skills simple if they were going to be useful for us in early childhood.

Of course, the danger is attempting to use this kind of immature, simplistic "primitive" black-and-white thinking when trying to solve the more sophisticated and complex adult world's problems and challenges. Splitting in the adult world almost always creates conflicts between those who believe they are right, and those who think they are wrong. *The primitive ego need to be "right" is the primary creator of virtually all of the conflict, violence, and suffering we see in the world today and historically.*

As we will see below, middlepath thinking (*the ability to intentionally search for the truths on both sides of every issue*) is a far more evolved, mature, adult, and useful thinking process when the problems and issues challenge us in a more sophisticated and complex, modern, adult world.

Early Childhood: Pleasure and Pain Come from the World and We Are Powerless

Because the formation of our inner-child psyche and its primitive ego takes place throughout the first six or seven years of childhood, our inner child and its primitive ego tend to reflect "all" of the learnings and experiences of early childhood; the good and the bad, the helpful and the unhelpful. For example, as young children, we learned that everything came to us from the world, and we *knew* we were virtually powerless. We were unable to get out of our crib and get what we wanted or needed, and we did not yet have the words to ask for what we wanted or needed, so we quickly developed the survival skill of opening our mouths and screaming until someone brought it to us. Because we wanted *what* we wanted, *when* we wanted it, we continued to scream until someone brought it to us. We were often angry and impatient in that "wanting" and "waiting." But in early childhood, it was a very effective way to get what we wanted.

Since most of the survival skills we learned in early childhood were designed primarily to keep us feeling safe and happy, the primitive ego of our inner child knew over time that embedding a sense of impatience and anger in our screaming was helpful whenever others dared to make us unhappy or wait. As we grew older, we used that anger to tell the world in no uncertain terms, "Don't even think about" taking our doll or truck away while playing with it, or attempting to withhold something from us that we wanted. Our primitive ego did *not* like the word "no." And it did *not* like to wait.

We *were* learning to survive childhood!

At the same time, we *knew* obedience and pleasing our caretakers, the *authorities* in our lives, was also necessary. We learned to be *obedient to authority*, but our primitive ego still did not like the word "no"!

I'm sure you're beginning to see the primitive and simplistic primitive-ego behaviors that we and others manifest as adults. *Intentionally* paying attention and becoming *self-aware* to these feelings and behaviors when *we (the collective consciousness of humanity)* manifest or unconsciously "knee-jerk" them into the world is the first step in learning to tame our own primitive ego. Seeing these feelings and behavior in others is easy. Seeing them in ourselves is more challenging. We will explore this concept in more detail in Chapter 2.

Visualizing Our Primitive Ego as a Human "Operating System"

A very useful metaphor is to imagine the primitive ego of our inner child as our invisible "operating system." Similar to the operating system on a computer, the only time we see our computer operating system is for a brief moment at startup. After that fleeting glimpse, the operating system becomes invisible, or "unconscious." *Every application, every document, and every visible or invisible function that your computer performs from that point on is controlled by the invisible operating system.* Your computer operating system functions out of sight in the background, *but your computer would be unable to perform without it.*

To understand your unconscious primitive ego, it's helpful to think about it as similar to your computer's invisible operating system. In much the same way, your inner-child psyche's unconscious primitive ego is your invisible human operating system. Our inner-child's memory contains everything we experienced and learned in childhood. We don't consciously see it functioning in the background of our life. Yet virtually everything that we do as an adult is unconsciously influenced or controlled by our inner child's unconscious primitive ego. *Until we learn to awaken and make this part of our psyche more visible and conscious through intentional growth in self-awareness, many of the choices we make in our adult life will continue to be unconsciously controlled by the immature, self-focused, dualistic black-and-white thinking process of a seven-year-old child!*

Until we become *intentionally* self-aware and begin to awaken our thinking to that of a more evolved and mature level of consciousness, our unconscious inner-child and all of its childhood beliefs and learnings will continue to *unconsciously split* the world into dualist categories of me versus the rest of the world, right from wrong, and good from bad! In other words, we will look like adults. We will even behave like adults *most* of the time. *But emotionally, we will be seven-year-old children "pretending" to look and act like adults.* If you are having trouble with this concept, think about the last time someone told you that you were *positively* and *emphatically* wrong! You were stupid. Or *"no,"* you can't *do* that. Or *"no,"* you can't *have* that!

When the beliefs that make up our primitive ego's unconscious self-identity are threatened, our primitive ego energy will come into full view! And all of that primitive emotional, negative, survival-of-the-fittest energy of childhood will be *unconsciously and aggressively "knee-jerked"* into the world! When that happens, the dualistic thinking of good and bad, right and wrong, will escalate conflict and violence. Our inner child will insist we are *right.* We will angrily explain in detail why the other person is wrong. And we will quickly add anger to our response if the other person continues to disagree with us. When we become aware of this *unconscious knee-jerk* energy coming from *ourselves*, don't judge, just pay attention. When we learn to *intentionally* pay attention, we are learning to tame our unconscious primitive ego intentionally. We are becoming less aggressive, reactive, and *more* conscious and aware. We are learning to *choose* our response to outside stimuli.

Our consciousness is evolving.

Despite the fact that it is rarely helpful having a 7-year-old inner-child attempting to unconsciously control our adult lives, the sobering reality is *that's exactly what most adults in the world today are doing.* Until we do the work of becoming intentionally *self-aware* of the energy we are sending into the world, our primitive ego's struggle for psychic survival and internal wholeness will never end. Stated simply, until we learn to *intentionally* tame our primitive ego and *intentionally* become self-aware (*of the beam in our own eye*), the unconscious primitive ego of our inner child will continue to use the immature thinking process we developed in childhood; the immature thinking process of childhood that *we will never fully or successfully transcend.* As a result, *we*, along with most of humanity, will collectively continue to be a species that insists on using an immature, unevolved, reflexively unconscious primitive ego to function in the day-to-day world. In metaphoric terms, that means that our average level of psychological intelligence is equivalent to that of rubbing two sticks together to make a fire so we can have hot coffee for breakfast each morning.

Primitive ego thinking is a form of species ignorance that we can no longer safely tolerate! As I stated above, until this primitive, early childhood ego of our inner child is intentionally tamed and evolved, *it will continue to be one of the most powerful and destructive forces threatening the extinction of the human species on this planet.*

You will see this simple reality when we examine the dangerous force-multipliers, existential threats, and economic triggers in Part 2 *created by immature primitive ego thinking.*

"We" are the problem.

24

The Birth of Self: The Birth of
Our Unconscious Primitive Ego

The primitive ego-consciousness that we will refer to in this book is simply the unconscious *primitive ego* of the unconscious 7-year-old *"inner-child"* that resides in each of us. As young children, we used the words "me" or "mine" to refer to those things we believe to be our own personal possessions. But their use subtly changed meaning when we refer to ourselves as "me" or "mine "after "me" becomes an internalized self-object. When this shift happens, our "unique and separate self" is born. We became *emotionally separate* from the rest of the created universe.

When we became aware that we are a unique and separate **me,** when we realized there is no other **me** like **me** in the whole universe, that is the moment we gave birth to *self. When that birthing of self happened, virtually all of the beliefs, opinions, fears, survival skills, expectations, habits, illusions, defenses, and assumptions that our primitive psyche created, learned, or adapted to cope with our experiences of childhood begin to slip quietly into our unconscious and become the primitive ego of our inner child.* From that moment on, our inner child determined who we could trust, what and who is dangerous, how to protect ourselves, how to get our needs met, how to toilet, how to take a bath, how to get dressed, what brings pleasure, how to avoid criticism, how to protect our sense of self, and the many thousands of other experiences, insights, and learnings we gleaned from childhood.

Most of our automatic, unconscious knee-jerk responses that make up our adult personality or self are simply the *survival skills* of our inner child becoming visible.

We continue to grow physically after seven to eight years of age. However, because very few of us make an *intentional commitment* to grow in self-aware-ness, we will remain unaware that the unconscious primitive ego of our inner child is the invisible operating system continuing to control our adult lives. That is, of course, until someone tells you no, be quiet, you're wrong, no you can't have that cookie, no you have to wait till next week, someone tells you you're a jerk, you're stupid, or you're an idiot, you did that wrong...you get the point.

Fundamental Problems of Inner Child and Primitive Ego Thinking

a. Its beliefs are not always accurate; they're immature and often rigid and well defended.

b. They manifest a high level of self ("me") focus.

c. They're designed to keep life simple, safe, pleasurable, good, right— that is, no nuance or gray, only black and white.

d. We may look like mature adults on the outside, but inside we continue to behave emotionally and cognitively as immature seven-year-old children.

e. When we feel threatened, we respond with aggressive, automatic *knee-jerk reactions* from our inner child's unconscious primitive ego. We continue to split the world into right and wrong, the source of most hurtful judgmentalism.

f. We tend to want what we want when we want it, and we tend to be impatient and exhibit very little ability to delay gratification.

g. The primitive ego of our unconscious inner child will get angry when someone says we are wrong. When they do, we will tend to imperatively present our beliefs as "THE" truth. We will tend to get angry and defensive when our beliefs are challenged, criticized, or when we are told "no."

In other words, as we do the work to intentionally become more self-aware, it will become clear that our childhood survival skills may have been beneficial in childhood, but if we continue using them as adults, they will cause us, and those around us, a lot of problems. Until we intentionally learn to develop a deeper, more enlightened (tamed) mature self-awareness, we will continue to journey through our lives with our unconscious inner child running the show.

As we begin to become more intentionally self-aware, the sober and frightening reality will be the realization that most adult humans alive today who we interact with every day will essentially all manifest the emotional consciousness and survival skills of a seven-year-old when they are under stress. Because no seven-year-old has the life experience or insights required to live a happy and productive adult life, we will begin to understand why so many of us are depressed and unhappy; and why there is so much narcissism, aggressive anger, conflict, and violence in the world.

Happiness in Life Requires an Intentionally Tamed Primitive Ego

Happiness is more easily achieved when (a) we have learned to live fully self-aware in the present moment and fully embrace the reality of "what is"; (b) we awaken to the reality that living in the past, emotionally and mentally trapped in the reality-distorting primitive ego of our unconscious inner child, is not an effective way to achieve happiness and success in life; and (c) we understand that primitive ego thinking will always leave us metaphorically and emotionally struggling with both feet mired deep in the emotional mud of childhood. Enlightenment, happiness, maturity, and an awakened and evolved adult consciousness all require the *intentional* taming of our primitive ego and the *intentional* growth of a fully conscious awakened self-awareness. There is no other viable path to enlightenment and happiness.

The intentional taming, evolving, maturing, and awakening of our primitive ego and intentional growth in self-awareness is critical. Until humanity's collective primitive ego consciousness is intentionally tamed, human civilization will continue to be defined by a seven- to eight-year-old child's level of emotional consciousness. It's no wonder the future of human civilization is facing possible extinction. I often wonder how we even got this far without destroying ourselves as a species. The conclusion I've come to is a golden arch concept of this book. *Immature primitive ego thinking is survivable in an isolated, immature human culture, but it's not survivable long term in a complex, systemically interconnected, interdependent, mobile, high-tech, global human culture.*

Digging Deeper:
The More Subtle Aspects of Primitive Ego Thinking:

1. The Primitive Ego Survival Skill of
Black- and-White Splitting, Tribalism, and Blame

As we explored above, one of the more basic dangers of childhood is the survival skill of black-and-white splitting. But there are other, more subtle, and dangerous unconscious consequences of splitting in the modern world. One is the tendency of splitting to create a sense of *otherness* and the harmful judgementalism we create when we *split* the world into categories of *us versus them*. The primitive ego too often emotionally experiences "otherness" categories of *"they"* or *"them"* as the enemy—some*one* or some group of potentially dangerous people.

This splitting of the world into them versus us is the root cause of tribalism. Tribalism, in a world that embraces splitting, is the foundation of ultra-nationalism, self-righteous competing religions, patriarchal sexism, all forms of institutionalism, racism, and other judgmental ethnic and homophobic labeling—to name only a few. Unfortunately, splitting and tribalism are endemic and common in a human culture that embraces immature primitive ego thinking. An immature primitive ego-driven culture splits virtually every part of its world into either/or categories. Even football games and other competitive sports are a form of tribalism that results from primitive ego splitting.

"Judgmentalism" also comes from the survival skill of splitting because the primitive ego believes that its tribe is special, that its tribe embraces *the truth,* and that the members of its tribe passionately believe that the tribe's definition of truth is *right.* Those who agree with our primitive-ego tribal beliefs are emotionally experienced as friends. Those who disagree are *wrong* and are angrily experienced as the dangerous and feared enemy—dangerous others who cannot be trusted. A primitive ego-based tribal culture believes safety requires that it must maintain control of others by establishing a vertical "power-over" relationship with them, a primitive survival-of-the-fittest kind of relationship.

When a primitive ego-based religious or political tribal culture believes that its religious or political tribal beliefs are imperative truth, its members tend to exhibit a very limited level of self-awareness. When self-awareness is low, the fragmented, or split off, shadow material of individuals in the tribe often gets unconsciously projected as derision or blame onto others; at times, even on other members of its own tribe. Through the process of *projection and blaming*, members of other tribes are unconsciously assumed to, in some way, embody the negative or shadow energy of the disowned and fragmented parts of the primitive ego's own tribal members. For example, we see this tendency very clearly in the dialogue between political parties (tribes). If we disown our own aggressive tendencies because we are not comfortable with them, we will unconsciously project our aggression onto others. In other words, "they" or "others" become the "aggressive" enemy to be feared and guarded against, *not us*!

The tribal "otherness" that comes from the primitive ego survival skills of splitting and projection are the root cause of virtually all of the world's violence and conflict. "We" are the good guys; "they" are the bad guys; the enemy! Either/or splitting creates the categories of right or wrong, good or bad, friend or enemy, and safe or dangerous.

In a more evolved and conscious human culture—a culture that (a) has intentionally tamed its collective primitive ego consciousness; (b) is awakened and mature; and (c) *intentionally* and deliberately embraced a deep level of self-awareness—would tend to manifest a high level of individual and tribal compassion, mutuality, and cooperation. They would use middlepath thinking and consensus decision-making; in other words, they would recognize the simple truth that there is *always* truth on both sides of every issue. They would also acknowledge the reality that no tribe or individual is smart enough to be "right" or "wrong" 100% of the time.

Until we reach this critical mass of intentionally awakened individuals in our global tribal cultures, the level of violence and terrorism we are experiencing in tribal conflict globally will continue to exist and increase. This increase in violence is called war.

We are the problem!

2. Embracing Change: Understanding Primitive Ego as an Iceberg

Until we have intentionally tamed the childhood consciousness of our immature primitive ego and its early childhood conditioning, our unconscious inner child and its powerful primitive (*early childhood*) ego will continue to be in control of our lives. A way to think about the unconscious primitive ego and how it unconsciously controls our daily lives is using the iceberg metaphor. In the eighteenth and nineteenth centuries, the captains of sailing ships often reported in their logs observing icebergs drifting in one direction even though gale-force winds were blowing in the opposite direction. They were unaware then that more than 90% of the iceberg was underwater, where ocean currents were far more powerful than the surface winds.

Anyone who has ever attempted to change their behavior by force of will through a New Year's resolution has undoubtedly experienced the power of the unconscious primitive ego. No matter how sincere the conscious "intention" to change (the gale-force wind), the unconscious beliefs and emotions of the primitive ego (the invisible ocean currents) will ultimately determine the course of our lives and how we will behave. Using the rider and elephant metaphor in the introduction, the elephant will always win.

Until we learn that the healing we need is embracing the internal work of *intentional* growth in self-awareness, we will devote most, or all of our life energy searching the external world for the gale-force wind "stuff" that we believe will change our lives, eliminate the pain, and make us happy.

Money, relationships, fame, possessions ("stuff"), and "success" are the familiar places our primitive ego will look for happiness; addictions are another.

The primitive ego will spend its life on this false path. Over time we will grow to become overly concerned with the speck in our neighbor's eye while unable to see the log in our own. We will attempt to maintain or increase our self-esteem by criticizing and judging others to feel superior. We will blame *others* for *our* feelings, a process that will cause unending conflict in our relationships and will virtually always leave us feeling powerless, angry, and victimized. We will struggle for vertical power over others, and we will use projection (blame) to feel superior. These common survival skills of early childhood reflect the current paradigm or world view of our world's primitive-ego-created human cultures, nations, religious, and political tribes.

We are the problem!

3. Changing a Belief is
Very Difficult for the Primitive Ego

Once we have developed an internalized sense of *self,* it is challenging to make changes in our self-identity. But until we do, no energy from our essential or true *self* can enter the world without first going through the reality distorting beliefs and illusions of our inner child's primitive ego. *Our primitive ego beliefs control our behaviors; therefore, our behaviors and actions often reflect our unconscious primitive ego beliefs.* If we believe we are superior and "right," we will assume we are better and smarter than *others,* and our behaviors and attitude will reflect that superiority.

Actual reality can never be contained in a word or a belief because *all* ego beliefs are created by the mind and cannot reflect true reality. *Reality is never static; it is always evolving, changing, and becoming.* As a result, reality can never be captured in a single word, belief, or concept; *it can only be experienced and reflected by an evolved, mature, observing adult consciousness.*

The primary danger with *all* ego beliefs is the primitive ego assumption; they represent both "absolute reality" *and* "absolute truth." When we assume our beliefs, views, and opinions reflect absolute truth, we can no longer effectively hear or see other realities. Any new information or input that challenges our self-image, world view, or beliefs is selectively ignored or distorted. This process is called cognitive dissonance. In other words, we are only able to accept input that supports our beliefs. We may have no memory of where those beliefs originally came from, but any information that challenges those beliefs will be ignored, and make us defensive, angry, and aggressive. We will aggressively assume that *we*, and our views and *opinions*, are right. Any input that challenges the "absolute truth" of our existing beliefs will be aggressively rejected or ignored... *because our immature primitive ego, and its early childhood conditioning, does not like to be told that it is wrong.*

I refer to this sobering inability to learn and take in new information as *intentional ignorance. This condition* reflects the consciousness of a vast majority of the humans on our planet.

We are the problem!

4. Our Childhood Experiences Are Important When Taming the Primitive Ego

Our childhood experiences are important when we begin the process of *intentionally* taming our primitive ego. If we got the necessary emotional resources from our primary caregivers—such as attention, unconditional love, empathy, and affirmation—our self-esteem would be stable and positive. We will be well prepared to continue growing into a mature adult ego comfortable with the anxiety of paradox, gray thinking, uncertainty, and not knowing. Our beliefs will be more flexible and open to modification or change. In other words, our ability to grow and learn will be mature and flexible.

Those who are fortunate enough to have experienced a functional, nurturing childhood will find it easier to achieve self-awareness. Our inner-child psyche will move into adolescence and adulthood relatively whole and unfragmented. That means we will have less unconscious shadow material to project onto others as blame or judgment. The task of awakening and becoming aware of our primitive ego will be relatively easy. Growth in self-awareness will come relatively easily. Our adult observing ego will mature relatively quickly. Our primitive ego will reflect an optimal stage of human development.

Conversely, the more a person was treated as an object instead of respected as a little "person" in childhood, the more a child would have experienced emotional and psychological wounding, trauma, and bonding and attachment difficulties in early childhood. Their inner-child psyche and sense of "self" will tend to be rigid, fragmented, and unintegrated.

If our childhood caregivers deprived us of the emotional resources we needed for optimum growth, it would be challenging for us to escape the prison of the reactive, primitive ego. Our primitive ego will manifest a false self, not our true self. We will become skilled at showing the world a "self" our primitive ego believes the world wants to see. We will experience vulnerability and intimacy as dangerous. Our self-esteem will be weak, and our self-image will tend to be brittle and negative. Our journey into self-awareness and wholeness will be more difficult and challenging.

We will tend to project the repressed or unconscious split-off shadow parts of our psyche onto others. Rather than feeling empowered to take responsibility for our own lives, we will tend to feel powerless and blame others for our feelings and our life circumstances. Stated simply, our awakening journey toward a non-reactive, mature, adult, observing ego will be virtually impossible until we have successfully healed the childhood wounds of our inner child's primitive ego.

Creating a healthy sense of "self" or the ego strength needed to move beyond our attachment to a wounded ego is often difficult work to do on our own. Taming a wounded primitive ego is best begun by seeking out a well-trained therapist. The gentle, reflective feedback from a mental health expert can be very helpful when we need to do this healing. But regardless of our childhood experiences and how we begin the healing process, *the intentional taming of our childhood primitive ego will require a life-long commitment to growth in self-awareness.*

Until we intentionally explore and fully understand the unconscious beliefs and survival skills we created to keep us safe in childhood, our primitive ego or "old brain" will unconsciously continue to use them to keep us safe, even in adulthood. Asking a child to run an adult life is never helpful because *no child* has the life experiences and maturity necessary to create or live a successful adult life in an adult world.

We are the problem!

5. Taming the Primitive Ego Requires New Learning and the Ability to Embrace Death

To grow and evolve both individually and as a species, we must learn to embrace life as an ongoing process of evolution and resurrection in which the *old self* dies to make room for the *new self* to be born. Because the primary focus of the primitive ego is the survival of *self,* it experiences *change* as a form of death. In other words, the primitive ego is deeply committed to a rigid sense of *self* that forcefully attempts to resist *all* change, *including its own growth.* To be successful in taming, evolving, and maturing our primitive ego consciousness, the will and courage to embrace new growth and change must come from the more evolved and "observing" adult part of our consciousness; the part that can *intentionally* pay attention to *whatever* emerges in the process of taming and awakening our self-awareness. And often, what emerges as we awaken and grow in self-awareness is painful.

Because there is no birth without pain, giving birth to the growth and change that happens as we awaken and mature our observing ego throughout adolescence and adulthood is seldom an easy process. It requires courage. Growth in consciousness and self-awareness is rarely achieved without struggle and pain. But that courage is critically needed in the world today. Only the "authentic self" of a tamed and matured primitive ego is capable of manifesting and sustaining the unconditional love and compassion that are so badly needed in the world today.

Until our mature, adult, observing ego has intentionally achieved this deeper level of self-awareness, the primitive ego of our inner child—which is extremely resistant to all growth and development—will continue to use its rigid, unbending beliefs to contaminate the *unconditional love of our essential self,* and unconsciously distort it with a *"because"* into the judgmental and hurtful *conditional* love that is so prevalent in the world today.

Stated simply, conditional love is always based on a *because.* I love you *"because...."* I don't love you *"because...."* Authentic love, in contrast, is simply offered.

Given the reality that we tend to see what we already believe or expect to see, the journey through adolescence and adulthood simply reinforces what we learned in early childhood; both the functional and the dysfunctional.

So How Do We Embrace Our "Authentic Self" and Begin to Live More Authentically?

How do we learn to say what we really mean, instead of saying what we think others want to hear? How do we become comfortable living in our skin, proud of the unique person we know we *are* inside? The work can be challenging, but the answer is simple; *intentionally tame your primitive ego consciousness and become self-aware.*

Until we *intentionally* do this important work, we will struggle with unhappiness and an inability to live authentically. We will avoid conflict in the fear that others will go away or abandon us; or the fear that they won't come back to us. We will live our lives convinced that we are somehow flawed or not OK just as we are, or that we don't belong, or that we're not lovable, smart, pretty, or special. The list is endless, but they all represent one common theme. *Because they are personalities constructed and artificially created by our childhood primitive ego, they do not represent our true essential or authentic self.*

Until we are willing to become *intentionally* self-aware and embrace the courage it takes to pay attention to the negative energy we feel inside, *and the negative energy we are knee-jerking into the world,* the yearning we feel to live more authentically will not bring about the transformation toward authenticity we so deeply desire. When we have the courage to intentionally look deeply into our behaviors and feelings, and sit with the childhood fears we have been reluctant to bring into our consciousness, only then will we begin to live into the authentic person we really are; the person we were born to be.

If we attempt to change who we are by force of will, it will only make the journey toward authenticity more difficult. It will only create another layer of false self; another "self" we *think* we *should* be. Only deep self-awareness can create or manifest the authenticity we hunger for.

We need to sit with our feelings and learn to pay attention to the behaviors and energy we are sending into the world, and then intentionally explore the fears and beliefs *behind* those feelings and behaviors. As we do this work, the layers of our *false self-personality* keeping our *authentic self* hidden will slowly begin to peel away.

It is important to remind ourselves that our childhood fears will never fully go away. They will simply become conscious. And like all fears, the more we move into them, the more comfortable we will be in acknowledging their presence, and the smaller they will become. Over time, our ability to live more authentically will begin to emerge.

Reality Distorting Bent-Nickel Beliefs of Childhood: The Source of Pain and Suffering

Bent-nickel beliefs are the unconscious primitive ego beliefs and early childhood conditioning that distort reality. When we attempt to ignore or distort reality, we *always* create pain for ourselves and others. *It is virtually impossible to create or experience a happy or successful life if you have attempted to build that life on a bent-nickel belief.*

In primitive ego workshops, I illustrated this concept by asking participants to build a stack of nickels. I would then congratulate them that their stack represented a happy, successful life. Great job! Then, I would give them a slightly bent nickel and ask them to build another stack of nickels with the bent nickel at the bottom of the stack. I would tell them that the second stack, which of course, would always be significantly smaller than their first stack, represented life with a bent-nickel belief at its base.

I would then point out that many well-meaning people would encourage them to *try harder in real life*. Of course, the only result of trying harder would eventually be depression and despair. *No matter how hard you try, you cannot build a successful life on a reality-distorting, bent-nickel belief.* It does not mean you are a "flawed" person, or that you are inadequate, or that you are not smart enough, or that you are incompetent…it simply means you picked up a bent-nickel belief that is distorting reality somewhere along your life journey; most likely in childhood. I would warn the workshop participants to be careful of your firmly held beliefs, since many are probably bent-nickel distortions of reality.

I would encourage them to remember the words of Mark Twain: "It ain't what you know for sure that will create problems in your life, it's what you know for sure that just ain't so." I would remind them that bent-nickel beliefs are *"just ain't so."*

Until we intentionally tame, evolve, and mature our early childhood's primitive ego-consciousness, nothing can enter the world without first going through the reality-distorting bent-nickel beliefs and illusions of our inner child's primitive ego. *Our beliefs control our behaviors; therefore our behaviors, choices, assumptions, expectations, and fears always reflect the "certainty" of our beliefs.*

We need to remind ourselves that:

The primary danger of all primitive ego beliefs is that the primitive ego assumes they represent both reality and "absolute truth."

When we presume to possess absolute truth, we can no longer effectively hear or see other points of view because any new information or input that challenges our self-image, our worldview, or our beliefs is selectively ignored or distorted.

Reality is never static. It is always evolving, changing, and evolving/becoming. Reality or truth can never be accurately captured in a word or a belief or a concept; it can only be experienced in the moment by an observing consciousness.

Here are some of the common bent nickel beliefs from the primitive ego workshops.

Examples of Common Bent Nickel Beliefs

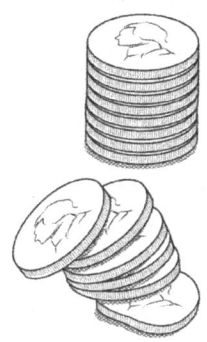

- I should be liked by everyone
- I should avoid conflict
- I should never get others upset
- I should never say no
- I should never disappoint others
- I should never ask for help
- Criticism is to be avoided at all cost
- I'll be happy when _____
- If you loved me you would "know" what I need without my having to ask
- I must correct others when I don't agree with them
- I have to be perfect
- My beliefs are "right" (Yours are wrong)
- Change is dangerous and should be avoided

Bent Nickel #1) Filling the Sense of Emptiness

Our primitive ego was conditioned in childhood to assume that getting what we need to fill the emptiness can only come from the external world. In childhood, that was often true. But in the adult world, *the world can only provide "stuff."* If we want to fill the emptiness, that lack of meaning, we have to turn our attention inward. What would give our life "purpose"? What were we born to do, to be? What thread of "interest" has always caught our attention...even in early childhood! Wrestling with these questions will begin to give direction and meaning to our lives. *More "stuff" won't.* True happiness results when we start living a life of purpose; the life we were born to live and be the person we were born to be. The great people of history are those who mastered their minds, not their environment.

Bent Nickel #2) Resisting Change Is "Pushing the River"

Change is like sitting on the edge of a river we call life. The river brings all things into our lives, and it takes all things away.

When we try to resist something the river is bringing us that we *don't* want, we are "pushing the river."

When we attempt to *cling* to something that the river is taking away from us, our "grasping" is again, metaphorically…"pushing the river."

We do this because our primitive ego hates change. As a result, we push the river by *resisting* things the river of life brings us that we don't like. Or we push the river by *clinging* to those things we like or want when the river of life takes them away.

The pain and suffering we experience in life are most often created by our attempts to push the river. For example, when we fight change by resisting or clinging, we experience the reality firsthand that we are powerless to avoid the reality of change. Our response to that sense of powerlessness is to slide into depression, weakness, helplessness, avoidance, denial, pain, addiction, anxiety, and suffering! *But it wasn't the change that created those feelings. It was our "pushing the river" resistance to change.*

One of the *more powerful survival skills* we possess, whenever something comes up that we would rather not deal with or accept, is *denial*. Of course, denial is simply another way of pushing the river and resisting the inevitability of the change that we want to avoid.

- When we attempt to push the river, we are either ignoring reality itself, or the existence of change.
- Reality *is* change. As we learned in the introduction, the cheese is always being moved!
- We are resisting the reality that life *is* change.
- We are resisting the reality that *nothing* is permanent in the external world!

- Learn to embrace reality by realizing that (a) change happens, (b) pushing the river is never the path to happiness, and (c) pushing the river always creates anxiety, stress, suffering, pain, and unhappiness in life.

- The path to happiness: Learn to embrace change and flow with the river we call life.

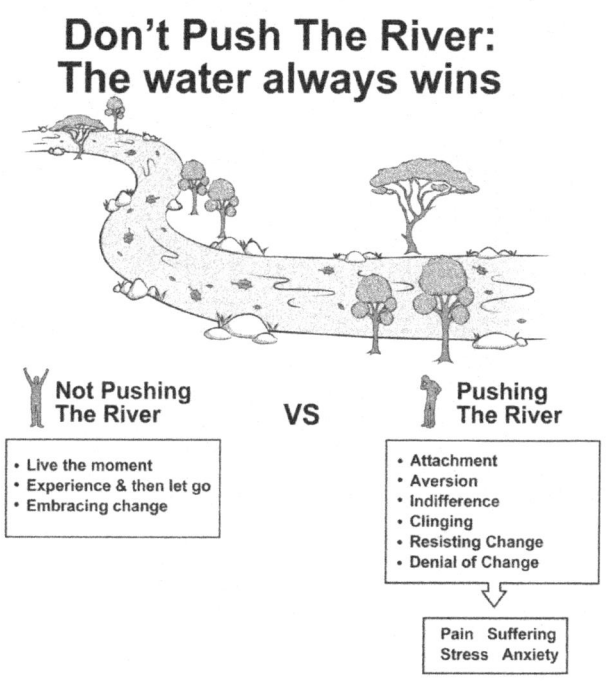

Change is the bedrock of all creation. Evolution *is* change. In *this* universe, change is inevitable. Everything in the universe is changing, evolving, and *becoming* something new and different. When we intentionally become self-aware and tame our early childhood primitive ego consciousness, we are also maturing, evolving, and becoming a new and different person.

Most of us are aware that we resist those things in life that create pain and suffering. For example, when we lose our health due to a cold or the flu, we count the days until we are back on our feet. We don't like being ill. We consciously resist illness. *What we don't see as clearly is our resistance to change itself.* When reality takes away things we like or want, we emotionally resist the reality of change. We are hard-wired to like safety and predictability in life. When things change, it causes anxiety.

Don't believe me?

Try changing where you routinely put your car keys or your glasses. Switch the cupboard you put your glasses in with the plates and vice versa. If you brush your teeth with your right hand, brush your teeth with your left hand. For a full week, try taking a different way to work each day. Stop watching all television for a week. Change the location of all of the credit and debit cards in your wallet. Go on a diet. Then watch what happens to your level of comfort internally. Life will likely feel out of control.

If you want an excellent example of how much you count on routine and consistency in your life, try doing all of the above for two weeks. It might drive you crazy, but it will show you very clearly how much your ego resists change.

Virtually all of the unhappiness that we experience in life is due to our inability, or lack of willingness, to embrace change. The universe *is* change. There is no permanence in the world of form. Happiness is achieved best when we learn to *intentionally pay attention to those times we are unconsciously pushing the river.*

Bent Nickel #3) It's Normal to Emotionally Knee-Jerk and Act Out Our Feelings

We need to acknowledge that our immature primitive ego will almost always act out whatever it is feeling; that it's *"normal"* to emotionally knee-jerk and act out our feelings.

It's not!

Emotionally knee-jerking whatever we are feeling onto others is why we so easily create conflict and hurt in our relationships with others.

Because we *have* a feeling does not mean we have to act on that feeling, and because we *feel unloving* does not mean we have to behave in an unloving way toward those around us.

We have an option. We can make a choice. We can learn to simply pay attention to the feeling and then make a conscious choice as to how we want to behave.

A helpful way to embrace this reality as we work to tame this bent nickel belief is to remind ourselves that contrary to what our primitive ego might believe, love is *not* a feeling. Love is a *behavior*. Compassion is not a feeling; it too is a behavior. Most marital conflict is created when one or both partners believe love and compassion are feelings.

Loving behaviors create happy relationships, and loving behaviors in our relationships with others *is always a choice that is separate from our feelings.*

Bent Nickel #4) Others, Especially Our Partner, Can Fix the Wounds of Our Childhood

Most people complain about not feeling loved in their marriage or significant relationships because their idea of love is a fantasy based on the illusion that *their partner* is a person who can heal the wounds of *their* childhood. This also applies to friends.

The yearning we feel is not the need to experience love; it's the need to be loved *in exactly the right way* so as to heal the pain and fill the emptiness we experienced in childhood!

For example, if we grew up invisible in childhood, we will be happy and feel loved when we are in our partner's vision, talking to us and listening to us. However, the moment our partner picks up a book to read or heads out to visit a friend, the loneliness and pain of childhood will come rushing back into our awareness. We will immediately feel unloved, and our happiness will quickly revert back to unhappiness that we assume our partner or friend created. (See Bent Nickel #3, above.)

We fail to understand that *no one* can fill the emptiness, the loneliness, or heal the wounds of our childhood. *We have to do that work for ourselves.* And it's a work that will never end because childhood is over. It *happened*. It is *history*. There is nothing that can remove the memories and the hurt that we are carrying. All we can do is learn how to love and care for ourselves. *This is a primary goal of intentional growth in self-awareness and the taming of our primitive ego.*

Until we are willing to accept this simple reality, we will continue to assume it's our partner's job to make us feel loved and happy; and when we continue to feel the pain of childhood, we will assume that it's because our partner doesn't love us. The danger in this kind of thinking is we begin to create unhappiness in our relationship because we criticize our partner for not trying hard enough, or we begin to fantasize that maybe there is someone else out there in the world who can rescue us from the pain we're feeling. Perhaps it's that pretty woman at the office who always smiles at us. Maybe it's that handsome guy sitting at the bar.

Loving ourselves means accepting that like 99% of all people, our childhood was not perfect. But we don't have to keep reliving our childhood story over and over. Our life story is not about who we "are." It's about what happened to us a long time ago.

We can begin to *rewrite* our life story.

We can begin to live the life we've always dreamed about living. We can embrace our life purpose and live the life we were born to live.

But all of this work is interior work, a work we have to do for ourselves. And it won't happen until we love our "self" enough to begin living the life we were meant to live.

Loving our "self" is simple, but it does take courage. It requires learning to live our life *authentically* and learning to be comfortable in our own skin. Authenticity happens when the person we are inside and the person we are outside are the same person. Authenticity requires taming our inner child's primitive ego-consciousness and doing the *intentional* work of becoming more self-aware.

We can't ask or expect others to somehow rescue us or make us "feel" loved when we haven't learned or embraced the courage to love ourselves.

And we can't heal the childhood wounds of our partner. We can be compassionate and understanding, but they have to learn to love themselves.

The dream of being rescued is an illusion. This primitive ego fantasy will keep us in bondage to our past and bring deep unhappiness and suffering into our lives and our relationships with others.

When we awaken to the fantasy that another person somehow can take away the pain of *our* childhood or fill the emptiness that *we* feel, it's not uncommon to find that we are already in a relationship with a person who loves us deeply. *They just show it in their way.*

A primary creator of unhappiness in life is the childhood belief that other people and events create our feelings. But no one can *make* us feel anything! Unless there is a real physical threat to us, the people and events in our life are not creating the feelings we are experiencing. They are only reminding us of the emotions and memories *we already possess*. This is a very difficult truth to fully embrace in day-to-day life, but it is indeed a reality. No one can *make us feel* anything that isn't already inside of us. They only have the power to remind us the feeling is already part of our life experience. What we do with that "reminder" is a choice, and every choice we make or fail to make *will* create a consequence or outcome.

Bent Nickel #5) The Primitive Ego Illusion of Separateness

As we discussed above, the primitive ego's sense of self as a *me,* a self that is unique and separate from the rest of the universe, is a childhood primitive ego belief called the *illusion of separateness.* This unconscious illusion of separateness is beyond a doubt one of the more harmful and dangerous beliefs held in humanity's primitive ego consciousness. It is (a) a primary creator of loneliness, isolation, and sadness; and (b) it is an unconscious illusion responsible

44

for humanity's lack of systemic thinking—the ability to embrace the reality that everything in the universe, including ourselves, is interconnected and interdependent on *everything else* in the created universe.

As children, we work hard to develop a sense of self-identity, a sense of self that's separate and apart from our friends and family. This illusion of separateness becomes so much a part of our unconscious self-identity, we rarely question the validity of this unconscious worldview as adults. We wonder why we feel lonely, unhappy, and isolated from those around us. We assume there is something wrong with us. It rarely dawns on us that our unconscious childhood illusion of separateness created in early childhood might be the source of the loneliness and suffering we so often experience in our adult lives.

The unconscious illusion of separateness that drives our feelings of isolation from others causes us to:

- Medicate ourselves to alleviate our feelings of depression, loneliness, and sadness

- Be overly judgmental of others despite the moral desire to be an empathic and compassionate person.

- Have an unconscious tendency to be competitive and self-focused when asked to share our gifts and resources with others compassionately.

- Experience an uncomfortable gap between who we would like to be and who we too often are in our relationships with others.

- Struggle with feelings of inadequacy and shame in our relationships with others.

- Feel that we must be flawed in some fundamental way.

- Tend to get trapped in a downward spiral of self-criticism that only adds to our sense of depression, isolation, and unhappiness.

But the most dangerous aspect of our primitive ego illusion of separateness is its ability to turn nature into an "it," an object to be used and discarded. We are destroying our planet and humanity's future as a viable species on our planet. We've lost the ability as a species to live *with* nature. This wisdom was deeply embedded in history's previous indigenous cultures. The indigenous cultures saw and honored the "spirit" embedded in every aspect of reality. Today we tend to think that ancient civilizations' indigenous focus on "spirit" was "religious." It wasn't. For the indigenous cultures, honoring the presence of spirit in the world around them was their way of embracing the interconnectedness and interdependence of reality. It gave them the ability to see everything in their world as a "thou" to be honored and protected. Today we would call that systemic thinking. The illusion of separateness has allowed us to view nature and her non-renewable resources as "things" to be used, consumed, bought, sold, and traded for financial profit…without any awareness or regard for how important, interconnected, and interdependent we are on those "things" for our long-term survival. The childhood illusion of separateness is a dangerous childhood bent-nickel belief that supports the voracious devouring of our planet and its fragile life-supporting ecosystems.

The existential force-multiplier threat called "lack of systemic thinking" is a major existential threat to the future survival of human culture and our human species. We will revisit this bent-nickel illusion of separateness in Part 2 and explore in more depth how it interferes with humanity's collective ability to embrace systemic thinking, a "thou" relationship with our planet, and our human ability to live sustainably with all of the other living systems on this planet.

Bent Nickel #6) Our Poor Me Life Story

Poor me thinking reflects our lifelong failures to connect our short-term choices with the long-term outcomes and consequences of those choices. Our primitive ego blames others, fate, the world, the family we were born in, our lack of (fill in the blank), and the unhappy, unsuccessful, boring, painful life we are living. Most of that blame is captured in the feeling of *poor me*. Over time, we turn those *poor me* feelings into our *poor me* life story, the *poor me* life story we tell ourselves that influences virtually every aspect of our life. We assume our *poor me* life story is an accurate belief. We blame the weather, the government, taxes, our spouses, our children, our boss, the fact that we didn't get a raise, the stress of too much to do, and not enough money. The list is endless. It's like a sad country-and-western melody we walk around humming called "I'll be happy when _____." Sadly, most of us are experts on *getting ready to be happy*, but we never quite seem to get there.

When we choose to blame others for the life *we have unconsciously chosen to live*, it makes us powerless. We have convinced ourselves that people and events outside of our control caused our unhappiness and the lack of success we experience in our life. We tell ourselves if it weren't for *them*, or what happened to us in childhood, our life would be better. In early childhood, that was often true. We were essentially helpless and dependent on the whims of others and fate.

But today, as adults, that narrative is not true. That is *not* the life we were destined to live.

We are responsible for the lives we are living. Period. Reality is simple and straightforward. It essentially offers us only two basic choices: (a) *Every* choice we make creates outcomes and consequences, and (b) *every* choice we *fail* to make also creates outcomes and consequences. Two choices. That's how it works.

We can:

a. Continue disconnecting *our* choices from *our* outcomes or consequences and spend our lives blaming others, our childhood, our parents, our spouse, God's will, bad karma, and living the powerless life of a victim unconsciously embracing our primitive ego's *poor me* life story, or

b. Accept the reality that *we* have the power to create the life we came here to live, and then *intentionally* do the work of *awakening* our consciousness and begin connecting *all* of our choices with *all* of our outcomes, and reclaim the power to determine how *we* want to live our lives.

Those are the two basic options that life offers.

The choice is ours: fully awakened responsibility for the life *we* have been creating for ourselves, or unconsciously blaming *others*. In the former, the outcome is empowerment and happiness. In the latter, we will continue to create our loneliness and unhappiness, living the life of a powerless victim.

Our destiny is not determined by fate or the *poor me* life story we created for ourselves.

The accuracy of our beliefs determines our destiny, and all of the great people in history are those who mastered their minds.

Bent Nickel #7) Survival of the Fittest Thinking

The primitive ego needs to have "power over," to be the best, to be in control, and to be "right." The primitive ego expends a great deal of energy avoiding the threat of vulnerability by making sure that we are better than someone else, and passionately defending our cherished "beliefs"—what our primitive ego absolutely *knows is right.*

This survival of the fittest need for "power over" others simply reflect the primitive ego's tendency to catalog the world in black-and-white, either/or terms of all good or all bad, all right or all wrong; the early developmental need for our primitive ego to keep the world simple; to easily define the *me* from the *not-me*. The creation of these *me/not-me* conceptual categories created by "either/or splitting" in the primitive ego consciousness is called *duality thinking* in Buddhist psychology.

Splitting enabled the primitive ego to protect its self-identity against criticism and any real or perceived threats from "others." Simply stated, the primitive ego always needs to be *right,* and it will create great conflict to defend its belief system from criticism. It will even go to war and die to defend and protect its beliefs. Unfortunately, too often those rigid, primitive ego beliefs come from early childhood conditioning and simply reflect the bent-nickel beliefs of early childhood conditioning that distort reality.

Until we have the courage to *intentionally* tame our unconscious primitive ego and *intentionally* mature our collective human consciousness, the collective primitive ego conscious of humanity will continue its destructive narcissistic need to have power over others; and the wars, violence, and conflict we have created throughout history will continue. Survival-of-the fittest thinking dominates virtually all aspects of human life and human thought. It is a core belief in neoliberal global capitalism and "what's in it for me" greed.

Conclusion of Bent-Nickel Beliefs

These unconscious, primitive ego, bent-nickel beliefs should not be labeled as either right or wrong. They are simply how our primitive ego birthed itself in childhood and young adulthood. However, we must understand these primitive bent-nickel beliefs are "not helpful" in our day-to-day *adult* relationships, especially if our goal is non-violence. They do not *reflect* reality; they are bent-nickel beliefs that *distort* reality.

Since no one grows up in a "perfect" family, each of us unconsciously brings reality-distorting bent-nickel beliefs, the seeds of conflict and suffering, into the world. Non-violence on our planet will not be achieved until humanity understands and accepts this uncomfortable reality.

The primitive ego is always self-serving. The primitive ego always knows how reality "should" be. The plumb line for right and good runs directly down the center of the primitive ego. The collective childhood primitive ego-consciousness is convinced that survival requires survival of the fittest thinking, not cooperation, middlepath thinking, or interdependence.

Thus, non-violence simply cannot be achieved using the primitive bent-nickel beliefs and their tendency to split the world into categories of "its" and "others." All of the castes and classes; all the gaps between the have and have-not nations; and all the racism, sexism, and painful judgment that comes from the label of "otherness"; have been created using the *me/not me, otherness, either/or splitting* paradigms of humanity's immature, unevolved collective, primitive human ego-consciousness.

One of my favorite quotes is this one from Stephen Covey:

How We See The World

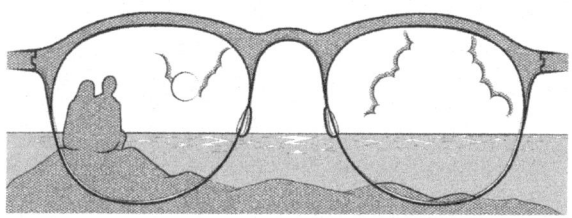

We do not see the world as the world is,
we see the world as we are.
~ Stephen Covey

Our perspective ultimately determines the construction of our world, and the people, places, and opportunities in it. The mood we're in that day, the things that have happened to us in life, the way we were raised, the things we have learned (or not learned, as the case sometimes may be) all affect how we view the world and, in turn, the world we create.

The sooner we can intentionally tame, mature, and awaken the collective primitive ego of human consciousness, the more intentionally we will create a sustainable, compassionate, and peaceful world for future generations. As we will see in Part 2, we are running out of time to awaken humanity's collective primitive ego-consciousness.

It is easy to forget how much our perceptions impact our day-to-day life. Simply taking a step back and thinking about a situation, person, or emotion from a different perspective can completely change that perspective and the reality that perspective creates. However, we often are so caught up in the moment that we tend to forget that it is through our eyes and our consciousness that this moment exists. The way we see it, the spin we put on it, is up to us. Every minute of every day, there is a chance to see things from a million different perspectives. The more accurately we can learn to "see," the more ability we will have to create a just world based on well-being and quality of life for all living beings on our planet.

Our world, and the worlds of those who interact with us, are impacted by the perspective we choose to embrace. It's not always easy to choose a positive perspective, but we will discover that the world around us improves every time we do.

Change your perspective! Don't let anyone tell us that we can't do it, because *we can!* We all can. And when we do, we *can change the world!*

What's in it for "me" greed, the need to be right, and the illusion of separateness are the three most dangerous beliefs of our collective primitive ego human consciousness. They create aggressive ideological tribalism that vilifies others and effectively destroys the ability to manifest compassion, kindness, "we-ness," cooperation, compromise, and middlepath thinking.

These three aspects of primitive ego thinking are the most dangerous threats to humanity's long-term survival, including the long-term ability to create successful, self-reliant local communities (the best realistic hope for the survival of human culture) we will explore in Part 3.

We can change the world. All we need is the courage to *intentionally* become self-aware and tame, mature, evolve, and awaken our immature, unevolved, unawakened early childhood primitive ego, the topic we will explore in Chapter 2.

CHAPTER 2:

Taming our Childhood Primitive Ego

Introduction to Chapter 2

Over the years, I have had many requests from readers asking me for a brief overview of the primitive ego theory and the importance of taming our primitive ego. As pointed out in Chapter 1, most of us attempt to change ourselves primarily through force of will and various well-meaning New Year's resolutions. But that rarely works!

The essential concept of change and growth in primitive ego theory is the adage that says, "We rarely grow and or change our behaviors using the force of will. We change our beliefs and our behaviors *when we realize our old beliefs and our old behaviors no longer make any sense to us.*" In other words, when we intentionally evolve and mature our thinking, and intentionally tame our primitive ego-consciousness to become more self-aware of the energy we are sending into the world. Primitive ego theory is based on the concept that *there can be no authentic growth in our consciousness without intentional growth in our self-awareness.*

Successful long-term growth in our consciousness requires a deep commitment to the evolution and transformation of our collective human consciousness. This is also true for the evolution, maturation, and growth of our *collective* human consciousness as a species. Achieving authentic growth individually or collectively as a species does not need to be confusing, nor does it need to come from blind adherence to a set of rigid ideological beliefs designed to create spiritual, religious, social, or political tribal unity.

There are many valid paths to enlightenment, but all successful paths to enlightenment include:

a. Intentional growth in self-awareness.

b. Becoming self-aware of the beams in our own eye.

c. Learning to stop "pushing the river" and resisting change.

d. Learning to embrace reality by living "fully present" in each moment.

e. As we evolve our consciousness on the path toward enlightenment and deep self-awareness, we:

f. Learn to manifest mutuality, empathy, and compassion.

g. Accept the fundamental and essential concept and importance of radical diversity.

h. Confront and mature the internal conflict and fragmentation of our primitive human psyche.

i. Embrace the profound systemic inter-relationship between ourselves and the rest of creation.

As we will discover in this chapter, we become significantly happier when we intentionally evolve and tame our primitive ego and its early childhood conditioning, and begin to take full responsibility for the creation of our own lives. As we consciously examine our unconscious childhood reality-distorting bent-nickel beliefs, we learn to embrace the wisdom of systemic thinking; the understanding and knowledge of ancient indigenous cultures; cultures that honored the *"spirit"* or sense of *"thou-ness"* embedded in every aspect of reality; the spiritual wisdom that sustainable indigenous cultures embraced successfully for centuries by living *with* nature rather than *using* nature. They recognized that the world around them was "family," and that "family" needed to be sustainably supported and protected for seven future generations.

When we intentionally do the work to become self-aware of our inner child's presence and the negative impacts that the reality-distorting primitive ego beliefs and unconscious conditioning of early childhood have on our relationship with others, we begin to embrace a more integrated sense of wholeness. The more self-aware we become, the more our relationships with family, friends, and others improve.

As we become more conscious of the survival skills we unconsciously adopted to navigate early childhood, we begin to grow in self-esteem. Those behaviors start to make sense when we see them through the eyes of childhood. We understand that we were simply using early childhood survival skills, which were effective in early childhood but were not helpful when we attempted to use them as adults. We begin to understand that there isn't anything "wrong" with us; we simply needed to develop more "adult" ways of dealing with the events and challenges in our life. We needed to become more mature, evolved, and self-aware.

Waiting to Intentionally Evolve Our Collective Human Consciousness is *Not* an Option

We are entering the third decade of the twenty-first century. Our climate is warming. Our storms are increasing in frequency and intensity. We are dealing with a COVID-19 pandemic. Our forests are burning. Floods are increasing. Our polar ice is melting. It is time that we learned how dangerous it is to allow our emotionally driven, narcissistic, what's-in-it-for-me, greed-based primitive ego thinking to continue unconsciously controlling our day-to-day choices and behaviors. We are well past the point in human evolution where growth in human consciousness and self-awareness can continue to be a hit-or-miss evolutionary process left to chance. We need to collectively embrace the courage to *intentionally* become a more self-aware species, and *intentionally* learn to tame, mature, evolve, and consciously awaken our collective immature, unevolved, unawakened early childhood primitive ego human consciousness *before we destroy our planet and its fragile ecosystem past the point of no return.*

Scientists are warning that we may have already passed some of those critical, irreversible tipping points.

In this chapter, we will look at what it means to "tame" the early childhood conditioning of our unconscious primitive ego...and why the future survival of our species on this planet will depend on how successful we are in that taming process. As we will see in Part 2, we are not running out of time to intentionally mature and evolve as a species—we are already out of time!

So How Do We Intentionally Tame Our Primitive Ego? How Do We Use the Material in This Book to More Intentionally Grow and Evolve?

We begin by recognizing that the existential force-multiplier threats and the massive existential changes those force-multipliers create in Part 2 are not *the problem. They* are *symptoms that we created. We* are the problem! *We* created the force-multipliers and their existential threats. *We* are responsible for the pain, suffering, aggression, conflict, violence, and massive existential changes that are coming. Stated simply, we are responsible and accountable for the massive existential threats and changes that our collective primitive, immature, unevolved human thinking has created...and continues to create.

The primary golden arch of this book is (a) the urgent need to *intentionally* tame, awaken, mature, and evolve the collective primitive ego-consciousness of humanity and its early childhood conditioning; and (b) the recognition that *waiting* to do this work is *not* an option if our goal is the long-term survival of our species on this planet.

"We" are the problem: Fundamental beliefs and illusions embedded in the collective consciousness of humanity:

a. "What's in it for me?" **greed**.

b. Need to be **"right"** (aggressive arrogance, extreme cognitive dissonance/confirmation bias).

c. Inability to replace *"me"* thinking with *"we"* thinking (compassion, mutuality, cooperation).

d. I want what I want **when I want it.**

e. **Blame** others for *our* feelings (inability to own our feelings).

f. Ignorance regarding the **danger of exponential growth** (e.g., COVID-19).

g. A lack of interconnected, interdependent **systemic thinking**.

h. Survival of the fittest thinking,

i. Black versus white, **zero-sum thinking** (*You* can't have that, it's *mine!*) (I win, you lose.)

j. An exaggerated, aggressive narcissistic self-focused sense of **entitlement.**

k. An inability to connect short-term choices with long-term consequences.

l. The **fear of change** (uncertainty, not knowing).

m. The unending, obsessive desire for **"more."**

n. The need for power "over" rather than power "with."

o. The illusion of separateness from the rest of creation (I'm a unique *me).*

p. The inability to embrace long-term thinking.

When you read this list at the beginning of every chapter, picture in your mind, a children's playground filled with six- and seven-year-old children. Then remind yourself that each of those children has spent the first seven years of their life becoming a unique "self." And each of those individual seven-year-old *primitive egos* had one fundamental task. And that task was becoming a unique person or *self* separate from every other *self.* Their primitive (*young*) ego-self used the concepts listed in this list to feel special, unique, loved, cared for, admired, accepted, and safe.

As we discussed in Chapter 1, seven is roughly the age that all of this childhood learning and conditioning quietly became the foundational thinking of their unconscious mind. This unconscious, early childhood "primitive ego conditioning" will become the basic emotional and cognitive foundation that every human consciousness will use to navigate the world until they do the work of *intentionally* taming their immature primitive ego consciousness and evolving a more adult, mature consciousness and thinking process.

As a mental health therapist, I was often asked, "Why is it so challenging to tame my primitive ego conditioning? Why is it so hard to evolve and mature my emotional and cognitive childhood thinking? Why haven't more people been able to embrace a more self-aware, mature, compassionate, evolved, adult thinking process?

To understand the answer to those questions requires an understanding of complex systems and how everything in a complex, interconnected, and interdependent system works to support the "wholeness" of the system. In this case, the *wholeness* refers to the individual human consciousness of *each person* on the planet. Until each person *intentionally* does the work to become self-aware, the collective primitive ego-consciousness of humanity will continue to be immature, unevolved, and fragmented.[2]

The most important way to understand the power of this early childhood primitive ego conditioning is understanding how *each of the items in the primitive ego aspects list above* unconsciously works together with all the other items in the list to "systemically" and mutually support each other. For example, the need to be special and important is supported by the need to be **"right"** even though the need to be **"right"** creates black-and-white, either/or, zero-sum, aggressive thinking and behaviors. The primitive ego assumption that our beliefs are always "right" and "true" is supported by our primitive ego's **narcissism** and our primitive ego's tendency to employ *confirmation bias* and *cognitive dissonance* to ignore any information that does not agree with our cherished beliefs. The need to be **"right"** is supported by the feelings of **entitlement**. The sense of **entitlement** is supported by a **narcissistic** sense of **"me-ness"** as a unique self separate from the rest of creation. The sense of **what's-in-it-for-"me"** **narcissism** creates **greed**. I want what I want when I want it creates **impatience**, and our impatience is supported by **entitlement and narcissism**. The primitive ego **fear of the "other"** supports our biases and

---

2   A consciousness fragmented into an infinite number of "me" and "not me" categories.

unconscious racism. Bottom line: The many aspects that make up the primitive ego-consciousness all work together, interconnectedly and interdependently, to systemically reinforce the primitive ego's illusion of separateness, a fragmented sense of "self" *separate* from the rest of creation.

OK, you get the idea. Taming the primitive ego is essentially doing the work of *intentionally* becoming more self-aware of this unconscious childhood conditioning. When you identify some aspect of primitive ego thinking, pay attention to the other elements of your primitive ego that are systemically and unconsciously supporting the part you *identified* and are attempting to tame.

Learn to Pay Attention and Not Judge When You Unconsciously Knee-Jerk Negative Energy into the World

Our early childhood primitive ego conditioning tends to unconsciously "knee-jerk" *negative emotional energy* into the world. These unconscious emotional knee-jerks are an excellent teacher if we learn to simply pay attention to them *every time we recognize that we are knee-jerking negative emotional energy into the world.* What triggered that negative energy? Use the list above to see what aspect of your unconscious primitive ego is getting triggered. The only energy we want to manifest in the world is mature, evolved, conscious, compassionate, empathic *tamed* energy based on a self-aware, *intentional choice.*

If we learn to pay attention and not judge ourselves every time negative, unconscious, emotional "knee-jerk" energy comes from us, it will help us identify those unconscious life events and experiences that tend to unconsciously trigger our primitive ego. Over time, those emotional knee-jerks will help us grow and become more self-aware. As we grow in self-awareness, the events that would have unconsciously "triggered" our primitive ego in the past will begin to lose their ability to unconsciously knee-jerk negative primitive ego energy into the world. When that day arrives, we will know we have started to *intentionally* evolve and mature our thinking; and the *intentional* taming of our primitive ego. Our adult *observing* consciousness will be more "awakened" and in control of our actions, behaviors, and the emotional energy we are sending into the world. Every time our *adult observing ego controls our behaviors, we can take pride in knowing that our journey toward an evolved and mature self-awareness has taken another important step toward enlightenment.*

Be patient with yourself. Enlightened teachers will tell you that growth toward a non-reactive, evolved, mature consciousness is a life-long process. The more you practice this kind of self-awareness, the more life will be non-reactive, rewarding, peaceful, and calm. The challenges the river of life brings you will continue, but how you deal with them will be different.

The Six Stages of Human Development: The Journey from Childhood to Enlightenment

In the chart below, we will focus on the first four stages of human development. The process of awakening and taming our childhood primitive ego is the primary evolutionary goal of **Stage 1:** Childhood; **Stage 2:** Reactive Adult; **Stage 3:** Awakening; and **Stage 4:** Observing Adult.

Until humanity achieves the primitive ego taming required to embrace the global *collective* human consciousness of Stage 4, the future survival of humanity on this planet will continue to be existentially challenged and threatened. Life as we know it *will* end, and humanity's *likely* extinction on our planet will remain high. Stated simply, our ability to live sustainably *with* nature on this planet will not be certain until the global *collective* consciousness of humanity has evolved to that of a Stage 5 consciousness. Achieving the ability to live sustainably *with* nature on our planet is essential for our survival as a species. It is a golden arch of this book.

Waiting to achieve this goal is not an option. We are out of time for waiting.

We will briefly explore the first four stages of human development in the chart below. For those interested in digging deeper into Primitive Ego Theory, I encourage reading my book, *Adult Spiritual Development: The Creation of an Authentic Spirituality for the 21st Century.* When I speak about "spirituality" in that book, I suggest that the reader interpret it to mean the wisdom of indigenous cultures and their ability to see "spirit" in all aspects of creation; in other words, the "the ability to embrace systemic thinking."

As you move from the left to the right in the chart below, use the diagram below the chart to describe the progress achieved as we evolve the human consciousness and our ability to become more self-aware.

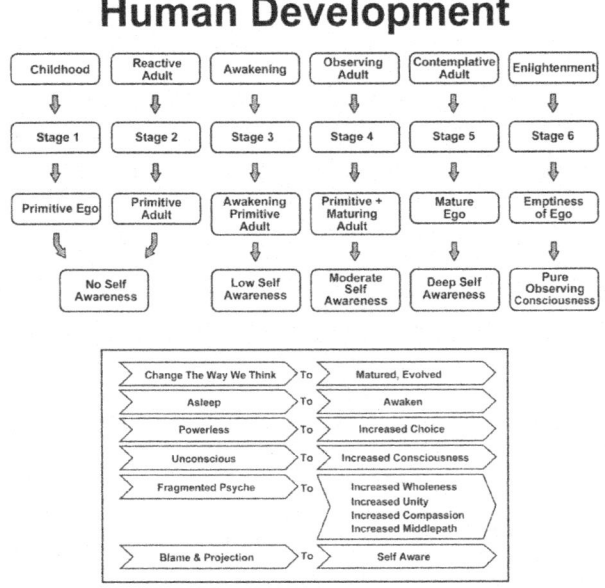

Human Development

Stage 1: The Collective Primitive Ego Consciousness That We Need to Tame and Awaken

As we learned in Chapter 1, the primitive ego aggressively resists all change because our human ego experiences all change as a form of death. This resistance to change will continue until we have achieved the enlightenment of Stage 6. The important point to remember when we say "taming our primitive ego" is the reality that our primitive ego essentially remains unchanged throughout our lives. It is the experience of our childhood. It is history. It happened. *What evolves is our adult observing consciousness.* This is our ability to evolve and manifest a more mature human consciousness as we increasingly become self-aware and conscious of the presence of our inner child's untamed primitive ego and its early childhood conditioning.

As we discussed in Chapter 1, the survival skills, beliefs, and other shadow material of our inner child's primitive ego are tightly interwoven and systemically supportive of our primitive sense of self. They work together to form a very effective barrier that enables our primitive ego to resist change and maintain a lifelong internal state of homeostasis, the ability to maintain a relatively stable internal state that persists despite changes in the world outside.

Until we are willing to mature our adult observing ego by intentionally paying attention to the unconscious shadow material of our childhood primitive ego and then doing the work required to deepen our self-awareness, our primitive ego will unconsciously control our lives.

Until we achieve the moderate self-awareness of a Stage 4 adult observing ego, humanity's ability to survive extinction will be highly problematic.

Our Primitive Ego Uses Childhood Fears to Challenge Our Ability to Live Authentically

As we evolve from a Stage 1 to a Stage 4 level of authenticity and personal growth; taming our inner child's unconscious primitive ego will be focused primarily on helping us discover the beams in our own eye. It will help us discover those fears and beliefs from childhood that have been creating so much of our unhappiness and lack of authenticity.

By the time we entered grade school, the *false self* created by the primitive ego conditioning of childhood had unconsciously become the unique and separate "self" personality known as *me*. Our childhood primitive ego created our false self or personality as a way to hide our authentic self so we could better ignore or shield ourselves from the powerful fears of childhood. In other words, our false *personality self* was the only "self" our childhood primitive ego decided was OK to show the world. Over time and by habit, this artificially created *false self* became who we "*are.*"

Until we do the work of taming our primitive ego and discovering how our primitive ego covered our true self under the layers of our false "personality self," we will live our lives *knowing* in our hearts that we are not living authentically; that our lives are not reflecting our authentic self.

Until we do the work of taming our primitive ego, the authentic or unique self we were born to be, will remain hidden. The person we were meant to be and the life we were meant to live, will remain unexpressed, hidden in the shadows of our false self.

The spiritual yearning that so many of us feel; that pervasive sense of emptiness; that sense that something important is missing in our lives; is our authentic, essential self struggling to assert itself, to make itself known. Until we awaken to the fears and reality-distorting beliefs of our childhood primitive ego, true happiness, our true purpose in life, and the person we were born to be, will continue to elude us.

So How Do We Begin to Live More Authentically?

How do we learn to say what we mean instead of saying what we think others want to hear? How do we become comfortable living in our skin, proud of the unique person we know we *are* inside? The work of *intentionally* taming our primitive ego and awakening our consciousness can be challenging, but the answer is simple: *The taming of our childhood primitive ego simply requires intentionally and consciously becoming self-aware.*

We all grow up avoiding various childhood fears. Until we have the courage to confront those fears, we will struggle with unhappiness and an inability to live authentically. For example, we will avoid conflict in the fear that others will go away or abandon us; or the fear that they won't come back to us. We will live our lives convinced that we are somehow flawed or not OK just as we are, or that we don't belong, or that we're not lovable, or smart, or pretty, or special. The list is endless. What we need to remember is the concept that *anything that could, in any way, threaten our sense of self in childhood, was experienced by our primitive ego as something to be feared.*

These fears are far too painful for us to fully understand or manage in childhood. So, as we saw above, our primitive ego steps in and uses its primitive understanding of the world to begin creating a "personality" or false self that will allow us to function in the world and keep our fears from entering our consciousness. Until we become more self-aware, those unconscious fears will continue to control and limit our adult lives.

For example, our primitive ego often uses black-and-white childhood thinking to create a "perfect" self by turning all of our beliefs into self-confident, absolute truths so-as-to avoid the possibility of criticism; in other words, our primitive ego always needs to be "right." Or it might use our tendency in childhood to be narcissistically self-focused as a way to eliminate feelings such as vulnerability.

Sometimes our primitive ego embraces vertical power, or survival of the fittest thinking, to create an assertive, controlling, or aggressive sense of self. This person is always in control to avoid feeling powerless.

Another common personality is a false self that becomes a compulsive "caretaker" of others and ignores self.

But the most common false personality type created by the primitive ego comes from the childhood assumption that everything good or bad comes from the outside world. The personality it creates is the false self that learned to value impermanent things or the "stuff" of the world as the source of happiness or unhappiness—a personality addicted to the consumption and collection of stuff: power, prestige, and financial success.

The combinations of traits and survival skills used by our primitive ego to create our personality can be almost unlimited in variety, but they all represent one common theme. Because they are personalities constructed and artificially created by our primitive ego, *they do not express our true essential authentic self.* Until we are willing to become intentionally self-aware and embrace the courage it takes to pay attention to the negative energy we feel inside, *and the negative energy we are projecting or sending into the world,* the yearning we feel to live more authentically will not bring about the transformation toward authenticity we so deeply desire.

When we have the courage to *intentionally* look deeply into our behaviors and feelings, and sit with the childhood fears we have been reluctant to bring into our consciousness, only then will we begin to live into the authentic person we are; the person we were born to be.

If we attempt to change who we are by the force of will, it will only make the journey toward authenticity more difficult. It will only create another layer of false self; another "self" we *think* we *should* be! *Only deep self-awareness can tame our primitive ego and its deep childhood conditioning. Only deep self-awareness can liberate our true self, the authenticity we hunger to manifest in the world.*

We need to learn how to sit *with* our feelings. Learn to pay attention to the behaviors and energy we are sending into the world. Explore the fears and beliefs *behind* those feelings and actions. As we do this work, the layers of *personality* that keep our authentic self-hidden will slowly begin to peel away.

It is essential to remind ourselves that our childhood fears will never "go away." They will simply become conscious. And like all fears, the more we move into them, the more comfortable we become in acknowledging their presence, the smaller they will become. Over time, our ability to live more authentically will begin to emerge. Our genuine, authentic self will become more visible.

Overview Summary of the Human Development Chart

Stage 1 Is Early Childhood

Stage 1 covers human development from birth to approximately seven to eight years of age. At about eight years of age, the experiences and learnings of childhood morph into our unconscious and become our felt-sense of self: the primitive ego of our unconscious inner-child experiences its-self as a unique and separate *me*.

Stage 2 Is Reactive

The reactive adult of Stage 2 is essentially the primitive ego of our inner child masquerading as an adult in an adult body. We are essentially functioning unconsciously out of our inner child's primitive ego and reacting unconsciously to emotional and environmental stimuli.

Note: Of the six stages of human development illustrated in the human development chart above, *most adult humans are stuck in the second developmental stage called the reactive adult.* This is a reactive **"pseudo-adult"** stage of development in which we look like adults, but we essentially manifest the emotional reactivity and thinking process of a young child.

We look like adults, but developmentally we tend to function most of the time out of the old brain or primitive ego of our seven- to eight-year-old inner child. In other words, we tend to *behave and perform unconsciously. We have relatively little choice in our behaviors, feelings, and thoughts. We tend to live our lives repetitiously, acting out of the primitive defenses and survival skills we developed in childhood.* People stuck in the emotional reactivity of Stage 2 tend to create a great deal of conflict, violence, and suffering in the world—for *themselves* and *others.*

Stage 2 pseudo-adults have virtually no self-awareness; they are often overwhelmed by a deep sense of powerlessness; they tend toward projection and blame[3]; and they are very guarded and defensive when relating to others. They are inclined to be oversensitive and very easily hurt by criticism. Their

---

3   A man piloting a hot-air balloon discovered he had wandered far off course and was hopelessly lost. He descended to a lower altitude, where he saw Nasrudin walking along the road. He lowered the balloon to within hearing distance and shouted "Nasrudin, Nasrudin! I have lost my way and I am running out of gas. I must find my way home quickly. Can you tell me where I am?"

Nasrudin looked up at the balloon, and replied, "Yes, you're in a hot-air balloon, about thirty feet above this field."

The balloonist shouted back in anger. "You are a fool, Nasrudin. What you told me is technically correct, but of no use to me."

"Well," Nasrudin shouted back as he continued walking along the road, "I am not sure who the fool is. You don't know where you are, or where you're going. I told you exactly where you are. You are obviously in the same position you were before we met, but now it's my fault!"

self-esteem is fragile. They struggle to achieve a healthy sense of wholeness but lack the tools to reach the psychic integration they hunger to experience. Depression, anxiety, feeling overwhelmed, and shame are everyday emotional experiences in Stage 2.

This is not to say that those of us stuck in Stage 2 are not capable of being loving and compassionate. The problem is because we lack self-awareness of the unconscious shadow material embedded in our primitive ego, we are very limited in our ability to maintain or sustain our intention to offer love and compassion for more than a few moments. In other words, our ability to love unconditionally is extremely limited, and the love and compassion we manifest *to others and ourselves* in Stage 2 tends at best to be *very* brief in duration and *very conditional.* (As we saw above, conditional love tends to have an unstated and often unconscious "because" attached to the love and compassion we offer others.)

Stage 3 Is Conscious Awakening

Stage 3 is the conscious *awakening* of self-awareness and self-consciousness; the moment we become consciously aware that we can intentionally grow in self-awareness. Another way to describe *awakening* is that we become aware of the speck in our own eye. *The focus of our conscious attention increasingly shifts from the outer world to our inner world.*

*Awakeni*ng is the birth of intentionality.

Awakening describes the moment we consciously or intentionally choose to awaken and align our lives with a higher purpose; to live life in a broader, less narcissistic self-focused context.

Awakening is when we intentionally commit to becoming spirit-centered rather than self-centered; to make enlightenment through growth in self-awareness a primary spiritual and developmental goal for our lives.

Awakening is understood in the traditional context of a spiritual awakening. In other words, we awaken to the reality that we are not a "self" separate from the rest of reality; we are a "self" systemically interconnected and interdependent on and with everything in the created universe. As we discussed above, this is not a religious awakening. It is awakening to the wisdom manifested by ancient indigenous cultures that saw and honored the *spirit* embedded in all creation; the insight and ability allowed them to live sustainably *with* nature and the natural world. This is what we would describe today as the ability for sustainable, systemic thinking.

Note: Stage 3 Awakening: The Primitive Ego Theory of Human Development Differs from Other Developmental Theories

The Primitive Ego Theory of Human Development presented in this book differs significantly from other developmental theories, because the third stage of "awakening" was virtually ignored in all other developmental theories. They were the products of their time, raised in a social context that defined spiritual growth as being linked to a person's strength or faith in God and adherence to a particular set of religious beliefs and teachings.

They assumed spiritual growth had very little to do with psychological development. Spiritual growth and psychological development were thought to be two very separate concepts. The idea that spiritual growth is directly linked to an increase in self-awareness would not have occurred to them, nor would it have been socially acceptable to their culture or colleagues. Many persons who embrace conservative fundamental black-and-white religious, political, or economic (neoliberal capitalism) belief systems do not accept this reality even today.

As a result, these earlier religious and developmental theorists did not understand that the spiritual awakening of Stage 3 needs to be thoroughly understood and *internalized as a unique and separate developmental "stage" of human development* before the unstable and *unsustainable "states"* of human evolution they were attempting to define could become the *stable* religious or social development they were proposing.

The developmental stages presented by these early theorists are very useful in understanding human moral, social, and ego development, but *states* of consciousness do not become stable *stages* of development until the psyche awakens and the required maturation of the primitive ego has taken place. As Ken Wilber[4] would say, the center of gravity of one's consciousness has to increase if one is to successfully achieve a *sustainable* higher "stage" of development. Stated simply, the human psyche is capable of awakening and achieving momentary glimpses of these mature but short-lived *states* of human development. Still, relatively few persons can maintain the more enlightened insights and long-term stability of those more advanced human development *stages* ...*religiously or socially.*

There are no short-cuts on our spiritual journey toward higher stages of human development and spiritual enlightenment. Until the awakening process has been successfully understood and integrated, and the consciousness of the observing ego has been tamed and matured through *intentional* growth in self-awareness to a higher center of gravity, the stable, developmental *stages* described by the Primitive Ego Theory of Human Development in the chart above, will be no more than occasionally experienced transient states of consciousness. *We might understand the "concept," but there will be no ability to sustain that level or stable stage of human development in one's day-to-day life.*

This includes the various developmental stages of the other developmental theorists as well. *States* do not become *stages* of development religiously, or socially, until the developmental and spiritual traits and qualities represented by the particular *stage* are *steadfast, unwavering, and sustainable, even when our primitive ego and our childhood beliefs and conditioning are being threatened, under stress, or directly challenged!*

Stage 3: Awakening As Metaphor: Riding on the Train

A useful way to think about the awakening process and learning to live fully conscious in each moment is to picture a metaphor of yourself riding in a passenger car on a train traveling through beautiful mountain terrain. All the

---

4   Ken Wilber is one of the foremost comprehensive philosophical thinkers of our time.

shades on the train are pulled down to cover the windows as we reactively live our life from moment to moment, virtually asleep and unaware of any reality other than what exists on the train.

Until the shades are raised, all we know is what we already know. All we see and hear is what we already believe to be true. All we can see or know is what is present in the car itself. There is little or no self-awareness. *We have no awareness that a larger world exists just outside the train window, a world we could easily see if only we could lift the shades covering the windows.*

In this metaphor, the passenger car represents the primitive narcissistic mind of our socially and culturally conditioned self. Our sense of self is confined to the pure primitive ego of Stage 1 or the emotionally reactive "pseudo-adult" primitive ego of Stage 2. The shade represents our primitive ego fears and self-focused narcissism that keeps us obsessively focused on our own needs and our own "self."

Awakening on the train is defined as that *first moment of awareness*; that moment that we get *our first fleeting glimpse of the incredible world that exists* just beyond the shades, and consciously see for the first time, the reality of another world that has always existed just outside of our narcissistic "self"-awareness.

A common description of those who have awakened is having the humility to see the world that exists beyond the limited awareness of our narcissistic self for the first time in our lives. For some, it may have come as empathy for another person or group of people. For others, it may have come as a momentary self-awareness that they were not the kind of person they wanted to be. For some, the moment of awakening and self-awareness is attached to a profound religious experience.

Unfortunately, our primitive ego's narcissism often turns the religious awakening experience into a "personal" faith experience with God. What began as a sacred moment of awakened self-awareness is quickly turned into our primitive ego's own unique and personal relationship with God; a relationship based on adherence to the rigid religious, tribal beliefs and the sense of belonging that comes from the unity of thought that is shared with other members in the religious community. It is not uncommon for Stage 2 "pseudo-adults" to get stuck in their religious beliefs and spend their lives narcissistically ensuring their admission into heaven rather than learning to manifest the unconditional love and compassion that comes from true awakening and authentic spiritual growth.

Awakening means that for one brief moment, for some often-unexplainable reason, we became consciously self-aware. The unspoken question at that moment was, "Will we come back for another look past the shade of our narcissism, or will we assume it's too much work and slide back into the unconscious primitive ego of our inner-child and live our life on the train, an unconscious prisoner of our primitive mind?" Many choose to live life on the train as Stage 2 "pseudo-adults," but this is not true for everyone.

For those who choose to grow, there is no real choice. Once they have even momentarily seen the reality that exists beyond the shades of their narcissistic primitive ego, the journey to conscious self-awareness becomes the only path with meaning for them. They can be said to have genuinely awakened and begun their *intentional* journey toward deep self-awareness and enlightenment.

Over time, those who choose to embrace compassion and enlightenment, and continue the journey of awakening into Stages 4 and 5, will find themselves increasingly able to lift the shades of narcissism that have kept them prisoners of their own mind for so long. As they awaken, become self-aware, and learn to pay increasing attention to the world that exists outside the confines of the train, the context that gives ultimate meaning to their life will begin to grow. Their life journey will no longer be just about themselves. Their "me" focus will have transformed into a "we" focus.

Our focus begins to shift from the primitive ego's self-centered consciousness to global or world-centric consciousness with true awakening. It is not long before we realize that it is not just about the growth of *our* consciousness that is important. We learn to embrace the evolutionary imperative that *it is the consciousness of our entire species that must awaken and mature.*

We find ourselves replacing our primitive ego's narcissistic self-focus as the primary driving imperative that gives meaning to our lives and embracing the critical need for growth in the evolution of *all* human consciousness. In other words, we shift from a "What do I want or need personally?" to an increasing global moral and ethical context that asks, "What is right for the evolution of humanity itself?"

We begin to understand ourselves, and our species, as an integral part of a more complex, systemically interconnected and interdependent world. In other words, an awakened consciousness that understands that everything in the universe is radically and systemically inter-related. The insight that we are more than a singularly unique and separate primitive-ego— *me*-self" riding on a train with the shades drawn.

But the journey forward can be very uncomfortable. Everything that we were so sure of in Stage 2 is now in question. All of our beliefs, opinions, and assumptions will undergo a transformation from the safety of *absolute certainty* to the *ambivalence and uncertainty of ego emptiness and not-knowing*. We will find ourselves with less and less to say. Less need to be "right." Less need to attach a "because" to our love and compassion. Less need to talk. Listening and simply paying attention will begin to manifest as humility. Our consciousness will no longer be an internal object we narcissistically seek to evolve. It will become the subject itself. We will find ourselves experiencing a more profound sense of unity with the "pure consciousness" embedded in the created universe's wholeness and oneness. The concept of "other" will have less and less meaning for us. The indigenous wisdom of honoring the spirit embedded in creation will become the way we experience reality.

Awakening is not comfortable. The danger of pulling down the shade in the train's windows and sliding back into the comfortable security of a Stage 2 consciousness will be significant for a long time.

Stage 4 Is Intentional Growth in Observing Ego

Stage 4 is the beginning of intentional growth in our observing ego. In this stage, we learn to more consciously direct our attention to manifest increased control over our internal thinking process and our emotional responses to stimuli from our outer environment. *In Stage 4, our observing ego increasingly develops intentional choice over what we manifest.* What we manifest in the world becomes more consistent with our psycho-spiritual attainment and what we know to be the truth beyond the train's windows.

Each new realization of truth leads to the clearing of old primitive ego beliefs and self-identity. Each establishes a new level of self-awareness that, in turn, leads to higher realizations of truth and reality, higher levels of consciousness. As we grow in Stage 4, we become less driven by our primitive ego's primitive survival consciousness and instincts, and *more responsible for the enlightenment of our entire human species.*

Evolution does an excellent job of moving us forward and learning new insights and truths, but it does a very poor job of clearing our consciousness of old, unhelpful primitive beliefs from our childhood. This growth in self-awareness and *the clearing of outmoded childhood beliefs is the work of Stages 4 and 5.* The primary change that we will experience as we move into the work of Stage 4 is *our observing ego's ability to simply pay attention.* We will continue to be emotionally reactive for a long time in Stage 4, but when we are reactive, our observing adult consciousness will increasingly manifest the ability to simply pay attention to how we are thinking, how we are feeling, how we are behaving; and the kind of energy we are manifesting into the world.

Because the primitive ego resists self-awareness with considerable psychic energy, the help of a well-trained therapist can be beneficial at this point in the journey toward full awakening and enlightenment. Learning to pay attention is a skill best learned with a competent teacher. Our self-awareness and ability to pay attention and intentionally observe what we are manifesting in the world will strengthen over time. The reactive pseudo-adult ego of Stage 2 will eventually mature and become a genuinely observing ego. The primitive ego of our inner child will continue to exist, but its ability to control our emotions, thoughts, and behaviors will have diminished significantly. Eventually, we will reach the consciousness of Stage 5 or the level of a contemplative adult.

Stage 5 Is the Beginning of a
True Sustainable Level of Self-Awareness

In Stage 5, our consciousness begins to develop and maintain a deeper contemplative self-awareness. Our need to "know" and be "right" is increasingly replaced by our need to *be with* and quietly pay attention to both inner and outer stimuli. Stage 5 consciousness means that we are beginning to manifest *a significantly evolved middlepath spirituality. We no longer need to split reality into concepts of either/or. We accept reality for what it is in each moment.*

In Stage 5, our contemplative consciousness and our ability for a non-reactive, deep self-awareness become more self-sustaining. Operating out of our essential or authentic self becomes more and more an expression of who we are, and our ability to manifest compassion becomes a choice that we have increasing control over. Our old attachment to the reactive primitive ego of our inner child has all but disappeared. We may occasionally need to talk with our inner child, but the inner child no longer controls our daily lives. I have practiced intentional self-awareness for many years, but I still occasionally need to go for a walk when I need to talk with my inner child. It's my opportunity to gently remind my inner child that he has taken care of me for many years, and now it's my turn to take care of him when he tries to take over my consciousness. I always talk to him out loud. I believe he "hears" me better when I do. But I'm careful to do that when he and I are alone.

In Stage 5, we see that our thoughts, beliefs, and feelings are transient illusions created in the mind, not the reality we once thought they were. Our consciousness moves increasingly into that of *the observer, a pure consciousness that can simply pay attention.* Our primitive ego is alive and active, but its power and ability to unconsciously control our behavior and choices have become a thing of the past. Stage 5's primary characteristic is the more sustained ability to embrace *ego-emptiness* or *not knowing*, the beginning of a true middlepath consciousness. We have learned to contemplate and pay attention to everything, but we *"know"* nothing. We are not affected by the anxiety of uncertainty, ambivalence, and not-knowing. *We have learned to live the questions and not seek so obsessively for answers.*

The primitive ego *always* needs the security of *"certainty"* and *"knowing"* the correct answer. It has virtually no ability to manage the anxiety that comes with uncertainty and ambiguity. Whatever the primitive ego believes to be true, it assumes that it is *The Truth.* A therapist helps develop a healthy sense of "self" or ego strength in Stage 4. Still, the work of moving beyond and letting go of our attachment to the ego in Stage 5 is best achieved with a well-trained spiritual director or meditation teacher.

Stage 6 Is Full Enlightenment

There have been many different descriptions and schools of enlightenment over the last several thousand years. Most have been primarily concerned with individual enlightenment. Spiritually and philosophically, I choose to believe *there can be no form without an initiating consciousness.* Because humanity can be intentionally and reflexively conscious and aware, the only enlightenment that makes sense to me in the modern twenty-first century is a *global* human consciousness that is fully conscious and self-aware. A global human consciousness that has the spiritual awareness to be fully responsible as co-creators with the Universe's Initiating Consciousness as humanity does the work of creating new forms. Including the ability to live our lives in the fully conscious awareness that in this local part of the universe, on the planet Earth, we are the co-creative, conscious result of a roughly 14.5-billion year creative evolutionary process. An evolutionary process that appears to be moving toward the increased complexity of all living organisms, increased levels of consciousness in living organisms, and increased communal cooperation between living organisms.

The final Stage 6 of human development is that of enlightenment, *a true middlepath pure observing consciousness. True enlightenment is simply an emptiness of ego,* the ability to live life in the pure observing consciousness that resides in each of us. In this stage, our observing attention and awareness are offered to everything because truth is found in all things. *Stage 6 enlightenment is having learned to ride in the train with the shades up all the time, simply paying attention to "what is" as one lives from moment to moment on one's life journey.*

In Stage 6, our inner-child's narcissistic primitive ego and the emotionally reactive "pseudo-adult" ego of Stage 2 are still present, but they are no longer visible. They are no longer in control because there is no longer any attachment to the fleeting illusions of our mind. We are no longer attached to the ongoing creations of our mind. *Our beliefs, opinions, fears, expectations, thoughts, and emotions are seen clearly for what they are; momentary illusions that come and go like clouds that float across the sky.* The enlightened mind simply pays attention to them, understanding that they are only illusions. Only pure attention to the reality of "*what is*" at the moment matters to an enlightened mind.

The enlightened, pure observing consciousness is not focused on itself because enlightenment is not an individual enterprise. All forms of creation are systemically interdependent and interconnected with all other forms of creation, and *the goal of enlightenment is the evolutionary growth of human consciousness itself.* The enlightened mind knows that *the purpose of life itself is to transform matter into deeper levels of consciousness.* The enlightened mind knows that the evolutionary imperative of all life is to survive, and all created form is evolving either upwards toward life and higher levels of consciousness, or downwards into chaos and death.

Final Thoughts: The Need for a Teacher: Therapy, Spiritual Direction, and Meditation

The primitive ego *always* needs the security of certainty and knowing the correct answer. It has virtually no ability to manage the anxiety that comes with uncertainty and ambiguity. Whatever the primitive ego believes to be true, it assumes that it is *The Truth.* Awakening from a lifetime of this kind of conditioning can be challenging, even when it is one of our deeper desires.

As I suggested above, a therapist can be very helpful when attempting to awaken and develop a healthy sense of "self" or ego strength in Stages 3 and 4. Still, the work of moving beyond or letting go of our attachment to the ego in Stage 5 is best done with a well-trained spiritual director or meditation teacher. To successfully mature and evolve our consciousness to the level of enlightenment required to intentionally and sustainably manifest compassion and unconditional love, we will need a teacher's help. ***Just as an eye cannot see itself, it is very difficult for our ego to see itself.*** Therapists, spiritual directors, and meditation teachers can be instrumental as mirrors for the ego in the process of awakening and evolving our self-consciousness. However, as Sam Keen[5] warns, when we head out of the house to look for a teacher or guide on our journey to self-awareness and enlightenment, we need to be certain that the batteries in our "bullshit" detector are fully charged. There are many therapists, new age "spiritual" directors, and religious charlatans out there who claim to be teachers, *and many of them have not done their own work.* Keen reminds us that *no one can lead us any further into the desert than they have gone themselves.* Interview your potential teachers carefully and be sure to check their training and credentials before you put your spiritual journey in their hands. Knowledgeable and competent teachers will welcome and honor such scrutiny. They will not be offended.

If they are, *beware.*

Stages 3 and 4 are the observing adult stage of ego development, the birth of intentionality. It's in Stage 4 following *awakening* that we first begin to *intentionally* pay attention to the many rigid beliefs and manifestations of our primitive ego; when we *intentionally* begin the long journey from the high reactivity of Stage 2 toward the pro-active enlightened middlepath consciousness of Stages 3 to 6. *This is a tentative but critical stage in human development.*

---

5   Sam Keen is a noted American author, professor, and philosopher who is best known for his exploration of questions regarding love, life, and religion. "The practice of philosophy is a way of life that results from falling in love with questions—the great mythic questions that can never be given definitive answers." "One day, out of nowhere, you realize you don't know who you are, and none of the cards in your wallet provide the slightest clue to your real identity." Quotes from Wikipedia.

Because the observing adult ego in Stage 4 reflects an increasingly intentional growth toward a more mature, integrated, and differentiated ego, a therapist can be especially helpful in this stage of our development. Birthing an awakened self-consciousness with the ability to pay attention to the present moment, the reality of "what is," and intentionally live in the reality of *now* is challenging work. Without a therapist, it is very easy to regress into the unconscious behaviors and thinking process of a Stage 2 "pseudo adult."

Taming the Primitive Ego: Some Basic Concepts

Concept 1: The Need for Change and Learning to Think Differently

In today's world, the primitive ego's illusion of separateness, the belief that creates the many categories of "otherness" is growing. Our collective primitive ego human consciousness and its need to have power over others is growing. The conflict that results from the primitive ego's obsessive need to be "right" is growing. We claim to value compassion. We preach about the importance of global peace. We acknowledge the growing gap between the "have" nations and the "have not" countries of the Third World, but the conflicts and focus on "me" created by primitive ego thinking continues to grow. We are clearly headed in the wrong direction. We need to tame our collective primitive ego-consciousness and do the work to evolve a more enlightened thinking process. Waiting to do this work is not an option.

The potential for the collapse of social and civil order due to social unrest is increasing as the force-multipliers, threats, and economic triggers created by our collective human primitive ego (discussed in Part 2) continue to increasingly threaten the survival of human civilization and the future survival of our species on this planet.

A more interdependent, interconnected systemic world view is very much needed. Global diversity, cooperation, and empathy must quickly become the primary goal of human consciousness. Global peace and non-violence urgently require a more evolved human consciousness, and the existential need for this evolved human consciousness is growing rapidly

So how do we let go of the collective primitive ego-consciousness of humanity, and its tendency for vertical power "over" thinking, and intentionally move toward a more evolved and mature interdependent, interconnected and cooperative human consciousness? *The question is, how do we accomplish that evolution in our collective human consciousness when the collective primitive ego of humanity so passionately resists change?*

Again, I believe the answer is obvious; the unconscious primitive human ego must be tamed and encouraged to mature and become conscious. In other words, humans must *intentionally* tame their collective primitive ego-consciousness and become more self-reflective and more self-aware.

We must become conscious by learning to become more contemplative. This will require us to pay attention, to reflect and contemplate who we are at a deeper level of self-awareness. It will require us to become more self-conscious because the simple reality is, **we cannot change anything that we do not see, understand, and accept about ourselves**. Once we begin to see and deeply understand that the conflict and suffering in the world are caused by our own unconscious and immature childhood primitive ego thinking, resisting change will make less and less sense for the primitive ego. *The collective human primitive ego will not change because of force of will; it will only change when the primitive beliefs and memes of childhood no longer make any sense in a modern, adult world.*

Through contemplation, the path into the future will become more evident. It will become increasingly more apparent to the collective primitive ego of humanity that in order to survive, it will be necessary to embrace the *horizontal power of cooperation*—the memes of empathy, diversity, and cooperation where everything is systemically interdependent and interconnected.

So how do we continue to create this new horizontal power paradigm? How do we accomplish this shift in consciousness? How can we accelerate the taming and maturation of the primitive ego?

Concept 2: Creating a New Human Language

Part of the problem interfering with the creation of a horizontal power paradigm of cooperation is the lack of *horizontal language* to articulate that new paradigm. The spiritual language currently available to talk about horizontal power of cooperation, compassion, and empathy comes from the world's various religions. Unfortunately, the world's religions are the bastions of vertical power thinking. When we attempt to use religious language, we get caught in the emotional baggage that has been attached to "religious" and "spiritual" language by thousands of years of *vertical power; the primitive ego struggles over who is right and who is wrong.*

When I suggest that the collective primitive ego consciousness needs to become more contemplative, I am simply encouraging us to intentionally look more deeply into the nature of reality to enable the spiritual growth of the human consciousness through the lens of deep self-awareness. Until we do, it will be all but impossible to talk about systemic thinking and the concept of spirituality in indigenous cultures and their ability to see and deeply honor the presence of "spirit" in all of creation. It's impossible to think about anything that cannot be described by language. So, until we begin to create a spiritual language to articulate and define the concept of horizontal "cooperation," compassion, empathy, and even "spirituality" itself, we are going to be very limited in what we can create.

In other words, we need to create a modern spiritual language that transcends all of the specific world religions; a spiritual language grounded in concepts of human consciousness and spiritual growth, not specific religious beliefs; a language that supports an intentional evolution, awakening, and maturation of our collective human consciousness similar to that of the ancient indigenous cultures' systemic ability to see "spirit" in all of creation.

Concept 3: Awakening: Understanding the Conscious Evolution of Humanity

A leader in the evolution of human consciousness was Jesuit paleontologist, anthropologist, and evolutionist Teilhard de Chardin, who worked to understand evolution and faith. He believed that when human beings developed reflexive consciousness, the ability to be "conscious of being conscious" was a radical step in evolution. The universe's 15-billion-year process of evolution gave birth to consciousness on this planet we call Earth. At that moment, the evolution of one species on one small planet at the edge of one galaxy in the universe of billions and billions of galaxies was no longer confined to simple biology. De Chardin believed that through the evolutionary birth of consciousness, we *became* evolution; we became co-creators with the consciousness of the universe. He believed the evolution of human consciousness would determine the future of evolution on this planet.

Another leader in the evolution of human consciousness was Jewish agnostic Barbara Marx Hubbard, an American futurist, author, and public speaker who is credited with the concepts of "the Synergy Engine," the belief that every single person on this planet has a direct influence on the evolution of the whole human race and the "birthing" of humanity. As an author, speaker, and co-founder and president of the Foundation for Conscious Evolution, Hubbard posited that humanity was on the threshold of a quantum leap if newly emergent scientific, social, and spiritual capacities were integrated to address global crises. She called this the meme of *conscious evolution,* an evolution based on our consciously choosing to change how we think…the belief that every person on this planet has a direct influence on the evolution of the whole human race.

Decades ago, their writing and ideas changed how I spiritually understand the creation, meaning, and co-creative purpose of human consciousness. I am grateful for the significant contributions they made in our understanding of human consciousness, the co-creative process of human consciousness, and the *co-creative potential that we possess as conscious human beings to change the future evolution of our species.*

They articulated clearly that we, as conscious co-creators, can choose to unconsciously continue creating pain and suffering through the inevitable conflicts created by our current primitive ego vertical power "over others" thinking, or we can intentionally awaken our human consciousness and create a new reality based on diversity, the horizontal power of cooperation, systemic interdependence, unity, and diversity; the reality of a truly compassionate, global, co-creative human community. The choice is ours. *As conscious co-creators, we can create that amazing future if we have the courage to try.*

They taught us that evolution is a process of similar elements (in this example, the similar element is "humans") coming together and freely sharing their essential energy to create the next step toward increased complexity and increased consciousness. But we will evolve as a co-creative human species only when each person's essential energy is freely connected and shared with the next person's essential human energy. *An integrated global community will be formed only by this person-to-person, center-to-center sharing of each member's essential awakened, self-aware energy, not their "primitive" egos.*

When we explore the creation of local communities in Part 3, it will be essential to remember the concept of embracing unity in those local communities will not mean that these integrated networks of local communities will be communities of amorphous oneness, but rather global, non-violent communities that celebrate and embrace the infinite diversity and uniqueness of each member of the community. We will explore this concept in detail in Chapter 10, when we unpack the concept of "self-reliant local communities."

To consciously birth this newly awakened human consciousness of connection and cooperation through the intentional taming of our collective primitive ego consciousness will be a significant challenge for the human species. Humanity can successfully embrace "cooperative community," but *only* when our collective human primitive ego need to be "right" and its illusion of separateness has evolved and been intentionally transformed and tamed so as to embrace *cooperative systemic thinking*. Until that taming and awakening of humanity's collective primitive ego-consciousness are achieved, its use of vertical power "over others" will continue to be invested in seeing itself as a separate and unique "self"-object that must survive.

Since we don't have good language to speak about a spirit-centered world view yet, and because our present vertical power language cannot adequately describe what a spirit-centered community's values and structure would look like, many of the social movements that are advocating for change will continue to have difficulty clearly articulating their deeper wisdom of a new horizontal power paradigm of cooperation. But I believe that these social movement demonstrators are beginning to manifest the spiritual wisdom of an awakened consciousness and the wisdom that *something needs to change*; an emerging spiritual awareness that the old ways of thinking are no longer making sense!

Concept 4: Changing the Way We View Ourselves: The Journey from Ego Consciousness to Universal Consciousness

We cannot create a compassionate global community and world peace using the outmoded primitive ego paradigm called survival-of-the-fittest thinking. The primitive ego can embrace the idea of peace, love, and compassion, only so long as the plumb line of what's "right and good" runs directly through the center of its own belief system. When our primitive ego feels threatened, the aggression and conflict created by vertical power "over others" will quickly emerge. So how do we move from primitive ego consciousness to a universal, enlightened consciousness?

The solution is twofold.

First, we must intentionally grow in self-awareness. We need that deeper level of self-awareness in order to understand ourselves well enough psychologically to see the log in our eye. Without self-awareness, our primitive ego will continue to focus on the speck in our neighbor's eye. *We must become aware that the seeds of conflict, pain, and suffering that come from the paradigm of vertical power over others' lives were sown deep in the conditioning of our childhood primitive ego.*

Second, we must learn to see who we actually are, our authentic and essential self. We must struggle to answer the age-old question humans have been struggling with since the beginning of reflexive consciousness. Who are we? Why are we? We must contemplate these questions by taking away, one by one, all the conceptual categories that the primitive ego uses to define it's "self." This is the work of awakening and growth in self-awareness.

The creation of an awakened, self-aware, enlightened, mature ego that can use a new paradigm of horizontal power, cooperation, and diversity to form a compassionate global human community; a freely chosen blending of our essential "i am" energies into an infinitely diverse global human family that manifests true agape love and compassion, will require a radically new definition of "self."

When the primitive ego has emptied itself of all its primitive, conceptual categories— including its self-identity based on a paradigm of vertical power—and the illusions of separateness, *what remains is who we really are; our essential observing self.* Over the ages, this has been described as our essential nature; pure consciousness; pure simple observer; the one who sees what *is* without ego distortions; the localized "i am" that rests in the larger reality of "I AM"; *the wave of pure consciousness that can never be apart from the universal ocean of consciousness.*

These were concepts that Jesus, Buddha, and all the great spiritual teachers have been attempting to teach us throughout history. They emphatically rejected the castes and class structures of a vertical power consciousness. They rejected the lord–servant paradigm. *They encouraged us to redefine ourselves in more spiritual terms; to be in touch with the essence of who we are, pure compassion, fully awakened co-creators with the creator consciousness of the universe.*

They understood that spiritual growth is directly proportional to the growth in self-consciousness. When we have consciously emptied ourselves of our conceptual categories, our various ego beliefs, and the need to judge everything relative to our self-esteem, then we will be free to accept the world as it is, and simply love. This place of ego "emptiness" and compassion is what I refer to as the middlepath; or the middlepath consciousness. The ability to walk between the black and white extremes and intentionally search for the truths that are always found on both sides of every issue; without the need to think in terms of who's right and who's wrong.

We don't know what a middlepath community might look like because it is a product of our human future. Until that time, we must have the courage to embrace a middlepath consciousness, a co-creative place of ego emptiness and not-knowing, where we can evolve into a new humanity, a human species fully able to manifest empathy and compassion for *all* of creation.

The only thing I am certain of is that the present primitive ego, driven by its paradigm called "survival of the fittest," has clearly outlived its evolutionary usefulness. It clearly has us on a path that will eventually destroy the universe's evolutionary gift of reflexive consciousness, at least on this planet. This reality is not rocket science. Just pay attention to the news. Our evolutionary life on this planet is not, as they say, a dress rehearsal. ***This is our one chance.*** *We will either evolve into a higher level of consciousness, or we may cease to exist. The "choice" is ours.*

The gift of consciousness was built into the very fabric of this universe at the moment of creation, but futurists and biologists such a Teilhard de Chardin tell us that our planet will never again produce the conditions necessary on this planet for conscious life to re-evolve. Mother Earth gave birth to consciousness. Her work is done. Now it's up to us to determine our evolutionary future. I am convinced we will learn to evolve consciously and quickly, or our future will be dire and very dark. Survival of the fittest thinking works fine when the battle is over a cave, and the weapons are spears. It doesn't work very well to settle ideological struggles when the weapons are weapons of mass destruction.

It is clear that a successful future for humanity will require a collective awakened and evolved level of human consciousness capable of creating a peaceful level of global cooperation and complexity—a global community in which the diverse gifts of every unique individual will be needed. No-one will be left out. The evolution to an awakened human consciousness will require all of our minds interdependently and cooperatively working together. *This ability to embrace diversity is not only the primary challenge of humanity in the modern world of the future; it is unquestionably the foundational prerequisite for the future survival of our human species on this planet. We will explore these concepts more in Chapter 10 as we do the work of creating self-reliant, sustainable local communities based on community well-being, not unlimited global growth based on profit.*

Concept 5: Changing the Way We View Ourselves— The Primitive Ego Believes That Everything Important Comes from the "Outer" World, Not the "Inner" World

A successful future for humanity will require the evolved and matured ability to recognize that happiness is an internal work; it does not come from the outer world. The unconscious reason we buy things and spend significant effort in life acquiring possessions when we feel depressed or unhappy is that our primitive ego has been convinced that happiness and pleasure come from the outer world, not the inner world. Our primitive ego would never think of looking inward for the source of happiness. Our early childhood conditioning taught us that the things that made us happy or unhappy nearly always came from the outer world. But as adults, looking outward for happiness only creates disappointment. When happiness fails to materialize, our primitive ego assumes that it needs to buy "more." This desperate search for happiness becomes a compulsive addiction for a never-ending need to acquire "more" and "more" and "more" stuff.

Happiness is achieved when we begin looking inside for meaning and purpose. Why are we here? What were we meant to do? What would satisfy our soul and create happiness in our life? How are we "pushing the river"? What or who are we blaming for our lack of happiness?

If we want to live a happy life, we must accept full responsibility to create that life. If we're going to create a different world, we must take full responsibility to create that world.

Of course, the reality is that what we choose to create in the outer world, consciously or unconsciously, is simply a reflection of our inner world. If we want to live a happy, more peaceful, and enlightened life, we must accept the responsibility for co-creatively creating that world by first changing ourselves.

Happiness is something we create through growth in self-awareness, not something we buy.

The first step toward that kind of change is the commitment to intentionally become more self-aware through the conscious evolution or the taming of our own observing ego. Only our more conscious and self-aware adult observing ego has the ability for self-empowerment, the ability to embrace the reality of what is, and accept full responsibility for the life we are currently living. We have to learn to be happy with *ourselves,* not with what we "have." This simple reality is primary learning and wisdom that comes from intentionally taming our primitive ego consciousness.

Concept 6: The Dangers Embedded in Our Collective Primitive Ego Entitlement, Narcissism, and the Need to Be "Right"

Three distinct behaviors unerringly point to the presence of a primitive ego that has unconsciously taken control of a person's consciousness. These three behaviors currently reflect the consciousness of a large majority of adults.

First is a strong sense of entitlement, the feeling that we *deserve* more.

- Entitled to more free government handouts.

- Entitled to more free health care.

- Entitled to more free unemployment benefits.

- Entitled to larger bonus checks at the end of the year.

- Entitled to purchase a nice home even when we know that we can't afford the monthly payments.

- Belief that the many problems and crises facing our nation such as climate change, our dependency on foreign oil, and the depletion of natural resources, are not our responsibility. They are someone else's fault. Therefore, it is **their** problem to fix them.

- Entitlement's bottom line is "it's the responsibility of the government to take care of us but *don't even think* about raising our taxes."

Second, a narcissistic, greedy "me first" attitude that reflects a significant lack of compassion or empathy for others.

- A deep prejudice and bias against immigrants and people different from us, (primitive ego fear of "other").

- The belief that "our" personal rights are more valid and important than the rights of others (primitive ego entitlement).

- The assumption that we live in a survival-of-the-fittest world, so it's OK to take what we want from others. If we don't take care of ourselves, who will? (Primitive ego *What's in it for "me?"*)

- It's OK to abuse, deport, imprison, torture, or execute immigrants and other terrorists who enter our country illegally (primitive ego racism and fear of "other").

- Winning the next election is more important than protecting the needs of the voters who sent me to Washington (primitive ego access to power "over").

- Amassing political power, wealth, and influence is more important than any crises facing our country (primitive ego "What's in it for me" greed).

And third, the imperative need to be "right," the inflexible attitude that "my" rigid black-and-white beliefs *always* represent absolute truth.

Abortions and homosexuality are wrong no matter what the situation.

- My anger is justified whenever another person dares to challenge my beliefs.

- It is OK to lie and distort the truth because I and my beliefs are always right.

- The ideology of *my* political party is absolutely right, and anyone who disagrees is obviously of questionable character, not very patriotic, and dangerous.

- It's OK to be radically partisan even if it gridlocks our nation because **my** beliefs and the beliefs of my political party are *always* right.

- **My** religion is the *only* religion that possesses the truth, so it's my right to go into the world and tell the members of other religions that they are *wrong*.

If you are becoming a bit uncomfortable that some of these behaviors are hitting a bit close to home for you, congratulations, you are a person who is ready to grow and evolve your consciousness. If this list has not made you uneasy or perhaps has even made you angry, you are apparently not yet ready to grow. But you can! The need to be "right" is not a terminal situation; it just means you're not ready to grow in self-awareness...*yet*. Read on.

Concept 7: Embracing Reality, Gratitude, and Manifesting Hope

When faced with challenges to our belief system, the unconscious primitive ego of our inner child becomes frightened. We begin to feel overwhelmed and powerless. We protectively pull inside. We shut down and begin to isolate. We convince ourselves that we are right, and those who dare to disagree with us are the enemy, and most importantly, we get angry and aggressive when they tell us "we" are wrong. This is a very dangerous behavior. Unfortunately, this is clearly what is happening to a growing number of people in the world today.

This tendency can be seen clearly in the emerging conservative global political parties. These growing conservative political movements are inevitably attracting the most ideologically inflexible, the most rigid, black-and-white, all-or-nothing primitive ego thinkers who are unconsciously under the unyielding, unconscious control of their inner-child's frightened primitive ego...and its aggressive need to be "right"!

When we recognize that our primitive ego is taking over our emotions and behaviors, we need to remind ourselves that **dealing with "reality" is not an option.** Our frightened primitive ego often ignores it, but "reality" is the *only* thing we *can* actually embrace. When something is "real," it means we *have* to deal with it. We have no choice! *The evolution of our consciousness requires that we are willing to engage with truth, facts, data, and reality, not illusions, distortions, and denial.*

If we want to create a more enlightened world, then each of us must be willing to become the change we want to create. We must we willing to expand our vision of the world. We must be willing to embrace the evolutionary possibilities waiting for us in the future, and most of all, we must be willing to bring hope into the world; to become the light in the darkness; to let go of our primitive "ego-self" and embrace our more enlightened, spiritually evolved observing "ego-self."

I am not referring to a "religious" concept here, but rather to a more basic spiritual truth. When each of us is willing to intentionally awaken our consciousness and pay attention, to become intentionally self-aware of the unconscious behaviors and energy we are sending into the world, only then will we successfully evolve the critically needed evolutionary growth of our collective human consciousness. This "conscious evolution" of our collective human consciousness will happen effortlessly when each of us accepts responsibility *to become* the change we want to see.

How will we know when we are awakening our consciousness? How will we know we are becoming more enlightened? How will we know our growth in self-awareness is authentic?

The surest sign of an evolving consciousness is the ability to sustain gratitude and thankfulness. As gratitude and appreciation grow, our ability to be happy and openly embrace the future will grow…even when confronted by the global crises and challenges that we are currently facing. Challenges we know need to be addressed and solved.

As our attitude of gratitude and appreciation grows stronger, like a snake shedding its skin, the greed and narcissism of our primitive ego will slowly give way to a more mature, enlightened observing ego consciousness. We will learn to listen more and talk less. We will learn to "hear" what others are sharing with us. We will learn to embrace the questions and give up the need to possess all the answers. In spiritual language, we will begin to empty ourselves and learn to embrace *not-knowing*. And most importantly, we will use middlepath thinking that intentionally looks for the truths that are always present on both sides of every issue.

Gratitude, appreciation, cooperation, and compassion are contagious attitudes and powerful energies. Never underestimate the power of an optimistic person, a person who exudes gratitude and compassion. When we are in the presence of a person who is more evolved, more enlightened than we are, their energy is appealing and catching. It transforms *our* consciousness. Over time, we too begin to change the consciousness of others. Mahatma Gandhi, Mother Teresa, Martin Luther King, Jesus, Muhammad, Nelson Mandela, the Dali Lama, and Desmond Tutu are each good examples of enlightened consciousness that changed the world. There are many more.

Our world is in crisis. We have given in to the helplessness of our frightened inner children…the unconscious thinking of our collective human primitive ego. The consequences of rigid primitive ego thinking are clearly visible in Washington, DC. And just as *we* can see it clearly in others, *others* can see it just as clearly in us.

Only as we become increasingly self-aware; only as we learn to intentionally pay attention to our own behaviors and beliefs, will we begin to see the primitive ego narcissism, the self-focus, the sense of isolation, and the me-first attitude that unconsciously resides in our own hearts.

Again, our primitive ego consciousness is not a terminal condition. It is the ego consciousness that formed during our early childhood. Every one of us can become more enlightened. The question we need to ask ourselves is, "When will I make the decision to become intentionally more self-aware and begin *my* spiritual journey into an awakened observing consciousness?"

The day we begin our own intentional journey toward a more enlightened consciousness will be the day that our nation, our species, and our world evolve and becomes more enlightened; more able to envision the world through new eyes; more able to create a new worldview that transcends the tribalism and primitive ego thinking we see today.

As you will discover in Part 2, I believe the world is likely to experience a very dangerous collapse of social and civil order and social upheaval in the coming years. This upheaval will convince us beyond any doubt that we can no longer continue on the current path called business-as-usual. When this upheaval arrives, we will see that continuing to use primitive ego thinking, entitlement, a narcissistic focus on *"me,"* and the primitive ego need to be "right" will only create more pain, suffering, and chaos in the world.

If we want to evolve our consciousness, we have no choice but to become more self-aware. We must first meet and understand the primitive ego of our own inner child. We must learn to love our inner child but recognize that we can no longer give the primitive ego of our inner child unconscious permission to run our lives. The first step toward authentic spiritual growth begins in learning to become self-aware, evolve and mature our consciousness, and love who we *are* and who we were born to *be.* Until we learn to love our true, authentic self unconditionally, our love for others will always be in danger of having a judgmental "because" attached.

We will move beyond the current violence created by primitive ego thinking only when we embrace the courage to walk a more authentic, evolved path into the future, a path born of deep self-awareness. Only then will we begin to create a more enlightened collective global culture based on gratitude, appreciation, cooperation, empathy, mutuality, and compassion. In philosopher Jean Gebser's words, "only then will we learn to become more appreciative of things that really matter."

Concept 8: Power "Over," the Primitive Ego Need to Control Others; and Perfectionism, the Need to Control Self

Our primitive ego's common behavior is the need for control; the need to win and be right; a vertical power-over others called "survival-of-the-fittest" thinking. Winning and aggressive competitiveness is a common childhood way of coping with perceived external threats. Or it may have simply been a way to earn praise and attention from our caregivers. Regardless of where the need to be in control and have power over others may have come from, it becomes a very negative internal emotion we tend to "project" onto others. The projection results because we believe it isn't *us* who has the "control" problem. It feels like we always have to protect ourselves from all those *other* "controlling" people. Because we believe we are surrounded by controlling people, we tell ourselves survival-of-the-fittest thinking is the only way to protect ourselves.

Perfectionism is a close cousin to survival-of-the-fittest thinking. In perfectionism, we attempt to control ourselves. We become "self"-critical. We embrace perfectionism to control ourselves and protect ourselves from external and internal criticism. The need to be perfect may have helped us avoid criticism and have the world feel safer as a child, but it is often a significant source of stress and anxiety for ourselves and others when we become adults. First of all, perfection is not possible. There is no such thing as perfection. It doesn't exist. Perfection is an illusion. Unfortunately, the primitive ego never learned that reality. No matter how well we accomplished something, it always felt like we *could* have done it a *little* bit better. Taming the primitive ego requires the self-awareness to know when we are attempting to control others and *when we are attempting to control ourselves*. Control of others, and control of self, are both attempts to push the river. *Both are illusions that make us powerless.* Both create significant stress and unhappiness in our lives and the lives of those around us.

Most of the anxiety, unhappiness, stress, and depression we experience in life comes from our primitive ego's unconscious struggle for perfection, the need to be "right," and our unconscious need to control others. These illusions can be very destructive to our self-esteem and our sense of well-being because they all attempt to "push the river." The negative energy associated with "self"-perfectionism is one of the most common ways we harm our self-esteem and our sense of well-being. Intentional growth in self-awareness is a powerful cure for these familiar self-inflicted creators of stress, anxiety, and powerlessness.

The model below illustrates the concept that when our goal is perfection or A+, then *everything we accomplish between total failure (F) and a solid (A) will be emotionally experienced as failure.* Becoming self-aware of the need for perfection will significantly reduce anxiety and increase our sense of well-being. Intentionally taming our primitive ego is an effective path to embrace when our goal is learning to be comfortable with who we were born to be.

A+ Model

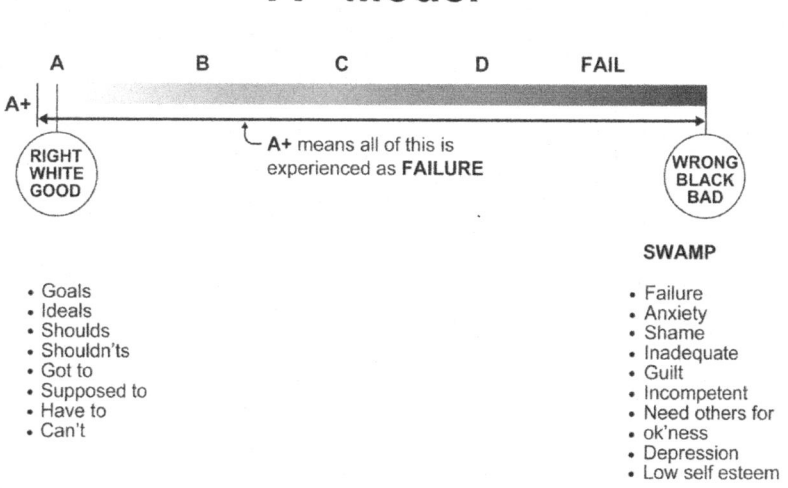

STRESS = Got to but can't because the goal is perfection

Concept 9: Our Primitive Ego Need to Blame Others for "Our" Feelings

Feeling powerless and victimized as adults comes from our primitive ego's unwillingness to accept full responsibility for both the choices and the consequences of those choices that we have made, *or not made,* in our lives. We, *not others or fate,* are responsible for the life that *we* have created. Our primitive ego prefers to blame the life situations and emotions that we experience onto others.

94

This is not to say that there are not times and situations where bad things may happen to us. The universe is neutral and impersonal, so sometimes, it seems like fate does indeed dictate what will happen in our lives. But regardless of what life brings us, we are still responsible for our choices, even if the only option we have is *our attitude.*

For example, our primitive ego is often convinced that others literally *make* us feel how we feel. So we blame them for our feelings *despite the reality that blame essentially means that we are powerless* until *others* change their behaviors that *we* don't like. When they say no or ignore us, or when we are certain that they are not going to change their behaviors, we get angry because *we know we are virtually powerless* until they decide to agree with us and change their behavior. That's when it is helpful through intentional growth in self-awareness to remind ourselves that *no one can make us feel anything that is not already inside of us.* Demanding that someone has to change their behavior for us to be happy is simply another example of "pushing the river."

A useful way to illustrate this concept is to suddenly hold up a snake in front of a person who is afraid of snakes. Their reaction will likely be angry and blaming *you* for scaring them! Then hold up your fluffy baby bunny rabbit for them. Their response will probably be wanting to hold it. *This simple test confirms that you cannot make anyone feel anything that is not already inside of them.* They already have a fear of snakes, so you simply reminded them of that fear. No matter how often you hold up the baby bunny rabbit, you will never scare them because they have no fear of baby bunny rabbits already inside them. This holds true for all feelings and emotions. The only exception would be if someone were actually to threaten your life. In this case, your ego, which is designed to protect you, would experience fear. Some might argue that the fear of death is already inside of you.

As you do the work of becoming more self-aware, you will find that *others* have lost their ability to create *your* feelings regardless of what they do. You will *know* they can't "make" you feel anything. They are merely *reminding* you that the feeling or emotion you are experiencing was created *inside you.* You will be more in control of your own emotions and reactions, and other people will be impressed at your ability to remain calm. This awareness is one of the more powerful insights you'll experience as you evolve and mature your ability to intentionally tame your childhood primitive ego and become more *self-aware.*

Concept 10: Middlepath: A Major Goal of Intentional Growth in Self-Awareness and Awakening

Middlepath is an awakened state of mind, not a place. We achieve middlepath thinking when our ego has been emptied of all beliefs, opinions, certainties, sense of duality thinking, and all concepts or judgment or categories of "otherness." As we get closer to a middlepath consciousness in our self-identity, happiness will increase, and the experience of depression, conflict, stress, and anxiety will diminish. A middlepath consciousness is content to simply *observe,* without judgment, the reality of the moment.

The best way to begin to understand middlepath is to picture two black-and-white primitive egos in a heated argument as to who is right on a particular issue. As discussed above, black-and-white thinking is an early developmental stage of childhood where the world is broken down or split into all good or all bad, all right or all wrong. In the model below, two young children are fighting on a playground. Each primitive ego is struggling to convince the other primitive ego that *its* view is the correct view. It will not be long before the discussion turns into an argument, and if continued, it will probably lead to conflict or violence.

Children Fighting

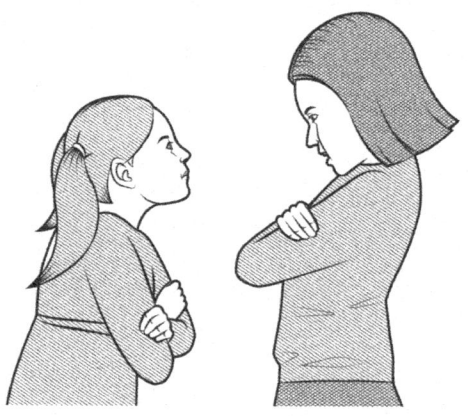

Two kindergarteners manifesting their primitive
ego's need to be "right".

These two young primitive egos will grow and mature physically. The bodies that carry their untamed primitive ego will grow into adulthood. But unless they embrace an intentional growth in their self-awareness, these adults will emotionally tend to remain children in adult bodies. The conflict and violence that immature, primitive egos can create in an adult body are virtually unlimited. *Virtually all of the conflict and suffering we witness in the world today is caused by "adults" using immature, primitive, black-and-white thinking, and the need to be right.*

Now let's picture these two primitive egos becoming a bit more open to the other person's point of view. What has happened? Well, first, each person's ego has now entertained the *possibility* that the other person's ego *might* be a little bit "right." In a metaphoric sense, they have each taken a small step towards each other. They are no longer defending their understanding of the issue as THE ABSOLUTE TRUTH. They have moved from pure black-and-white thinking to a slightly grayer point of view. They have become less reactive and are not experiencing each other as a personal threat. They no longer experience each other as "the enemy" who is trying to tell their primitive ego that it is "absolutely" wrong.

They are beginning to embrace middlepath thinking. They are intentionally seeking the truths embedded in the other's position. When they have achieved a deeper level of self-awareness, they will recognize that *no one* is smart enough to be absolutely "right" or absolutely "wrong" 100% of the time.

They are now beginning to listen a little more closely to what each other has to say. The noise level is starting to drop. They are beginning to accept the possibility that there might be a bit of truth in what the other person is saying. They have moved from *absolute certainty* to a place of *not-knowing-for-certain*. The potential for conflict and violence between them has lessened. They are beginning to experience each other as people who simply think differently about the subject they are discussing.

The model below illustrates the process of creating a more middlepath consciousness. A consciousness that has tamed its primitive ego and emptied itself of absolute certainties, rigid beliefs, absolute truth, judgment, and replaced them with acceptance, not "knowing," empathy, and compassion for others.... even when the other person might disagree with them.

Emptiness of Ego

Response is:

Input ⇨	Certainties Beliefs Absolute Truth	Certainties Beliefs Absolute Truth	⇨ Violent Judgemental Reactive Angry

EGO   ⇧ No Space No Emptiness   EGO

| Input ⇨ | Beliefs | Emptiness Of Ego Space Some Time To Choose Response | Beliefs | ⇨ Chosen Measured Response |

EGO   EGO

| Input ⇨ | Middlepath Emptiness Of Ego Conscious Choice As To The Energy We Manifest | ⇨ Compassion |

EGO   Middle path thinking is actively searching for the truths found on both sides of every issue / conflict   EGO

These two primitive egos have begun to mature. They are moving toward a middlepath consciousness:

- A place where some truth is always found in both points of view.

- A non-reactive place of silence and increased listening.

- A place of openness and not-knowing.

- A place where the beliefs and absolute certainties of the primitive ego have been let go, or emptied.

- A place where there is less conflict and violence.

- A place where each person feels safer, heard, understood, and valued.

- A place of increased diversity.

- And most importantly, a place where black-and-white, right/wrong, either/or duality thinking has given way to concepts of gray, systemic, interconnected, and interdependent thinking; a wholeness/unity way of thinking where listening is as important as speaking. A place of wholeness, where the unity of all things is experienced, where "spirit" is found in all of reality, and where both persons experience each other as "thou" or "kin."

If the ego in each person in our model above scenario continues to mature, they will eventually experience the unity of the middlepath; a spirituality of silence and non-violence where there is no "otherness"; a place of radical and infinite diversity. When a person has achieved emptiness of ego or a middlepath consciousness, a place in which they don't *do* compassion, they *become* compassion.

We view ourselves and view the world as a mental journey that begins with the primitive, black-and-white ego of childhood and moves toward a middlepath consciousness called enlightenment. Thus, all growth in self-aware-ness, all increase in self-consciousness, is movement toward a middlepath consciousness or a middlepath spirituality. Without growth in self-conscious-ness or self-awareness, spiritual growth is not possible. The journey toward a middlepath consciousness needs to become the future of human evolution.

The current path we are on is not sustainable; it is headed toward suffering and the likely extinction of our species on this planet.

Stated simply, a middlepath conscious is not merely a good idea. Growth in self-awareness and middlepath thinking are essential for humanity to avoid the collapse of social and civil order as humanity struggles to cope with the massive changes, existential force-multiplier threats, and economic triggers (described in Part 2).

Waiting to intentionally evolve the consciousness of humanity is no longer an option. To avoid the rapidly growing possible extinction of humanity, I believe a tamed, middlepath thinking or middlepath consciousness is the most critical skill humanity will need to embrace for human culture and human civilization to survive the massive changes and existential threats that are coming.

Concept 11: Learning to Pay Attention and Focus on Primitive Ego Knee-Jerks

The essential point here is the concept that the primitive ego of our inner child adopted the beliefs, habits, and survival skills necessary to take care of us in early childhood. Still, as we explored at the beginning of this chapter, these primitive "old brain" defenses and survival skills have become our *unconscious* emotional *knee-jerk* responses to similar adult-life situations that we are now encountering as adults. Because they are so common and so easily create conflict in our relationships with others, we will close this chapter by taking a more in-depth look into the concept of knee-jerks and their ability to create violence.

We understand that no child under six to seven years of age has the wisdom or maturity to successfully function in an adult world. For example, hitting someone or yelling at them when we are angry with them may have worked in childhood, but this kind of behavior is often ineffective and dangerous in the adult world.

Developmentally, most adults in the world today manifest a relatively low level of self-awareness. They unconsciously attempt to use their primitive ego templates from childhood to cope in the adult world of their day-to-day life. They may look and talk like adults, but the sobering reality is the narcissistic, self-focused, primitive ego of their inner-child, and its early childhood conditioning, is the level of consciousness cognitively and emotionally in control of their adult lives.

This early childhood, primitive ego energy tends to come into the world as emotional knee-jerks, *not* carefully thought out responses to external stimuli or triggers. For example, when someone disagrees with us, tells us no, tells us we are wrong, ridicules our beliefs, or becomes judgmental of us, we immediately and *unconsciously knee-jerk* defensive anger into the conversation. Our body language changes, our ability to process ideas decreases, we emotionally become defensive, our blood pressure increases, we experience the other as dangerous and critical, and our primitive ego need to be "right" immediately kicks in, and we increasingly become aggressive.

Intentional growth in self-awareness is learning to pay careful attention when we have these common emotional knee-jerk reactions. When they happen, we are increasingly able to calmly remind ourselves that no one can make us *feel*, we recognize that our primitive ego consciousness is knee-jerking the need to be "right" and unnecessary aggressive emotional energy into the conversation. This recognition allows us to consciously engage our mature, evolved, awakened, self-aware adult consciousness. We begin to intentionally look for the truths we *know* are embedded in the other person's understanding of the issue. The potential conflict shifts to that of a more adult and helpful conversation in which both people can walk away as friends.

I recognize that many readers will assume this scenario to be unrealistic. And they are probably right, given the tendency of most adults to knee-jerk emotionally charged defensive primitive ego childhood energy into conversations when there are differences of opinion. But I offer this scenario as a possible reality if we could intentionally tame the collective primitive ego-consciousness of humanity and embrace a more evolved, mature, awakened, and "self-aware" collective adult human consciousness.

It is becoming ever clearer that we need to learn how to awaken and put the light of our conscious attention on our unconscious behaviors, feelings, and thoughts; to become self-aware and make our primitive ego more conscious. The need to control, perfectionism, insisting on the need to be right, and survival-of-the-fittest thinking all come from the unconscious shadow energies of our primitive ego. If we could learn to look within, become self-aware, and take full responsibility for what we have been unconsciously projecting onto others, the scenario I offered above just might become the way humanity could resolve differences of opinions and more creatively solve the problems that we have unconsciously created using our collective, untamed, immature, primitive ego consciousness.

I believe that most people would prefer working to create this kind of human culture. I think most people are tired of the conflicts, the angry conversations that so often happen when people disagree, the thinly veiled threats of violence that seem to be a growing part of human culture. I believe that humanity is not only capable of creating this more evolved and adult world, I think most people would be open to begin actively working to create that world.

We will look at that possibility in Chapter 10 when we talk about hope, and the possibility of creating self-reliant local communities based on well-being, and the evolved, matured, collective middlepath "self-aware" consciousness of the scenario I presented above.

Conclusion of Part 1

We have covered a lot of material and primitive ego concepts in Part 1. The material was presented so that the primitive ego concepts could be easily accessed for review as we move into the chapters of Part 2. The more we can link the primitive ego concepts of Part 1 with the material we'll cover in Part 2, the more clarity we will have that *we* are the problem.

Waiting to intentionally tame and evolve the collective childhood primitive ego-consciousness of humanity to become a more awakened and self-aware species is *not* an option. I believe it is the most essential work humanity has ever been called on to do. I am convinced that dealing with and creatively solving the existentially dangerous force-multipliers threats that we'll cover in Part 2 will illustrate both the need for a deep understanding of this primitive ego material and the urgently needed collective awakening and evolution of our human consciousness.

Human civilization's future and our survival as a species will depend on how well and how quickly we can evolve our collective human consciousness. We have run out of time to prepare or mitigate the threats we'll cover in Part 2. Each of the individual existential threats in Part 2 has the force-multiplier strength to systemically collapse human culture. When the existential force-multiplier threats and economic triggers in Part 2 begin to systemically cascade toward collapse, they will systemically reinforce each other in that collapse. When that happens, the collapse of social and civil order will shift from a likely possibility to an inevitable certainty.

The future is *not* what it used to be. And that future is not *coming. It's* here. We need to begin *now* preparing for the massive changes and challenges that are coming. The material in Part 2 will amplify the urgency of preparing *now.*

A Word of Hope

Before we dive into the dire and dark realities of Part 2, I want to offer a word of hope. I believe the material on self-reliant local communities in Part 3 will offer the best and most realistic hope for humanity's survival and future generations. Creating self-reliant, sustainable, local community's is ***the*** golden-arch reason I am writing this book. Future generations are inheriting a world they did not create. We created it for them. The future generations will need our wisdom and the collective taming of their primitive ego consciousness to successfully deal with the life-altering challenges they *will* face. I believe humanity's viable long-term future will depend directly on the successful taming and evolution of the collective human consciousness.

The future will be dire and dark, but there is reason for hope, and that hope is realistic if they have the courage to intentionally grow in self-awareness and do the work that will be required to tame and evolve the collective human consciousness of the members of their individual self-reliant local community's. Not everyone will accept this challenge, but I believe many will. And the successful, sustainable, self-reliant local communities they create will, in time, "seed" the sustainable future of humanity on our planet.

I wrote this book as a blueprint of hope for future generations that begin to prepare *"now"* for the massive changes, challenges, and existential threats that are coming.

Now onto the dark and the dire.

PART 2:
THE EXISTENTIAL FORCE-MULTIPLIER THREATS AND ECONOMIC TRIGGERS THREATENING HUMAN CIVILIZATION

In Part 2, we will take an in-depth look at the primary and secondary black swan existential force-multiplier threats and economic triggers that *will* continue to stress the fragile and vulnerable social, civil, and economic systems that support human civilization and humanity's essential social structures.

When these fragile economic and essential social structures begin to systemically collapse, the social and civil collapse will quickly follow. Preparation, to create the sustainable resilience that will be needed for survival when that social and civil collapse happens, needs to begin *now*. Resilience requires preparation *before* a crisis arrives, not after it arrives.

Each of the black swan existential force-multiplier threats and economic triggers we will explore below in Part 2 were created by our collective immature primitive ego human consciousness. As writer Paul Gilding[6] reminds us, "We have come to the end of Economic Growth, Version 1.0, a world economy based on consumption and waste, where we lived beyond the means of our planet's ecosystems and resources." As one writer said as a response to the concept of a black swan event, the many force-multipliers threatening humanity, including those listed in Part 2 of this book, "are not black 'swan' events, they are better described as a herd of stampeding black elephants racing towards us, and they *will* create the likely/inevitable collapse of human culture and life as we know it. And the first victim to experience systemic failure and collapse will likely be neoliberal global capitalism."

---

6   https://en.wikipedia.org/wiki/Paul_Gilding.

In the chapters of Part 2, we will examine:

a. How each of the existential force multiplier threats were created by the immature, unevolved collective primitive ego-consciousness of humanity and its early childhood conditioning.

b. How it's only a matter of time until one or more of those existential force-multiplier threats, or economic triggers, will create a destabilizing economic or social event that will precipitate a systemic cascade of economic, social, and civil collapse.

These growing existential force-multiplier threats and economic triggers are already destabilizing our world's political systems and our neoliberal global economy. Today it's COVID-19. Tomorrow it will be the climate crisis, storm intensification, declining oil production, powering down from fossil fuels, intentional degrowth of the global economy, massive and growing global debt, another global pandemic, or simply the social and political lack of will to intentionally tame our immature collective primitive ego human consciousness. We will explore all of these existential threats below.

We Are the Problem; the Root Cause

The golden-arch reason I decided to write this book is the concept that *we* are the problem; *we* are the root cause and creator of the black swan existential force-multiplier threats and economic triggers that are currently threatening the future survival of humanity.

Each of the existential force-multiplier threats and economic triggers that we will explore in Part 2 has the potential to eventually create or trigger the social and civil collapse of human culture. But the economic triggers and existential force-multiplier threats are only the *symptoms.*

We are the problem. We are the root cause. Our collective immature primitive ego, human consciousness, and early childhood conditioning created each of the existential force multiplier threats and economic triggers in Part 2. And only "we" can solve those threats/symptoms. Only "we" can reduce their growing threat to the survival of our human culture, human civilization, and the future of our species.

But solving them will not be easy or straightforward. Because interconnected and interdependent systems are always extremely complex, the solutions required to solve those threats/symptoms will also be complicated and complex. This is especially true when we talk about systemically interconnected and interdependent *global* systems such as the global economy and neoliberal capitalism.

But reducing that threat will require paying *more attention* to the *root causes* (the collective, immature, unevolved primitive ego-consciousness of humanity and its early childhood conditioning) and *less attention* to the massive *changes and symptoms* these economic triggers and existential force multiplier threats are creating. *Until we deal with the root cause, the symptoms will only continue to increase rapidly in both severity and social impact.*

Immature, primitive, unevolved thinking in a primitive local human culture is survivable. But immature and unevolved, primitive thinking in a scientifically advanced global culture is *not*. When essential social systems systemically collapse, they *will* trigger a massive social and civil collapse, and that social collapse *will* end human civilization and life as we know it. And as I will illustrate in this book, we are far closer to that reality than most people believe possible or are prepared to survive.

Taming the collective primitive ego-consciousness of humanity is unquestionably, and undeniably, the most critical and essential challenge humanity has ever faced. Until we intentionally and collectively do that work, our collective immature primitive ego human consciousness and its dangerous early childhood condition will continue to be the root cause, threatening the likely collapse of human civilization, and the growing possibility of extinction of our species on this planet. Waiting to rapidly and intentionally evolve the collective human consciousness is not an option.

Corporations and Greed-Based Business-As-Usual:
Neoliberal Global Capitalism's Focus On Profit

One of the main factors accelerating our rush toward global social and civil collapse is the underlying design of our global corporate economic system. We can look at corporations as artificial life forms that humans have created. They were designed to have one purpose: to survive and compete in the artificial game that we also created called the global stock market. We gave these artificial life-forms only one prime directive: "maximize financial profit and shareholder value to survive and win the game." And that is precisely what corporations do—they survive regardless of the impact *their* survival has on the planet, other life support systems, or other living species on the planet. It's called business-as-usual.

If a corporation can only survive and win its game by maximizing financial value, then it naturally must work to overcome anything that stands in the way of that goal. For instance, a corporation must seek to evade environmental restrictions that reduce its profit margins. If the health and diversity of local ecosystems or communities stand in its way, it must prioritize its corporate survival. Given that the corporation is designed with the purpose of profit and survival, it must also naturally self-select CEOs and leaders who have no ethical compunction or concern for externalities. Evading restrictions, corrupting governments, polluting the atmosphere, exhausting non-renewable natural resources, and minimizing workers' wages to increase profits, are simply examples of what corporations were designed to do.

Similarly, our global economic system was designed to manifest similar kinds of behavior. The global, debt-based currency issued by private banks, and backed by government loans, is designed to support corporate growth and profit, minimize competition, produce products in Third-World emerging nations where wages are far below that required for worker survival, and intentionally create artificial scarcity to maximize corporate profit, and intentionally create a global environment of zero-sum corporate winners and losers.

A good definition of neoliberal global capitalism is this quote by W.B. Yates on social and civil collapse:

Turning and turning in the widening gyre
The falcon cannot hear the falconer;
Things fall apart; the centre cannot hold;
Mere anarchy is loosed upon the world,
Surely some revelation is at hand;
And what rough beast, its hour come around at last,
Slouches towards Bethlehem to be born?
– W. B. Yates

We will begin Part 2 by exploring in more detail the existential force multiplier threat of neoliberal global capitalism. Unarguably, and unquestionably, neoliberal global capitalism is the most fragile structure in the foundation of human civilization. *When* it collapses, the inevitable social and civil collapse of humanity and life as we know it will quickly follow.

Black Swan Force/Existential Force-Multiplier Threat and Economic Trigger: Neoliberal Global Capitalism

Our resistance to intentionally evolve our collective human consciousness blinds us to the changes that need to be made in the foundations of human civilization.

We are the problem: aspects of humanity's collective, unconscious, unevolved primitive ego, and its early childhood conditioning, that work together to systemically reinforce and support each other.

In neoliberal global capitalism, the primary "We are the problem" is "What's in it for me?" **greed**. (Keep in mind that all of the primitive ego aspects in the list below work together to systemically support the primitive ego's "What's in it for me?" greed.)

* *

Primitive ego early childhood conditioning:

a. "What's in it for me?" **greed**.

b. Need to be **"right"** (aggressive arrogance, extreme cognitive dissonance/confirmation bias).

c. Inability to replace *me* thinking with *we* thinking (compassion, mutuality, cooperation).

d. I want what I want when I want it.

e. **Blames** others for *our* feelings (inability to own our own feelings).

f. Ignorance regarding the **danger of exponential growth** (e.g., COVID-19).

g. A lack of interconnected, interdependent **systemic thinking**.

h. Survival-of-the-fittest thinking.

i. Black versus white, **zero-sum thinking** (*You* can't have that, it's *mine!*).

j. An exaggerated aggressive, narcissistic self-focused sense of **entitlement**.

k. An inability to connect short-term choices with long-term consequences.

l. The fear of change (uncertainty, not knowing).

m. The never-ending, obsessive desired for **more.**

n. The need for power "over" rather than power "with."

o. The inability to embrace long-term thinking.

* *

Introduction to Neoliberal Global Capitalism: Unquestionably the Most Fragile Structure Vulnerable to Collapse in the Global Foundation of Human Civilization

Neoliberal global capitalism[7] is the global economic system that drives the global economy. It is also the most fragile and vulnerable social system to all of the existential force-multiplier threats that we will examine in Part 2. The potential of the existential force-multiplier threats in Part 2 to trigger the eventual economic collapse of neoliberal global capitalism is exceptionally high.

Because capitalism is the most fragile and vulnerable economic structure supporting human civilization and life as we know it, neoliberal global capitalism's economic collapse *will most likely be the trigger event that creates social and civil collapse.* Because of this sobering reality, we will begin Part 2,

---

7 **Neoliberalism** is contemporarily used to refer to market-oriented reform policies such as "eliminating price controls, deregulating capital markets, lowering trade barriers" and reducing state influence in the economy, especially through privatization and austerity.

Chapter 3 by taking a detailed look at some of the dangerous concepts and ideologies embedded in neoliberal global capitalism.

a. Neoliberal global capitalism institutionalized the immature primitive ego concept of "What's in it for me?" greed. It is based on never-ending growth and profit. When growth and profit end, capitalism as an economic system will collapse and die. Stated simply, when the money stops flowing, capitalism will begin to collapse as a viable economic system. It is the most dangerous and fragile economic system ever created by humanity. When it collapses, and it *will*, social and civil collapse is all but certain to follow.

b. Neoliberal global capitalism is an addictive global economic system that functions without regard for the external impacts it has on the ecosystems of the planet that it's rapidly devouring, or the people living on the planet. Its primary goal is essentially the creation of wealth for the *few* by encouraging the world of the *many* to blindly purchase and consume a never-ending debt-creating supply of "stuff" that we've been conditioned to believe is the source of happiness. Neoliberal global capitalism is designed to flow wealth to the 1% and intentionally increase wealth inequality. The need to end the immoral greed, unlimited growth, and the creation of wealth for the 1% that drives neoliberal global capitalism is urgent. Wealth inequality itself is a potent existential force-multiplier threat that is already destabilizing human cultures globally by intentionally creating lower wages, which tends to increase global poverty.

c. COVID-19 has very clearly illuminated the systemic vulnerabilities built into neoliberal global capitalism. And the facts are sobering. We will take a look at why this is true. Neoliberal global capitalism is an existential force-multiplier threat. Still, it is *not* the *problem*. It's the economic *symptom* that *we* created *using humanity's collective, immature, unconscious, unevolved primitive ego, and its immature early childhood conditioning.*

d. This is also true for each of the existential force-multiplier threats that we will examine in Part 2. They are all existential force-multiplier threat *symptoms* that *we* created. We are the root cause. We are the problem! And until we collectively and intentionally do the work of taming our collective primitive ego and becoming more evolved and *self-aware*, humanity's future extinction will continue to become increasingly likely.

e. Each of the primary and secondary existential force-multiplier threats we will explore in Part 2 has the ability to destabilize neoliberal global capitalism and create/support its collapse.

f. Neoliberal global capitalism simply unleashed our collective primitive ego thinking, our primitive ego behaviors, and our collective greed-based "What's in it for me?" thinking, including our need to have **more**...more wealth, more power, more control, and more unlimited economic growth and profit. The need for more in neoliberal capitalism supports the need to essentially take over the world.

g. The only "less" that neoliberal global capitalism has created is less governmental regulation, fewer international banking controls, and less access to wealth for the majority of humans working to create trickle-up wealth for the 1%.

The Existential Catch-22 Paradox
of Neoliberal Global Capitalism

This chapter will explore both the vulnerabilities discussed above and the significantly dangerous and critically important Catch-22 paradox embedded in neoliberal global capitalism. Neoliberal global capitalism is the most critical and vulnerable crack in the social foundation of human civilization in the twenty-first century. When neoliberal global capitalism collapses, it *will* trigger massive social and civil collapse and end human civilization as we know it.

The Dangerous Catch-22 Paradox
in Neoliberal Global Capitalism

There is also a dangerous Catch-22 paradox built into neoliberal global capitalism. Neoliberal global capitalism is not only the most vulnerable structural foundation supporting global human civilization, it is the most fragile human-created structure likely to collapse. It is also the most powerful existential force-multiplier threat on the planet, *creating* the global climate crisis. Stated simply, neoliberal global capitalism is working hard to create the climate warming crisis. The climate warming crisis is ramping up to increasingly stress neoliberal global capitalism and threaten its inevitable collapse.

The sobering reality of this paradox is the recognition that they are fighting each other systemically to "win" their war against each other. And I believe capitalism will win. Because of the rapidly growing cracks and vulnerabilities in the foundations of global capitalism, the probability is high that it will be the primary existential force-multiplier threat most likely to collapse and create a social and civil collapse. In other words, the collapse of neoliberal global capitalism will undoubtedly create social and civil collapse well before the impacts of climate change and storm intensification becomes intense enough to create financial havoc and trigger the economic collapse of neoliberal global capitalism. That day is coming, but I believe neoliberal global capitalism's failure as a viable economic system will happen far sooner. COVID-19 is a virtually invisible virus, but it is already becoming a serious threat to neoliberal global capitalism.

Regardless of which system wins, I believe social and civil collapse is inevitable in the near future. Whether it's capitalism or the global climate crisis, we *will* experience social and civil collapse and the end of life as we know it on this planet. And it's worth repeating: social and civil collapse is coming far sooner than most people will be prepared to survive. Unless we begin to prepare now for that inevitable collapse, very few people will be adequately prepared to cope with or survive the massive life-altering changes and challenges that social and civil collapse will create.

Each of the existential force-multiplier threats and economic triggers that we will explore in Part 2 has the potential *on its own* to aggressively threaten the fragile foundations of human culture. But because of its vulnerability for collapse and its potential to create a cascading social and civil collapse, I consider neoliberal capitalism unquestionably the most vulnerable system to the dangerous existential force-multiplier threats that we will explore in Part 2. The need to better understand the flaws and defective ideologies embedded in global capitalism is urgent. If we understand the weaknesses and flawed ideologies in neoliberal global capitalism, we will better understand the urgency of beginning to prepare for its existential and likely collapse.

I recognize and understand that imagining the collapse of neoliberal capitalism will be a significant challenge for some readers, given how deeply the underlying concepts and ideologies of greed-based "What's in it for *me?*" capitalism is embedded in the human consciousness. For many, *it would be easier to imagine the end of the world than to imagine the end of capitalism.*

Because our future as a species on this planet is so dependent on our understanding the dangers of modern neoliberal global capitalism, we will explore this topic as thoroughly and as carefully as possible.

Before we begin, remember the quote by Alvin Toffler that I included in the Introduction: "The illiterate of the 21st century will not be those who cannot read and write, but those who cannot learn, unlearn and relearn."

I believe we are at a critically grave and perilous moment of truth for humanity. A moment that will profoundly challenge what we have been led to believe are the unquestionable economic truths in the gospel of neoliberal global capitalism. I think the words that best capture this moment are "The future isn't what it used to be," and Mark Twain's warning that "It ain't what you know for certain that is dangerous, it's what you know for certain that just ain't so."

There are many ideological "truths" in neoliberal capitalism that we've been conditioned to believe are indisputable gospel truth. Still, as we will see, much of that indisputable ideological conditioning *"just ain't so."*

We need to embrace those words of wisdom as we struggle to create a more sustainable human future; a future based on the sustainable, self-reliant local communities and local economies of Chapter 10; self-reliant local communities that are based on the creation and attainment of well-being rather than wealth and profit.

Neoliberal Global Capitalism:
The Economic Assumptions, Limitations, Flaws, and Ideological Beliefs That Make It Vulnerable to Collapse

Neoliberal (fossil-based) global capitalism is often referred to as "*free-market fundamentalism.*" Unfortunately, many of the assumptions and beliefs we have been encouraged to accept as *reality* and *unquestionable truth* in the modern world are now exposing some of their embedded dangerous and life-threatening flaws. As we will see, this is especially true as we unpack some of the sacred economic assumptions that neoliberal global capitalism ideologically embraces as unquestionable fundamental truths.

The information contained in this book is offered to inform you so you can do your own research. I have tried to confirm the information included below from multiple sources to ensure that it is as accurate as possible. As I stated above, my purpose is *not* to convince or force my subjective personal beliefs on the reader. What I do encourage is following the facts. Follow the science. In a world where information is too often biased to support the corporations, political parties, and the 1%, truth matters more than ever.

Because neoliberal global capitalism is a systemically complex interdependent and interconnected economic "system," we would do well to keep in mind the sobering truths (usually attributed to Vladimir Lenin) regarding the collapse of complex systems: "There are decades where nothing happens, and there are weeks where decades happen. They usually move at glacial speed with the seeds of collapse being sown over years, if not decades. The problem being, we never know where the spark will come from that triggers the avalanche."

In the examples below, I will identify the flaws and assumptions embedded in capitalism and illustrate the dangerous economic limitations and consequences of those beliefs and ideologies. In every example of neoliberal capitalism that follows, we will see how the immature primitive ego assumptions and flaws that we explored in Part 1 tend to be an integral and fundamental part of neoliberal capitalism's over-arching ideologies of free-market fundamentalism. These primitive ego assumptions include:

a.   What's in it for me greed. Power "over" rather than a collective, cooperative power "with." Unlimited growth—that is, the rejection of limits. Maximum profit. Sense of entitlement. Lack of systemic thinking. Elimination of regulations. Disregarding the danger of exponential growth. Inability to connect long-term consequences to short-term thinking.

b.   How these same immature primitive ego concepts that initially *created* the assumptions and flaws embedded in neoliberal capitalism's over-arching ideologies now *aggressively support* the inevitable consequences of those dangerous flaws and assumptions.

As we explore the vulnerabilities of neoliberal global capitalism in the pages that follow, it will be essential to understand that any *single aspect* of capitalism is not what makes neoliberal capitalism vulnerable to collapse. It's the total of all of neoliberal capitalist beliefs and ideologies that systemically *network together* to create the vulnerabilities that will lead to its inevitable collapse. This reality can't be overstated. And when neoliberal global capitalism collapses, it *will* trigger the inevitable collapse of our human social and civil structures and the foundations of human civilization as we know it. And that collapse of social and civil order could threaten the viable future of humanity itself.

Some believe that capitalism can be an effective, democratically regulated, and well-managed fair and just economic system. But until humanity has intentionally tamed, matured, awakened, and evolved its collective primitive ego consciousness, *I see no way that neoliberal capitalism and its greed-based, unregulated free market fundamental ideology, or any other form of profit-based, unregulated capitalism, will ever be a sustainable economic system for human civilization.*

Any economic, religious, or political system that embraces a rigid ideological fundamental thinking process that is intentionally disconnected from evidence, facts, science, and reality will ultimately fail to survive. I am convinced that neoliberal global capitalism, and its unregulated free-market fundamental ideology, will not survive much longer as a viable global economic system. If it does, the implications for the survival of human life on our planet will be dire.

Reality: When things are unsustainable or harmful when they no longer make sense, they will eventually change, evolve, be abandoned, be replaced, and come to an end.

The Collapse of Capitalism
Will Create Desperation and Chaos

When we contemplate the collapse of capitalism, it is essential to think systemically. For example, when our economic system collapses, people will lose their jobs and income. Rents won't be paid. Landlords will evict people from their homes and apartments. Unemployed workers won't pay taxes. Local, state, and national governmental programs that are already experiencing massive debt, will lose their funding. Every category of "consumption" will decline. Access to food, water, toilets, showers, cooking equipment, summer air conditioning, and winter heat will no longer be possible.

The economic collapse of global capitalism *alone* is not what will create the eventual collapse of our human social structures. The global financial collapse *will* create massive social and civil unrest as fear, hunger, desperation, loss of jobs, poverty, suffering, anxiety, and chaos create a growing climate of hopelessness. Desperate people are dangerous because they have nothing to lose. Their anger and frustration will create waves of chaos and violence that will destroy the functional viability of the few weakened social structures that are still standing following an economic collapse.

A growing populist backlash against wealth inequality and a declining middle class is already visible globally. And COVID-19 has already begun to create this desperate and frightening climate of social unrest as I write this book. Reports of violence and right-wing extremism are growing. The emotional and social struggle between opening the current shutdown economy to ensure the survival of global capitalism versus the growing number of deaths caused by COVID-19 is already stressing the governments of nations worldwide. The cracks and vulnerabilities of neoliberal global capitalism are already beginning to emerge. Supply lines are stressed. Food shortages are growing. Unemployment is reaching depression levels. Corporations, local businesses, and local and national governments are already experiencing financial stress; jobs are being lost, people are being evicted from their homes and apartments, people are frightened and stressed, schools are closing, death tolls are rising;, and COVID-19 has only been around for ten months.

Complex Systems Require Complex Solutions

It's essential to recognize that systemically interconnected and interdependent human social cultures, and global economic systems, are very complex. When they collapse, recreating the systemic stability required to successfully rebuild a functional human global social culture and a healthy global economy will be extremely difficult. Human civilization and the social/economic systems that support it are far more complex and vulnerable than most of us realize. Even if rebuilding a functional global financial system is successful following COVID-19, I believe that the rebuilding process will likely take several years, perhaps even a generation, to accomplish. I believe we will see many of the systemic realities I listed above, as the global economy attempts to "re-set" after the COVID-19 pandemic, and its destructive health and economic impacts are brought under control.

As we will explore below, even more sobering is the realization that many of the existential force-multiplier challenges, threats, and economic triggers that we will explore in Part 2 are *already* beginning to threaten the inevitable collapse of neoliberal global capitalism, and they *will be far more powerful and disruptive* than the COVID-19 pandemic.

The future isn't what it used to be, and we need to begin preparing for that future *now.*

Neoliberal Global Capitalism: Definitions, Dangers, Assumptions, and Flaws That Will Eventually Lead to Its Collapse

The Shift from Symptoms to Root Causes

Neoliberal capitalism is only an economic *symptom* created by the *root cause:* the collective immature primitive ego-consciousness of humanity and its unevolved early childhood conditioning. Neoliberal capitalism simply unleashed and institutionalized our immature collective primitive ego thinking, behaviors, and greed-based "What's in it for *me?*" thinking.

Neoliberal global capitalism and deregulated free-market fundamentalism allowed transnational corporations to "buy" the support of politicians, privatize and own essential public resources, deregulate governmental attempts to limit their power and wealth, limit social programs that would benefit the "commons," use natural disasters to exploit the social vulnerability and increase their control over the commons[8], leave the vulnerable in the commons at risk, and reflect a massive lack of moral awareness and empathy for the consequences of their actions on the vulnerable, the well-being of the planet including its warming atmosphere and oceans, and its fragile life-supporting ecosystems. Neoliberal global capitalism enthusiastically embraced our collective primitive

---

8   The **commons** is the cultural and natural resources accessible to all members of a society, including natural materials such as air, water, and a habitable earth. These resources are held in common, not owned privately. Commons can also be understood as natural resources that groups of people (communities, user groups) manage for individual and collective benefit. Characteristically, this involves a variety of informal norms and values (social practice) employed for a governance mechanism.[1] Commons can be also defined as a social practice of governing a resource not by state or market but by a community of users that self-governs the resource through institutions that it creates. Wikipedia

ego's tendency for short-term thinking, its lack of interconnected and interdependent systemic thinking, and its propensity to essentially ignore the dangers of exponential growth on a limited planet.

During the COVID-19 pandemic in the United States and worldwide, the commons did not have the health care systems and infrastructures needed. Still, the fracking companies, the cruise ship industry, and the airline corporations almost immediately received massive economic emergency funds to "save" the economy. Political attention was primarily focused on how fast the workers could go back to work and get the economy rolling again. In the United States, financial aid for those in the commons took several months to arrive. Some had to wait even longer. Many got no financial help as governmental relief systems were overstressed, ideologically gridlocked, and unable to cope with the vast number of requests for help and support. Critical materials required for testing were outsourced to China and India, where they could be produced using underpaid labor. The massive global outsourcing of essential chains of supply to increase profits seriously limited the world's ability to cope with COVID-19 when it began spreading.

In Neoliberal Capitalism, Things Go to Those Who Are Able and Prepared to Pay the Most for Them

Wealth inequality visibly reinforces the division between the haves and the have- nots. Created by a greed-based primitive ego thinking process focused on *What's in it for me?* thinking and a strong sense of entitlement, wealth inequality creates social poverty and a dangerous lack of access to the benefits of the human culture for those in the commons. This is especially true for black, brown, and Native American populations and communities. *Wealth inequality and the lack of access to the benefits of capitalism in the commons inevitably leads to increased social resentment and anger, social unrest, and the potential for future social and civil collapse as critical social structures are already being stressed by the existential force-multiplier threats and economic triggers described in Part 2..*

Historically, wealth inequality and anger in the commons has been a primary cause of empire collapse. A primitive ego lack of compassion creates wealth inequality, a sense of entitlement, greed, and the judgmental assumption by the entitled wealthy elite that people in the commons "get what they deserve" and "if they want "wealth," they should have worked harder." The anger and resentment created by wealth inequality are visible and growing globally in the commons in the United States and around the world.

When things are unsustainable or harmful, when they no longer make sense, they will eventually change, evolve, be abandoned, be replaced, and come to an end.

In Neoliberal Capitalism, the "Needs and Survival" of Those in the Commons Tend to Be Socially Ignored, Invisible, and Unimportant

This immoral invisibility in neoliberal global capitalism is created by the collective primitive ego, and it's narcissistic "it's all about a *me*" greed-based thinking process. When an entire global economic culture is based on this kind of greed-based primitive ego thinking, the moral values of compassion, mutuality, and empathy for others tend to be low to non-existent. Over time, this invisibility and suffering in the commons creates deep social resentment and anger because everyone *knows* their suffering is invisible and irrelevant to their government leaders, their politicians, and to the expensive local, state, and the national health care institutions they can't afford to access. They *know* the system is rigged against them. While prices continue to rise, they are painfully aware that the 1% are getting richer while they haven't seen a net increase in real income and wages in decades. This resentment will significantly increase social and civil unrest when neoliberal global capitalism collapses.

When things are unsustainable or harmful, when they no longer make sense, they will eventually change, evolve, be abandoned, be replaced, and come to an end.

The Economic Ideology of Neoliberal Capitalism Leaves as Much as Possible to Be Determined by the Freedom of Market Forces

In neoliberal global capitalism, market forces and trade treaties are essentially controlled by powerful transnational corporations, their unrelenting focus on unlimited growth and profit, upper management, and stockholders. It creates tax cuts for the rich, reduces income for the working and middle-class, eliminates trade unions, and encourages nations to embrace deregulation. The use of money is decided by the wealthy corporations and is based on maximizing *their* profits and wealth, not the well-being of the people in the commons. Money is lent mostly to more affluent people. This financial disparity creates wealth inequality and a deep social "class" division between the haves, and the have nots. This class division between the wealthy and those in the lower "commons" is creating a deep and growing social resentment and anger. The Black Lives Matter movement *and the fact that it is increasingly supported by white demonstrators globally* is an excellent reflection of this growing social resentment.

Neoliberal global capitalist ideology, and the free market fundamentalism embraced by powerful transnational corporations, displaces and eliminates small local businesses and local food production. Land that historically supported small farms producing food for local markets worldwide is now being taken over by transnational agribusiness corporations as small farmers lose their ability to remain competitive.

Neoliberal global capitalism created by greed-based primitive ego and "what's in it for me?" thinking not only lacks compassion, it intentionally ignores the global suffering it causes in the commons. This ruthless domination of the global markets creates a growing frustration, social anger, a sense of powerlessness, and deep and angry resentment in local small business owners and small farmers worldwide.

When things are unsustainable or harmful, when they no longer make sense, they will eventually change, evolve, be abandoned, be replaced, and come to an end.

In Neoliberal Capitalism, the Moral Significance of Interest Is Never Questioned Despite the Suffering It Causes

In the 2008 global financial crisis, the banks that caused the crisis got bailed out, while an estimated 10 million American homeowners lost their homes to foreclosure sales between 2006 and 2014. The banks got bailed out, and the CEOs of those banks were never prosecuted. CEO salaries increased. The anger and frustration that were created are still palpable and present in American culture today. The concept of the wealthy living off the interest created by loaning out their wealth is not only based on a primitive ego narcissistic sense of entitlement and greed-based "What's in it for me?" thinking that lacks compassion, but it also hides the judgmental assumption held by the wealthy elite that *no one* should expect to get an income (socialism) without working for it...except of course for *them*, because *they* have wealth to loan. The unregulated power of transnational corporations and the growth of the neoliberal capitalism they support create a dangerous level of social unjustness, anger, unrest, powerlessness, and frustration globally. All seeds of social unrest.

When things are unsustainable or harmful, when they no longer make sense, they will eventually change, evolve, be abandoned, be replaced, and come to an end.

Neoliberal Capitalism Is Best Described as a Predatory Economic System Based on the Concept of Human Predators versus Human Prey

Capitalism is based on primitive ego black or white, zero-sum thinking: the idea that for *some* people gain at the expense of others, *some others* will need to lose. The concept of win/win is rarely embraced in neoliberal capitalism. The three important ideological principles embedded in capitalism are (a) who profits, (b) at the expense of whom, and (c) morality and compassion are always secondary to profit. It's important to note that these three fundamental belief systems embedded in capitalism are based on the benefits and usefulness of those beliefs for the predators. Not their victims. Predators are defined as people who gain at the expense of others. The predator belief systems that justify their exploitation of others include racism, anti-migration for whatever reason, and sexism. Humanity's collective primitive ego fear of "others" has always tended to create suffering, hunger, and the persecution of "dangerous others." The goal of profit is used to justify the predator's exploitation of the prey. It is based on a primitive survival-of-the-fittest thinking, and primitive ego greed-based hunger for *more*. Prey can also be defined as slavery, debt, wealth inequality, our planet's ecosystems, and even nature herself.

Neoliberal global capitalism is a predatory economic system that *intentionally creates economic scarcity:* the intentional *scarcity of jobs* to keep wages low (including outsourcing production for even lower wage costs); the *deliberate scarcity of wealth* in a culture that defines itself *by the achievement of wealth*; and the *intentional scarcity of goods* produced so as to keep prices high while increasing the consumption of "stuff" in a working-class that has been conditioned to equate *more* with happiness.

Neoliberal global capitalism is a profit-maximizing economic machine. Its overriding need is maximizing the return on invested capital. It is not loyal to any nation, person, corporation, or ideology. *And that includes the well-being of the planet, justice, fairness, human rights, and moral values. It will do whatever it needs to do to make a profit.*

Neoliberal capitalism routinely outsources critical life-supporting resources to maximize profits; an economic practice that violates the fundamental concept never to outsource *and lose control of essential resources on which you need to live and survive.* The supply-line problems created by COVID-19 demonstrate the wisdom and truth of that fundamental wisdom.

Neoliberal global capitalism is an international economic process centered on deregulating trade and finance to enable businesses and banks to operate globally. These financial practices are responsible for (a) the emergence of a single global world market dominated by powerful transnational corporations, (b) the intentional destruction of local cultures and local economies, and (c) the imposition of monocultural farming practices.

The Ideology of Progress:
The Economic System Called Neoliberal Global Capitalism

Neoliberal global capitalism is the combined total of all the interactions between our human species and the natural environment. It's a complex, systemically interconnected, and interdependent economic system created by humanity to include virtually every human on the planet in a social, political, and economic system based on an ideology of "progress." It's a global system that is clearly *not* green, pro-poor, climate-friendly, or sustainable. And if it continues to function as "business-as-usual" in human civilization, it is all but certain to end life as we know it, and likely to cause the extinction of humanity itself. It urgently needs to be replaced. And waiting to create that replacement is not an option. Unfortunately, assuming this will happen voluntarily is dangerous, Tinker Bell thinking. There is no way the 1% and the wealthy elite will intentionally kill the goose that is laying the golden eggs that have created their wealth. Until capitalism collapses under the pressure of the force-multipliers, existential threats, and economic triggers, *neoliberal capitalism, and those who profit from it, will take whatever steps they need to take to aggressively continue their support of global capitalism.*

To Summarize What We Know About
Neoliberal Global Capitalism

The moment neoliberal global capitalism *stops* growing, it dies. But wait! That seems to contradict what we know about cancer. Cancer represents unlimited growth, and if not checked, it always leads to death. So, what had cancer? In other words, what body died? What organ had cancer?

Answering that question will twist your brain a bit until you recognize clearly what has cancer. As soon as you understand that reality, the facts support what we know about cancer. Namely, cancer represents unlimited growth, it often kills the organ, and the organ kills the host body.

As you can see from the diagram below, when neoliberal capitalism dies, it only represents the "organ" that dies. The "body" that dies is human civilization as we know it. When it dies, human civilization as we know it dies, but the planet survives. In other words, *human civilization had cancer! We* created the body called human civilization and infected it with a cancerous growth called neoliberal global capitalism that is now killing it. *We are the problem that created the symptom!*

Cancer In Neoliberal Global Capitalism

In the human body, when the organ with cancer dies, the human body dies, but humanity survives. When Neoliberal Global Capitalism dies, human civilization as-we-know it dies, but the planet survives.

Organ with cancer	What dies	What host body survives
Individual Human Organ	Human Body	Humanity
Neoliberal Capitalism	Human Civilization (as we know it)	The Planet

- Neoliberal global capitalism generates wealth and power for a small fraction of Earth's seven billion people (growing to ten billion by mid-century). At the same time, it trashes the planet and threatens humanity's very survival as a species.

- As a predator/prey-based economic system, neoliberal global capitalism strives to keep most of humanity needy and desperate.

- Neoliberal global capitalism is a financial system that extracts wealth to benefit a tiny elite called the 1%.

- Neoliberal global capitalism creates artificial scarcity, cheap labor, low taxes, and lax environmental measures and social protections.

- Neoliberal global capitalism is a human-created economic system in which our way of life, and virtually every need to sustain that "way of life," is imported and then "sold" to a consumer who only the corporations can supply; a global economic system that intentionally creates, anxiety, fear, disempowerment, and insecurity. *And insecure people can be easily manipulated by false narratives of governments and autocratic politicians that encourage the commons to focus their blame onto enemy "others" for their poverty, insecurities, and fears.* This technique is the historical playbook of fascism, autocratic leaders and governments, extreme national populism, destabilizing extreme right political movements, and ultra-nationalism.

- The world is already destabilizing under the growing social pressure and economic costs of the climate crisis and the COVID-19 pandemic. These are only two of the existential force-multiplier threats and economic triggers. These two force-multipliers are already significantly increasing the risk of social anger and unrest, powerlessness, frustration, and the growing likelihood of social and civil collapse.

- Neoliberal global capitalism is fed by never-ending growth and profit. Any external force-multiplier/existential threat or economic trigger that stops that growth will create the death and collapse of neoliberal global capitalism, and that death *will* trigger the social and civil collapse of human culture and life as we know it.

Reimagining the Replacement of Neoliberal Global Capitalism

Neoliberal global capitalism is a global economic system created and supported by humanity's immature primitive ego "What's in it for *me?*" greed; narcissistic entitlement; a narcissistic self-focus; never-ending consumption; zero-sum thinking; survival-of-the-fittest competition; the need for power "over" and control of others; short-term (profit and growth) thinking; the lack of interconnected and interdependent systemic thinking; a lack of understanding of the dangers represented by exponential growth on a limited planet; and psychopathic treatment/disregard of nature and the needs of others.

Bottom line: The collective primitive ego-consciousness of humanity needs to be intentionally tamed, awakened, matured, and evolved. Until that happens, I have little confidence that humanity will have the political or social courage, or will, to re-imagine and implement a sustainable, viable global economic system capable of replacing neoliberal capitalism as our global economic system. Until that happens, neoliberal capitalism will continue humanity on the path toward a very dark future.

The one hope that I believe is possible is the subject of Chapter 10; the creation of small, self-reliant, local communities based on long-term sustainability and well-being, not profit and growth. Before we move on, here is a brief outline of what we will examine in detail in Chapter 10.

Local Communities, Local Economies, and the Wisdom of Ancient Indigenous Cultures

We need to reclaim the values, goals, and collective behaviors of an enlightened species and replace neoliberal capitalism with the local communities and ecologically sustainable local economies discussed in Part3. Local communities and local economies are focused on well-being and quality of life, not wealth and profit. We need to reimagine a sustainable global economy based on (a) the enlightened wisdom of the ancient indigenous cultures and b) *their ability to see the "spirit" embedded in all of creation; what we would refer to today as the wisdom to embrace systemic thinking and intentionally protect the well-being and health of all living systems for seven future generations.*

We need to recover that ancient wisdom and the ability to embrace nature as an ecologically sustainable and interconnected living network of interdependent systemic relationships; the ability of those ancient cultures to promote the common good and maintain their cultural integrity for thousands of years. Like those indigenous cultures, we need to (a) acknowledge the reality that we are part of the interconnected planetary web of life, and (b) recognize that the future of our species is dependent on a healthy planet, the well-being of the commons, and a "well-being" quality of life…*not* the obsessive accumulation of wealth and power!!!!

We need to radically redesign our current destructive global economic thinking, intentionally tame our collective primitive ego human consciousness and undertake the challenging work of reimagining a long-term human presence on this planet based on the concepts of well-being and sustainability. *And waiting to undertake this reimagining is not an option.* We are out of time to begin the intentional transition to a powered-down, simplified human civilization and rediscover some of the low-technology techniques and tools of previous generations to create a genuinely sustainable and viable long-term global human culture.

The ethic of greed, business-as-usual, and reckless never-ending growth has to end. Siphoning off wealth by the privileged elite, at the expense of the commons and the workers, needs to end. We do not need to redesign our global economic system because we *want* to; we need to redesign it because the viable future of human civilization *demands* it. Nature demands it. The planet requires it. We have to embrace the concept of "limits" and refocus the local economies of Chapter 10 in Part 3 toward justice and sustainability.

The survival clock is rapidly approaching midnight. We need to end neoliberal global capitalism and reimagine the creation of a sustainable global economy for humanity while we still have time. Our global neoliberal capitalist economy is exploitive and self-destructive. The current economic balancing act between unlimited growth, and the inevitable reality of collapse without that growth, is destroying our planet. The *intentional* lack of attention on the existential importance of embracing limits embedded in neoliberal global capitalism has to end. And *soon*.

The Realities to Embrace as We Contemplate the End of Neoliberal Capitalism

Climate change is warning us that life as we know it is rapidly coming to an end for our descendants and us. The future isn't coming. It's already here! It's only a matter of time before our lives, and the lives of our descendants, will experience significant disruption as catastrophic climate intensification, economic turmoil, and destabilizing environmental impacts *continue to intensify and change life as we know it.* The continued denial of global warming, climate change, and growing climate intensification is inviting a dangerous future. The assumption that our global economic system and neoliberal capitalism will remain strong and stable—while the rapidly growing economic impacts of the climate crisis continue to increase financial pressure on governmental and social economies that are already suffering from massive debt and underfunded social programs—is a form of *intentional ignorance* that reflects extreme and dangerous *Tinker-Bell thinking.*

"Our economic systems and our planetary systems are now at war" (Naomi Klein). We are spending trillions on endless wars, massive subsidies for fossil fuels, and funding bank bailouts, all while intentionally ignoring the urgent need to fund the transition of our global economy to that of a sustainable and resilient global economy *that aggressively supports a rapid decrease in CO_2 emissions.* We are clearly heading in the wrong direction. And we are rapidly running out of time to address the problem. We need a shift in values from extractivism to those of a regenerative economy, the values that are deeply embedded in the local communities that we will explore in Part 3. Capitalism's collapse is all but inevitable. Nature is warning us of that reality. Environmental scientists are warning us of that reality. The only question is *when, not if.*

As I write these words, the COVID-19 pandemic is having a massive economic impact on the global economy, an effect equivalent to that of the Great Depression of the 1930s. *And a pandemic is only one of the existential force-multipliers threats and economic triggers that have the potential to collapse our global economy and create the social and civil collapse of human culture.* Our future will *not* be what it used to be. We need to begin preparing for that new future *now if we want to survive the massive impacts and changes that are coming.*

A Simple Reality: We Can Save Neoliberal Capitalism, But We Can't Save the Planet If We Do

A sobering but straightforward reality. The current commitment to global neoliberal capitalism is social and civil suicide! As we will see when we dig deeper, we need to intentionally re-prioritize the critical needs of human society, the commons, and the environment at the local, national, regional, and international levels. In other words, we need to embrace intentional simplicity; reduce consumption; embrace degrowth; power down from fossil fuels; focus on well-being rather than profits; create socioeconomic equality; eliminate extreme differences in income and wealth inequality; focus on bottom-up movements; create the right to adequate food, housing, medical care, education, social services, and a comfortable retirement; liberation from the treadmill of consumerism and the production of unnecessary and harmful products and services; and radically redefine the meaning of "standard of living."

Unfortunately, these priorities only represent some of the existential force multiplier threats and economic triggers; and *each one of those existential force-multiplier threats **alone** has the power to collapse neoliberal global capitalism and life as we know it!* The reverse of the sentence above is also true: ***We can save the planet if we incorporate the concepts above, but we can't save neoliberal capitalism if we do.***

We Have to Change the Conversation

Reimagining neoliberal capitalism alone will not change the dark future humanity is heading towards. We have to *intentionally* awaken our collective human consciousness and deal with the current immature, collective primitive ego thinking process of humanity; a thinking process that insists on short-term thinking, a status quo bias that embraces resistance to change, either/or polarized thinking that creates a dangerous and aggressive need to be "right," and the illusion of separateness rather than a more enlightened and mature interdependent and interconnected systemic thinking. Until the collective immature primitive ego-consciousness of humanity is replaced with a more enlightened and evolved level of thinking, the consciousness that created the problems embedded in neoliberal capitalism is not going to change. We need to embrace a mature and evolved social dialogue focused on creating the more viable and sustainable local communities and local economies of Part 3.

As I stated previously, creating these more mature and viable local communities will first require the intentional taming of the collective immature primitive ego-consciousness of every member of the local community. Without the intentional evolution and awakening of the local community's collective human consciousness, they will not be successful in creating the long-term sustainable and viable economic systems needed to replace neoliberal capitalism and save our planet. As Einstein warned us, *"You cannot solve a problem using the same thinking process that created that problem."* Only when the local communities of Chapter 10 have been created and have intentionally evolved their local community members' collective consciousness will the creation of a long-term viable local economy be possible. When these concepts are successfully combined, the best—and perhaps only—realistic hope for humanity's future will be realized.

Only when the structural design of a local self-reliant community and its local economic system are focused on the well-being and the public good of the commons instead of profit, will the creation of a hopeful and long-term viable future for humanity be more achievable. What is existentially necessary and obvious is that humanity must end greed-based neoliberal capitalism if we want a sustainable and viable future for our species on this planet.

Unlimited Economic Growth on a Limited Planet Is Intentionally Ignorant Tinker Bell Thinking

The odds are extremely low that unlimited economic growth on a limited planet can continue much longer. Nature is already employing catastrophic climate change to ensure that it doesn't. The oceans are warming. The ice is melting. Forest fires are increasing. Droughts and flooding are increasing. And nature will continue to increase these natural feedback responses to ensure that the current use and burning of carbon fuels will be radically reduced in the near future. Global warming impacts, and the massive reduction in the use of carbon energy, will both radically decouple future economic growth from its current level of fossil fuel emissions. Stated simply, nature *will* win the war humanity is currently waging on her and our planet's fragile ecosystems. *Unlimited growth on a limited planet violates the laws of physics. It's not sustainable. It is simply not possible.* A precocious seven-year-old recently told me very emphatically, hands on her hips, that it was impossible. I simply nodded and smiled at her wisdom. I couldn't help but wonder how a seven-year-old possessed such wisdom and insight. It bolstered my sense of hope for the future.

I chose not to share with her my belief that neoliberal global capitalism and the future of humanity are both increasingly vulnerable and under attack by multiple existential force-multiplier threats that *will* inevitably ensure their collapse. She is only seven. She will experience that sobering reality soon enough.

Many believe that an economic collapse would be a significant crisis. I agree that it will change life as we know it. But I think it will ultimately create a very positive and hopeful future. I prefer to believe it will protect humanity's future from the growing certainty of extinction if we insist on continuing to protect the unsustainable "business as usual" path we are currently using to create our future. The future is a choice, not a given. I choose hope.

Economic Growth Is Similar to a Drug Addiction.

When we lack the strength or courage to confront an addiction, it's human nature to sink deeper into denial and begin an intentional journey into the dark night of the soul. This is also true for individuals addicted to drugs, and it is also true for global economies addicted to profit and growth. Humanity has a tough choice to make. We either confront the denial, recognize the addiction, and change direction, or we are going to arrive at the destination we are currently heading toward. Denial of the addiction will only make the future survival of humanity significantly less likely. And the destination we are presently heading toward is not a future any of us would voluntarily or intentionally *choose* to create.

The Purpose of an Economy Is to Meet Basic Human Needs

Unfortunately, our planet cannot sustain an economic system based on never-ending growth and a never-ending consumption of its natural resources. The hidden danger of neoliberal global capitalism is the sobering reality that the *Tinker Bell, brainwashing, Kool-Aid litany of the "benefits" of neoliberal global capitalism* have become the embedded, entirely accepted, unquestioned, unconscious, fundamental ideologies of neoliberal global capitalism that controls an overwhelming majority of the people on the planet. *Virtually every economic transaction on the planet is based on someone making a profit.* And the greed driving that system is unconscious. *It's just the way it is! It's never questioned!* The collective immature, unevolved, primitive ego-consciousness of humanity's unconscious inner child is entirely in control.[9]

The End of Capitalism Is Unthinkable.

Unfortunately, we are trapped between a rock and a hard place because the end of capitalism is unthinkable. A continuation of the "status quo" or "business as usual" is also utterly impossible! And unthinkable! *The future will not be what it used to be.* This future is a reality we need to begin emotionally embracing and stop avoiding. We need to focus on the path toward local communities discussed in Part 3 and shift our attention from economic growth and financial wealth to our deeper goals and values of economic well-being, cooperation, compassion, and sustainability. "When we speak of economic growth in a world of physical limits, we always have to ask ourselves growth of what, growth where, growth for whom, with what impacts, and for how long?" (Ian Christie.)

---

9   an excellent podcast on this subject was recently published by the Post Carbon Institute. It is a Season 2 podcast titled "The 10,000 Mile Cod and Insane Global Trade" by Crazy Town. It's well worth the time to listen to this podcast. https://www.postcarbon.org/crazytown.

Human Culture and Human Society Are Not "Things"

Human culture is not an "it." A thing. It's an organic communal behavior of individuals and groups, social bonds, habits, values, and memories of sharing. Human culture is a system much like the human body. Every part of the system is based on interdependent cooperation and collaboration, a living organism in which each part of the organic, interconnected system benefits by being integral to and focused on the larger whole's well-being. Unlimited growth in any part of the human body is called cancer. And that cancer too often leads to death.

When we talk about unlimited growth in the economic system of human culture, we are not talking about a "thing." Like unlimited growth in the human body, unlimited and endless growth in our human economic system is also a form of cancer. Both result in the death of the host. The concept of endless growth in neoliberal global capitalism, and the assumption that unlimited growth is somehow *even possible* on a limited planet, are dangerous and deadly cancerous memes. Both reflect the presence of a fatal ideological planetary cancer—an ideological meme deeply embedded in the collective early childhood unconscious primitive ego of humanity.

The global capitalistic economy, the fossil energy system, and the planetary environment all evolved and function together systemically. Like the human body, they represent an interdependent wholeness that requires all resources in the system to be shared to maintain the whole system's health and well-being. Much like the human body, unlimited growth in our planetary system represents a form of cancer. And untreated cancer always leads to death. Unlimited growth in neoliberal global capitalism has already exceeded the limits of growth on our limited planet. It is a form of cancer, and we are choosing to ignore or acknowledge that obvious reality. But nature and our planetary environment are clearly warning us that neoliberal global capitalism has cancer and is *rapidly* reaching the end of its life on this planet.

Unfortunately, a neoliberal global capitalist economy is the global economy on which many people depend on to meet their basic needs. When the neoliberal global economy collapses, and massive employment increases and workers are no longer able to "sell" their labor for income, resilience will be critical for survival. Waiting to prepare for that future is not an option.

Local Communities Are the Path to a Viable Future When Neoliberal Global Capitalism Collapses

When neoliberal global capitalism collapses, humanity will need to have prepared for that collapse by starting to create the critically needed small, local, self-reliant Localization Communities that will be discussed in-depth in Part 3. And the long-term success of those self-reliant, local communities will require the *intentional* taming, maturation, and evolution of the local self-reliant community's *collective* consciousness. If our goals for the future of humanity is resilience and survival, we will need to begin creating those local communities *now*. Waiting is *not* an option.

As I pointed out above, the collapse of neoliberal capitalism is coming far sooner than most people believe or are prepared to survive. When growth and profit end, the death throes of neoliberal capitalism will very quickly emerge. The COVID-19 pandemic has shone a sobering and powerful spotlight on neoliberal global capitalism's fragility *and its systemic inability to successfully avoid collapse when stressed.* When neoliberal global capitalism collapses, our global human culture's social and civil collapse will inevitably follow very rapidly. And that systemic collapse will happen far sooner than most people believe. But if we began creating the small, fully self-reliant, sustainable local communities and local economies based on well-being, not profit and growth, as described in Part 3, they could offer younger generations a realistic, credible, and viable path forward.

A golden arch concept of this book, the reason I chose to write it, is my belief that the local communities described in Part 3 need to be created *now, before* the collapse of capitalism. After capitalism and our social and civil structures collapse, building a viable local community will be far more challenging than if we begin now. Post-collapse, the tools, skills, and resources needed for long-term survival will be far more challenging to acquire. Also, those local communities will need to have embraced the intentional taming and evolution of their collective immature primitive ego-consciousness, as described in this book. As a mental health therapist, I have been studying and developing primitive ego psychology for three decades. I am convinced that taming the collective primitive ego-consciousness of those local communities would be critical for their long-term success.

If the creation of those local self-reliant "seed" communities could begin to form now, the local communities that intentionally and aggressively embrace the taming and evolution of their collective community consciousness could provide the foundation for an enlightened and successful future human culture.

After the inevitable collapse of our current economic and social systems takes its place in the annals of human history, self-reliant local communities could be the long-term, viable, sustainable, self-reliant future human culture of humanity that not only survives but offers future generations a sustainable, environment-centered, cooperative economy focused on community well-being and the social well-being of a thriving, long-term, human culture on our planet.

Summary of the Flaws in Neoliberal Capitalism Created by Primitive Ego Thinking that Make it Fragile and Prone to Collapse:

1. The over-exploitative ways we treat nature and her fragile ecosystems that support life on this planet.

2. The lack of equitable sharing of our planet's natural resources

3. Inability to embrace a sustainable relationship with nature and the planet's ecosystems.

4. Failure to embrace "do no harm."

5. Inability to limit population growth.

6. Failure to reject the concept of unlimited economic growth on a limited planet.

7. Inability to think more systemically (interdependence, interconnectedness, and cooperation).

8. Failure to protect and restore planetary habitat and ecosystems.

9. Failure to embrace intentional simplification and scale back consumption to sustainable levels.

10. Inability to shift from economic *me* thinking to economic *we* thinking—i.e., from competition to cooperation.

11. The collective unwillingness to intentionally tame our collective primitive ego-consciousness, intentionally become more self-aware, and intentionally evolve our collective primitive ego thinking.

12. Inability to protect our forests and water and soil resources.

13. Failure to recognize and embrace the wisdom of systemic cooperation that is written into our cells.

14. Inability to recognize that any unlimited growth is a form of cancer and eventual death.

15. Failure to shift our focus from wealth and profit to a focus on well-being.

16. Inability to change from a focus on wealth to a focus on caring for nature and our planet.

17. Failure to acknowledge the health of living systems over short-term wealth accumulation.

18. Inability to acknowledge the requirements and limitations of the land we live on.

19. Inability to protect the soils and water that grow our food.

20. Inability to identify or care for the local species of plants and animals that need to be protected.

21. Unwillingness to value cooperation and well-being rather than exploitation and profit.

22. Reluctance to embrace sustainability and self-reliance by creating local gardens and growing more of our food.

23. The inability to recognize that insecurity (lack of self-reliance) makes people susceptible to the false narratives of governments and autocratic leaders who tend to blame other "enemies" for the problems. This is a technique taken directly from the fascist playbook. Insecure and disempowered people can turn to anger and extremism, populism, polarized ideological tribal thinking, lack of compassion, increased "What's in it for me?" competition, and irrational fear of immigrants; and are easily manipulated by false narratives designed to increase their insecurity. We will explore this concept more in Chapter 8.

24. Inability to recognize that in the pursuit of profit, we have turned critical resources that we need to survive over to global supply lines over which we have little to no real control.

25. Inability to acknowledge neoliberal global capitalism's addiction to profit in a world where money rules have made us powerless to survive. Most people have no land for fruit trees or gardens to grow food or raise chickens, goats, pigs, cows, and so on. We have lost control of our ability to embrace self-reliance and our survival. Without intentional preparation, now, many and perhaps most, will not survive when collapse arrives.

Realities to Consider as Neoliberal Global Capitalism Approaches Collapse

- *Every* **existential force-multiplier threat to the future of human civilization that we are facing today** has been directly and intentionally created by the collective, immature unconscious primitive ego-consciousness of humanity.

- **Truth matters. Facts matter. Reality matters. Nature matters. Science matters**. Any belief that we can continue neoliberal global capitalism or business-as-usual without support from the above realities is hazardous and uninformed Tinker Bell thinking.

- **Uninformed personal, subjective assumptions** and those who claim to possess "absolute truth" in their belief that neoliberal global capitalism will continue in the future reflects an intentional ignorance. As a wise teacher once said to me, "When you go out into the world, **be sure to check the batteries in your bullshit detectors,** because there are a lot of folks out there selling it as absolute truth."

- **Self-awareness is often defined as becoming aware of the beams in our own eye.** The journey toward growth in self-awareness is a journey of awakening that requires the courage to embrace the shadows that live in the consciousness of all of us, and the willingness to keep the light of our consciousness on those shadows until they become a conscious part of who we are. As a therapist, I understand how challenging it can be to intentionally awaken our human consciousness and become self-aware. It requires courage, profound humility, and recognizing how important that work is for the future survival of humanity.

- **The great people of history, the people who we honor, all learned to master their minds.** I am convinced that the failure to tame and evolve our collective immature primitive ego consciousness is the most dangerous primary existential force-multiplier threat humanity has ever faced. As I noted above, a collective primitive ego human consciousness is survivable in a primitive culture, but an unevolved, collective primitive ego-consciousness in a modern technological human culture is absolutely *not*. Every force-multiplier/existential threat and economic trigger threatening the survival of our human species on our planet, was created using the immature, unevolved, untamed, collective primitive ego-consciousness of humanity. Despite three decades of urgent warnings from our environmental scientists, we have done nothing to effectively address the collapse of the biological and environmental processes that we have unleashed. According to those climate scientists, half of the greenhouse gases in the atmosphere have been added since 1989, and *we knew* the dangers we were creating for future generations.

- **We have clearly reached the limits of neoliberal global capitalism and its insane litany of *unlimited* economic expansion.** Those who think differently in the face of overwhelming scientific evidence are caught in the dangerous trap of Tinker Bell thinking. Unfortunately, for too many, it seems that *it is easier to imagine the end of the world than to imagine the end of capitalism.* The promise of wealth and power that capitalism offers has become a deeply embedded addiction to growth and greed in much of humanity's consciousness. Like any addiction to a drug, the addictions to growth and greed *will* lead to the destruction of our lives and the lives of future generations. It's sobering to realize that we have intentionally and knowingly caused the breakdown of a climate system that has been relatively stable and supportive of life on our planet for over 800,000 years in roughly a few generations. The current COVID-19 tension between those *focused on saving lives* and continued to stay at home isolating to fight the spread of the virus, versus those *focused on saving the economy* by opening the economy and opening business and ending the stay at home isolation, continues to intensify. My concern is growing that neoliberal capitalism will win. Profit and growth will almost always take priority over the massive loss of life that experts are telling us will result if we end the stay-at-home orders. If neoliberal capitalism wins this conflict, I suspect that social and civil stress will grow exponentially in the near future as anger, desperation, and frustration in the commons comes to a head and takes to the streets. The truth of this statement will be confirmed in the days and months ahead.[10] There is no herd immunity to protect us from the "What's in it for me?" primitive ego greed that is spreading neoliberal global capitalism. The only solution for that illness is the courage to *intentionally* tame

---

10   Two good articles on this topic: COVID-19: Neoliberalism Is Not Going Down without a Fight, Daniel Vargas-Gomez, resilience.org; and Tomgram: Nomi Prins, A Rendezvous with Destiny? / TomDispatch.

our collective primitive ego human consciousness. And waiting to do that work is *not* an option.

- **Reality:** When things are unsustainable or harmful and no longer make sense, they will eventually change, evolve, be abandoned, be replaced, and come to an end. Do we stop life to allow capitalism to continue??? Or do we tame and evolve our collective immature primitive ego consciousness and stop neoliberal global capitalism to allow life to continue? The answer to that question will, more than any other, define humanity in the months ahead.

- **Humanity will not survive "business as usual."** A tamed, evolved, matured, and awakened primitive ego consciousness would embrace the simple ethic that every person, and every generation, has an equal right to the enjoyment of the planet's natural wealth. This ethic would be a foundational concept in humanity's consciousness in the self-reliant local communities of Part 3. *Creating these self-reliant local communities is the only realistic and hopeful path forward for humanity. Waiting to begin that process is not an option. Resilience and survival both require intentional preparation.* I believe starting the creation of these local communities is now one of the most urgent and critical decisions facing us. *How we respond at this moment will, more than any other decision, define the future of humanity and our survival as a species.* There are three significant realities that I believe are in our future: the all but certain collapse of neoliberal capitalism in the near future, the collapse of social and civil infrastructures that support human civilization that the collapse of capitalism will trigger, and the realistic hope for the future on humanity embedded in localism and the creation of self-reliant local communities and local economies. A post-capitalist human culture based on localism will define human civilization's future economic systems and human cultures. Localism will also determine the likely end of *global* trade and *global* economic systems. The days of "individual and national *me*" focused economies will be replaced by "collective and national *we*" focused economies.

146

Successful national identities will also need to embrace this more collective human *we* focus. I do not believe that "global" will define our human economy in the future. Local community "networks" might be possible, but trade between these networked communities would be based on collective well-being. Survival and well-being will be the focus of local trade in the future, not profit and growth. The transition to self-reliant local economies described in Part 3, Chapter 10 is the only viable future that protects our planet and the living systems that depend on the life-supportive resources our planet provides. And only the *intentional* taming and evolution of our collective primitive ego human consciousness will create a collective human consciousness mature and evolved enough to accomplish that transition.

We will explore the creation of self-reliant local communities in depth in Chapter 10. But we'll take a brief look at self-reliant local communities below as a way to transition from neoliberal global capitalism and its greed-based focus on profit and unlimited economic growth, and illustrate what an economic system designed to create community well-being and long-term survival would likely look like when neoliberal capitalism collapses.

The Creation of Local Communities: The Best Long-Term Viable Option to Replace Neoliberal Global Capitalism When It Collapses

Localism = The Evolution of Human Culture from Globalism to a Post-Capitalist Future

The systemic ideologies embedded in neoliberal global capitalism are threatening the future of humanity. They require profound structural, systemic change. **Because the global economy** is an extremely complex, interconnected, and interdependent global economic network or system, the systemic changes that will be needed would require equally complex solutions. They will require a level of courage and collective "we" thinking that neoliberal capitalism is incapable of offering. The complex systemic changes our global economy needs will *not* come from the divisive, competitive, greed-based, *me* focus of neoliberal global capitalism.

Waiting for global, national, or state-based governmental action to end neoliberal capitalism's growth is not a realistic or viable option *because those profiting from capitalism won't let the end of growth happen.* Unlimited economic growth is the golden goose that lays the golden eggs that increase their wealth. And even if, by some miracle, the intentional end of unlimited economic global growth does take place in the future to build a more humane economic system, it will not happen in time to save the planet or avoid the suffering that will result as the climate crises continues to intensify rapidly. In other words, it may not happen in time to prevent the possible extinction of the human species.

I am convinced that the only viable path forward for humanity; the path that could create the in-depth structural, systemic change solutions required; the path that would offer real hope for the future of humanity and doesn't involve dangerous Tinker Bell thinking; is the creation of the self-reliant, local communities that we will explore in-depth in Part 3. To contrast these self-reliant local communities from neoliberal global capitalism, self-reliant local communities would require the *intentional* taming, evolution, and maturation of the collective childhood primitive ego consciousness of *all members* of the local community, and would be *we*-focused on the long-term, sustainable well-being of *all* members of the community; not *me*-focused growth, profit, and greed. The community members would trust and depend on each other to sustain that sense of trust and well-being, and they would work sustainably *with* nature, not *against* nature.

These sustainable and self-reliant local communities could begin to create the resilience needed as the world starts to experience the massive changes that are coming. They would intentionally embrace the ancient wisdom that resilience is only built through early and intentional preparation. Our obsession with growth and affluence is coming to an end.

The unlimited growth and profit focus of neoliberal global capital-ism cannot continue. Global warming cannot continue. Unlimited access to endless fossil energy cannot and will not continue. Pandemics, however, *will* continue. Food shortages *will* increase. Storms *will* intensify. Flooding *will* increase. Eventually, and sooner than most people believe, these realities will have a massive impact on our lives. *The only viable path for the future survival of humanity will depend on community and cooperation with others.*

The resilience to survive the changes and existential threats coming *will* require preparing *now* for the day they arrive. Our current denial, ignoring and discounting the existential danger of their reality, and the threat they pose to humanity's future will be an option *until they arrive.*

We are co-creators. We created the world we live in through our human consciousness.

The global economy we have created on this planet must be redesigned to blend harmoniously into nature's ecology. Our planet and her fragile ecosystems are a "thou," not an "it." We need to embrace the wisdom of past indigenous cultures that lived sustainably by honoring the "spirit" embedded in all of cre-ation. Many reject this way of seeing the world as too religious, too primitive. They are wrong. It wasn't. Indigenous cultures simply understood that they were a part of a *systemically interconnected and interdependent community called nature.* They recognized their actions and decisions had to embrace that reality if they were to survive long-term. Unfortunately, we have chosen to ignore that wisdom. We turned the planet's ecosystems and nature into an "it." An "it" that could be extracted, consumed, polluted, wasted, sold, chopped down, owned, and traded for personal profit. We need to embrace the indigenous wisdom of honoring the presence of "spirit" in all of reality and intentionally embrace the critical importance of "systemic thinking" by intentionally tam-ing and evolving our collective immature primitive ego-consciousness and its unconscious immature early childhood conditioning.

And waiting to do this work is not an option.

We live in a conscious, living universe, and we must become more active and more intentional in the co-creation of our human reality. We stand on the brink of maturity, and ancient wisdom can give us guidance. The childish competing, grabbing, fighting, "What's in it for me?" greed path we are on has us headed for extinction. It has to end. Our collective human consciousness has to *intentionally* evolve and mature.

Neoliberal global capitalism (free-market fundamentalism) intentionally ignores the reality that unlimited economic expansion on a limited planet is impossible. This belief is more than Tinker Bell thinking. It is a form of intentional ignorance. Scientists tell us that a sustainable human footprint on this planet would be roughly 2 billion people. We are over 7 billion and headed toward 10 billion within a few years. *And virtually every person on the planet wants to live the middle-class lives that people in the developed world are currently living.* Ignoring the impossibility of these realities will destroy our planet.

The growing climate crisis and storm intensification created by global warming cause a rapidly growing economic hardship on individuals, municipalities, states, national governments, insurance companies, and pension funds. It creates financial distress and suffering as people are forced to relocate when they can't afford to replace their homes. Insurance companies are increasingly refusing coverage in areas subject to flooding, storms, and forest fires. Climate chaos is growing rapidly. The intentional ignorance is created by the collective primitive ego conscious of humanity and its massive lack of compassion for other living systems, the illusion of separateness, a lack of systemic thinking, "What's in it for me?" greed, entitlement, and the inability to connect the long-term consequences of our short-term actions.

The climate crisis is a rapidly growing force multiplier on the global economy. When the commons begin to experience the impact of climate change on their lives more directly, their denial will be replaced by a rapidly growing level of social anger, frustration, and powerlessness.

Those in the Western world who have enough food to eat, water to drink, a decent paying job, and access to health care live in what has historically been a relatively safe and reasonably secure bubble. They have not experienced the pain and suffering that many in the world are already experiencing. So, denying global warming and the growing climate crisis has been relatively easy. But those days are coming to an end. The number of people acknowledging the reality of climate change is growing, and growing rapidly. The lack of an appropriate global governmental response to the apparent fact that unlimited growth on a limited planet is causing global warming and climate change is already beginning to create a growing level of social anger. This is especially true in the younger generations that will inherit the world we are creating. The frustration and social anger over the massive lack of systemic thinking and intentional ignorance being reflected by governments worldwide are rapidly coming to a moment of truth.

I would suggest a different interpretation of these realities.

Capitalism is based on a very simple concept—the sobering reality that it continues to grow in size and profits, or it dies. And every politician in every governmental body on the planet knows that neoliberal capitalism is the golden goose that lays the golden eggs that support their access to wealth and power. Their "What's in it for me?" greed-based primitive ego thinking encourages them to prioritize profit and wealth over the individual suffering of others or the destruction of the planet.

They know our finite planet cannot sustain an economic system based on ever-expanding consumption. They know they have to pretend that all is well, while climate and other force-multipliers reveal the deeper reality that we are clearly in the end game days of capitalism. They know the moment they acknowledge this reality publicly, the golden goose dies, and their access to wealth will end. Their collective intentional refusal to slow down carbon emissions created by neoliberal global capitalism's embrace of unlimited economic expansion is based on the reality that ignoring reality is better for them than the end of profit. So they ignore the validity of the growing climate crisis and continue to support the narrative that everyone should embrace neoliberal global capitalism and become part of the destructive system that equates happiness and success in life with the accumulation of "stuff" and financial wealth.

The unwillingness to openly speak the truth is based on a reality far more profound and dangerous reality than simple greed.

I believe their unwillingness to speak the truth comes from their recognition that when neoliberal global capitalism dies, the world, and life as we know it, will come to an end. As I noted above, neoliberal global capitalism is an extremely complex, interdependent, and interconnected global economic system. And like all complex interconnected and interdependent systems, they are like a house of cards. They are fragile and susceptible to sudden cascading collapse when the right card is pulled out of the system. And when the collapse of neoliberal global capitalism begins, stopping it will not be an option. When neoliberal global capitalism collapses, *life as we know it will end. Period!*

As I write these words, my concern is growing that the COVID-19 pandemic could be that critical economic trigger, the card that creates the collapse. It is turning out to be a potent force-multiplier on the global economy.

Capitalism is designed for profit maximization, job creation, and perpetual, never-ending growth. Under neoliberal global capitalism, transnational corporations are *not responsible for society's only shareholders*. And these fundamental concepts cannot be challenged even in the face of the climate crisis, climate change, storm intensification and frequency, COVID-19 pandemics, massive global debt, declining fossil fuel production, climate change, increasing global political and economic tensions, and all of the other force-multipliers and destabilizing economic triggers listed in Part 2 of this book that are increasing their pressure on capitalism.

I believe the global economic crisis and vulnerabilities built into the design of neoliberal global capitalism are rapidly coming to a head. We are currently overconsuming every resource on the planet, increasing storm intensification and frequency, and driving ourselves and countless other species toward extinction. And these growing force-multipliers and all of the other force multipliers we have been examining in Part 2, were already happening *before* COVID-19.

Given the reality of all these force-multipliers and economic triggers, can the neoliberal global economy and neoliberal capitalism survive the impact of COVID-19? And if so, for how long? And I suspect a lot of governmental leaders around the world are asking themselves that same question. By the time you read this book, we will know the answer to that question.

We need to remember the reality that when things are unsustainable or harmful, when they no longer make sense, they will eventually change, evolve, be abandoned, be replaced, and come to an end.

The pressure on neoliberal global capitalism is growing rapidly.

We need to rethink our values, goals, and collective behaviors and increase our collective focus on our global civilization's economic realities. We need to embrace a *more systemic way of thinking* and seeing reality as an *ecological network of interdependent and interconnected relationships* that maintained their integrity for thousands, even millions of years. We need to shift our attention from wealth production to the health of our planet's living systems, and the realization that we are all interconnected in the web of life; including the reality that our long-term human prosperity is dependent on a healthy planet, well-being, and quality of life, not the accumulation of wealth and power.

The world is already destabilizing under the pressure of only two of the economic triggers and existential force-multiplier threats: a climate emergency/ crisis and a COVID-19 pandemic. They *alone* are dramatically increasing the likelihood of social collapse as social anger, frustration, unrest, fear, powerlessness, frustration, food shortages, job loss, and loss of income continue to grow.

Realities to Remember as We Explore the Existential Force Multiplier Threats and Economic Triggers of Part 2:

a. The urgent need to tame our collective primitive ego human consciousness and undertake the challenging work of radically reimagining our old modes of economic thinking, our economic social structures, global capitalism, and the long-term sustainability of our human presence on this planet will become more apparent and urgent.

b. The recognition that we are out of time to begin the intentional transition to a powered-down, simplified human civilization and undertake the task of rediscovering some of the low-technology techniques and tools of previous generations to create a truly sustainable long-term global human culture will also become more apparent and urgent.

c. The reality that waiting to undertake this reimagining is no longer an option will also become more apparent and urgent.

d. The ethic of greed and reckless growth has to end.

e. The siphoning off of short-term wealth by the privileged elite needs to end.

f. We do not need to redesign our global economic system because we *want* to. We need to redesign it because the future of human civilization *demands* it.

g. We have to embrace the concept of "limits" and refocus the local economies of Part 3 toward justice and sustainability.

h. We have to decouple well-being from growth. Unfortunately, our global capitalist economy is exploitive and self-destructive. It is always poised between the reality of growth or facing the reality of collapse if growth is allowed to end.[11]

---

11 We will continue this conversation in Part 3 as we challenge the self-interest and intentional lack of attention on the concept of "limits" of our current global economic system and begin the creation of local communities and local economies and their long-term sustainability—local communities that intentionally embrace the ethics and organizational structures of worker owned cooperatives and the consensus decision-making governance of its members.)

I believe, and many economists would concur, that the collapse of fragile neo-liberal capitalism is the most dangerous existential force-multiplier threat and economic trigger threatening the social and civil collapse of human civilization. Many economists believe the inevitable collapse of neoliberal capitalism and human civilization may have already begun. It's just not equally distributed and visible in many of the developed nations. The COVID-19 coronavirus is a black swan economic triggering event that is currently creating massive economic supply chain interruptions that threaten a global economic system collapse. *And there will be more global pandemics in the future*. And health experts are warning that some of those future pandemics will likely be more deadly and disruptive than COVID-19.

The existential force-multiplier threats and economic triggers threatening social collapse will be a challenge to read and embrace. But I believe COVID-19 might be a blessing, a wakeup call that will help us take those existential force-multiplier threats and economic triggers more seriously. Their potential to be more disruptive than COVID-19 is high—and it's not a question of *if*, it's only a question of *when*—COVID-19 is a long-overdue wake-up call for humanity to increase our self-reliance, especially our ability to provide our own food.

I see no realistic way of reforming neoliberal global capitalism. It's not that it's too big to *collapse;* it's too systemically complex to *survive!* It is an extraordinarily complex and fragile, systemically interconnected, interdependent house of cards. When the right card is pulled out, the system *will* begin to collapse under the weight of its own complexity. The existential force multiplier threats all threaten capitalism's collapse, and all of them are powerful and growing rapidly.

Global capitalism is a complex global system built to function at a very different time in human history when fossil energy was inexpensive and readily available. Today, the oil fields produce less oil, of a lower quality, and the (EROI), or energy return on investment, is negative in most fields. In other words, the energy return on energy from fracking is a significant warning sign for the future of fossil energy. When neoliberal capitalism is no longer able to get the energy it needs to survive, or when it can no longer burn carbon fuels to support a global economy for 8 to 10 billion people, its collapse is inevitable. Again, it's not *an if. It's* a *when.* COVID-19 is already creating oil company bankruptcies.

The vulnerable cracks in neoliberal global capitalism foundations are beginning to weaken and head toward inevitable collapse. The massive debt financing required to continue economic growth is reaching its limits. The hydrocarbon energy reserves and sources are dwindling and declining, and the global population supported by capitalism is heading rapidly to over 10 billion. It's only a matter of time before neoliberal capitalism experiences a cascading systemic collapse from the weight of its own success and the growing external pressures threatening the structural flaws built into its original design by the immature, unevolved collective primitive ego-consciousness of humanity.

Because of the extreme vulnerability of capitalism to the existential force-multiplier threats and economic triggers listed in Part 2, *I believe there is no way that global capitalism will be able to avoid collapse and trigger the inevitable social collapse of human culture and human civilization as we know it.* And when that collapse happens, humanity's future will depend in no small measure on how successful we have been in creating the self-reliant, sustainable local communities and local economies we will explore in detail in Part 3.

Summarizing Chapter 3

The growth imperative of greed-based neoliberal global capitalism is the greatest threat to global democracy. It is growth-as-governance—that is, anything that threatens, impedes, or limits growth and profit, is essentially ignored or legally removed.

The people get no vote in the process.

The politicians and the 1% get wealthy.

Wealth inequality increases.

Global poverty increases.

Neoliberal global capitalism is an extremely complex, interdependent, and interconnected global economic system. It is well beyond this book's scope and golden arch to explore neoliberal global capitalism in depth. So, I have kept the material in this chapter on neoliberal capitalism focused on providing a comprehensive overview of the flaws and consequences of neoliberal global capitalism, not an in-depth study of its details and complexities.

To quote Thomas Friedman from his *New York Times* article on capitalism entitled "How We Broke The World," "Diverse ecosystems, in nature and politics, are always more resilient than monocultures. Monocultures in agriculture are enormously susceptible to disease...one virus or germ can wipe out an entire crop. Monocultures in politics (and economics) are enormously susceptible to diseased ideas." Neoliberal global capitalism is a perfect example of a worldwide monoculture economy.

As you undoubtedly recognize as you read the material in this chapter on capitalism, the underlying "ideas," concepts, assumptions, flaws, and ideologies embedded in capitalism tend to be repetitively linked to the same immature, untamed, unevolved "ideas," beliefs, assumptions, and thinking our primitive ego, and its early childhood conditioning, uses to live and function in the adult world. I encourage readers to refer back to Chapters 1 and 2 to increase their ability to link these immature primitive ego-thinking beliefs and assumptions to the ideas in this book, and especially this chapter on neoliberal global capitalism. The more effectively we can link our *collective* immature, unevolved primitive ego thinking and human consciousness to that of our own *personal* thinking, the more we will be engaged in the *intentional* taming of our own primitive ego and the evolution/awakening of our own consciousness.

Change is not only a reality; it's inevitable.

It doesn't happen "to us."

It just happens!

We are not committed to neoliberal global capitalism. We can create a new human economy. If we want to change and evolve our thinking, we can. It's possible. If we want to reimagine the future we would like to create, we can. And as we will explore in Chapter 10, humanity's future economic system *can* be local.

The globalization of our economic system creates interlocking fragility. It gives *the appearance of stability, but in reality, it creates dangerous and fragile vulnerabilities* to many existential force-multiplier threats, threats that are capable of creating its collapse. Globalization has created a complex systemic system of interconnections and interdependencies. When one part of the system fails, it creates other interconnected system failures that systemically begin to cascade.

There will be fewer crises in a globalized system, but they will be severe when they arrive. The COVID-19 pandemic is shining a bright light on our global economy's fragility and the vulnerabilities that happen when everything is connected with everything else.

After the pandemic is dealt with, we cannot return to business as usual, because business, as usual, is the problem! Neoliberal global capitalism is a failed experiment!

It is also the most fragile, collapse-prone, existential force-multiplier threat to social and civil collapse that humanity's immature, unevolved collective primitive ego consciousness has ever created.

Black Swan Force, Threat Multiplier, and Economic Trigger: Climate Crisis, Climate Intensification, Global Warming

Our resistance to intentionally evolve our collective human consciousness blinds us to the changes that need to be made in the foundations of human civilization.

"We" are the problem: Aspects of humanity's collective, unconscious, unevolved primitive ego, and its early childhood conditioning that work together to systemically reinforce and support each other.

In climate crisis, climate intensification, and global warming, the main parts of "We are the problem" from the list below, include (a) "What's in it for me?" greed; (g) a lack of interconnected, interdependent systemic thinking; (j) an exaggerated aggressive narcissistic self-focused sense of entitlement; (k) an inability to connect short-term choices with long-term consequences, and (m) the never-ending, obsessive desire for "more."

* *

Primitive ego early childhood conditioning:

a. "What's in it for me?" greed.

b. Need to be "right" (aggressive arrogance, extreme cognitive dissonance/confirmation bias).

c. Inability to replace "me" thinking with "we" thinking (compassion, mutuality, cooperation).

d. I want what I want when I want it.

e. Blames others for "our" feelings (inability to own our own feelings).

f. Ignorance regarding the danger of exponential growth (e.g., COVID-19).

g. A lack of interconnected, interdependent systemic thinking.

h. Survival of the fittest thinking.

i. Black versus white, zero-sum thinking ("You can't have that, it's mine!).

j. An exaggerated aggressive, narcissistic self-focused sense of entitlement.

k. An inability to connect short-term choices with long-term consequences.

l. The fear of change (uncertainty, not knowing).

m. The never-ending, obsessive desired for "more."

n. The need for power "over" rather than power "with."

o. The inability to embrace long-term thinking.

* *

Introduction to Chapter 4:
Global Warming is the Most Disruptive and Dangerous Force-Multiplier and Existential Threat to the Future Survival of Humanity

The collapse of our planet's life-support system due to global warming is *the* primary threat to humanity. It's bigger than pandemics, war, famines, or even economic collapse, but climate change will likely release all four of those dangerous and significant force-multiplier realities as human social and civil structures weaken and cascade into collapse. As we saw in Chapter 3, the collapse of neoliberal global capitalism will be the first and most likely force-multiplier to create a social and civil collapse. Still, the global climate crisis is clearly the force-multiplier most likely to threaten humanity's extinction.

Global warming and climate change are unquestionably *the* two most immediate and existential crises facing humanity. Unfortunately, we are not acknowledging the growing severity of their impacts, nor are we paying attention to the urgent warnings of our climate scientists who are warning us about the ever-increasing dangers of irreversible climate tipping points.

As we saw in Chapter 3 regarding the unwillingness to address the dangers of neoliberal global capitalism, the *solutions* to global warming and climate change are as economically damaging and impactful as the *problem*. This is especially true in global warming. Global warming and climate change are far worse and more impactful than politicians are willing to acknowledge. The early predictions of climate change, storm intensification, and climate change were understated. Still, as the scientific data began to emerge, and our climate scientists' warnings became more realistic and grew in urgency, politicians realized the solutions to global warming were so impactful on the global economy that voters would view them as unrealistic alarmists.

Even now, in 2020, the political and social will to aggressively deal with climate change and the massive changes that would be needed to realistically reduce CO2 emissions, and the growing impacts of global warming and storm intensification, are still not subjects that humanity or our politicians are ready to embrace or openly acknowledge.

While the world dithers, the financial impacts of storm intensification, polar ice melt, flooding, rising ocean water levels, droughts, forest fires, the increasing economic costs to insurance companies (that are already refusing to insure coastal properties), and the growing costs and tax burden on cities, local municipalities, states, and nations are all force-multipliers and economic triggers on the vulnerable and fragile social and civil structures that support human culture. And these force-multiplier threats and economic triggers continue to grow in strength every day we intentionally ignore their economic and social impact.

For decades, scientists have warned us that global warming above 1.5 degrees Celsius will dramatically increase the threat to human civilization and life as we know it. We are currently at 1.1 to 1.3 degrees Celsius and rising rapidly. Above 2 degrees Celsius, the impacts will be far more dramatic. And scientists tell us we are now on course to warm between 2.6 and 3.2 degrees Celsius by the end of the century! We are already seeing 1000-year rainstorms, forest fires, droughts, species loss, rising water levels, increased ocean acidification and warming, and melting icecaps. It's hard to imagine what people living in a 2.5 to 3.2 degrees Celsius world will experience.

And the most sobering change climate scientists have reported in their predictions is the alarming reality that the changes and potential tipping points that will accelerate the warming rate are coming significantly faster and far sooner than they originally forecasted!

It's becoming clear that climate change *will* create severe economic, financial, social, and civil impacts and consequences in the very near future even if carbon emissions are aggressively addressed *now*. Inaction on climate warming *will* destroy the global economy. Given the overwhelming lack of social and political will to address the problem, I believe the climate crisis is destined to be a major force-multiplier that *will* create the all but certain systemic social and civil collapse of human civilization and the possible extinction of our species. And aggressive action to reverse global warming *will also* radically impact human culture and significantly change life as we know it far sooner than most people believe possible or are prepared for.

Massive change is coming, and we are not preparing for its arrival.

To quote Bob Litterman, Chair of the Commodity Futures Trading Commission's Climate Risk Working Group, "Ignoring climate warming, not pricing in the systemic risk, and not creating appropriate incentives to reduce emissions are tragic and potentially catastrophic mistakes."

Sarah Bloom Raskin, a former member of the Federal Reserve Board of Governors, said, "Climate change constitutes a material financial stability risk. If we ignore climate change, we, in essence, destroy the economy." (March 12, 2020)

The extreme weather that the United States experienced this year (2020) was *not* an anomaly. The flooding that broke all previous records, the hundreds of tornadoes and the relentless rain bombs, and massive forest fires (including similar environmental impacts around the world) were *precisely* what was predicted by our best climate scientists. "This is *not* a new normal. This is just the beginning of the middle phase of accelerating global warming, and according to our best climate scientists, it's going to get a *whole lot worse!* " (And this quote from Lawrence Wollershein, Job One for Humanity, was made on June 4, 2019!)

Climate change and storm intensification are increasing droughts, and atmospheric river rain-bomb flooding creates food shortages. Current trends continue to grow as ocean warming continues to add more moisture to the atmosphere. (Bob Litterman, Chair of the Commodity Futures Trading Commission's Climate Risk Working Group.)

Scientists warn that the threat of more severe pandemics will also increase as we continue to warm the planet, melt the ice, thaw the permafrost, and damage the ecosystem. They predict that future pandemics could be far more infectious and contagious than COVID-19 due to global heating.

The Rock and the Hard Place of Reality

Unfortunately, governments will not act until the global warming consequences *do* get a lot worse because, as we saw above, they are caught between a rock and a hard place. The impacts of climate change on human civilization and our global economy, and the impacts of ending CO_2 emissions between 2025 and 2050, as proposed by the recent IPCC reports, *are almost identical.* They know that social and civil collapse is all but certain whether they ignore the problem and do nothing, or whether they take action. *Either approach will create an economic, social, and civil crisis.* Until social pressure from voters demands change and forces politicians to publicly recognize global warming and climate change as an existential emergency, politicians will continue to kick the can down the road.

Despite the warnings that will continue to come from our climate scientists—warnings that will continue to create *decision paralysis*—we will continue to ignore or discount the severity or magnitude of the coming changes. *Why?* Because they've never happened before! We have no history to draw on or guide us. We are moving into an unknown future. The only thing that seems inevitable in the future is the sobering reality that the future that's coming will not be what it used to be, including life as we know it.

COVID-19 is an excellent example. Pandemic scientists have warned for decades that a global pandemic was inevitable. And even as I write these words, we are reopening the economy in the middle of COVID-19 despite warnings from the health experts that the worst is yet to come. We can't imagine the massive impact of a global pandemic even as it is happening!

Nobody believed the scientists who warned us COVID-19 was coming, and those same scientists and health experts are now warning that the 2020 winter could be even worse. They believe the social and economic impact of COVID-19 is going to be far more disruptive and longer-lasting than most economists and politicians believe. Systemic collapse is hard to imagine and even harder to repair, or recover from, once it begins. We already see social stress when people are being shot simply because someone asked them to wear a face mask. What will happen as unemployment increases? How will people afford food? Pay their rent or house payments? Or put gas in their cars? What will they do when they are evicted from their homes and apartments when they can no longer pay their rent or mortgages? What will they do when they lose access to food? The likelihood of social and civil collapse is growing rapidly. And we are only dealing with eight months of COVID-19 as I write these words!

It reminds me of the wisdom of one of our more well-known philosophers (John Wayne), who reminded us that "you can't fix stupid." Massive changes are coming, and uninformed personal *subjective* opinions and beliefs are putting our lives and the lives of those we care about in danger. We need to get informed. We need to listen to scientists. *Facts* matter. *Data* matters. *Truth* matters. And we are already out of time to prevent or avoid the impacts of global warming that will continue to increase for generations...even if we ended all carbon emission *today*. We have more carbon in our atmosphere than any time in the last 15 million years, and 2020 is on course to be the hottest year on record. In the words of David Wallace-Wells, author of *The Uninhabitable Earth*, "we *need* to panic." Waiting is not an option.

I see no way we will avoid a social and civil collapse in the years ahead.

I recently had a conversation with a climate denier who told me that all these sobering warnings about global warming and climate change have a less than 10% chance of actually happening. So I asked him, "Would you get on a plane that had a 10% chance of crashing?" The silence was deafening. I quietly reminded him that we are booking that flight for his children and grandchildren to take ten years from now...*or sooner*. Again, the silence was deafening.

We need to take decisive action to eliminate CO_2 emissions *now*. Climate change is not something we can fix. It's not a treatable "condition." The only options we have are (a) shutting down carbon emissions and (b) preparing for the climate changes that are already baked into our future. As you read the material in this book in the days and months ahead, you will likely already grasp the concept when I warn that social and civil collapse is not only inevitable, but the extinction of human life of this planet is a rapidly growing possibility.

Global Warming: The Existential Changes, Challenges, and Threats That Are Coming

The Golden Arch: We Are the Problem

We are the problem. We are not a viable species. We are a gigantic, voracious, invasive super- organism continuously transforming and devouring our planet's limited resources; resources that future generations will need to survive the planet we are leaving them. Global warming is the most existential crisis humanity has ever faced as a species. And *we* are the problem. *We* are the root cause of global warming and the other force-multipliers listed in Part 2 that threaten our future; the force-multipliers that we will explore in-depth below. We need to *intentionally* evolve and tame our collective primitive-ego human consciousness and remind ourselves that this is our *only* planet. And we need to wake up to that sobering reality. *Now.* Waiting is no longer an option.

Unfortunately, humanity is currently trapped in decision paralysis. We don't know where to begin or what to do. The golden arch of this book is the urgent reality that *step one* is the need to intentionally tame our collective primitive ego human consciousness; deal with our primitive illusion of separateness; learn to embrace systemic, interconnected, interdependent thinking; end our intentional ignorance, political cowardliness, cynical denialism, and irresponsible dithering; and begin aggressively tackling the problem of climate change. *Until we intentionally tame our collective primitive ego consciousness and embrace a fundamental reorientation of our human values, behaviors, institutions, economies, and technologies, we are nothing more than an invasive species merely marking time until we go extinct.* We are behaving like the guy who jumped off the top of the building and, on the way down, shouted, "No big deal, no harm has come to me yet," as he plummeted toward the pavement below.

We are living on a sinking ship!! We are trapped in decision paralysis. And all we are doing is mindlessly moving the deck chairs around as we sink. Our "future," the future we are promised by the elite, the 1%, the transnational corporations, and our global governmental politicians, is *more* material progress, *more unlimited* growth, and *more* business-as-usual. The concept of sustainable development or a sustainable future is not part of our "official" future.

The crisis of climate change is an existential opportunity for humanity to replace cultural norms and reorganize itself for long-term sustainable survival. We live *in* nature. It's time we began to cooperate *with* nature. She's been around for a long time. We need to embrace her hard-won ecological wisdom before she recognizes us as an invasive species and employs her ability to drive invasive species into extinction! She has a lot of experience and wisdom on how to get rid of invasive species, and she is clearly warning us that she's not playing games. We need to become a sustainable species that cooperates *with* nature or prepare to face the consequences of her wrath.

And she is growing more and more impatient. She is clearly warning us that we are rapidly running out of time to *intentionally* mature and evolve our collective human consciousness!

"Today, at just under 2 degrees Celsius of warming, the planet is already hotter than it has ever been in the entire history of human civilization…it as though we have landed on a new planet, with a new climate, and have to sort out what parts of the civilization we've brought with us can survive these new conditions, *and what cannot.* How different will things get? The last time there was as much carbon in the atmosphere as there is today, there were palm trees in the arctic."[12]

Digging Down into the Life-Altering Changes and Climate Impacts That Are Coming

The material to follow is a brief overview of the life-altering changes and impacts that are coming. It's not meant to cover all the scientific material available, nor is it intended to convince the reader that global warming is real or created by human behavior. The climate science is clear. Global warming is real, and it has been created by human behavior and actions. I do not embrace the concept that an *uninformed,* personal *subjective* belief or *opinion* is more important or more reliable than the highly trained climate scientists' collective scientific data. And I would suggest that the reader not embrace it either. Follow the data. Follow the facts. Stay focused on the severity of the impacts that scientists tell us *are* coming. Resilience requires preparation *before* the crisis, not *after* it arrives.

Facts matter. Data matters. Truth matters. Our future as a species will be determined by how well we use scientific facts, data, and truth. Keep John Wayne's words in mind when you encounter uninformed climate denial, uninformed *"they say"* personal subjective opinions, and intentional distortions of

---

12   Article: "Welcome to the End of the 'Human Climate Niche'", David Wallace-Wells, May 19, 2020.

the climate science community's data, facts, and truths. "You can't fix stupid." So don't waste time attempting to convince those who deny science. You can't push the river, and you can't fix stupid. Stick with the facts, data, and truth… your future depends on it.

The scientific data is growing almost daily. Given how fast the scientific climate data is emerging, I encourage readers to do their own research. Job One for Humanity is an excellent resource. Resilience.org, Post Carbon, Inside Climate News, and Google are also worth checking out. Some of the material in this overview came from articles written by those sources and are listed in the bibliography at the back of the book. Our scientific knowledge is increasing rapidly; so be sure to do your own research and stay updated on the scientific findings. What you will discover is the forecasts environmental scientists made a few years ago were far too conservative. The changes, impacts, and tipping points they warned about are coming sooner and more destructively than initially reported.

It's Not Just Scientific Data: It's *Personal*

The data and facts contained in this chapter, and the chapters to follow, need to be read and digested through the lens of personal suffering, hunger, starvation, dislocation, deaths, homeless, those who can't afford medical care, those who have no voice, and those who are powerless. This includes millions of people around the world who are already suffering from global warming and climate change. Most of the data presented by the scientists and media will have no human context or meaning in terms of personal impact until *we* provide the *meaning*.

Until we recognize the severity of the data personally, it will go in one ear and out the other. Empathy, compassion, and care for those already suffering, or who will be suffering in the days ahead, will continue to be absent in how we collectively humanize, personalize, respond, and process the scientific data. We will continue to live in a cold, uncaring, dehumanized world. Our humanity demands that we respond and take action to reverse global warming while there is still time to prevent some of the suffering.

An excellent example of this happened this morning as I was writing these words. We were told that we are now over 200,000 deaths from COVID-19 in the United States and almost one million deaths globally. Just numbers. Just data. Not personal. A commercial followed it. The meaning and importance of that data will become *real* in our consciousness only when we can hold in our consciousness the fact that every one of those deaths was a real person... fathers, sons, daughters, brothers, sisters, mothers, children, friends, or neighbors...including those who now have to cope with the grief and loss of those "persons" who died.

Unless, and until, we personalize the data and make it *human,* we will experience no impulse to change our behaviors, priorities, actions, values, and understanding of what is happening to our planet and those people who died. Or empathically embrace the grief that their death is creating for others. We will just process the information as data and move on with business as usual, life as usual. The golden arch of this book is the need to mature and evolve our thinking. The need to mature and evolve our collective consciousness. The need to embrace reality and *intentionally* tame the self-focused early childhood conditioning of our collective narcissistic "me"-focused primitive ego human consciousness.

Until we do this work of *intentionally* taming our primitive ego and *intentionally* becoming more self-aware, mature, evolved, and adult in our thinking, we will continue to ignore the data because it will have no human meaning. Another way to say this is, we will continue to ignore reality, we will continue to live unsustainably, we will continue consuming, devouring, and destroying the only home we have. The home we call planet Earth.

And in time, the human species will fade from the memory of the planet. The universe will move on with one less invasive species to worry about.

In Part 3, we will explore the creation of local communities and what I believe could be our most hopeful and viable future as a species...assuming, of course, that humanity is willing to *intentionally* tame and evolve our collective human consciousness. If we are unwilling to intentionally do that work, I see no viable long-term future for our species. And waiting is no longer an option. We are out of time.

We are the problem. We created the world we are living in. And only we can create a sustainable world that honors and respects all of the living systems and entities that, like us, depend on the life-supporting resources our planet provides.

Storm Data

The importance of storm data is best viewed through the lens of *personal impact* discussed above, the financial impact on the social and civil foundations of human culture, human civilization, and neoliberal global capitalism. As the cost of climate change and storm intensification continues to increase, we need to ask ourselves (a) *How* are we going to pay for that increase? (b) *Who* is going to pay? (c) *Who* is going to carry the debt until that debt is paid and for *how long*? and (d) *Who* is going to pay the interest on that debt given the fact that in 2020 we are already approaching $261 trillion of debt globally in a global economy that was struggling to maintain 2% growth…*before* the COVID-19 pandemic arrived? The U.S. debt is about to cross $61 trillion.

For example, here are some of the dollar numbers from recent climate change storms and global warming:

- Hurricane Michael alone cost the Tyndall Air Force Base over $5B, and that is only one of roughly 12 climate/weather disasters to cost over $1B each.

- Hurricane Florence cost the U.S. Marine corps, Camp Lejeune, approximately $3.6B, and North Carolina around $17B.

- Snowstorm in the Northeast U.S. in March 2018, $2.25B.

- California Paradise forest fire cost over $18B.

- Hurricane Harvey cost over $125B.

- Hurricane Katrina had an approximate cost of $161B.

- The cost of Hurricane Michael, October 2018, was $25B, and $5B at Tyndall Air Force Base.

- Hurricane Sandy in 2012 cost $5B.

- Hurricane Harvey in 2017 cost $125B.

- Hurricane Sandy and the forest fires in 2019 were both in the $300B range.

- In the last 100 years, severe storms have increased by 300%, and they continue to grow in severity.

- Despite a $16B bailout in 2017, FEMA's National Flood Insurance Program was over $208B in debt *before* the start of the 2018 hurricane season.

"Increased global warming is a massive failure of imagination and courage. Climate change is now reaching the end game, where very soon humanity must choose between taking unprecedented action or accepting that it has been left too late and bear the consequences. The level of greenhouse gases in the atmosphere is now greater, and the earth is warmer than human beings have ever experienced."[13]

Denial in human consciousness is high. Our immature primitive ego-consciousness prefers short-term thinking (immediate gratification) over long-term thinking. We pay attention when pain is close to us, when it is *personally* impacting us, or if we believe it *will* personally impact us in the *very near* future. We ignore pain when it is far away in the distant future. We assume we have more immediate, pressing issues and problems.

Unfortunately, when it comes to climate change and storm intensification, we have too many issues and too many problems to choose from. Too many possible solutions. We are overwhelmed with *decision paralysis*.[14] But the

---

13 8/22/2018, Prof. Hans Joachim Schellnhuber, 20-year head of the Potsdam Institute for Climate Impact Research.

14 *Switch: How to Change Things When Change Is Hard*, by Chip and Dan Heath.

cost of inaction will significantly outweigh the cost of taking action *now*. As we learned in the Introduction, change requires clarity. We need to know *precisely* the change we want to create. And that change needs to begin internally.

Step one in dealing with the force-multipliers of Part 2, especially the force multiplier called climate change and global warming, is *intentionally* taming our own primitive ego consciousness. As we discovered in Chapter 2, if we choose not to intentionally do that internal growth in self-awareness and tame our primitive ego consciousness and early childhood conditioning, we will use the same thinking to create the solutions we originally used to create the force-multiplier problem.

Immature, primitive ego thinking created the global warming crisis, the most critical threat to human survival that humanity has ever faced. That threat is growing while we choose to avoid even talking about the impacts that will result until we aggressively take action to reduce CO_2 emissions. Our species' future will depend on how quickly we are willing to take that first step that each of us needs to take to embrace the courage to *intentionally* tame, evolve, and mature our own collective primitive-ego human consciousness. As was pointed out in the introduction, until a significant number of us are willing to take that critical first step, viable solutions to the problem of global warming and the other force multipliers in Part 2 will continue to use the same immature, primitive, unevolved thinking that was used to create the problems originally.

In each of the topics listed below, keep in mind that *we* are the problem. Every one of the existential threats, challenges, and life-altering changes listed below in Part 2 was *created* by our collective immature primitive-ego human consciousness and is now *sustained* by that same collective immature primitive-ego human consciousness.

a) Droughts, Flooding, and Food Shortages

Changes in weather patterns due to global warming and increased water vapor in the atmosphere create droughts and floods that impact farmers and food production in the United States and globally.

Climate scientists warn that global warming has the American West heading into the worst mega-drought on record, the worst in several thousand years. Dry periods were common in the past 800 years, but the droughts created by global warming will last for centuries. There is growing conflict over well-drilling rights and access to groundwater aquifers as water management legislation attempts to protect the underground aquifers for irrigation in Nevada. Lake Mead's water level recently dropped to an all-time low, and predicted to fall below 1080 feet above sea level for the first time in 78 years. As droughts continue to afflict the American West, the dire situation at Lake Mead will continue to have consequences for Arizona, Nevada, and California, which draw their water supply from Lake Mead.

Another low-snow winter in 2020/2021 would trigger the first emergency declaration in the basin, forcing states to deal with water cutbacks. "Never has the question of "what will the winter be like?" loomed larger than it does now in the Colorado River Basin. Water management experts warn, if the snowfall is anything like last year when only two-thirds of the usual snow fell, it will trigger the first emergency declaration in the basin, forcing states to deal with cutbacks in the water they are appropriated. *And even if it is a big snow year, it will likely only delay what now seems inevitable.* The last time Lake Mead was full was 1983. Since then, it has slowly declined. It is now 40 percent full, and experts warn it may never be full again. Currently, at 1,082 feet above sea level, when it reaches 1,075 feet, it will trigger the first Tier 1 water cutbacks.[15]

"The pressures on the river raise the possibility that Lake Powell or Lake Mead—or both—could cease functioning as designed. Water levels could become too low to produce power, to go boating, to store water, and, in Powell's

---

15   Lake Powell is also threatened by climate change and dropping water levels. On May 13, 2020 the *Washington Post* reported the Upper Missouri River Basin was the driest it has been in 1200 years; even more parched than during the disastrous Dust Bowl of the 1930s. The drop in water levels in the Missouri is due to reduced snowfall in the Rocky Mountains in Montana and North Dakota, according to climate scientists.

case, to meet downstream delivery demands." [16] The 40 million people who depend on Colorado River water need to prepare for a significantly drier future.

Not dealing with climate change is Russian roulette. We need to prepare for systemic cascading collapse as interconnected and systemically interdependent systems collapse and create changes we've never seen before! Again, changes are coming that we can't even imagine.

While some areas experience drought, others are dealing with "rain-bomb events" and dangerous flooding. As the climate warms, water levels in the atmosphere are increasing. Atmospheric rivers 250 to 500 miles wide and up to 2 miles deep are becoming more common. *These atmospheric rivers often contain twice as much water as the Amazon river.* Rainfall from these atmospheric rivers creates dangerous flooding risks and increased frequency and intensification of hurricanes and severe storms. Scientists warn that annual rainfall will grow and continue to generate more rain and flooding. But most of the water will run off to create river flooding. It will not flow into the aquifers, be absorbed into the soil, or end the drought conditions.

For example, atmospheric river flooding in March 2019 in Nebraska put two-thirds of Nebraska's 93 counties under a state of emergency. Costs to the economy were estimated at over $1.5B in crop losses and infrastructure damage. Bankruptcies and delinquent loan payments increased.

b) More Pandemics and Zoonosis

Health care experts and climate scientists are warning that global warming *will* increase animal-to-human virus transmission, according to the World Health Organization (WHO). This is called Zoonosis. It's estimated that roughly two-thirds of all human infectious zoonotic diseases and three-fourths of new emerging zoonotic diseases come from animals—i.e., zoonotic viruses. As the climate warms and polar ice and permafrost that contain both trapped carbon

---

16   Brian Maffly, the *Salt Lake Tribune* (https://www.sltrib.com/news/environment/2019/01/20/lake-powell-could-become/).

and ancient viruses continue to melt, they will create the significant tipping points that scientists are increasingly concerned about.[17]

c) Global Challenges

Job One for Humanity has published a report called "Climageddon Scenario," in which it has listed what it believes to be some of the worst and most critical problems created by global warming. Here is a summary of their predictions.[18]

1. **Overpopulation.** The carrying capacity of our planet is roughly 2 billion. We are now at 8 billion, headed for 9.4 billion by 2050.

2. **Resource depletion and food shortages.**

3. **Global economic instability,** including poverty and wealth inequality, increased the national debt, and growing pension deficits, will increase.

4. **Political instability** created by increased wars, conflicts, terrorism, massive migrations created by food shortages, climate changes, droughts, ocean water rise, and heatwaves.

5. **Global pandemics,** which were anticipated *before* COVID-19 arrived, will increase due to the intentional dismantling and deterioration of our global health systems and services.

6. **No global government** with legislative or social enforcement ability and no international consensus. (When this reality is added to the massive lack of social or political will to deal with climate change, I believe social and civil collapse is inevitable in our near future.) Because there is no social or political will to deal effectively with the

---

17   Article: "Q&A: Could Climate Change and Biodiversity Loss Raise the Risk of Pandemics?" (www.carbonbrief.org/Q-and-A).

18   Global One for Humanity "Climageddon Scenario," Job One For Humanity: 20 Worst Consequences of Global Warming (now irreversible for the next 50 years). (https://www.joboneforhumanity.org/20_worst_consequences_of_global_warming.)

Also see article: "What Are the Seven Greatest Global Adaptive Challenges Facing Millennials, Younger Generations, and Humanity as a Whole?" (https://universespirit.org/what-are-seven-greatest-global-adaptive-challenges-facing-millennials-younger-generations-and-humanity as a whole.)

rapidly growing global warming crisis, it will take centuries to reverse the warming we have *already* created.

7. **We are not even close to the required CO2 emission reductions** of 50% by 2025, another 50% by 2030, and another 50% each additional decade until we reach net-zero CO2 emissions.

8. **Experts tell us it would take hundreds of years** to achieve a 100% replacement of fossil energy. Assuming we could replace fossil fuel energy with solar or wind and continue to grow the economy and continue to live the lives we are presently living (*i.e., what experts consider to be hazardous short-term Tinker Bell thinking*).

9. **New technologies** will not save us *in time*.

10. **Global warming is increasing, and unstoppable.** Experts currently see no way to stay below 550 ppm as we continue business-as-usual! That is the extinction-level of global warming.

11. **Increased methane is 86 times more potent than CO2**...and the fracking industry is currently intentionally hiding methane emission numbers.

12. **Tipping points** such as polar ice melting are increasing (irreversible system collapse).

13. **The IPCC is underestimating** where we are by 25% to 40%.

14. **Business as usual** will have us cross 500 to 600 ppm...***soon.***

d) Irreversible Tipping Points

Tipping points are a function of complex systemic interconnected and interdependent systems. Our planet, ecosystems, human civilization, and global economic systems are examples of complex interconnected and interdependent systems. Changes in any part of a complex system *will always* create changes in the other parts of the complex interconnected system.

Complex systems in nature are self-sustaining and self-correcting. And more importantly, *every part of a complex system works for the benefit of the whole system.* The human body is an excellent definition of a complex interconnected, and interdependent system. Every part and organ of the human body shares in the body's resources and energy resources. The well-being of the *whole* body is the prime goal of the complex living system we call our human body. Complex systems work fine until one organ or part of the body tries to take over and hoard or monopolize the body's resources and energy systems. Cancer and its goal of unlimited growth at the expense of the other organs in the living system is an excellent example of monopolizing. When unlimited growth or monopolizing happens, the whole or living system called our human body, or the living system called our planet's complex living ecosystem, collapses and dies.

The unlimited growth of a cancer cell, or a COVID-19 virus, are good examples. When they begin to monopolize or hoard the body's energy resources, it's only a matter of time before the other organs and cells in the interconnected and interdependent "wholeness" of the body begin to die. The system *starts* to collapse. We call this condition an "illness." The illness will continue to worsen until the *collapse or death* of the body or system is *irreversible*. When it passes this irreversible tipping point, the body dies. It may take time for the body to die, but once a critical irreversible tipping point is triggered, the process of dying is irreversible.

In systems theory, a tipping point is the beginning of an irreversible cascading collapse of the system.

We live *inside* nature. We are part of her complex living ecosystem, and we depend on nature to be sustainably supportive of life. And we take that reality for granted. But scientists are warning that we may have already passed some critical irreversible tipping points. The unknown is whether the planet can recover, rebalance, and continue to support life. And right now, we can't answer that question. We know the planet is ill, it has a temperature, and its life support systems are stressed. What is yet unclear is whether our world is merely sick or whether it has triggered irreversible tipping points that will lead to its death—that is, to the inability to support carbon-based life.

What *is* becoming more apparent is the sobering reality that we are already entering into the Anthropocene,[19] a new geological age for our planet. We will discover the long-term future influence and impact humanity will have on the climate and the planet's ability to support carbon life. Global warming due to carbon emissions in the atmosphere is heating the oceans, and the ocean currents are taking that heat up to the polar ice caps and melting them. Scientists are warning us that this could be a significant, irreversible tipping point for our planet's future. Now some climate deniers want us to believe that this is no big deal. *But let's change the narrative. Let's see how much heat we're talking about before deciding how big a deal it is or isn't.*

Changing the Narrative

The oceans have absorbed roughly 90% of the heat captured by carbon emissions in the atmosphere. When the water warms, it expands, and scientists warn that the top 2300 feet have warmed 0.3°C since 1969. The last time the oceans were this warm was 100,000 years ago, and sea levels were 20 to 30 feet higher then.

The oceans have warmed so fast there hasn't been time for the polar icecaps to fully melt. But that melting is currently happening far more quickly than scientists predicted. When it does finish melting due to the *current* global warming, New York, London, and Miami are just three of the coastal American cities that would be significantly impacted by a 20- to 30-foot level sea rise.

And global warming is continuing *to increase.* The temperature is climbing and will continue to grow warmer based on CO2 emissions that are *already* in our atmosphere...and our carbon emissions are continuing *to increase.* Bottom line: Ice melt *will* accelerate.

---

19 Anthropocene: the current geological age, viewed as the period during which human activity has been the dominant influence on climate and the environment; an influence that began with the Industrial Revolution—i.e., the period during which human activity has been the dominant influence on climate and the environment. We, humanity, have become a major force of nature in this new Anthropocene epoch.

The ocean warming is equivalent to one atomic bomb per second for the past 150 years. Or another way to say this is five nuclear bombs (Hiroshima) per second over the last 25 years. That equates to roughly 228 sextillion joules of heat. Even more troubling is the realization that ocean warming is not only increasing, but the rate of warming is also growing! Since 1993, ocean warming has more than doubled. The last time the oceans were this warm, water levels were 40 to 50 feet higher than they are now! (Remember: it takes time to melt the ice). In 2019, we added a record 40.6 billion tons of CO2 to the atmosphere. But even more concerning is the fact that ocean warming is shifting ancient ocean patterns. That means the oceans are moving heat to different parts of the planet, which will change weather patterns and intensity—the heat transport system is global. It's a major, irreversible climate tipping point that is changing rapidly!

As we pass more and more global warming tipping points, the worst global warming consequences will increase faster and faster, growing exponentially over time. Once we cross the 2025 tipping point, any realistic or practical control of our global warming future is all but over for centuries to thousands of years. If we pass four critical deadlines and tipping points (see footnote), mass human, animal, and biological extinction, as well as economic, social, and political chaos, will be a widespread inevitability *within our lifetimes!*[20]

These are the critical changes that are keeping the scientist awake at night.

They know this level of global warming is unsustainable. They just don't know how long we can explode five (Hiroshima) atomic bombs per second until "it" (you can fill in the blank) hits the fan. Many believe we have already passed the *irreversible* tipping point of global warming. Based on the research I've done and my years as a mental health psychotherapist, I see no way to avoid social and civil collapse as the existential force multipliers threats and economic triggers in Part 2 put existential pressure on the foundations that

---

20   This footnote is an excellent reference to review for the four most critical tipping points (425–450 CO_2 ppm tipping point, ice melt, methane, and runaway warming). (https://www.jobone-forhumanity.org/the_4_most_critical_global_warming_deadlines_and_tipping_points). (https://www.joboneforhumanity.org/the_global_warming_extinction_emergency_plan_b).

support human civilization. The collapse of social and civil foundations that support human civilization can and likely will happen far sooner than most people believe possible. Remember, complex systems collapse rapidly once they begin. Repairing them, or putting them back in place, is complicated and rarely attainable. Even when the repair is possible, the time-frames to re-establish planetary ecosystems can take thousands of years or more.

So, I ask the question again. Do you believe that global warming is "no big deal"? Or do you think, like me, that we need to take decisive and aggressive action as a species *now* to reverse it and prepare for the inevitable changes already baked into the system; the changes that are coming?

Some of those force-multipliers might be reversible, but I do not believe global warming is one of them. We have kicked the can too far down the road.[21]

e) A List of Potential Problems, Economic Triggers, and Social Impacts Intensified by Global Warming

- Conflicts and wars over food, water, and land to live on.

- Increased water vapor (atmospheric rivers).

- Rising sea levels due to polar ice melt.

- Methane time bombs.

- Financial stress caused by global warming.

- Pandemic impacts on our global economy.

- Animal attacks due to human encroachment into their wild habitat.

- Tsunamis due to tectonic plates shifting as ice melts.

- Increased volcanic activity.

- Toxic air pollution.

---

21 20 Worst Consequences of Global Warming (now irreversible for the next 50years.) (https://www.joboneforhumanity.org/20_worst_consequences_of_global_warming) and What Are the Seven Greatest Global Adaptive Challenges Facing Millennials, Younger Generations, and Humanity as a Whole? (https://universespirit.org/what-are-seven-greatest-global-adaptive-challenges-facing-millennials-younger-generations-and)

- Increased heat.

- Increased droughts.

- Less food.

- Water costing more.

- Desertification.

- Fires and wildfires.

- Ocean acidification and marine death.

- Loss of biodiversity.

- Loss of breathable air (from acidification death of phytoplankton).

- Mass climate migrations.

- Jet stream disruption.

- Ocean heat current migration changes.

- Shrinking sea ice and ice shelves.

- Shrinking glaciers and snowpack.

- Flooding.

- Melting tundra and permafrost.

- Increased potential for disease and pandemics.

- Increased financial costs to municipalities and governments already in massive debt.

- Insurance companies no longer insuring vulnerable properties.

- Massive underfunded pensions.

- These are some of the existential threats and economic triggers we have set in motion and intensified through global warming.

- Weather patterns will continue to become increasingly unstable and unpredictable on food availability and production, coastal and wetland flooding, property values, property tax income, insurance costs, insurance availability, heat waves, droughts, and flooding.

- Where do we begin? What should we do?

These questions are an excellent example of decision paralysis created by too many choices.

The Path Forward

First: The golden arch answer to those questions is begun by (a) an *aggressive* reduction in CO_2 emissions and (b) *intentionally* taming our collective primitive ego human consciousness. Not only are these two essential paths forward, they are something that every person can do to begin the healing of our planet. They are the only way we can avoid using the same immature and unevolved collective human consciousness to solve the problems in the list above, *the consciousness that humanity used to create those problems!*

When I talk to people about the taming and evolution of our collective human consciousness, they say there are far more important things we should be doing. I disagree. The window to effectively deal with global warming has essentially closed. The impacts of global warming are going to continue to increase. And whatever we do to reverse global warming will create the collapse of our neoliberal global economy we discussed in Chapter 3. We need to do what we can to aggressively reduce CO_2 emissions, but the only realistic path forward is preparation for resilience and long-term survival. *And a critically important part of that preparation for long-term survival needs to be the maturation and evolution of our collective human consciousness.* Without that taming, the solutions we use to prepare for long-term survival will themselves eventually become victims to our immature, greed-based, "me"-focused collective human consciousness. When that happens, we will simply recreate the exact conditions that created the collapse of human culture we are attempting to avoid. We will explore this concept in depth in Chapter 10 and the creation of self-reliant local communities. In the meantime, *the intentional maturation and evolution of our collective human consciousness is essential for the future long-term survival of human culture and human civilization.*

Second: We need to debate policy, not the reality of scientific facts! We need to trust the data, trust the facts, trust the evidence. And that evidence is extremely sobering. Because of our dithering, two billion children alive today will live in the future that we have created, *and you and I would never intentionally choose that reality for ourselves! But we have created that future for our children and grandchildren!* Our collective shame should mobilize every adult on the planet to do what we can to aggressively reverse our planet's warming, even if that means intentionally and willingly embracing a massive reduction in our current standard of living.

f) Social and Civil Collapse and Extinction

In the last 100 years, severe storms have increased by 300%, and they continue to grow in severity. The conversations on climate change, global warming, and storm intensification ignore the very high likelihood of social and civil collapse long before these hothouse and climate change estimates arrive. We are already in irreversible global warming.[22] Climate change and storm intensification damage are already having significant impacts on food production and governmental operating budgets. The future we are talking about is already here! It's just not evenly distributed yet.

Given the growing levels of CO2 emissions, as storm intensification continues to increase, the probability of mass climate migration is becoming a certainty. Because of the fragility of human civilization's underlying structures, which we will explore in the chapters to follow, assuming social collapse will be avoided is highly unrealistic. As we will discover in the chapters to follow, I see no way to prevent social and civil collapse. COVID-19 is already a significant existential force-multiplier and economic trigger on our economic, social, and civil systems. It is shining a much-needed bright light on the unconscious systemic racism, racial inequalities, and the sobering social vulnerabilities of the poor, the marginalized, and the disenfranchised.

---

22   Article: "Global Warming is Now Irreversible." https://www.joboneforhumanity.org/ irreversible_global_warming_is_here_now.

Given the growing levels of CO_2 emissions, as storm intensification continues to increase, *the probability of mass climate migration is becoming a certainty.* Because of the fragility of human civilization's underlying structures, which we will explore in the chapters to follow, assuming social collapse can be avoided is *highly unrealistic.* As we will discover in the chapters to follow, I see no way social and civil collapse can be avoided.

My concern is that we will continue doing nothing to prepare for social and civil collapse or reduce CO_2 emissions. When we finally wake up to the existential threats and sobering reality of the climate crisis, it will be too late to avoid the impacts that it will have on our social and civil structures. People will react emotionally. Desperation, fear, and a sense of powerlessness will create disruptive social anger and violence. They will look for someone to blame for their pain. My concern is we are doing nothing to reverse or change that inevitable future.

COVID-19 is very much like climate change. They are both putting a chokehold on global economic activity. As we learned in Chapter 2, neoliberal global capitalism grows, or it dies. We need to prepare for the unimaginable future headed our way; more severe pandemics, collapsing ecosystems, shrinking native habitats, increased virus transmissions to humans, prehistoric plagues, and virus release by melting polar ice and melting permafrost.

Systemic collapse happens when a complex interconnected and interdependent system is pushed past its limits. Climate impacts are already disrupting social, economic, and civil structures and pushing them past their limits to survive and support human culture as we know it. Debt is reaching catastrophic levels and growing rapidly; people are being evicted for non-payment of rent and mortgages, migrations of desperate people are growing and creating social and financial unrest in a growing number of nations around the planet.

I believe there will be massive severe and destabilizing economic, political, social, and civil impacts in almost all areas of the world. Preparation for that day needs to begin now. In 10 to 15 years, we will need the emergency preparations of the self-reliant local communities discussed in Part 3 to survive and adapt to the coming changes.[23]

Martin Luther King said it as clearly as anyone I've ever heard, when he reminded us that *"A riot is the language and voice of the unheard."*

The poor of the world are *not being heard.*

The Black and Hispanic communities in America and other nations are *not being heard.*

The people displaced by climate change in the emerging nations around the world are *not being heard.*

The climate migrants seeking a place to live around the world are *not being heard.* Yet experts warn that because of global warming alone, before 2030, the world will see hundreds of millions of climate refugees.

The massive inequalities between those who *have* and those who *don't* are *not being heard.*

The day *is* coming when their voices *will* be heard.

And when that day comes, *our* survival and the survival of all those *unheard voices* will depend directly on our collective ability to (a) achieve more control over the necessities of life and (b) increase our skills to be more self-reliant than most people are today.[24]

Global warming is already in a dangerous state of irreversibility that will last for hundreds to thousands of years, and CO2 levels are rising rapidly, supersizing storms and accelerating irreversible tipping points.

When we do research on global warming and begin to prepare for the coming changes, we need to remind ourselves that all *weather* is local, but climate and *storm intensification* are global. The voices that Martin Luther spoke about *will* be heard, and they *will* be global.

---

23   We will explore this subject in detail in Part 3 when we look at the need to create self-reliant local communities.

24   See Part 3 and the creation of self-reliant local communities and local economies.

Our future as a viable species on this planet will depend on how well we prepare for that day and how well we hear their voices today.

g) Global Warming and Climate Change in the Post-Carbon Era

Swedish chemist Svante Arrhenius was the first scientist to suggest that the planet was warming due to emissions of carbon dioxide, and that was in 1896! NASA recently reported that CO2 levels are higher than at any time in the past 400,000 years! Thirty years ago, Exxon Mobile, Shell, and BP already knew that we were about to start cooking the planet based on reports from their own scientists.[25]

Naomi Klein, author of the book *This Changes Everything,* reminds us that "saving the planet does not mean the planet is fragile...that's not true! The planet will be fine; it's humans and other organic life that's fragile and needs saving."

She reminds us that one way or another, we *are* going into a completely new phase of history called "The Post-Carbon Era."

The consequences of global warming are dire. Scientists are telling us that we have already reached the point where we will get a minimum of a 1.5 degrees Celsius increase in temperature, and it's highly likely that number will be significantly higher, and that's assuming we halt carbon emissions *now*. Even 1.5°C will result in sea level rises of roughly 20 inches, life-threatening heat waves, massive flooding, and multiyear droughts. The impacts on farming and food production will be severe.

A 1.5°C target limit will require a 45% CO2 emission reduction by 2030! And even this is now considered far too conservative. Tough decisions are needed, not more empty promises. And we need *actions* with clear, realistic deadlines to focus that action! And we need them *now*. Waiting is not an option.

We are currently on track for 3°C to 4°C warming!

---

25   Article: "The Climate Emergency: From Bad to Cataclysmic," Jonathon Porritt).

And the recent IPCC report, which scientists warn is far too conservative, is now reporting that polar ice melt is more vulnerable to 1.5°C warming than initially believed.

Irreversible tipping points are kicking in and accelerating the impacts of global warming.

The 100 climate scientists who wrote the 2018 IPCC report (U.N. Intergovernmental Panel on Climate Change) estimated in 2018 that we only had roughly 15 years to take significant action to avoid a major crisis.

Today, 2020, fewer than 3% of American adults ranked the environment as the most critical problem facing their country today!

Climate change and storm intensification are already creating significant financial impacts at national and regional scales, social disruption (as we cross critical social system collapse thresholds), food shortages, floods, and climate migration.[26]

Fossil fuel increases planned for the next ten years will shatter the Paris Climate Limit. Coal, oil, and gas production will more than double current CO_2 emissions (emission levels that are already 50% over allowable CO_2 emissions to avoid 1.5°C warming and stay under 2°C by 2030.)

Subsidies and tax incentives are aggressively promoting greater fossil fuel development and increasing the number of permits required to drill. In the IPCC's words, "The next decade is existentially critical and consequential. We need to drop our CO_2 emissions by 45% by 2030 to stay below 1.5°C."

---

26   The climate commitments made in Paris comprise only a third of the reductions needed to limit warming to 2 degrees...and even if fully met, they put us on track for a potentially catastrophic 3+ Celsius degrees mean global warming. Climate scientists tell us that the world is currently on track to experience 3 to 5 Celsius degrees warming. Five degrees warming would be catastrophic and likely fatal to civilized existence. Even a "modest" 3-degree increase implies disaster enough to inundate coastlines, empty megacities, destroy economies and destabilize geopolitics. The current pace of reducing fossil energy consumption is totally inadequate. Worse yet, global energy use and carbon emissions are rising exponentially at the same rate they were four decades ago! (The Tyee, "Memo from a Climate Crisis Realist: The Choice Before Us," 3/5/2020).

In other words, the current Paris pledges, *even if fully implemented,* would lead to a world 3° to 4°C warmer.

A 1.5°C climate target is no longer possible.

We are already blowing past 2°C.

We are currently on course to pass 4°C by mid-century.

Job One for Humanity reminds us that "the IPCC reports are telling us that the planet will reach the crucial threshold of 1.5°C (2.7°F) above pre-industrial levels as early as 2030. 1.5°C will increase the risk of extreme drought, wildfires, floods, and food shortages for hundreds of millions of people."

To hold at 1.5°C, we need global CO2 emissions to drop by 45% from 2010 levels by 2030 and reach "net-zero" by 2050. The most sobering reality of all these predictions is that most climate scientists believe the Paris targets in the IPCC reports tend to be far too conservative!

The new slogan for Job One for Humanity is "Adapt to Global Warming Extinction." Job One for Humanity is telling us that "if we fail to accept climate emergency openly, worldwide, and make the necessary changes… *we will not survive.*

Climate change is happening faster than scientists expected; it's bad, and it's going to get much, much worse—that's the bottom line.

Job One For Humanity warns that the global warming emergency is much worse than we are being told. We will see mass starvation due to crop failures and 70% to 90% human deaths in the next 30 to 50 years! Climate scientists are warning the world that we are currently headed toward a 3° to 4°C rise.

The global warming window is closing rapidly.

Even at 1.5°C, the impacts will be widespread and significant.

We need "unprecedented changes," and the next few years are critical.

Mother nature is sending clear warnings.

And Job One For Humanity, which is science-based, is warning that the reductions in CO_2 emissions needed are dangerously low if survival is our goal. Even the IPCC reports warn that a 1.5° to 2°C rise is considered a cliff. And 3 to 4°C is regarded as a minefield.

And it's important to remember the IPCC reports fail to mention the threat of "tipping points" or the black swan force-multiplier/existential threats and economic triggers in Part 2.

Oil demand to support business-as-usual is currently increasing by 1.5% per year, and few analysts believe oil demand will decrease in the next decade.

The International Energy Agency (IEA) (https://www.iea.org) tells us they believe oil demand will increase for the next 20 years and will reach125 million barrels per day by mid-century.

Economic growth is acting as a planetary-level cancer. We are blindly traveling down the road, doing business as usual, focused on unlimited growth, progress, short-term profit, and the endless pursuit of "more."

We need to end this mad trance we are under…we need to *intentionally* tame our collective primitive ego consciousness. And waiting to begin this taming is "no longer an option.

Continuing business-as-usual is Tinker Bell thinking in the extreme!

In May 2018, we reached 411 ppm, and that number has been increasing roughly 3 ppm per year over the last six decades, and this rate is increasing every year.

Every additional 25 ppm carbon added to the atmosphere will increase global temperatures another 0.5°F.

At 500 ppm (2042 to 2067), all ice and all glaciers on earth will go into complete meltdown. Historically, when the 500 ppm threshold was reached (4 to 7°F), ocean water levels were 230 feet higher.

If we cross 500 ppm, the probability is high that we will reach 600 ppm within another 25 to 30 years. Somewhere between 5 and 9°F of warming, the extinction of humanity will become a certainty.

Global warming is already an existential crisis that will change life as we know it. And unfortunately, the crisis continues to grow amid denial and apathy. Scientists already believe that global warming will lead to severe, pervasive, and irreversible changes on our planet. Disastrous climate change and energy shortages are near certainties and are coming far sooner than most people believe or are prepared to survive.

The planet can anticipate more and longer heatwaves/droughts, desertification, tropical deforestation, melting permafrost, methane releases, regional water shortages, failing agriculture, local famines, rising sea levels, the flooding and eventual loss of many coastal communities, abandonment of overheated cities, civil unrest, mass migrations, collapsed economies, and possible geopolitical chaos.

At 4°C, the number of climate refugees would reach hundreds of millions! Climate change is not an "issue"; it is the *reality* in which every climate "issue" we identify as critical to the future of humanity will be played out. And we are running out of time to recognize that reality and respond accordingly. This means that *we can't get caught up in the individual "issues." We need to stay focused on the reality of climate change itself!!!*

Humanity will continue to be focused on climate change, and its growing ecological impact, for generations. *It will be a subject that will define our future as a species!!*

Merely reorganizing the deck-chairs to keep the Titanic from sinking is no longer an option. It's Tinker Bell thinking! We need to focus on converting those deck chairs into life rafts. The climate crisis is grounded in the extractivist logic of neoliberal global capitalism and its exploitative relationship with the planet and the world around us!!!

We need to stop thinking "something bad" will happen in 2030. It's happening now! We are adding roughly 40 billion metric tons of CO_2 in the atmosphere every year. And we are already experiencing social and civil stress in the growing defiance of "authority" over the COVID-19 pandemic response and the non-issues of wearing masks and social distancing.

The primary threat of climate change is social unrest and disruption. The financial and social impacts of climate change on human life, property, ecosystems, heat waves, droughts, floods, fires, storm intensification, ocean acidification, and sea-level rise (coastal) will continue to increase.

To briefly summarize the information in this section g) on global warming:

- Global warming is currently only 1.2° to 1.3°C.

- The impacts of 1.5°C, 2°C, or more will be far, far worse.

- The battle for our planet's future will not be going away, and *some scientists are warning climate change might be a lot worse than the estimates are warning!* This is our only planet, and we need to wake up to that sobering reality.

- Declining snowpack resulting from climate warming is causing **water availability** in the Colorado River to fall 20% from historical levels. This amounts to a loss of 1.5 billion tons of water annually. This loss is equal to roughly the annual water consumption of 10 million Americans.

- As flooding, storm surges, and ocean water levels increase, it compromises **septic systems** and increases the threat of waste pollution. Droughts make it difficult for septic tanks to get the volume of water they need to function in some areas. Florida is especially vulnerable. The state has over 2.6 million septic systems, or roughly 12% of all the country's systems. And many of those systems are in flood-prone areas. The repairs that will be required will exceed the financial ability of many homeowners. Some estimates suggest replacing a septic system with a sewer system could cost between $15,000 to $50,000. As the sea levels rise, the water table also rises. And that means that the cost of protecting drinking water supplies will also increase.

- The ppm of CO_2 in the atmosphere is already 100 ppm higher than any time in the last 15 million years. By 2050, the CO_2 levels in ppm will be roughly the level our planet reached just after the extinction of the dinosaurs 50 million years ago! That is, ~3.4°C.

- When carbon reaches 425 to 450 ppm, the temperature increase will be roughly 2° to 2.7°C.

- Over 425 ppm, the temperature will increase above 2°C faster than any time in geologic history, and the rate of temperature increase will grow quickly. *At 450 ppm, we will have reached an extinction scenario for humanity. Many scientists believe this is inevitable by 2050 if we continue business as usual.*

- Recent estimates warn that crossing the carbon 500 ppm threshold has happened repeatedly in the earth's geological history. When this occurred, the sea level inevitably rose to the 70 meters (230 feet) range. At our current annual carbon ppm emission rates, we will reach this catastrophic carbon 500 ppm range by roughly 2042. If you were born this year, you would be 22 years old when this ppm figure is reached. Climate change is not *coming;* it's *here.* It's *now.* And yes, we *are* out of time.

- Washington and international gridlock and denial of climate change is a massive failure to embrace systemic thinking.

    1. We are not getting the truth from political leaders in Washington or other nations.

    2. The consequences are worse and coming far sooner than we are being told.

    3. We are locked in the implications and impacts of global warming and current $CO2$ emissions for the next 30 to 50 years regardless of what we do.

    4. We have 5 to 6 years at best to significantly slow down $CO2$ emissions and avoid the worst of the consequences of global warming.

    5. We need to start now to prepare by creating the self-reliant local communities we will discuss in Part 3.

6. In 2018, the International Energy Agency (IEA) reported that energy consumption in 2018 rose at the fastest rate in a decade, which means we are doing nothing to reverse the coming climate change crisis. We are increasing the rate of CO2 emissions.

h) Wrapping Up The Data:
Flooding and Small Farm Loss

One of the most visible threats of global climate change is flooding. When the climate warms, the atmosphere can carry more water vapor. Flooding is already among the costliest climate-related disasters. This increase in water is creating the *atmospheric rivers* we discussed above. Atmospheric rivers cause most of the flood damage in the Western United States already, and they are projected to intensify *significantly!*

Atmospheric rivers create rain-bombs that dump more water in a few hours than would be expected to fall in months. Most of the water comes down so fast and heavy, it runs off to flood local rivers, not into the local aquifers. They increase storm severity, storm frequency, storm destruction, life-threatening dam breaches, and valuable topsoil runoff. Centuries of forest clearing, overgrazing, lack of organic regenerative farming practices, and monoculture agriculture that removes ground cover crops make much of the topsoil on our farmland vulnerable to runoff from atmospheric river rain-bombs. Urban towns, cities, housing projects, parking lots, paved roads, office buildings, and shopping centers built in flood-prone areas are also seeing dangerous atmospheric river flooding. And the rains are expected to increase as the atmosphere continues to warm and carry more water vapor. Building cities, towns, and housing projects in flood-prone areas and wetlands needs to end.

U.S. National Climate Assessments recently reported, "Any warming above 2°C will lead to grave and likely catastrophic effects on health, livelihoods, food security, water supplies, human security, and economic growth. *Floods in 2018 to 2019 were reported to be the wettest in U.S. history going back to the 1850s and the start of record keeping.*"

In 2019, the *New York Times* reported that globally, 150 million people live on land that will be below the high tide within the next 30 years. Most of those 150 million climate refugees will be forced to migrate into an increasingly hostile and walled-in world! In 2019, the Army War College reported, "The Department of Defense is precariously unprepared for the national security implications of climate change-induced global security challenges."

The sea level is rising faster on the East Coast (due to land sinking) and Gulf coasts. Scientists estimate that ocean levels will be up 8.2 feet by 2100 compared to 2000. This sea rise will directly impact much of the 40% of the U.S. population that lives in or near coastal areas. It's also important to note that sea-level predictions are increasing due to accelerated polar ice melt (an irreversible tipping point). As water levels rise, the sea levels will begin rising on the West Coast also. If you live on or near the ocean coastline, your life will be impacted. In the United States, clean-up costs from storms and flooding will continue to rise into the billions of dollars.

The future has arrived. Our planet is warming outside our control. The world will be reformed with or without action on our part. The water is coming! Septic tanks will be at risk of flooding. Dams will collapse. Rivers will rise. People will be forced to migrate.

Droughts and unexpected weather changes are already harming farmers and impacting food supplies. Farm debt is the highest in history. *Time* magazine recently reported, "the closing days of 2019 find small farms pummeled from every side: a trade war, severe weather associated with climate change, tanking commodity prices related to globalization, political polarization, and corporate farming defined not by a silo and a red barn, but technology and the efficiencies of scale."

It is the worst crisis in decades.

Chapter 12 farm bankruptcies were up 12 percent in the Midwest from July 2018 to June 2019; they're up 50 percent in the Northwest.

Tens of thousands have simply stopped farming, knowing that reorganization through bankruptcy won't save them. The nation lost more than 100,000 farms between 2011 and 2018; 12,000 between 2017 and 2018 alone. Farm debt, at $416 billion, is at an all-time high. More than half of all farmers have lost money every year since 2013. Farm loan delinquencies are rising.

The current warming trajectory could bring 100-year rainstorms as often as every 2.5 years by 2100…storms that could massively flood cities and farms in the decades ahead. The National Academy of Sciences projects large increases in these mega-storms. "We have very high confidence of extreme precipitation in the future. Flash flooding is going to be an increasing concern as well."

David R. Easterling, a climate extremes researcher and director of the U.S. National Climate Assessment, warns, "We're going to see increases in extreme events, and we need to be prepared." He went on to say that most current infrastructures, such as dams and bridges, were designed to deal with rainfall levels experienced in the 1950s and were not built to withstand the more frequent extreme rains identified by the new research.[27]

i) Realistic preparation for the changes that are coming

Over-reacting to the data above is not possible. I included this material for only one reason. And that reason was to emphasize the urgency that each of those statistics are meaningless numbers and facts and data and statistics and warnings. They mean only one thing; the reality that the survival of our lives, our children's lives, and the lives of our grandchildren are going to depend entirely on our ability to take the above data seriously and begin *now* to prepare for the future that is coming. Without preparation for resilience, our future survival is highly problematic. The survival of our children and grandchildren is not possible without intentional and aggressive preparation. The numbers don't lie. They are not exaggerated. In fact, most scientists will tell you they are dangerously understated.

The golden arch of this book is focused on the necessity of preparing for the realities that are coming. The data presented above by environmental

---

27 "New Study Shows Global Warming Intensifying Extreme Rainstorms Over North America." Bob Berwyn, InsideClimate News, 6/2/2020.

scientists is real, and ignoring that data will create unnecessary suffering for our children and grandchildren. I believe that careful preparation will create the resilience they will need to survive. However, they will require us to aggressively begin that preparation now while there is still time and opportunity to create the resources and skills they will need for resilience and survival.

All of the material and concepts presented in this book are focused on giving readers the insights needed to begin preparing *now*. Waiting is not an option. The above data is real and *understated,* not *exaggerated.* And it will take *years* to gather the resources and learn the skills that will be required for long-term survival.[28]

Don't Follow the Crowd

Because individual preparation; and the implementation of net-zero carbon emission goals will cause massive changes in life as we know it, humanity in the developed nations will aggressively resist the necessary changes until it's too late to avoid the existential impacts of global warming and climate change.

We know what we have to do to solve the problems of global warming. Scientists have warned us of the changes listed in section g), above, that we need to make. We have the information, but those changes will not be implemented until a sufficient and critical number of people do the work of *intentionally* taming and evolving their self-focused primitive ego-consciousness, and *intentionally* begin preparing for resilience and survival *now.*

Preparation for increased storm intensification and the climate changes that are coming is critical, but few will begin to embrace that preparation. Don't follow the crowd. Without preparation *now,* there will be no resilience for survival when those storms and climate change impacts arrive. There will not be a "new normal." The only "normal" will be *more* change. And those changes will continue to intensify and grow *more* destructive, not *less.* Carbon pollution has ended the era of stable a stable, "normal" climate.

---

28   See Chapter 10 on the creation of self-reliant local communities, which what I believe is the most realistic hope for the future survival of our children and grandchildren.

Climate change, storm intensification, droughts, floods, 1000-year storms, and COVID-19 are already exposing the vulnerabilities and inequalities of the world's black, brown, and poor populations. The climate crisis is already here. It just isn't evenly distributed *yet*.

Preparation for the massive changes that *are* coming will be critical for future generations to successfully create the resilience they *will* need to survive. That preparation is a primary focus of Part 3 of this book. Life as we know it will look very different in the years to come. Creating local, self-reliant communities that have embraced the *intentional* taming of the community's collective primitive ego consciousness is the most likely and hopeful preparation we can undertake to ensure our long-term survival and avoid our extinction as a species. Resilience requires preparation *now, before* the crisis arrives.

The self-reliant local communities, and local sustainable economies of Part 3, are focused on the collective self-organization and social values of traditional human cultures that historically created resilience by embracing cooperation, well-being, degrowth, justice for all living organisms, and radical simplicity; rather than profit and unlimited economic expansion. As self-reliant local communities, they would embrace the values and systemic thinking found in the indigenous early human cultures, the ability to see and honor the presence of spirit in all of reality. The spiritual values and capacity for systemic thinking that we lost as we became "more civilized."

Climate Change Is a Lens to View the Future That's Coming

Climate change is a lens that is allowing us to see the future and remind humanity that despite our differences and our traditional boundaries, we are a species sharing a climate reality that will force us to come together and remind us just how tightly we are bound together as one species and one human community.

And climate change will also require us to shift our thinking from fixing the problem to *the more fundamental issue of addressing the underlying cause of the problem;* the ability to recognize the importance of cooperation, the need to create a shared future, and the need to power down from fossil fuel energy and begin more intentionally focusing on the urgent need for humanity to make the shift to intentional simplicity and sustainable renewable energy. And most importantly, the need to create a socially "just" sharing of the planets limited resources with all of the other species and living ecosystems on our planet. In other words, the need to begin re-imagining what a truly "just" system would look like, a system that is ecologically sustainable, evenly shared, and just for *all* life, not just human life. The transition to a more sustainable way of living is inevitable, *but social justice for all is not!*

These changes are not only necessary and needed; they are urgent.

Unfortunately, I see no way humanity will incorporate the above values and ethics until a significant percentage of the human culture has the courage to intentionally evolve their primitive ego consciousness and its childhood illusions and delusions of early childhood. Humanity is currently on a path toward social and civil collapse, and I see no realistic way to avoid that reality. The only viable path forward that embraces a realistic sense of hope is creating the self-reliant local communities and economies of Part 3. Every other "solution" to the problems that face us simply reflects dangerous Tinker Bell thinking.

Climate change is here!
It's going to get a lot worse before it gets better!

We need system change moving forward, not more "business as usual" that favors the wealthy at the expense of the 99%! We need to build and co-create a new society from the bottom up. A global human culture that embraces radical social change and radical social transformation. "Business as usual" is not an option!!! Doing nothing is not an option!! *Waiting is not an option!!* I believe that creating self-reliant local communities and local economies is a crucial part of the system change that could help humanity avoid extinction. Humanity knows how to survive after a significant crisis. It's called cooperation. Localization and creating self-reliant local communities would use that model of cooperation and become a long-term system change that just might allow us to survive and function as a sustainable species moving forward!!!

We need to be in the right relationship with our planetary home and with each other!

We need to embrace diversity, stay open to learning, embrace change, and explore which skills might help create a radically new social transformation and society. We need to break with the existing order and power structures and better connect with the working people, farmers, the poor, indigenous communities, immigrants, and the many current victims of neoliberal global capitalism.

We need to phase out of fossil fuels, phase in clean energy systems; create local food production, distribution, and economic systems; restore soil fertility; eliminate factory farms and polluting agribusinesses; build public transport networks, reduce the need for private trucks and cars; eliminate manipulative advertising and its power to increase consumption; build energy-efficient homes and buildings; transform the military into voluntary teams charged with restoring ecosystems; increase the availability of high-quality health services; do reforestation; de-grow our wasteful and harmful economies and their carbon footprints; eliminate wealth inequality; supply clean, abundant energy to all global citizens; pay or make reparations for colonial and imperialist exploitation; ex-militarize down to the bone; become a planet and its people focused on who we are as global species, not a species that sees itself as a collection of fragmented, separate nations.

We are headed toward catastrophe. We need to embrace realism and facts over Tinker Bell thinking.

If this generation doesn't step up, we're in trouble. This is the generation that's going to be on the business end of climate change for as long as we live.

– Pete Buttigieg, April 2019

We need to base our decisions on facts and data, not on our personal assumptions or unexplored, uninformed personal beliefs. We need to do our work, tame and evolve our collective immature primitive ego-consciousness, and then decide on the best course of action that will keep us and those we care about safe for seven sustainable generations into the future.

Summary of Chapter 4:
Summary of Existential Threats Created by the Force-Multiplier Called Global Warming

There was a lot of material presented in this chapter. It is easy to get overwhelmed. It's easy to experience decision paralysis. I know. I get it. I'm writing about it, and it overwhelms me at times. You don't need to digest all the material presented in this chapter in minute detail. *The importance of this chapter is simply recognizing that global warming is the primary existential threat facing the future of humanity, and we need to begin preparing now.* That recognition is far more critical than the specific details of global warming and climate change. The collapse of neoliberal global capitalism will bring human civilization to its knees in the near future and threaten social and civil collapse. Still, global climate change is the primary existential force-multiplier threat that could put humanity under the gravestone of history if we continue to ignore it.

An existential force-multiplier threat event is defined as an unexpected and usually unanticipated high-consequence event. Force-multipliers threaten the structures that support the foundations of human culture. COVID-19 is a significant force multiplier event that is currently threatening the collapse of our fragile global economy. Tom Friedman of the *New York Times* recently described the black swan threats facing humanity as more like "a herd of stampeding black elephants multiple, predictable, and economically catastrophic events that everyone knows are coming, but our political and business leaders have consciously chosen not to deal with." He was reminding us of the simple truth that choices (made or not made) have consequences.

And the essence of this chapter is recognizing that global warming is the most massive existential black elephant force-multiplier leading a herd of existential force-multiplier threat elephants stampeding toward humanity.

Only when we have the courage and wisdom to face the existential threat that climate change and global warming represent for the future of humanity and our planet will we begin to act. And when we act, pray that enough of our human population has tamed and evolved their collective primitive ego consciousness and childhood conditioning. If they haven't, we will be condemned to use the same immature, unevolved thinking crafting the solutions to the problems that past generations used to create them. The longer we fail to act, and the longer we fail to evolve our thinking as a species, the more dire the consequences will be. The hour is fast approaching when it will be too late for effective action. Waiting is no longer a viable option. We are already out of time.

We need to embrace the simple truth that "we," the human species, and our grossly immature and unevolved thinking, are the root cause of all the charging black elephants. Until we do the work of *intentionally* taming and evolving our collective primitive-ego human consciousness, that herd of stampeding elephants will be headed directly toward human civilization. Regardless of where you live on the planet, the stampeding dark cloud of dust is already visible on the horizon. If you listen carefully, you can hear the thunder of their hooves.

The climate crisis is the greatest threat to humanity's future survival, but those profiting from neoliberal global capitalism are unwilling to acknowledge that reality.

I will end this chapter by saying we *know* what we have to do to solve global warming. We know it has to be addressed *now*. It's not rocket science. But those solutions will not be implemented until a sufficient, critical number of people have intentionally tamed their immature, unevolved, self-focused primitive ego-consciousness, and have embraced the wisdom, courage, and urgency of acting now.

Waiting is no longer an option. We've kicked the can as far down the road as we can, and for as long as we could.

Intentional preparation for long-term survival is already late getting to the table.

The only question now is will we take action and begin aggressive preparation in time to make a difference.

We are already well beyond the category of *catastrophic*.

The next stage is likely *extinction*.

CHAPTER 5

Existential Force-Multiplier, Threat-Multiplier, and Economic Trigger: Resistance to Change

Our resistance to intentionally evolve our collective human consciousness blinds us to the changes that need to be made in the foundations of human civilization.

We are the problem. The aspects of humanity's collective, unconscious, unevolved primitive ego, and its early childhood conditioning, that work together to systemically reinforce and support each to resist change include:

(b) the need to be "right," (g) a lack of interconnected, interdependent systemic thinking, (j) an exaggerated aggressive narcissistic self-focused sense of entitlement, (k) an inability to connect short-term choices with long-term consequences, (l) the fear of change (uncertainty, not knowing), and (o) the inability of our collective primitive ego to embrace long-term thinking.

* *

Primitive ego early childhood conditioning:

a. "What's in it for me?" greed.

b. Need to be "right" (aggressive arrogance, extreme cognitive dissonance/confirmation bias).

c. Inability to replace "me" thinking with "we" thinking (compassion, mutuality, cooperation).

d. I want what I want when I want it.

e. Blaming others for our feelings (inability to own our own feelings).

f. Ignorance regarding the danger of exponential growth (e.g., COVID-19).

g. A lack of interconnected, interdependent systemic thinking.

h. Survival-of-the-fittest thinking.

i. Black versus white, zero-sum thinking ("You can't have that, it's mine!").

j. An exaggerated aggressive, narcissistic self-focused sense of entitlement.

k. An inability to connect short-term choices with long-term consequences.

l. The fear of change (uncertainty, not knowing).

m. The unending, obsessive desired for "more."

n. The need for power "over" rather than power "with."

o. The inability to embrace long-term thinking.

* *

Introduction to Chapter 5

Change is a fundamental reality of this universe.

Without change, our universe would not exist.

Without change, evolution would not be possible.

Without change, *we* would not exist.

Without change, creating the *new* would not be possible.

Without change, diversity would not be possible.

Without change, correcting the *old* would not be possible or necessary.

Without change, the future would not be possible.

And without change, preparation would not be possible or *needed* because nothing could change to require preparation.

Without change, even the concept of "reality" would be meaningless.

Fortunately, in this universe, change *is* a fundamental reality. And because it is, anticipation and preparation for change are not only necessary but also *existentially* necessary. Without the ability of anticipation and preparation, humanity would be powerless. We would be condemned to passively accept whatever the universe chooses to bring us. Fortunately, we do have the ability to anticipate change and prepare for change. Which is a good thing, because change is precisely what *reality* does in our universe. *It changes!*

Without the ability to anticipate and prepare, some of the changes that reality brings could change life as we know it. Some of those changes could even be fatal to the future survival of our own life, or the survival of our species.

So, since reality *does* exist, and change *does* happen, we need to anticipate and prepare for some of the changes that reality brings us because we are back to the original premise that "change is a fundamental reality of this universe."

Stated differently, we have no choice; we have to accept the reality of change, we need to anticipate the changes that might come, and we need to prepare for those changes when they could be life-threatening.

If the paragraphs above seem a bit obvious and a bit like preaching to the choir, I would agree with you. But I included them because much of humanity is behaving as if change is an alien concept. They act as if change *might* happen on other planets, but certainly not here on *our* planet. They would argue:

Besides that, change is dangerous. It creates the unknown. And that's scary.

Besides that, what I'm doing is *right,* and change would imply that I'm *wrong.*

Besides that, I'm living the way I *want* to live, the way I'm *entitled* to live.

So, I prefer to pretend that change is not necessary or desired.

So, thank you very much, but no, thank you! Life is fine just as it is.

Therefore, you must be wrong, or an alarmist, or believe in conspiracy theories.

You get the point.

How do I know much of humanity is thinking this way?

Because:

a. Most people are intentionally ignoring or acknowledging the reality that massive change is here, and more is coming.

b. Extremely few are actively preparing for those massive changes.

c. A majority of humanity is aggressively rejecting, denying, ignoring, mocking, and labeling as extremist most of the warnings of change that highly trained environmental scientists are virtually shouting from the rooftops for us to hear.

To avoid the inconvenience of change, they assume their subjective opinions are more accurate and "right" than the facts and data of the scientists and experts.

I refer to this "uninformed assuming" to reflect a condition called *intentional ignorance.*

It reminds me of Mark Twain's quote that "It isn't what you know for certain that harms you; it's what you know for certain *that just ain't so.*"

Assuming that change isn't coming *just ain't so.*

Assuming that the change that is coming is not life-threatening *just ain't so.*

Assuming that the scientists don't know what they're talking about *just ain't so.*

Assuming that the coming changes will not threaten humanity's survival on our planet *just ain't so.*

Assuming that facts don't matter, truth doesn't matter, and data doesn't matter, *just ain't so.*

Massive Change Is Already Here, and More Is Coming

Massive change *is* coming, and the reality that we are not preparing for its arrival is a primary golden arch focus of this book. Because I see social and civil collapse as a high probability, I tend not to talk about the book with most people because I know it is usually met with rolling eyes, scorn, dismissal, and aggressive denial. One person recently suggested I need to grow my beard longer, get a sign that says "Doom Is Coming," and find a corner to stand on while I preach about "end times." I didn't tell him that I would do that if I thought it would be helpful.

Given the amount of effort and time it has taken to research the subjects covered in this book, and the many hours and months to do the writing, I tend to avoid engaging in meaningless conversations. I simply recognize the wisdom in Gordon Peterson's advice that "When people stop listening, stop talking." When I have finished writing, people can either read the book or not. For those who do, I sincerely hope it is helpful and encourages them to begin actively preparing for what's coming. Our ability to survive the massive changes that are coming will depend entirely and directly on how well we have prepared for them.

Having lived several decades homesteading and living off the land in upstate New York, my concern is that it will be easy for most people to under-estimate the hard work and costs involved in gathering tools and equipment, acquiring land, putting in wells and septic systems, and learning the skills required to live the "simple life" of our ancestors. It takes a lot of time, energy, and intentional preparation to create a self-reliant, sustainable way of life.

When my grandparents told me stories about working from morning to night, I used to think they were exaggerating. You know, "the having to fend off wolves on the way to school five miles away" story. But I quickly learned that they were understating the reality of their experience. I discovered they were telling me the truth.

My experience of homesteading and living off the land was a very reward-ing way to live, but cutting and splitting firewood to heat and cook on a wood stove, milking goats, raising pigs, processing beehives, watering and processing gardens, picking fruit trees, drying fruit, building out-buildings, processing and preserving food, dealing with coyotes, deer, and raccoons living under the porch, and shoveling snow in upstate New York was hard work and took long hours. But I would do it again in a heartbeat if I were a bit younger.

My wife and I are now retired, living full time in a motor home doing volunteer work around the country. As I write this, we are working this summer as volunteer groundskeepers for a small community rodeo and fairground in central Washington. We are surrounded by wheat farms. Most of the farmers in the community know what growing food and raising animals means. They think nothing of working all day, and then harvesting, raking, and bailing all night. Like most farmers and those called to living their lives closer to the land, growing food, and raising animals, they would say "that's just life" when you're farming and working with nature. "You work when the work needs doing."

Preparation for the massive life-altering changes that are coming requires preparation to begin now to create the skills and resources necessary for self-reliance and the resilience needed to survive in the years ahead. The sooner a person starts that preparation, the more likely they will be prepared to survive the future that's coming; the future that isn't what it used to be.

Massive Change Is Not Coming, It's Already Here

The future isn't what it used to be, and waiting to begin preparing for that future is no longer an option. The future is already here. It's just not evenly distributed *yet*. The poor around the planet know this reality. The marginalized around the world know this reality. Blacks and browns and people of color know this reality. The folks in Bangladesh and southeast India and the other Far East nations know this reality. They struggle to survive the droughts, the storms, the heat waves, and lack of water and food. Many have been displaced and forced to migrate and are struggling to enter neighboring countries that have closed their borders.

Protected by their wealth and more stable social and civil infrastructures, the privileged in the developed nations have managed to avoid most of the negative impacts of the massive changes. But given their current lack of preparation, that protective shell of privilege *will* end far sooner than they will be prepared to successfully manage. Rich or poor, resilience for self-reliant survival requires significant preparation and skills *before* the crisis arrives, not *after*. And that wisdom and knowledge is not something that can be bought. It comes from experience. Waiting to begin preparing for the future and the massive changes already here is *no longer a viable option*...assuming you want to survive those changes.

The scale of preparation required to survive the coming changes will require a significant focus and commitment of time, resources, and energy. For many, it will likely involve relocation (acquiring land for gardens and live-stock) and time to learn the survival skills that will be required for gardening, composting, food preserving equipment and skills, working with livestock, animal processing, the tools that will be needed for independent survival, water sources (wells), wood heat and wood cooking equipment (including access to wood, saws, axes, sharpening equipment), solar and wind for local energy (lights and battery charging for hand tools), and blacksmith skills and equipment. The preparation will be overwhelming unless preparation begins now. The skills and equipment you will need to survive are the everyday skills and tools people two or three rural generations in the past learned to work with every day while they were growing up.[29]

When the impacts of the changes that are coming begin to increase in intensity, preparation goals will need to assume that water, electricity, gaso-line, propane, sewer systems, garbage, and the other social services will likely experience significant interruptions. Some will even cease to exist in rural areas where land will be available to create self-reliant, small local communities.[30]

The words of Spencer Johnson, the author of "Who Moved My Cheese" that I quoted in the Introduction on the reality of change, have hung on the wall of my office for decades. They are my constant and straightforward reminder of

---

29   This kind of preparation will require years of effort and the creation of a supportive local community, which we will explore in Part 3.

30   We discuss the creation of local communities in detail in Part 3.

the realities of change and the wisdom I wrote about above. Essentially, the fact is that *change happens*, somebody is *always* moving the cheese, so *deal* with it.

We Are the Problem

As I've written above, this book's golden arch is the reality that *We* created the structural problems that are now threatening human culture and human civilization. Our collective unconscious immature, unevolved, early childhood primitive-ego conditioning created, and then ignored, virtually all of the existential-force multiplier threats and economic triggers threatening humanity we are reviewing in Part 2 of this book. Our political systems, our legal systems, our policing systems, our economic systems, our corporate and banking systems—none of them are going to change until the internal, cultural, interpersonal thinking process of our collective unconscious and unevolved primitive ego and its early childhood conditioning mature.

Change in our human culture happens only when *we* change.

It evolves only when *we* evolve.

It becomes more just and compassionate only when *we* become more just and compassionate.

And thinking otherwise is Tinker Bell thinking.

Preparation for the massive changes that are coming will require us to embrace physical, emotional, and mental changes. And as I illustrated above, some of that change will be very challenging. Changing our beliefs, assumptions, illusions, and values will be just as challenging as changing the way we live our lives.

Digging Deeper into the Reality of Change in Our Collective Human Consciousness

All of the aspects of immature, primitive ego thinking listed at the beginning of each chapter are offered to describe our unconscious primitive ego and its early childhood conditioning and, most importantly, how they contribute in this chapter to our collective inability as a species to embrace change. The three primary aspects of unconscious primitive ego thinking that most directly and intentionally resist change are (a) the need to be "right," (b) decision paralysis created by a lack of clarity that results from the primitive ego's inability to embrace the *not knowing* and the *uncertainty* that change creates, and (c) the inability of our collective primitive ego to adopt long-term thinking.

We'll briefly look at these three critical primitive ego impediments to change in the material that follows. It's always important to keep in mind that our unconscious primitive ego aspects work together to mutually support each other. None of them stand alone. Taming the primitive ego requires paying attention to how they are present in our thinking and actions every time they emerge. As we will see in Part 3, our individual and collective survival in the years ahead will depend in no small measure on how well we do that taming.

Our Resistance to Change:
Our Immature Primitive Ego's Need to Be "Right"

As we discussed above, one of the more dangerous beliefs and delusions of our immature and unevolved collective primitive ego human consciousness and its early childhood conditioning is the aggressive need to be "right." The need to be "right" was a powerful childhood defense against criticism, and we used it aggressively in childhood to protect our fragile early childhood ego. But like most of our unevolved, unconscious early childhood survival skills, we unconsciously attempt to use them to manage our adult lives. And when we do, we are essentially asking a seven-year-old child to function effectively in an adult world. Unfortunately, *no seven-year-old has the life experiences or wisdom to function successfully in the adult world.*

The need to be "right" (a) creates an aggressive tendency to reject or criticize anyone who disagrees with us, and more importantly (b) it creates an internal *cognitive dissonance,* the tendency to reject or ignore information that conflicts or challenges any of our beliefs. Some refer to this as *confirmation bias,* the tendency to seek out information that already agrees with our beliefs and avoid information that doesn't. Of course, cognitive dissonance and confirmation bias effectively shut down our ability to grow, learn, and embrace new knowledge. They are common psychological techniques employed by the primitive ego consciousness to resist change. The need to be "right" is essentially a form of intentional ignorance. It allows us to ignore the wisdom to *always* pay attention and focus on the *consequences* of our beliefs, *not* the *belief* itself.

Beliefs always create consequences.

Consequences create our lives.

The cognitive dissonance and confirmation bias created by the aggressive need to be "right" intentionally and aggressively ignores the three important wisdoms I shared in the introduction.

Mark Twain: "It ain't what you *don't know* that gets you into trouble; it's what you know for sure *that just ain't so.*"

Alvin Toffler: "The illiterate of the 21st century will not be those who cannot read and write, but *those who cannot learn, unlearn, and relearn.*"

Eric Hoffer: "In times of change, *"learners" inherit the earth,* while the *"learned"* find themselves beautifully equipped to deal with a world *that no longer exists.*

When we are confronted by others telling us we are wrong, our primitive ego gets angry and aggressive. The need to be "right" also increases our tendency to belong to "tribes" that agree with our beliefs. Our tribal identity not only increases cognitive dissonance and confirmation bias, it legitimizes the aggressive anger, judgmentalism, and openly hostile energy we project toward those in other tribes who dare to imply we are wrong…simply because they believe differently.

The primitive ego's aggressive need to be *right* has created most of the conflict, wars, and lack of compassion in human history. The primitive ego's need to be right increases tribal ideological extremism, political division, and endless conflict. We see this tribal conflict and ideological rigidity in the polarized tension between the Republican vs. Democrat, conservative vs. liberal, left vs. right, and red vs. blue in American politics. This aggression towards those in other tribes also explains our social ability to ignore explicit racism and racial bias, and the unconscious aggression we project onto *others* who look and think differently from those in our tribe. We see this antagonism toward "others" religiously, politically, nationally, racially, economically, pro vs. anti-science, wealthy vs. poor, educated vs. uneducated, "normal" vs. lesbian, bisexual, gay, transsexual, or queer…essentially, unconscious aggression toward any anyone, or any tribe, who is perceived as "other."

However, it is also essential to acknowledge that the arrogance and aggression toward others are sometimes fully conscious and intentional. When we arrogantly know we are right, we intentionally shut down our ability and openness to learn and grow; our ability to embrace innovation, creativity, or creatively imagine *what if* the other person is right. When we *know* we are *right,* it supports the creation of cognitive dissonance and shuts down our ability to embrace middlepath thinking, the ability to actively search for the truths that are always embedded in both sides of every issue. As Wendell Berry reminds us in his classic book, *The Unsettling of America: Culture and Agriculture,* the wilderness on each side of life contains essential insights. But we can't live or survive in those wildness areas alone. Life has to be lived in the middle ground between those wilderness extremes where the wisdom from both wilderness areas can be *intentionally* incorporated in our lives.

I've always found it helpful to remember the concept that "No one is smart enough to be right or wrong one hundred percent of the time." And yes, this sign also hangs on my writing room wall.

The primitive ego need to be *right* ignores this simple middlepath reality.

The primitive ego need to be *right,* and the aggression it creates in the world, is simply a primitive and unevolved way of thinking that embraces the unconscious ego conditioning of early childhood. The need to be right is not genetically predetermined. If we want to change and evolve our thinking, we *can*. It's *possible*. We *can* change. If we want to reimagine the future we would like to create, we *can*. That, too, is possible. But the ability to embrace change and the arrogant need to be right are *not* compatible. They *cannot* coexist together.

We need to remind ourselves that our immature, unconscious primitive ego is emotionally impatient. It is narcissistically "me" focused, and it wants *what* it wants...*now!* We learned very early in life that people would do our bidding if we screamed long enough and loud enough. But in the adult world, authentic and lasting change often happens slowly. We need to remind ourselves that *everything* in the created universe is in the process of changing, evolving, and becoming something new...but some changes take time. And if we are patient with ourselves, even the intentional evolution, awakening, and taming of our primitive ego human consciousness are achievable.

A good rule of thumb to use as you read the material to follow in in this book is to remind yourself of the certainty that:

a. When things are unsustainable or harmful, when they no longer make sense, they will eventually change, evolve, be abandoned, be replaced, and come to an end. And that includes our collective immature primitive ego-based human consciousness.

b. Change is not only a reality; it's inevitable.

These simple concepts, when applied to the reality and inevitability of social and civil change, and likely collapse, are two of the primary golden arches of this book.

Our Resistance to Change: Decision Paralysis

As we learned in the Introduction, our human *resistance* to change is often nothing more than *decision paralysis*: a lack of clarity regarding the exact changes the rider (logic) needs to embrace. And when the *need* for change is unclear or missing, our primitive ego's (the *emotional elephant's*) need to emotionally avoid uncertainty and not knowing will always choose immediate, short-term gratification. [31]

Until there is crystal clarity on the *exact changes* required to meet the *clearly defined goals*, the rider's mind will become exhausted by too many choices as it attempts to make a decision. When this happens, *decision exhaustion* will kick in and (a) change will not happen or (b) a decision will be made, but action to implement the decision will be short-lived. A basic tenet of sustainable change is always having crystal-clear clarity on what we want to change. In other words, if we want to avoid decision paralysis, we have to have absolute clarity on the change we want to achieve.

The first and primary change needed to effectively prepare for the massive changes and threats of Part 2 that are coming is finding the courage to intentionally tame our individual primitive ego consciousness and its immature thinking process. Until we do that work, we will continue to use the same thinking process to solve the problems facing us that were used when humanity created them. Change starts with us. We are the problem. We are the root cause. And only we can solve the problems we created. But we need the clarity that only a tamed and evolved consciousness and matured thinking process can provide.

The second primary requirement for significant and lasting change is defining the compelling *need* for the change. Until there is clarity on the need for the change, the primitive ego (*emotional elephant*), which loves predictability, sameness, routines, habits, and same old-same old, *will always take the short-term goal of immediate gratification* over the sacrifices that the long-term goals of the rider who wants to embrace long-term change. The elephant's hunger for immediate gratification will take priority.

---

31   I recommend reading *Switch: How to Change Things When Change Is Hard,* by Chip and Dan Heath, Broadway Books, 2010 for excellent material on these concepts. This is one of the best books I've read on the subject of change. The metaphor of the rider (logic) and the elephant (emotions) that the authors use to talk about change is a powerful and helpful way to think about change.

When (a) the rider (left hemisphere logic) is immobilized by decision paralysis created by indecision and too many choices, and (b) the elephant (right hemisphere emotions of the unconscious primitive ego) lacks a compelling motivation or emotional *need* for the change is unclear, (c) the powerful emotions of the elephant (*unconscious primitive ego*) will take control. It will deny the change, resist the change, or dismiss the change using unconscious cognitive dissonance.

Even when presented with science, robust evidence, predictions, or warnings, they will be ignored by most people's unconscious primitive ego (emotional elephant). They will continue to assume the threat is not real because it has never happened before.

The severity or size of the threat will make little difference until the danger is personally experienced by the individual. Even then, most people's primitive ego (emotional elephant) will delay action until the scale of the threat becomes an existential crisis. By that time, adequate preparation for resilience will be too late. Until that day arrives, the primitive ego (emotional elephant) will choose the rewards and certainty of stability and sameness over the long-term negative consequences of inaction.

To Briefly Summarize...

This, in a nutshell, is the existential dilemma confronting humanity today. This is the situation that most people are struggling with when confronted with the massive changes the scientists are warning us are coming. They *need more clarity* as to the exact critical moves that these massive changes will require. And unfortunately, *that clarity is not being provided.* The "authorities" that would typically provide that clarity are struggling with their own political and economic decision paralysis. They are caught between the need to protect the economy and social stability while at the same time struggling with the need to protect the planet and human civilization from the massive changes that are coming.

Until this conflict is resolved, the rider (logic) of the primitive ego (emotional elephant) in most people will continue to embrace the same-old, same-old routines and habits of stability and sameness. The *urgent need for change will die, stillborn.*

Change will happen only when the emotional elephant (primitive ego) is engaged. We need to (a) increase the focus of our attention on the *need* for change; (b) better articulate exactly how the massive changes that are coming will directly impact individuals, including their values of compassion and empathy; and (c) increase the sense of *now-ness* of the threats...not on their arrival "someday" in the future, and not on the "debate" as to whether the threats are real. And as one writer said, climate change is *now*, and it's time to panic. And also (d) we need to listen to the voices of those in poor, less-developed nations who have already experienced the early arrival of some of the massive changes that are coming; the voices of the unheard who currently have no voice in our developed countries. They understand the need to panic and the need to prepare before the crisis arrives. We need to hear their voices. They can teach us about systemic collapse. They've experienced it first-hand. They can teach us about desperation and lack of preparation. They've experienced them first-hand.

The massive changes we will explore in the chapters to follow are coming whether we believe them or not. They *will* create social and civil collapse. We will explore an important and realistic method of preparation for the resilience and survival of those existential changes in Part 3.

Our Resistance to Change: The Inability to Embrace Long-Term Thinking

The lack of ability to engage in long-term thinking and use current data to *imagine the future that is coming* directly interferes with our ability to prepare, to save money for emergencies, for retirement, for the down payment on a home or car...all the things that some people would prefer to label those who do prepare as being "lucky." But long-term thinking is not luck. It's the ability to think about the unthinkable and then prepare for it. Long-term thinking is the ability to see "trends" and then imagine the future and the logical conclusions of those trends. Not preparing for the COVID-19 pandemic is an excellent example/consequence of "short-term" thinking, not unluckiness. The scientists have been warning for several decades that a pandemic was inevitable and coming.

Long-term thinking allows us to (a) "see" trends, (b) imagine and anticipate the changes that might be coming as a result of those trends, and (c) begin to prepare for the day they arrive to limit the ability of those changes to create pain and disruption when they do arrive.

Complex systems are vulnerable to change and system collapse. The changes that complex systems create when they begin to collapse are often unpredictable in both the kind of change they will create and the timing of that change. And complex systems require complex solutions when they collapse. Applying simple solutions to the collapse of complex systems is extremely dangerous Tinker Bell thinking. Failure to prepare is also dangerous Tinker Bell thinking.

The force-multiplier existential threats and economic triggers in Part 2 are warning us that massive change "is" coming. They are warning us of the inevitability of environmental changes, storm intensification, economic changes and threats, social and cultural changes, ecosystem changes, massive extinction events, loss of diversity, and energy changes. They are future existential threats that have the potential to threaten the survival of human culture. Ignoring them reflects a dangerous level of intentional ignorance. Not preparing for them also reflects a dangerous level of intentional ignorance. These are not simple problems that can be solved simply. They are massive, complex systems that will create equally massive and complex consequences and require complex solutions. Waiting until they arrive to begin embracing the reality of these existential force-multiplier threats also reflects a dangerous level of intentional ignorance. Our human activity on our planet created these complex systems. The consequences they will create when they create massive change, or outright collapse, *will* require massive and complex adaptation, matured and evolved long-term thinking, and complex long-term solutions.

Our primitive ego is desperate to maintain a sense of control and keep our lives small and manageable. Predictable. It doesn't want to *see* the existential threats that are coming, or the *need* to begin preparing for those changes *now*. But the longer we wait to embrace long-term thinking and begin to prepare for the arrival of those consequences, the more pain and suffering we will experience. The more likely we are to face the end of human civilization, life as we know it, and even the possible extinction of our species on this planet.

It is clearly time to panic. Intentional ignorance has us headed toward disaster.

Summary of Existential Threats Created by Humanity's Resistance to Change

"To embrace change and tame our primitive ego, we need to ask ourselves some important questions:

What are we living *for*? Creation of wealth? Profit? A good job?

What is the *most important* thing in life? Financial success? A big home? A fancy car?

What is of *ultimate significance*? Fame? Pride? Dying wealthy?

And what changes do we need to make in our lives to embrace our answers to those questions? What changes do we need to make in our lives to express those answers in the world? We need to ask these questions and think carefully about the answers, because our lives and the lives of our children and grand-children depend on it. At the end of the day, we need to ask ourselves, how did I live my life today? Did I do everything I could to live in accord with the deepest truths I know? To align with a higher purpose? Where could I have given more? What changes do I need to make in my life to more authentically live my answers to those questions?

And most importantly, am I responsible for manifesting intentional ignorance to those around me? How am I doing that? What would I need to give up or let go of to align with the evolutionary impulse to embrace change and 'become' a vessel for greater intelligence and power in this world? To embrace my most authentic self?"[32]

I read this quote from Craig Hamilton many years ago. It is another of the life-changing quotes hanging on the wall in my writing room. It called me to wrestle with the question, "where do we begin as a species to prepare for the massive changes that we know are coming? How do we awaken, evolve, and mature our collective human consciousness? Where do we start? The answer for me as a mental health therapist, having studied and developed primitive ego psychology for decades, is doing the work to begin *intentionally* taming our collective primitive ego-consciousness and teaching others the critical importance of doing that work. The questions Hamilton asked in that quote are what called me to write this book.

I know that structural change requires public participation. Until a sufficiently large number of individuals awaken, mature, and intentionally evolve their unconscious childhood primitive ego conditioning, human civilization's social and economic structures will continue to function exactly as our collective unconscious and unevolved human primitive ego-consciousness designed them to function. And these structures and ways of thinking that define our human culture and human civilization, the systems *we* created, are everywhere.

These include greed, "me"-focus, the aggressive need to be "right," short-term thinking, a lack of systemic thinking, the illusion of separateness, sense of entitlement, fear of change and "other," narcissistic behaviors, survival-of-the-fittest thinking, immediate gratification, black-and-white either/or thinking, and blaming others for our own feelings.

---

32   Quote by Craig Hamilton, founder of Evolving Wisdom.

We need to recognize these sobering realities and begin the work of intentionally maturing, evolving, and taming our own collective primitive ego consciousness so we can begin to more intentionally create social structures that are more awakened, mature, compassionate, and evolved—structures that are based on "we" rather than "me." Structures based on the equality and well-being of our human communities, our planetary ecosystem communities, and all of the non-human life communities that share the planet with us, not just our own invasive, narcissistic, "me"-focused individual and personal well-being and wealth.

As you will see in the chapters in Part 2, it's time for humanity to grow up. Waiting is no longer a viable option. Our species' survival will depend on how well we recognize that we are the root cause of the force multipliers listed in Part 2 and do the work of re-creating the structures that we created; the structures that are threatening the survival of our species on this planet. We are an invasive species devouring our world. We need to evolve.

This book is about getting clarity before we begin to embrace the change process. We need to know our destination if we want to avoid decision paralysis. Embrace the *"need"* to evolve. And the place to begin that work is finding the courage to intentionally tame our own individual primitive egos, so we don't use the same thinking process to solve the problems in Part 2 that were used to initially create them. Change starts with us. We are the problem. We are the root cause!

As we saw in the introduction of this book, the cognitive side of our human brain, the side we refer to as the rider, is the side that needs clarity. Without that *clarity*, the rider will be overwhelmed with decisions, and decision paralysis will set in. It will become helplessly caught up spinning its wheels. The rider is very small compared to the emotional elephant. The emotional elephant has to see the *need*. If the rider and the elephant disagree, the elephant will win, the rider will lose, and the future of our species on this planet will continue to be problematic and short.[33]

---

33   To learn more about the science of change, I urge readers to read the book *Switch: How to Change Things When Change Is Hard*, by Chip and Dan Heath. It's an excellent book on the subject of change.

CHAPTER 6

Existential Force-Multiplier Threat and Economic Trigger: Debt

Our resistance to intentionally evolve our collective human consciousness blinds us to the changes that need to be made in the foundations of human civilization.

We are the problem. The aspects of humanity's collective, unconscious, unevolved primitive ego, and its early childhood conditioning that work together to systemically reinforce and support each other in the creation of debt, include the following: (a) "What's in it for me?" greed, (g) a lack of interconnected, interdependent systemic thinking, (j) an exaggerated aggressive narcissistic self-focused sense of entitlement, (k) an inability to connect short-term choices with long-term consequences, and (o) the inability of our collective primitive ego to embrace long-term thinking.

* *

Primitive ego early childhood conditioning:

a. "What's in it for me?" greed.

b. Need to be "right" (aggressive arrogance, extreme cognitive dissonance/confirmation bias).

c. Inability to replace "me" thinking with "we" thinking (compassion, mutuality, cooperation).

d. I want what I want when I want it.

e.   Blaming others for our feelings (inability to own our own feelings).

f.   Ignorance regarding the danger of exponential growth (e.g., COVID-19).

g.   A lack of interconnected, interdependent systemic thinking.

h.   Survival-of-the-fittest thinking.

i.   Black vs. white, zero-sum thinking ("You can't have that, it's mine!").

j.   An exaggerated aggressive, narcissistic self-focused sense of entitlement.

k.   An inability to connect short-term choices with long-term consequences.

l.   The fear of change (uncertainty, not knowing).

m.   The unending, obsessive desired for "more."

n.   The need for power "over" rather than power "with."

o.   The inability to embrace long-term thinking.

* *

Introduction to Chapter 6: Debt

This has been a very challenging chapter to write. Attempting to pin down debt statistics is a challenge. The data is hard to research, and the numbers continue to increase. As I researched the data and articles on debt, it became clear that the complex local, state, national, and global financial interconnections make it almost impossible to get a solid consensus on debt estimates. The various corporate and governmental bureaucracies have created interwoven international and national financial systems so complex that even the experts can't agree on exact numbers when it comes to debt. However, what is consistent is the reality that most of the economists and financial experts around the world are sounding the warning that we are in a massive debt bubble.

I've listed the numbers below that I have obtained general agreement on from multiple sources. But they are rough estimates at best. By the time you read these words, (a) the numbers will be significantly higher than presented;

also, as you read the numbers below, remember that (b) they represent debt in *trillions* of dollars; and (c) all of these estimates were based on the assumption of a growing economy. And almost none of the debt was created to prepare the economy for an economic downturn, a COVID-19 pandemic, or a general recession/depression. Yet all three of these economic realities are either happening or predicted to occur in the near future.

Much of the debt was designed to finance *profits*, not *growth*.

Pensions

A pension is essentially deferred compensation. The employer and the employee agree to set aside a portion of the employee's salary that will be payable upon retirement. The pension is funded by deductions from an employee's paycheck, current workers contributing to the pension fund, contributions from the employer, market-invested earnings of the funds, and taxpayers. Pensions are assumed to be self-sustaining. In economic slowdowns, when market investment returns go negative, government income also tends to be down. This leaves legislators with little appetite to raise taxes to put more money into the pension fund.

The money owed to retirees is a non-renegotiable bankruptcy-protected debt, so funds continue to flow out of the pension fund even in downturns in the economy. When government pensions are underfunded, the shortfalls have to be covered by increased taxes, public services reductions, or increased contributions from current workers. Most public-sector employees in the United States have pensions linked to their final salary.

Unfortunately, the federal government has been lax about putting aside enough money to cover these promises. Most pensions are set up assuming future returns will be in the 7% range. But the reality is a bit more sobering. People are drawing more from the pot because (a) they live longer after retirement, (b) the economy has been growing less than 2%, not 7%, and (c) the 2% growth was reality *before* the long-predicted major downturn in the economy or the unexpected massive economic impact of COVID-19.

Here are some of the statistics. ($T = trillions):

- Global debt: $257T.

- U.S. national debt: $26T. (Estimated to exceed $50T by 2050)

- U.S. household debt: $14.3T.

- Corporate debt: $72T.

- U.S. corporate debt: $10T.

- Corporate and public pensions: $6T.

- Underfunded corporate and public pensions: Over $1.6T.

- State and local debt: $3T.

- Unfunded Social Security and healthcare: $100T.

- The number of workers supporting each SS recipient:

  1940 = 160

  1950 = 16.5

  1960 = 5.1

  1970 = 3.7

  1990 = 3.4

  2010 = 2.9

  2030 = 2.3

So, let's put these numbers in a different narrative or context. As we saw in the previous chapter on change, data like the above only creates decision paralysis. The information tends to be meaningless and gets ignored because it doesn't get internalized in a context that can be emotionally understood. Let's take a look at what a "trillion" feels like emotionally.

a. A **million** seconds = 12 **days.**

b. A **billion** seconds = 31 **years.**

c. A **trillion** seconds = 31,000 **years.**

Let's look at the debt numbers above in terms of years if each $1 of debt was equivalent to one second. Keep in mind, these are debts that have to be paid back at some point *down the road.*

$1.6 trillion seconds (underfunded corporate and public pensions) = 49,600 years.

$1.6 trillion seconds (student debt) = 49,600 years.

$3 trillion seconds (state and local debt) = 93,000 years.

$10 trillion seconds (U.S. corporate debt) = 310,000 years.

$14.3 trillion seconds (U.S. household debt) = 443,300 years.

$26 trillion seconds (U.S. national debt) = 806,000 years.

$35 trillion seconds (U.S. national debt) by 2029 = 1,085,000 years.

$100 trillion seconds (unfunded Social Security and healthcare) = 3,100,000 years.

$257 trillion seconds (global debt) = 7,967,000 years.

$400 trillion seconds (global debt) by 2030 = 12,400,000 years.

- And these numbers are growing exponentially every year.

- We use *more* debt to pay off existing debt *plus* the interest payments on that debt. Stated simply, this is unsustainable. All we are doing is creating massive economic cracks nationally and globally in our fragile social and civil financial structures. *(Cracks that will inevitably lead to systemic collapse in the foundations of the social and civil systems that support human culture and human civilization.)*

- Many economists have been predicting that the debt bubble is all but certain to lead to a global economic collapse similar to the crash of 1929 in the near future.

- The probability of a debt bubble collapse and the underfunded pension crisis has been growing for years.

- System collapse was only a matter of time.

- We have built our global economic system on trillions of debt, not real economic growth.

- Economists have known for decades that this debt bubble is unsustainable and headed for collapse in the near future.

- As we saw in Chapter 3, capitalism requires us to continue business-as-usual, which is a handy euphemism called "kicking the can down the road"…*until we can't.*

Debt: The Over-Stretched Rubber Band That's Ready to Break: Some Realities to Consider

Reality: Debt is always an *asset* on someone else's financial ledger.

- Credit card, auto, student loan, and mortgage loans are measured in trillions of dollars.

- It's essential to remember that debt is *quality of life* now, today. But it will be the *poverty of life* tomorrow.

- It's important to focus on needs, not wants, learn to live life simply, and save until it hurts. You will be glad you did.

- Stay out of debt, especially at this point in history.

- The economic myth of today is the idea that debts can and should be paid back. This is true for the bottom 85% to 90%. For the top 5%, governments and corporations, debt tends to grow much faster than the ability to pay it back. Eventually, debts that can't be paid won't be. When that happens, the person, bank, or agency holding the asset (the lender that expects to be paid with interest) loses that "asset." Given that the economy "*has*" to keep growing, the fed covers the debt loss with more loans…..and the merry-go-round goes round and round…. until it can't. When that day arrives, the future will look a lot darker.

Phantom Wealth

- The deregulation of finance has flooded the growth economy with debt-based money, which banks and financial institutions can create out of thin air through their loans.

- This phantom wealth provides cheap capital for corporate expansion while luring increasing numbers of people and whole nation-states into a debt spiral from which many cannot escape.

- Corporations and financial institutions use their wealth to purchase political power: they hire armies of lobbyists, make substantial political campaign contributions, and fund think-tanks to influence public thinking on issues important to them.

- Free trade treaties include Investor State Dispute Settlement (ISDS) clauses that allow corporations to sue governments if laws or regulations might impinge on expected profits. The result is a subversion of democracy: interlinked multinational banks and corporations now constitute a "de facto" global government that is unaccountable to any electorate. (Post Growth Localization, Helena Norberg-Hodge, and Rupert Read)

Reality: Debt is one of the more powerful force-multiplier threats and economic triggers that we will explore in Part 2. Keep in mind, all of the debt numbers above have a "$**T**" after them. The longer our economy is under stress, the deeper the damage will be, and the longer it will take for the economy to recover. Indebtedness, the condition of owing money, bankruptcy, lost wages, reduced purchasing power, and supply-chain choke points will be complex economic issues to overcome.

- Governments will pour massive economic credit and stimulus into the economy. This will add more debt to a level of debt that is already massive and unsustainable. Our global economic systems are already over-indebted, so *more debt* is only going to further increase the severity of future financial crises.

- Our economic resilience is already seriously compromised in the event of future economic stressors and the existential force-multipliers of Part 2. The systemic, interconnected nature of our global economic systems radically increases the probability of cascading global economic collapse.

- Global climate change will be a significant force-multiplier on an already compromised global economic system.

- The COVID-19 coronavirus that is happening as I write this book is already a massive and growing threat to our global financial and economic systems. And experts are telling us that the impacts of this virus will be a severe shock on our global economy. Not very encouraging!

- Recession and depression are growing realities. *The only question is which of the force-multipliers listed in Part 2 will create the tipping point that leads to a cascading collapse of our global economy.* In a systemically interconnected, interdependent world, shocks can cascade rapidly.

- Each of those force-multipliers gives increasing credibility to the concepts that "the future isn't what it used to be" and "waiting to prepare for resiliency is not an option." We need to prepare for the increasingly turbulent years and changes that are coming. We are a tightly interconnected and interdependent global social and economic system. The possibility of global, social, civil, and economic collapse will grow increasingly more likely as we lose access to basic needs that have become increasingly dependent on the interconnected global economic system and its flow of goods and services.

Resilience requires preparation *before* the crises, not *after.*

Reality: Government deficits are essentially a loan that needs to be repaid, a form of buying the future "on time." When you or I finance a car or a home through a bank loan, the loan's retirement or payment is measured in years. When a government loan is created by the Federal Reserve, the retirement or payment of the loan is measured not in years but by the term *"down the road."*

Reality: Our global economic system is built on trillions (**$T**) of dollars of debt backed by nothing but the creation of more debt and more *down the road* loans. When the Federal Reserve prints "phantom" or "printed/manufactured" money, they are essentially creating more federal debt, money that needs to be paid back at some point in the future *down the road*.

Reality: The role of government and federal loans is supposed to protect the vulnerable, not pad the bank accounts of the elites, banks, and corporations with bailouts.

- Unfortunately, too often, the money "loaned" to corporations and banks is used for stock buybacks that reward executives and shareholders, not long-term investments to create a more robust economy in the future.

- Keep in mind federal "printed/manufactured" money is a debt that must be repaid, *an obligation that creates less money available for investment in the future.* Debt reduces future growth and the financial assets that our children and grandchildren will need to support *their* economic future. Those future generations will not have the ability to create strong future economies if their limited financial assets are required to pay off the loans and the interest payments of those loans acquired by their ancestors. When future generations learn how we misspent their future, they are not going to be happy.

- As we saw in Chapter 3, capitalism is an *intergenerational* predator. Stated simply, the global financial system has become a predator enslaving and plundering the future generations of the world of their wealth and resources. When debt levels rise to the point where repayment becomes impossible, the resources required to finance future "growth" are simply no longer available. Their future is being buried under a mountain of debt and interest payments.

Reality: We are passing the point of no return. Some 97% of the money circulating in the economy today *is backed by nothing but debt.*

- This never-ending addictive debt cycle is increasing rapidly, and every dollar (again, measured in the trillions) is an anchor around the neck of future GDP growth. In addition to that anchor of debt, there *will be* recessions in the future.

- COVID-19 is having a massive impact on the global economy, and scientists tell us there *will be* more pandemics in our future. We need to remember, a growing number of economists are warning that given the current debt bubble, a significant 1930s-like reset of the global economy is *inevitable*.

Reality: The bottom line here is the future is going to be rocky. The debt bubble is already beginning to burst. Cities and states are already filing for bankruptcy as budget deficits increase.

- And the future collapse of social and civil structures that support human culture and human civilization only grows more likely with every dollar (measured in trillions) of debt printed by the Federal Reserve. The massive and increasing debt required to cover all of these growing deficits is simply *another* debt or liability that must be repaid or restructured (liquidated).

- We are digging the hole deeper every day.

Reality: Eventually, the rubber band has to break.

When a debt *disappears* or is "retired" (for whatever reason or by whatever means), an "asset" on someone's books disappears. If you are a bank, a municipality, a state, or a corporation holding an asset that disappears, or a bill that can't be paid due to a lack of funds, the solution is to apply for another loan (more debt) to cover the loss or lack of funds.

- Again, this unlimited, unending cycle of more debt to cover bad debt cannot continue forever. Eventually, the rubber band has to break. The economy will begin to collapse.

- Cash and financial resource required to support future economic growth will begin to dry up. The economy will slow. The poor and less privileged will suffer the most and be the first victims of economic collapse. Unemployment will increase. Foreclosures will increase. People will get desperate. Social unrest will increase. Businesses will close or go out of business. Banks will stop lending money. Unemployment numbers will increase dramatically. Fragile civil and social systems will begin to crack. Services will be cut. Taxes will increase.

- Given the reality that there has been no real "recovery" since 2008, the social unrest and anxiety that will come with the next financial crisis will be significant. Many of the pension funds have money invested in the financial markets.

- When we experience the predicted major market collapse that's coming, the pension funds required to support the retirements of retirees (whose numbers are growing at the rate of roughly 10,000 a day for the next decade) will be significantly compromised. Stated simply, the force-multipliers and existential threats covered in Part 2 will increase the pressure on the complex interconnected and interdependent financial systems. In time, they *will* begin to experience economic, social, and civil collapse.

Those who believe this is a vision that's too extreme, too apocalyptic, are not paying attention to the rapidly growing financial impacts of COVID-19. The future is already here, and it's growing more dire daily.

Reality: Capitalism and the lifeblood of capitalism called profits *have to grow*, or capitalism begins to collapse and die.

- Not only are retirement and pension programs already in crisis, the average retiree has only $136,000 saved for retirement.

- These insolvent pension programs and massive savings shortfalls do not bode well for future social stability.

- As we saw in Chapter 3 on neoliberal global capitalism and Chapter 4 on global warming, the global addiction and dependency on unlimited growth and money creation called "business as usual" needs to end if we want to survive the future that endless growth is creating on our limited planet.

- The ability of debtors to fulfill their loan commitments is critical in a capitalist economy. They are the cash flow that validates debt and encourages future debt and investment. When the cash stops flowing and debt obligations are not paid, the neoliberal global economy based on growth and profit will quickly grind to a halt. Stated simply, neoliberal global capitalism will slide into a financial crisis.

Reality: Social debt essentially transfers consumption from the future to the present. It is based on the immoral assumption that the economy will continue to grow, and that continued growth will enable future generations to pay *for the lifestyle that we enjoy now.* What they will inherit are interest and principal payments that will cripple future infrastructure investments and needed social programs.

Reality: To summarize, the neoliberal dependence on ever-increasing debt and unlimited exponential growth is impossible on a limited planet. To assume differently (on a finite and limited planet) is extremely dangerous, Tinker Bell thinking.

- In primitive ego terms, *our collective immature and unevolved, untamed human primitive ego can't get everything it wants when it wants it,* especially on a limited planet when everyone else on the planet also hungers for the same lifestyle as those living in the developed nations.
- The above concepts described on a humorous and lighter note: In the words of Erik Lindberg (relilience.org), "Debt is only part of the chorus that makes this great sucking sound as 6% of the global population demands almost a quarter of its goods."

Or, Kurt Cobb's favorite New Yorker cartoon shows a man in a coat and tie standing at a podium who tells his unseen audience the following: "And so, while the end-of-the-world scenario will be rife with unimaginable horrors, we believe that the pre-end period will be filled with unprecedented opportunities for profit."

Or, his second favorite story, of a man in a tattered suit sitting cross-legged near a campfire with three children listening to him intently as he says this: "Yes, the planet got destroyed. But for a beautiful moment in time we created a lot of value for shareholders" (resilience.org, The Financialization of the End of the World).

And lastly, financial writer Paul Farrell wrote a piece for MarketWatch entitled "How to pick stocks for the near term when long-term trends say collapse is near." ((https://www.resilience.org/stories/2020-06-21/the-financial-ization-of-the-end-of-the-world/?mc_cid=846dc39558&mc_eid=6adeb9989e)

- These quotes are humorous, but there is a sobering reality embedded in that humor. When empires begin to collapse, instead of adapting to new realities, the primitive ego resistance to change only increases the futile Tinker Bell efforts to maintain the current fragile system despite the economic and social vulnerabilities exposed by COVID-19 and the beginning of what might be the next Great Depression.

- Given the all the evidence and fragility COVID-19 has exposed in our global economic systems, the inability of our human species to deal with the reality behind our greedy primitive ego delusions and Tinker Bell thinking and see what it means for our future as a species, is both sobering and alarming. Taming and evolving the collective primitive ego-consciousness of humanity will be critical to our future as we struggle to become a viable species on our planet.

Summary of Chapter 6:
Summary of Existential Threats Created
by the Force-Multiplier Called Debt

- Debt has been described as termites in the social and civil woodwork, a bubble getting closer and closer to collapse. It tends to grow faster than the ability to pay it down. This is especially true in periods of economic slowdowns and recessions.

- Most people are unaware that almost all the money in circulation today is not backed by real growth in the economy. It is essentially approved debt, and *more* debt. *More* manufactured, printed, phantom money.

- Interest payments on the national debt are roughly $500 billion a year. By the end of the decade, it will be over $1 trillion/year. Some believe this estimate to be too conservative.

- It's been estimated that roughly 97% of the trillions of dollars circulating in the global economy today are backed by nothing but debt. *Every time a private bank issues a loan, more phantom money has been "created."* Much of this money is used for speculation and future profit, not the needs of the commons. This kind of debt creation and profit speculation created the 2008 recession and is setting the world up for another even more massive financial bubble collapse when this debt can no longer be paid back.

We Are Borrowing Money (Debt)
Faster Than We Are Creating Wealth

When the debt bubble collapse arrives, it will make a simple financial recession look like a sunny day in the park. And it *will* collapse.

Permanent federal deficit spending is now part of our global economic system.

"More" requires "more."

When *"more"* ends, the global financial system will collapse.

And debt is only *one* of the many force-multipliers/existential threats facing humanity that we are looking at in Part 2.

We need to acknowledge the reality that "the future isn't what it used to be." And preparing for that darker future requires that we begin that preparation *now.*

As we will explore in Part 3, I believe building small, self-reliant local communities that focus on community well-being, rather than growth and profit, is the best and perhaps only realistic hope for our species' future survival on this planet.

We have to end our presence as an invasive species on the planet before nature ensures our extinction. Climate change is increasing, and storm intensification is growing in intensity. The signs are clear that nature is growing impatient with the immature behaviors and actions of our species.

Unlimited growth on a limited planet is a level of ignorance and insanity that has to end.

As a growing number of economists would say, "the debt clock is ticking." Unlimited debt is dangerous. In March of 2000, the total public and private debt in the United States was $27 trillion. Today in 2020, that debt has grown to roughly $75 trillion.

Debt gives us the ability to bring the future into the present, but debt eventually has to be paid back. In the words of one anonymous source talking about debt, "Modern slaves are not in chains, they are in debt."

When you borrow from a lender, you are also borrowing from your future self. A time in the future in which you will need to spend less than you make so you can pay it back, *with interest!* The question that has to be asked is, how long would it take for an economy that is growing at a rate of 2% to pay back $75 trillion, including interest?

That same question could be asked of both national and individual debt.

Debt is increasingly becoming a critical and fragile vulnerability in the foundation of human civilization, and in the neoliberal global capitalist religion of unlimited economic expansion, profit, and wealth accumulation.

- The **current** U.S. national **debt** is $26T and growing roughly $1T/ year, and that was *before* the coronavirus arrived!

- Eventually, the interest payments will become more than the economy can bear.

Student loan debt is over $1.5T, and 23% of those loans are in arrears.

- In 2020, Americans owe nearly $1 trillion in **credit card debt**, and that's a record high according to a report from the Federal Reserve.

- In February 2020, the Federal Reserve reported that household debt balances hit $14 trillion, an all-time high.

- For many in the United States, making ends meet is a constant daily struggle…especially for those in the bottom 60%.

When I was going through college, I worked a part-time job to help make ends meet. My first house was small, but I could afford it. My first job as a graduate with a bachelor's degree in Electrical Engineering was a good-paying job at General Motors. I made $6000 a year. Life was good. I took out personal loans to go to college, but it took me less than ten years to pay them off. Repaying my college loans represented a tiny and affordable percent of my monthly paycheck. And yes, I recognize that I am pretty much revealing my age.

Today, people feel like the economy is rigged against them.

- Achieving stability is far more difficult for the younger generations than it was for me.

- Saving for the future is all but impossible for most people.

- They have nothing left after expenses.

- Today, in the United States, almost all saving occurs in the top 20% to 30%.

- In the bottom 60% to 80%, savings are non-existent and negative. In other words, they are just hanging on or going into debt.

These are just numbers unless you recognize the vulnerability of the bottom 60% to 80% as they struggle to cope with COVID-19. When 60% to 80% of our population lived hand-to-mouth *before* COVID-19, *it should be a massive wakeup call as to how precarious our nation is to civil unrest and the potential for social and civil collapse.* A level of social and civil unrest that already includes Black Lives Matter, the likelihood of a significant COVID-19 recession or depression, mass unemployment, rapidly increasing health care costs, and a commons that has little to no savings to cope with the changes that are destabilizing our national and global economy.

Before COVID-19, it was estimated that by 2030 two billion people would be living in urban slums. And that number is likely to be significantly higher and come sooner due to the economic impact of COVID-19.

We Need to Keep Our Focus on the Future

- *The economy and the stock market are seriously out of sync.*

- Before COVID-19, the U.S. economy was struggling to hang onto a 2% growth rate. The primary thing supporting the financial market was the trillions of dollars being pumped into the economy by the Federal Reserve, even as the U.S. federal debt was over $26 trillion and continues to rise rapidly.

- Every dollar of the trillions of dollars being pumped into the economy is a national debt that will be unavailable to cover future slowdowns, future recessions, future pandemics, future infrastructure investments, and future increases in forgivable loans and unemployment benefits support or paycheck protection programs.

- Our nation is already burdened with over twenty-five million unemployed due to COVID-19, and future Social Security, Medicare, and Medicaid payments, and social entitlements that are already *underfunded.*

- When we (a) add unemployment numbers that are growing as the recession continues to deepen, and (b) talk about a guaranteed Basic Income grows—which, when added to current entitlement spending, would add an estimated $2+ trillion a year to the federal deficit—the cast-iron anchor around the neck of future generations is becoming alarming. And assuming federal investments in future economic growth is rapidly approaching Tinker Bell thinking.

- We need to focus on those living in poverty and keep in mind that debt, and the interest payments to retire that debt, will seriously limit future growth in the economy. It will also restrict badly needed national infrastructure investments, which would support the national economy and provide jobs for the unemployed.

- We need to process these realities through the eyes of the bottom 60% who have no savings for emergencies or retirement, no education, no job, no income, limited social services, living in poor communities, and the sobering reality that we are talking about 60% to 70% of the U.S. adult population! *These sobering realities are not a hopeful context for a stable society when debt bankrupts a nation where 60% to 70% of the culture is desperate and powerless!*

Pensions Are Based on the Employer Being a Borrower, and the Workers Are the Lenders

When the economy slows or goes into recession, the workers are the ones who get hurt. This is also true for Social Security recipients.

In 2018, the Congressional Budget Office reported that by 2041, federal debt would require all federal tax revenues just to support Social Security, the various health care programs, and pay interest on its loans. Politically, the Social Security payments to retirees will probably continue, but the taxes on those benefits are very likely to increase. And that is an outcome better than some form of debt liquidation.

Bottom Line, the Rubber Band Will Break: Debt Is Moral Issue

Unlimited growth in debt is not possible. The road ahead is going to get very rocky. Preparation will need to include eliminating personal debt and a reduction in lifestyle where possible. Not comfortable, *possible.*

Offering workers a defined-benefit pension, where an income based on final salary is paid for the rest of their lives, is an expensive proposition, especially as life expectancies lengthen. Pension shortfalls are common across America, with the average public pension just 72.4% funded. That adds up to a collective shortfall of more than $1.6T. The bill for taxpayers seems certain to rise substantially. For the states with the most significant pension holes, the political conflict will be inevitable.

Debt and the interest payments on debt needs to be paid back. And we are hanging that debt repayment and those interest payments around the necks of future generations. *Think about this reality in terms of less flexibility to respond to existential future crises, which every force-multiplier in Part 2 will create.*

Debt is fundamentally a profound and overwhelming moral issue on future generations that we are choosing to ignore. *We are spending their future and 60% to 70% of the people in our country.*

We need to begin *now* to *intentionally* evolve the immature collective narcissistic primitive ego of humanity or future generations will curse our immoral existence and the massive lack of compassion we had for our children and grandchildren. They will *not* be happy… or *peaceful.*

History's Collapse of Empires

We need to pay attention to history. We need to remember that *wealth inequality* and a *desperate commons* have been the underlying cause of every empire collapse in human history. Like a coronavirus, *wealth inequality is a cancer* already present and growing in our country. And massive levels of debt are destined to become a significant factor in the future spread of that cancer.

- *Social instability is not the friend of an empire.* And the United States is currently headed in the wrong direction. Gun violence. Political gridlock. Massive wealth inequality. Racism. Lack of action to reverse global warming. Massive debt. Unevolved primitive ego thinking. *The list of cracks headed toward instability and collapse is growing.* I do not see debt as the trigger for collapse. I see it as dry rot in our nation's structural foundations and our global economy, a dry rot that will weaken those critical structures when the winds and storms of systemic change begin to blow and threaten them.

- The American empire and our global economy are both facing the powerful existential force-multiplier threats of Part 2. Preparation for resilience in the future that's coming is critical, and it needs to begin now. We'll look at more existential force multipliers in the next chapter.

CHAPTER 7

Existential Force-Multiplier Threat and Economic Trigger: Powering Down from Fossil Energy

Our resistance to intentionally evolving our collective human consciousness blinds us to the changes that need to be made in the foundations of human civilization.

We are the problem. The primary aspects of humanity's collective, unconscious, unevolved primitive ego, and its early childhood conditioning that work together to systemically reinforce and support each other in order to resist powering down from fossil energy include (a) "What's in it for me?" greed; (c) inability to replace "me" thinking with "we" thinking; (f) ignorance regarding the danger of exponential growth; (g) a lack of interconnected, interdependent systemic thinking; (j) an exaggerated aggressive narcissistic self-focused sense of entitlement; (k) an inability to connect short-term choices with long-term consequences; (m) the unending, obsessive desired for "more"; and (o) the inability to embrace long-term thinking.

* *

Primitive ego early childhood conditioning:

a. "What's in it for me?" greed.

b. Need to be "right" (aggressive arrogance, extreme cognitive dissonance/confirmation bias).

c. Inability to replace "me" thinking with "we" thinking (compassion, mutuality, cooperation).

d. I want what I want when I want it.

e. Blaming others for our feelings (inability to own our own feelings).

f. Ignorance regarding the danger of exponential growth (e.g., COVID-19).

g. A lack of interconnected, interdependent systemic thinking.

h. Survival-of-the-fittest thinking.

i. Black vs. white, zero-sum thinking ("You can't have that, it's mine!").

j. An exaggerated aggressive, narcissistic self-focused sense of entitlement.

k. An inability to connect short-term choices with long-term consequences.

l. The fear of change (uncertainty, not knowing).

m. The unending, obsessive desired for "more."

n. The need for power "over" rather than power "with."

o. The inability to embrace long-term thinking.

* *

Introduction to Chapter 7:
Powering Down from Fossil Fuels

I consider the inevitable powering down from fossil fuels to be one of the top four most likely, and unavoidable, force-multipliers to existentially threaten the future of human culture and human civilization that humanity is facing. Neoliberal global capitalism, global warming, and massive debt are the other three.

Fossil energy return on investment (EROI) is negative. In other words, the cost of extraction is increasing, and the return on investment is decreasing. Production from existing oil fields is declining, shale oil companies are already in or headed toward bankruptcy, new oil field discoveries are not large enough to replace production declines in existing fields, CO2 emissions are continuing to rise, and it's only a matter of time before climate warming *will* trigger a socially mandated powering down from fossil fuels.

The inevitable powering down from fossil energy (a) will radically change life as we know it, and (b) the powering down from fossil energy will happen far sooner than most people believe or are prepared to survive or cope with when that day arrives.

Politicians, corporations, and the voices of neoliberal global capitalism will continue to resist powering down as long as possible. Still, the day is coming in the near future when the "commons" worldwide will take to the streets and demand that politicians and world governments power down human civilization from its use of fossil fuel energy. *If they don't, the future of humanity will be dire.*

Forecasts made twenty years ago assumed that post-peak-oil and the inevitability of oil depletion would threaten human civilization. Then came the fracking revolution, which began to produce natural gas and oil using new horizontal drilling and hydraulic fracturing advances. This new supply of oil, combined with the Federal Reserve's low-interest-rate subsidy policies, gave the fracking industry access to cheap financing. The threat of oil depletion ended and was replaced by an unrealistic, dangerous Tinker Bell euphoria.

The reality that no one wanted to look at too closely was the fact that shale oil and gas were too costly to produce at a profit. Shale oil was a financial and technological illusion that did indeed create a short-term abundance of fossil energy that allowed business, as usual, to continue pumping CO2 emissions into the atmosphere. The collapse of this illusion is rapidly becoming a significant "powering down" force-multiplier on the future of human civilization. The reality of "powering down" is no longer a "future" reality. It is a current reality that is destabilizing the fossil energy industry. No one wants to talk about it, but powering down from fossil energy is rapidly becoming a force-multiplier reality that will change human civilization as we know it in the near future. The fact that "powering down is coming will increase rapidly as the world increasingly embraces the global climate crisis as an existential threat.

The two questions that I often pose in this book about *intentional change* are (a) will the intentional change, in this case *powering down* from fossil energy, happen in time to avoid the existential impacts of global warming? And (b) can we prevent the social and civil collapse that powering down will create?

Scientists are already warning that we are out of time to avoid much of the suffering that will result if we continue business-as-usual. The longer we wait to power down from the burning of fossil energy, the more unnecessary suffering we will create. They warn if we wait too long, the next generation will have to prepare for massive threats to the future survival of humanity, even the likely possibility of extinction.

I see no path forward that realistically avoids the necessity of powering down. Because the entire global economy runs on fossil energy, powering down from fossil energy will create social change so massive and disruptive that social and civil collapse will be unavoidable. If we want to avoid massive suffering and the possible extinction of human life on this planet, we need to begin that powering down *now*. We are out of time, and waiting is not a viable option. The sooner we start an intentional and mandated powering down from fossil energy, the more likely we will survive climate warming and *minimize* some of the inevitable impacts of social and civil collapse.

The Courage to Power Down Will Have to Come from the Commons

I do not believe that the current generation of leaders and politicians will ever have the courage, or the political will, to force the powering down of human civilization. Still, I am hopeful that the younger generation of activists *will* have that courage and force the powering down of human civilization from fossil energy. The future of humanity will be primarily determined by their courage to (a) publicly confront the political power structures, politicians, and economists that aggressively support the business-as-usual of neoliberal global capitalism; and (b) embrace the creation of small, self-reliant, sustainable local communities and local economies we will explore in Part 3. Self-reliant local communities and local economies that are focused on sustainability and well-being rather than our current greed-based global focus on wealth, growth, and profit.

Our addiction to growth must end, *and it must end soon.*

The growth-focused neoliberal global economy that has been created by petroleum and neoliberal global capitalism will *not* survive the changes that powering down will create. The chapter in human history called unlimited economic expansion is coming to an end. And the world is unprepared to cope with the massive changes that will be created by powering down as it changes life as we know it for most of the planet. The primary impacts of powering down will be experienced by the developed nations, but few cultures will avoid some impact.

But I am hopeful. I do believe that local networks of small self-reliant local communities and sustainable local economies that are focused on the well-being of all members in the community *will* survive and *could* be the future foundation of humanity and human culture if we have the wisdom and courage to begin intentionally creating them *now.*[34]

Avoiding Tinker Bell Thinking as We Power Down from Fossil Energy and Create a New Sustainable Human Future

There are many green energies and "green new deal" (GND) plans that promote the idea that our global economy can continue to *grow* and survive if we switch our energy creation from fossil fuels to "renewable" energy. I believe survival is achievable using renewable, green energy. But the belief that green energy will continue to support *growth* is extremely dangerous Tinker Bell thinking. First, the energy required to manufacture and construct that massive green energy infrastructure buildout, and the enormous battery storage capacity infrastructure required to distribute and store that energy because of the intermittency

---

34 It will take time to create the skills, tools, and resources for self-reliance, so beginning to create them *now* is critically important for them to survive as a future, long-term foundation of human culture. We will explore the creation of these local self-reliant communities and sustainable local economies in detail in Part 3 of this book.

of green solar and wind energy, would alone push CO2 emissions well past levels that human civilization could survive. Second, fossil energy dwarfs the energy available from green, renewable sources. We will explore in more detail below the massive energy that fossil fuels currently provide to power our current global economy and human civilization as we know it. We are talking about a level of energy countless orders of magnitude greater than renewable, green energy would ever be able to supply. Powering down from fossil energy is an existential force-multiplier threat that *will* end life as we know it.

The bottom line that we need to embrace in our thinking about powering down from fossil energy is the reality that there *will* be significantly fewer humans on the planet in the future, and those considerably fewer humans will be consuming *significantly* fewer of our planetary resources. To ensure long-term sustainability, the human footprint on the planet will need to be carefully limited to the consumption of resources that our one planet can *sustainably* support.

We need to embrace the realities embedded in *powering down*:

a. To sustain the current footprint of the United States and the developed world *alone*, we would need *five planets the size of earth*.

b. Adding the rest of humanity currently living on our planet *who also aspire and deserve to enjoy the lifestyles of those in the developed world*, it's evident that the *sustainable* standard of living of those living in the developed world would have to be roughly 90% to 95% lower than their current lifestyle.

c. I see no future for humanity that does not include the reality that *the future will not be what it used to be*.

d. We need to prepare for the massive changes powering down will create. *And waiting to begin that preparation is not an option.*

Green Energy Is Not "Renewable"

The Tinker Bell belief that green energy is *renewable* energy does not reflect reality. Forests and plants *are* renewable. Nature *is* renewable. Solar panels and wind turbines *are not renewable*. *They* are manufactured.

And the commonly held belief that green energy will solve the global warming problem and allow the global economy to *continue growing* is an extremely dangerous Tinker Bell myth currently being circulated in the media. As we discussed above, there is no energy source known to humanity, or currently imagined by humanity, that could replace fossil fuel energy *and successfully continue current global growth and business as usual.*

The modern world was created by, and is now sustained by, fossil fuel energy. If you calculate the amount of energy that is consumed every day by our growing human population and our increasingly global economy; including the energy that would be required to manufacture and maintain that "renewable" green energy infrastructure, you quickly recognize there isn't a solar system or wind system that could come even close to creating that level of energy without pushing $CO2$ emissions to human extinction levels.

Powering down from fossil energy is essential for our survival, and it *will* end life as we know it.

Green, Renewable Energy Will Not Replace Fossil Fuel Energy

The best estimate I could find was from 2009.[35] Even in 2009, **155,481 Terawatt-hours** of green energy would be required to replace fossil energy. One terawatt hour = one trillion watts for one hour. Now multiply that times 24 hours a day, times seven days a week, times 52 weeks a year. No hand calculator goes that high.

---

35   This number would be significantly higher in 2020, but it gives you an idea of just how much power and energy we're talking about.

Even if it were possible to create that much green energy, the solar panels, wind turbines, and battery storage facilities required would cover every square foot of the planet several times over.

The bottom line: Green, renewable energy will *not* replace fossil fuel energy. While we wait for some genius to invent a clean, *portable*, green, renewable energy system that replaces fossil fuel energy, we need to power down and end CO2 emissions so that we still have a human civilization around to enjoy that new energy system.

Until some form of new, sustainable energy far more robust and portable than wind and solar is discovered or developed in the future, powering down from fossil energy and global warming are both existential crises that will (a) create social and civil collapse and (b) end greed-based *growth* as a goal of human culture. We have to move beyond capitalism's growth imperative, but assuming this new magical energy will be available *before* powering down creates social and civil collapse is incredibly dangerous Tinker Bell thinking.

Reality: Life As We Know It
Is Coming to an End

In the meantime, we will have to be content knowing that the day we begin to take *powering down* from fossil fuel energy seriously, it will be the tipping point that will bring down our global human civilization as we know it. And I see no way we can avoid having to embrace that dark reality. If we attempt to ignore the need to power down from fossil energy and attempt to continue business-as-usual, the future of our world will eventually get even darker than the social and civil collapse that powering down will create. The extinction of humanity is *inevitable* if we continue business-as-usual and continue to ignore the climate change realities that face us.

It's clear: Humanity is currently "consuming" and "burning" far more of our planet's natural non-renewable resources than the earth can provide. Many critical minerals and life-supporting resources are already facing depletion. Nature is running out of patience with us, and she is already beginning to trigger environmental forces that will eliminate us as an invasive species from the planet. Extinction is a process nature that nature has a lot of experience employing when she needs to protect herself. And she *always* gets to bat last!

A Brief Summary of this
Introduction to Powering Down

I am not writing this book to predict doom and gloom. It is being written to show the reader that massive change *is coming* and the need to prepare for that change *now* is urgent.

Resilience for survival requires preparation before a crisis arrives, not after.

And yes, I recognize that I am repeating myself. I consider that sentence to be a primary golden arch focus of this book. The second golden arch objective is to encourage and support the younger generation in that need for preparation. I believe the younger generation is the generation that will have the will, the courage, and the vision needed to embrace the life-altering changes that need to be made.

Because these changes are so critical for the survival of humanity, and because they will be so impactful to life *as we know it*, the demand for change will have to come from the bottom up, *not* the top down.

Politicians and world governments will *not* embrace these realities in time...and waiting for them to act is no longer an option. Neoliberal global capitalism, fossil fuel depletion, declining energy return on investment (EROI), powering down from fossil fuel energy to reduce CO_2 emissions, and the reversal of global warming are the significant, existential, life-altering challenges of our time. Continuing to ignore them is not an option. The time for action is *now*.

As I stated in earlier chapters, the facts and data I will present below are not meant to convince the reader that our world is standing on the cliff of collapse. Anyone who is paying attention already knows this sobering reality. My goal in writing this book is to encourage the younger generation on the importance of acting *now*. Aggressive powering down from fossil fuels needs to begin *now*. We have a few *years*, not *decades*, to successfully accomplish this powering down and prepare for the social and civil collapse powering down will create. We are out of time. Waiting to begin that preparation is no longer an option.

As we saw in the chapter on change, the energy required to successfully create lasting and significant change has to come from the emotional elephant, not the rider's logic. As we learned in the chapter on change, the emotional elephant is motivated to support change most effectively when the need for that change is clearly defined. The data below is presented to (a) illustrate the urgency of the changes that are *needed*, and b) engage the only *emotional elephant energy* large enough to successfully create these critically necessary changes; the collective *emotional elephant energy* of the younger generations who are inheriting the unsustainable world we created for them.

Our collective future as a species on this planet is literally in their hands. But we in the older generation *can* actively support them as they fight for the massive changes our collective human future and survival require.[36] And they *will* need all of the support, skills, resources, and encouragement we can offer them.

Some Miscellaneous Facts and Data That Support Powering Down

I find data-dense narrative hard to digest, and all but impossible data to see when I want to review it for use later. To avoid "dense narrative fatigue," I will present the following data in the form of a bulleted list for easier consumption and more accessible later review.[37] As we power down from fossil fuels, aggressively reduce CO_2 emission, and prepare for the inevitable social and civil collapse that powering down will create, having data and information that supports the need for powering down will be an essential resource to support preparation for the changes that powering down will create.

---

36   See Chapter 10 on Localization, and the creation of self-reliant local communities.

37   The facts and data come from the Scientific American Blog Network, and other energy related organizations.

We also need to keep in mind that powering down is systemically inter-connected with all of the other existential force multiplier threats covered in this book. However, given the reality of global warming, global climate change, storm intensification, and the social impacts they are creating, *including* the fact that fossil fuels are in decline, powering down and the collapse of neoliberal global capitalism have the potential to be the first existential force-multiplier threats that will be triggered in the near future. As we will discuss in Chapter 10 on Localization, they are also threats that we can begin to aggressively prepare for now.

Petroleum Fossil Fuels Are the Primary Energy Source Driving Human Civilization

This reality is also a primary problem for human civilization! Our modern, global human culture is deeply embedded in an insatiable addiction and hunger for energy. Some 80% of the world's energy comes from fossil fuels. Our human civilization was created and is now sustained by the use of fossil fuel energy. Almost everything in modern human culture and human civilization is produced using fossil energy; powered by fossil energy; and transported, extracted, recycled, and replaced by fossil energy.

Unfortunately, as we saw above, global petroleum production is declining, and shale oil production is near its peak. Still, shale oil production has never achieved a positive energy return on investment. In simple terms, shale oil production has never created a profit for investors. It has been described as a Ponzi scheme that's been massively funded by investors and government subsidies. In other words, it has been financed by a debt that will never be repaid to those investors. Many of the major shale oil companies are already in bankruptcy court.

We Are Already Powering Down

Production costs are increasing, the quality and energy embedded in the petroleum being extracted is declining, and the EROI is decreasing. According to a recent article from *Barron's*, the fracking industry has lost hundreds of billions of dollars. It is now saddled with debts (estimate to be over $71 billion) that will never be paid back as the fields continue to play out, and EROI continues to be increasingly negative.

Investors are backing away from investing more money in the shrinking number of shale producers. If the industry has arrived at peak debt, peak production is likely to follow. Tier one acreage (sweet spots) is declining. As reported by Mark Papa, then-CEO of shale company Centennial Resource Development in 2018, "A lot of the good geological spots have already been drilled." In January of 2020, Papa, who is now chairman of Schlumberger, said, "A change is coming." He said *resource depletion is a big issue.* He also reported that the Bakken in North Dakota and Eagle Ford in Texas have already peaked.[38] And this was before COVID-19 arrived.

Fossil Fuels Are Not Cheap Energy, Especially when External Costs Are Included

External costs include forest fires, global warming, droughts, storm intensification, rain-bomb flooding, health impacts including the increasing threat of more pandemics due to rising global temperatures, global warming, ice melt tipping points, CO_2 emissions, food shortages, climate refugees, and so forth.

Oil Company Denials of Global Warming Are Very Similar to the Tobacco Companies' Playbook

Greed-based corporate propaganda has intentionally created doubt and denial about the dangers their product has been creating for decades. Like the risks of cigarette smoking, the dangers of global warming and climate change *are not unsettled!* Global warming is real, climate change is real, storm intensification is real, and their impacts are existentially harmful to the future of humanity and our planets' ecosystems. They *have* been directly created by human activity on the planet.

---

38   (Article: "Peak Permian Oil Production May Arrive Much Sooner Than Expected." Justin Mikulka, 2/28/2020, resilience.org).

Facts matter. Science matters. Data matters. Truth matters. Don't settle for less.

Uninformed, *subjective* personal opinions presented as absolute truth without supporting facts and data *do not matter.*

They reflect *intentional ignorance,* the ideological Kool-Aid disseminated by those who continue amassing wealth through *business as usual* and their addiction to *unlimited growth and profits.*

Fossil Fuel Subsidies and Subsidy Removal

Fossil fuel subsidies total roughly $5T / year and are designed to offset net energy declines and the growing negative energy return on investment, and to ensure that oil companies remain viable. "Viable" essentially means out of bankruptcy court.

Researchers estimate that CO_2 emissions reductions from subsidy removal alone would be in the range of 500 million to 2 billion metric tons of carbon dioxide a year by 2030.

Some say these emission reduction numbers are far too conservative. They could be significantly larger.

The North American oil market has been grossly overcapitalized by unsustainable subsidies/loans. Petroleum and financial experts are warning that *no shale company has made a profit.* In other words, the cost of petroleum production exceeds the sale of that petroleum production, a concept called negative EROI or negative energy return on investment. And the money to (a) extract petroleum from existing wells and (b) tier one acreage land that's available for purchase (what is known as sweet spots, or "good rock" for production) are both running out. More and more Permian oil companies are going bankrupt, and the wells are producing lower quality oil.

Decentralizing Large Generation Systems

Since large electric power generation plants require many customers to remain viable, decentralizing large generation systems to *small, self-reliant, local community-based renewable energy generation* could effectively lead to complete decarbonization of electrical power.

If local, self-reliant, renewable power generation was combined with *intentional simplification* and *reduced consumption*, the community ownership costs of supplying affordable renewable local energy could be realistically met by these small sustainable, and self-reliant local communities.

Food Is a Basic Need and Needs to Be Produced Locally As Much As Possible

Much of the food in developed nations is shipped in from other countries around the world. It violates the wisdom that essential resources required for survival should never be supplied by supply lines we have no control over.

Our food is not only coming from long distances. It is shipped on cargo ships that consume vast amounts of fossil fuels. To avoid significant food shortages when the inevitable powering down of fossil fuels arrives, we need to rapidly *re-localize* food production in the developed nations.

Because the energy costs of shipping food worldwide are significant, and because local and global transportation of food is almost entirely dependent on fossil fuels, we also need to begin a rapid and aggressive phasing out of food from centralized, large-scale agricultural corporations in the agribusiness industry.[39] Creating local food sources is a critical preparation that needs to begin *now* for those living in developed nations in anticipation of the inevitable powering down from fossil fuels.

Avoiding social and civil collapse will be all but impossible when we power down from fossil energy. We need to begin creating post-growth *policies* and a *new vision of human culture* and *human communities now.*

---

39 See Part 3 for a deeper look at the creation of self-reliant, sustainable, local communities and local economies.

I believe that the "localization" seed communities, which we will explore in Part 3, are the reimagined vision of human culture that we need to pursue and promote as vigorously and as quickly as possible. They will offer a new vision of what human community life could look like moving forward.

The essential concept that needs to be embraced is that of beginning to prepare now. Powering down is coming, and preparation for that day will take time and energy to be successful. Those who fail to prepare *now* could face critical food shortages in the future. *Every* person, *every* family, and *every* community should be growing their own local food as much as possible.

Powering down from fossil energy is inevitable. We are nearing the peak of global oil extraction and petroleum's inevitable future demise as a usable energy source for our global society. Still, we *are dangerously unprepared for the day we have to face its irreversible decline.*

Unlimited Extraction of a Non-renewable Resource on a Limited Planet

The unlimited extraction of a non-renewable resource on a finite planet is *extreme Tinker Bell thinking.* It is driven by humanity's unevolved collective primitive ego failure to embrace limits, systemic thinking, or the dangers of exponential growth. We are effectively unprepared to stay warm in the winter or cook food when powering down from fossil energy begins its irreversible decline because of the need to reduce CO_2 emissions, and resource depletion.

Intentional Planning for Peak Oil and Powering Down

Intentional planning for peak oil and powering down are significant challenges. Both will collapse the social and civil foundations of human civilization as we know it, but so will ignoring the problem! They represent the metaphor of being caught between a rock and a hard place. I believe the only realistic solution to those coming realities is preparing for their arrival by creating the self-reliant local communities of Part 3, and waiting to begin that preparation is not an option. Peak oil and the social imperative to reduce CO2 emissions are both coming in the near future.

A Brief Summary of Chapter 7:
Key Concepts in Powering Down from Fossil Fuels

We are light-years from the conversations we should be having, and the actions we should be taking to prepare for powering down from fossil energy.

We need to shift our focus to the *causes* that created the problems, not the *symptoms* the problem *created*.

We need to tame our collective human primitive ego-consciousness, its greed-based "What's in it for me?" thinking, and the myth that unlimited economic expansion is even *possible* on a limited planet—i.e., existentially dangerous Tinker Bell thinking.

We need to wake up and pay attention to reality.

a. **Reality is telling us we are already beginning to power down!** It's happening *now*, not sometime in the future! Production costs *are* increasing, EROI *is* decreasing. Existing fields *are* depleting, production in new fields *is not* replacing the depletion levels and production losses of existing fields, and the quality of energy present in new oil *decreases*.

b. **Until we focus on the reality that the post-carbon transition is already underway**, we will continue to unravel and destabilize global politics. Economic growth will continue to decline, and global social and political unrest will continue to increase. We need to remember the simple reality that *"when people can't afford bread, they head to the streets."*

c. **When *intentional* powering down begins,** social and civil unrest *will* increase significantly and dramatically. And we are not preparing for that reality.

d. **We are already on the downslope** toward an inevitable powering down from fossil energy. According to the experts, *we hit peak oil in November of 2018.* Because social and civil collapse is unavoidable as we power down from fossil energy, we need to prepare for the reality and certainty of that collapse when it arrives. We are caught in a no-win Catch-22. If we ignore the powering down that is already happening, social collapse and unrest are baked into our future. If we *intentionally* embrace the reality that we have to power down if we want to avoid extinction, social collapse and social unrest in our future is also guaranteed. Both paths will lead to the end of human civilization and life *as we know it. Still, if* we embrace reality and take aggressive action to prepare for power down *now,* including the social and civil unrest that powering down *will* create, we *might* significantly improve the odds that we could avoid the extinction of our species. It's our call. It's our time to act.

e. **The global economy needs to put massive carbon taxes** not only on non-renewable fossil energy but taxes on *all* non-renewable resources. This simple action could reduce CO_2 emissions and create the necessary financial resources to move toward a net-zero carbon emission future. *The capital created by these taxes should be legally required to be spent only on CO_2 reduction programs.*

f. **Future financial resources will be severely limited as our economy struggles to recover from COVID-19.** The fragile cracks in our global economy are becoming more visible. As we saw in the chapter on debt, the COVID-19 coronavirus is showing us that a Federal Reserve that is printing money looks good on paper, but "manufactured money" is not real growth. Real growth and real wealth require real economic growth, not more credit and debt. *In other words, rapid recovery from the virus crises is not going to be realistic or possible. The Fed is running out of ammunition.*

g. **I believe the future is going to be far more challenging than most of us are prepared to embrace *or prepare for.*** The future will ultimately reveal how accurate my concerns are and how they impacted our economy. *But I see the challenges that are coming as a gift.* They will show us clearly where our global economic systems are fragile and need a redesign. That visibility will help us to pay attention and direct our resources. If our global economic system is too large, too interconnected, too interdependent, and too complex to handle a simple crisis like COVID-19, or any of the other force-multipliers in Part 2, the challenges of powering down from carbon energy are going to make COVID-19 look like a sunny day in the park.

h. Powering down from fossil fuels and global warming are the most dangerous threats that human civilization and the existential future of humanity has ever faced. They are also two of the most dangerous threats we have ever faced that are *inevitable.*

Both of them are out of our control to avoid. Yet we are doing our best to ignore their reality and leave our future in the hands of fate. *It's time to wake up. We are out of time.* Waiting for things to get worse before we take action is an excellent example of intentional ignorance and existentially dangerous, Tinker Bell thinking.

We need to prepare, and we need to begin that preparation, *now.*

Conclusion of Chapter 7: The Burning of Fossil Fuels in the Near Future

Fossil energy *is* global capitalism.

Fossil energy *drives* the neoliberal global economy.

Fossil energy *drives* national economies.

Fossil energy *drives* the world as we know it.

Energy *drives* creation and the universe.

Nothing can happen without energy, nothing can be produced or manufactured, and without energy, life itself would not exist.

The global economy is based on fossil energy. The modern developed world was created by fossil fuel energy. And *when fossil fuel ends, the modern human civilization and life as we know it will end.*

State lawsuits filed in 2020 indicated that public pressure on ExxonMobil, Koch Industries, Flint Hill Resources LP, Flint Hills Resources Pine Bend and American Petroleum Industry (API) was already growing for alleged deception and intentionally casting doubt on the climate impacts of the burning of fossil fuels, misleading statements about climate change and the urgency of the problem, and creating a false controversy when they knew there was no legitimate controversy.

As the global heating crises become more visible, public push-back will increase pressure on the need for more aggressive *powering down* from fossil fuels.

The record high temperature of 100.4°F recorded in the Siberian Arctic in 2020 shocked climate experts who were not expecting this degree of heating until the end of the century. This resulted in experts warning that this represents the reality that the planetary climate emergency has reached a far higher level of "dire" to the threat of our future survival. The Arctic has switched from a carbon sink to a carbon source, and has been referred to the Arctic as a "greenhouse gas time-bomb."

These events are clear indications that the powering down from fossil fuel energy is not only inevitable, it is also growing evidence that the powering down from fossil fuel burning will come far sooner than most people believe as efforts increase to keep global warming below 2°C and 2025 fossil fuel reduction targets.

As we move into the future, *life as we know it* will not be what it used to be….nor will our *global economy.*

In June 2020, COVID-19 had already created a 20% reduction in oil consumption and exposed the shaky financial ground the oil and gas industries are standing on. The U.S. shale oil and gas industry appears to be on shaky legs. It faces the threat of industry-wide bankruptcies as oil companies struggle to cope with the steep collapse in petroleum demand and the steep descent in petroleum prices created by COVID-19. An estimated 30% of U.S. shale is technically insolvent. Eighteen oil and gas companies have defaulted on their debt, according to an S&P Global Rating tally in June 2020. Analysts are warning that dozens more U.S. oil and gas companies may succumb as well.

Oklahoma-based Chesapeake Energy, a shale-drilling pioneer, has filed for chapter 11 bankruptcy protection, and Exxon reported its first quarterly loss since 1999 ($610 million). At this writing, its share price has dropped more than 93% since January 2020, to $11.85.

Royal Dutch Shell announced that it would reduce its dividend for the first time since 1945.

Whiting Petroleum and Diamond Offshore Drilling have already filed for bankruptcy.

As of this writing, the oil and gas industry's near-term future looks like an uphill struggle. Recovery from COVID-19 impacts on the energy market could take months to a few years, and that's assuming the future recovers to its starkly unimpressive less than 2% annual growth before COVID-19.

Energy return on investment (EROI) was originally very high (oil gushers). Today, the oil comes from thousands of feet below the ocean, and low-yield fracking requires drilling down thousands of feet. It's clear we've picked the low-hanging "oil," and the quality of energy we're getting from a barrel of oil today is dropping.

Before COVID-19, the global consumption of petroleum was roughly 100 million barrels a day.

As of this writing (mid-2020), the consumption level has dropped to roughly 90 million barrels a day.

Future consumption is likely to continue to drop as the global economy struggles to get traction for future growth. We are already in a recession. With unemployment well above 10 million (some estimates are closer to 20 million), and 30% of mortgage holders failing to make payments in June 2020, many economists predict a 1930 Great Depression level collapse in the financial market is possible.

Many experts also believe that COVID-19 may be giving us a look at what the world after COVID-19 might look like in the reasonably near future. Beyond that, only time will tell whether we learned anything from a world pandemic as our planet continues to heat toward 2°C.

We can say with a high degree of certainty that the future isn't what it used to be, *and that's not a good thing.*

As I stated at the beginning of this chapter, because of (a) the global warming crisis and (b) the decreasing energy return on investment (EROI) as petroleum becomes increasingly expensive to extract and process, *powering down from fossil fuels will be the first, and the most powerful, and the most likely force-multiplier to impact human civilization in the years ahead.*

When humanity recognizes the urgent need to power down and begins to deal with the life-altering impacts that will result when that aggressive powering down begins, the social and civil collapse of human civilization will be unavoidable and apocalyptic if we fail to prepare now for the reality of its arrival. And powering down from fossil energy is a reality that will arrive far sooner than most people believe.

A powering-down future *will not be what it used to be…*and as I said above, *that's not a good thing…especially if we are not prepared for that future.*

We need to reinvent how we live and work.

We need to be *aggressively* reducing our use of fossil fuels, but we are currently *increasing* fossil fuel energy use as I write these words.

We need to put humanity on an energy diet and end the world's gluttonish and insatiable appetite for energy. And COVID-19 is currently giving humanity a sobering look at what that future might look like.

It's time to tame and evolve our collective primitive-ego thinking and our tendency for "What's-in-it-for-me?" thinking and begin to intentionally embrace the more evolved "we" thinking that will be needed to create a viable post-carbon human culture.

Talking to the Elephant:
Some Interesting Statistics to Change the Narrative

I will end this chapter by talking directly to the collective elephant of every person reading this book. The following facts and information are from Crazy Town Podcast #2 and #3.[40]

I encourage readers to listen to these podcasts. I include them here to illustrate the concept that assuming our modern world can survive or continue to exist as we know it *without* fossil fuels is utterly insane, ignorant, dangerous, and unrealistic Tinker Bell thinking.

Consider the following:

- **A healthy and fit person on a bike, peddling as hard as possible for one hour, can only generate about 1 watt of energy at best.**

- The average home uses approximately 30,000-watt hours of energy per day.

- One load of laundry uses about 500 watts.

- Toasting one slice of bread uses about 700 watts.

- A kilowatt from oil costs roughly .13 cents (i.e., extremely inexpensive).

- **1 barrel of oil** = 5,800,000 BTUs (Source: Louisiana Oil and Gas Association). (Human labor to produce energy of 5.8 million BTUs would = roughly 4.5 years of human labor or approximately $140,000.)

- **1 gallon of gas** = 125,000 BTUs (Source: US Department of Energy).

---

40   Crazy Town: #2 and #3 One Point Twenty-One Jigawatts and Punching Ronnie in the Mouth (https://www.postcarbon.org/one-point-twenty-one-jigawatts-episode-3-of-crazy-town/) or https://play.google.com/music/listen#/ps/I5weece3tb67w32nj6ugci7hpku.

- **1 barrel of oil** contains the energy contained in 46.4 gallons of gas (5,800,000 divided by 125,000 = 46.4 gal).

- **1 gallon of gas = 500 hours of human work output.**

- **1 barrel of oil = 23,200 hours of human work output.** In other words, the energy equivalent of 46.4 gallons of gas per barrel of oil × 500 hours of human work output per gallon of gas = 23,200 hours!

- One person can now do the work of five, ten or even a hundred people through the use of ingenious *machinery powered by fossil* fuels.

- It's estimated that 98% of physical labor is performed using machines, and 85% of those machines burn **petroleum**!

- One barrel of oil = roughly 5.8 million BTUs and costs about **$40**. In other words, a barrel of oil (roughly $40) = about 11 years of human labor.

- If an average person in the United States consumes about 50 barrels of oil = 500 years of human labor, at $45K per year, **this equals about $500,000 of human labor.** (*Remember, this figure represents the amount of "human labor" that will **not** be available when we begin to aggressively power down from fossil fuels. And global warming is telling us that our powering down from the burning of fossil fuels needs to be massive (and "now") if we want a viable future for humans on our planet.*)

- An estimated 50% to 75% of all petroleum has been burned, 50% of that since 1991, 75% since the 1970s; and we are consuming over **100 billion barrels/year!**

Stated simply, *the big oil companies are already ushering in the twilight years of fossil fuel energy!* Preparing for a low carbon world is the world we need to be aggressively preparing for in the months and years ahead. This data is a sobering look at just how different life as we know it will change in the near future.

And this change is *not* optional. It *will* come.

So, we need to intentionally and aggressively begin to prepare for its arrival *now*. Pay attention, "elephants." Our future is depending on you.

Imagination is more important than knowledge.

– Albert Einstein

I recommend listening to the entertaining crazy town podcasts to clarify the above data.

(i.e., Crazy Town: #2 and #3, **One-Point-Twenty-One Jigawatts** and **Punching Ronnie in the Mouth** (https://www.postcarbon.org/one-point-twenty-one-jigawatts-episode-3-of-crazy-town/) or https://play.google.com/music/listen#/ps/I5weece3tb67w32nj6ugci7hpku.

In Chapter 8, we'll look at the close cousin of powering down called *degrowth*…and degrowth may not mean what you think it does.

CHAPTER 8:

Existential Force-Multiplier Threat and Economic Trigger–Degrowth and Intentional Lifestyle Simplification

We are the problem. Our collective resistance to evolve our thinking keeps us blind to the changes that need to be made. Our inability to embrace degrowth and intentional lifestyle simplification, include (a) "What's in it for me?" greed, (d) an "I want what I want when I want it" attitude, (j) an exaggerated aggressive narcissistic self-focused sense of entitlement, and (m) the unending, obsessive desired for "more."

* *

Primitive ego early childhood conditioning:

a. "What's in it for me?" greed.

b. Need to be "right" (aggressive arrogance, extreme cognitive dissonance/confirmation bias).

c. Inability to replace "me" thinking with "we" thinking (compassion, mutuality, cooperation).

d. I want what I want when I want it.

e. Blaming others for our feelings (inability to own our own feelings).

f. Ignorance regarding the danger of exponential growth (e.g., COVID-19).

g. A lack of interconnected, interdependent systemic thinking.

h. Survival-of-the-fittest thinking.

i. Black versus white, zero-sum thinking ("You can't have that, it's mine!").

j. An exaggerated aggressive, narcissistic self-focused sense of entitlement.

k. An inability to connect short-term choices with long-term consequences.

l. The fear of change (uncertainty, not knowing).

m. The unending, obsessive desired for "more."

n. The need for power "over" rather than power "with."

o. The inability to embrace long-term thinking.

* *

Introduction to Chapter 8:
Degrowth and Intentional Lifestyle Simplification

Degrowth is the simple post-growth concept that we have *too many people*, consuming *too many non-renewable resources* on a *limited* planet. Stated simply, our future as a viable, sustainable species on this planet *will* require far fewer humans, consuming far fewer resources.

Degrowth and lifestyle simplification directly challenges the unlimited growth ideology of business-as-usual in neoliberal global capitalism, and the sense of entitlement that we always deserve *more*. Degrowth emphasizes a more sustainable interconnected systemic human–earth relationship; a commitment to respecting ecological limits and protecting long-term planetary sustainability.

The way I prefer to think about degrowth is the need for humanity to embrace the indigenous Native American tribal belief common for centuries that *"spirit"* is a *"thou"* deeply embedded in all of nature and all of reality; *not* an *"it."* They saw "spirit" in nature, the soil, every tree, every plant, every living organism, every rock, the atmosphere, the water, the wind, and every other human or animal being on the planet. The indigenous cultures *intentionally* used and protected the natural resources that supported their lives, and most importantly, *the lives of those who would need those natural resources for seven generations into the future.*

Degrowth is based on not only a deeper spiritual connection with nature, it also requires the ability to embrace systemic thinking and *relearning and embracing* the indigenous *we-ness* embedded in a *just* human–earth relationship with other living systems and species; in other words, a sustainable interconnected, and interdependent systemic relationship with our planet. A systemic relationship with nature that neoliberal global capitalism, extractivism, unlimited growth, profit, greed, private land ownership, colonialization, massive wealth inequality, and our collective *me*-focused primitive ego human consciousness has mangled, crushed, and corrupted beyond recognition. The entitled, self-focused, narcissistic way of living that has put our human species on the fast track to unimaginable suffering and likely extinction.

Degrowth requires embracing the concepts of self-determination, self-reliance, sustainability, re-generativity, and resilience; the concepts that honor, and listen to, the voices of those directly impacted by decisions that define their lives. Voices that include the planet's ecosystems, the animals, the insects, the birds, the trees, the soil, the rivers, the oceans, and the voices of those unjustly marginalized and silenced by our current global, greed-based economic systems.

Degrowth also embraces the concept of *intentional simplicity.* We have far too many people, consuming far too many non-renewable resources on a resource-limited planet. To embrace the concept of degrowth, the global economy would require those in the developed nations to better respect ecological limits, embrace local and planetary sustainability, and become more self-reliant by producing more of the food, energy, and necessities they require to support a simpler way of life; a lifestyle that is more connected to the ecosystems of the land they live on, and the local community around them.

The future is not what it used to be, and preparation for that future will need to include the concepts of degrowth, self-reliance, radical simplicity of lifestyle, and the creation of self-reliant local communities. The days of unlimited growth and profit will need to be replaced by concepts of well-being and supportive, self-reliant, cooperative communities.[41]

The evidence is clear that our current business-as-usual global economy is unsustainable. Continuing to advocate and support unlimited economic growth on a limited planet is not only intentional ignorance, it's insane Tinker Bell thinking. We are destroying our planet and creating deeply unstable social inequalities and cruel injustices in the process. We need to reimagine a more innovative, sustainable, compassionate, and inclusive future that is more equitable and just. A future that embraces the imagination, and degrowth goals of a simplified *post-growth, post-fossil energy* world; the *post-global* values of sustainable, self-reliant local economies; and the *post-collapse* values of a *we*-based human culture that's focused on well-being rather than unlimited consumption, profit, and growth. Stated simply, degrowth is essentially the anthesis of unlimited growth.

I am convinced that preparation and adoption of a degrowth lifestyle is urgent and *not* an option. Without *intentional* preparation that begins now, the existential force-multiplier threats in Part 2 will change life as we know it far sooner, and far more dramatically than most people will be ready or able to survive. To be successful, degrowth and intentional simplification are not goals that can be achieved without years of deliberate preparation, skill development, strong local community support, teamwork, and cooperation.[42]

Acquiring the skills required to live a self-reliant lifestyle need time and practice to learn and develop. Two decades of homesteading in upstate New York taught me that acquiring the land for crops, tools, equipment, livestock, water systems, renewable energy systems, honeybees and hives, and

---

41   Chapter 10: Localization.

42   We will explore this subject in more depth in Part 3.

food-processing equipment to live a self-reliant lifestyle can easily require four to five years for most people.

The primary golden arch message in this book is the urgent need to begin preparing *now* for the changes that *are* coming. Waiting is no longer a viable option. Survival in the coming world will require a high level of self-reliance, preparation, commitment, and intentionality. I encourage readers to think about the children and grandchildren of the next generation. Like children in previous generations, the skills and knowledge required to thrive in a degrowth culture that embraces a self-reliant simplicity lifestyle, are best learned and acquired as a natural part of growing up.

Given the massive changes coming, I encourage readers to prepare *intentionally* and begin *now*. Be ready for a significant amount of ridicule as you help the next generation begin to prepare for the future that's coming. Simply stay focused on truth, facts, and data. They matter more than the opinions of an intentionally uninformed general public. Stay informed. Stay awake to the changes that are both coming and inevitable. Simply remind yourself, "A person is *not* an alarmist when the threats coming *are actually alarming.*"

I believe the changes that are coming are massive, inevitable, and existentially beyond alarming. The next generation will need your help as they prepare for a future that isn't what it used to be.

Degrowth: The Path Toward a Viable Future

Degrowth is a voluntary transition towards an ecologically sustainable society that embraces well-being, the benefits of an intentionally simple lifestyle, and the elimination of the stress created from living a life in which happiness is defined as the accumulation of wealth and a never-ending desire for "more."

Degrowth, and intentional simplicity of lifestyle, both require consuming less of the "stuff" we *want,* and more of the things we *need.* It requires the desire to end the frantic life of a squirrel trapped running in a circular cage generating wealth year after year for those who already have obscene levels of wealth. It requires the simple recognition that waiting hopefully for some of that wealth to trickle down somehow is unrealistic Tinker Bell thinking.

Massive wealth inequality in the top 10% is showing us that wealth trickles up, not down!

Degrowth and intentional simplicity of lifestyle not only create a radically different economic system. They ground us in a different reality. They give us more control and security over our lives. As our lives become more "intentionally simple, local, and self-reliant," we begin to experience first-hand the sobering reality that the promised benefits of growth were *far* less valuable than the personal and social *costs* we were paying to acquire that growth.

We begin to recognize that the never-ending growth of our current global economy was *not* natural, necessary, or desirable, and it continues to be rapidly destroying our planet. The more self-reliant and sustainable our lives become, the more we can better experience and understand the sobering reality that growth-based economies are *designed* to collapse when *never-ending* growth and profits end. We begin to experience first-hand the sobering reality that *never-ending* growth has *always* been based on exploitation, extraction, and the creation of waste and pollution.

Degrowth and intentional simplicity are essentially the opportunity to "awaken" to the security and sense of well-being that comes with self-reliance and the "well-being support" of a self-reliant, sustainable local community.

The next generation needs our help for them to experience that way of life and begin learning the life skills they will need in the years ahead.

The Real Costs of Unlimited Growth Are Becoming Visible

The existential dangers embedded in the myth of *unlimited* expansion and growth are becoming visible. But the conflict between *change to save the world* and *no change* is also growing. Degrowth and intentional simplicity of lifestyle mean less production and profit, less accumulation of wealth, and more focus on the realities of *increased* sharing, *less* consumption, *increased* focus on well-being, the common good, scarcity, freedom from debt and interest payments, and the burdens of monthly repayment.

Degrowth is awakening to the reality that we have been conditioned from childhood to embrace the Tinker Bell illusion that happiness and success in life are defined and determined by how much we own, how much we earn, and how much wealth we can accumulate. We know that is not true at some level of consciousness, but we don't know how to get out of the squirrel cage. What would we do? How would we survive? How would we live?

In Part Three, Chapter 10, we will attempt to answer those questions as we explore the concept of localization and the intentional creation of self-reliant local communities. For now, it's essential to recognize that we have been conditioned to live an illusion called unlimited growth capitalism. This illusion is rapidly destroying our planet and threatening the possible extinction of our species. Only when we fully embrace and accept that reality will we have the courage to intentionally tame our primitive ego and the conditioning of early childhood in order to awaken our consciousness enough (a) to walk away from the life-smothering lives we have all been conditioned to live, and (b) embrace the possibilities of living life in a supportive, self-reliant local community with others who have also awakened to that life-stifling oppressive reality. Connectedness, sustainability, and shared well-being in a self-reliant local community with others are the gifts that come with degrowth, intentional simplification, and self-sufficient living.

In Part 3, we will see that not only is that life possible, but given the reality of climate change and storm intensification, we will learn that a sustainable and self-reliant local community may be the best way to prepare for the changes that are coming. The preparation concepts discussed in Part 3 will help create the resilience we will need to survive the existential changes that are coming. We will also see more clearly in Part 3 that degrowth and self-reliant local communities are paths of hope that could support the future survival of humanity and human culture.

We need to remind ourselves that COVID-19 impacts and degrowth are two very different subjects. The economic slowdown created by COVID-19 is not degrowth. It is, however, an excellent example of the unsustainability and fragility of neoliberal global capitalism and our current way of life. COVID-19 is also showing us that intentional degrowth and change is possible. Degrowth shows us we *can* change the ways we function as a human culture when faced with a significant crisis. Those changes are challenging, but they are possible.

Degrowth is an *intentional*, long-term commitment to the downsizing of production and consumption; a commitment to reorganize how we have structured our human culture. If a virus like COVID-19 can cause this much havoc and disruption in our global social and economic systems, it's a clear wakeup call that we need to imagine different and better ways to organize our human culture and our global economy. Degrowth is an intentional transformation of human culture in the developed nations. It emphasizes the importance of a self-reliant local economy that supports and restructures how we work together to grow our food and live more sustainably in small local self-reliant communities.

Degrowth is essentially reduced consumption, intentional simplification of lifestyle, and more self-reliant local solar and wind energy production. Stated simply, degrowth offers a more resilient, sustainable, interdependent, cooperative way of organizing human culture. Degrowth also illustrates clearly the difference between (a) the unlimited growth and profit of our systemically complex global capitalistic economy and (b) the simplicity and reduced consumption of a sustainable local economy that's based inside a self-reliant local community that's focused on the well-being of every person in the community.

A Brief Overview of the Basic Concepts Embedded in Degrowth and Intentional Simplification

a. **Degrowth is essentially a post-growth movement that challenges the litany and paradigm of infinite growth and neoliberal global**

capitalism's intention to continue aggressively supporting business-as-usual regardless of consequences.

Degrowth embraces care for the earth's ecosystems, its people, and the redistribution of surpluses back to the land and the people who produce those surpluses, not the elite 10%.

Degrowth is not only a new way of managing and defining the social economy. It intentionally supports the vision of a systemically based humanity based on interdependent cooperation, teamwork, autonomy, sufficiency, and well-being. A post-growth vision of a self-reliant local community could become a "seed" concept for the sustainable future of human civilization that we will explore in Part 3.

b. **Degrowth shines a bright light on what needs to be unlearned.**

Unlearning is a fundamental golden arch goal of this book, an unlearning based on doing the work of intentionally taming, maturing, and evolving our collective primitive ego human consciousness and its unconscious childhood conditioning.

Much of what we learn in early childhood is unconscious and far too self-focused and immature to be viable or useful in the modern adult world. Intentionally taming our primitive ego is best defined as *unlearning* the myths, illusions, and distortions of early childhood through intentional growth in self-awareness and our ability to intentionally embrace and reflect a more evolved, mature, adult consciousness.[43]

To be successful long-term, degrowth and self-reliant local communities will require collectively *unlearning* the life-long conditioning that created and aggressively supports the dangerous myth of unlimited growth.

---

43 The intentional taming of our collective primitive ego human consciousness is described in Chapter 2.

The concepts of well-being, autonomy, self-reliance, and sufficiency all need to become part of our economic language as we redesign the values of our economic systems to ensure that those who have been deprioritized, disenfranchised, and exploited by neoliberal global capitalism are fully visible, and their voices heard. Sufficiency is the concept of distributive justice. Everyone today and tomorrow should have enough to satisfy their fundamental human needs, and no one should have more than they *need* relative to the sustainable "limits" of our planetary resources and ecological boundaries. The sufficiency principle would reflect the Seventh Generation Principle, the ancient teaching and concept embraced by indigenous Native American Iroquois tribes and their longhouse culture; the concept that decisions made today should result in a sustainable world seven generations into the future.[44]

c. **Degrowth requires a supportive self-reliant local community.**

A local community based on cooperation and well-being, community-based renewable energy self-reliance, and food production that is local and regenerative.

d. **Survival in "the future that *is* coming" *will* require the support, teamwork, and cooperation of a self-reliant local community.**

Individual efforts would lack the flexibility, caring, and teamwork that only a supportive local community could provide. Because the concept of private land ownership creates wealth and power inequality, degrowth replaces private land ownership with cooperative community ownership of land. Community "ownership" would also include the sharing of tools and equipment used by the community. The primary goal of a local community would be focused on the well-being of all persons in the community, not individual profit or wealth accumulation.

---

44 See *Unlearning: From Degrowth to Decolonization* by Jamie Tyberg for more excellent material on these concepts.

e. **Our planet has physical limits.**

We have intentionally ignored this obvious reality in our global pursuit of profit, greed, and "unlimited" economic expansion. Degrowth reminds us that long-term "sustainability in nature", and the long-term "sustainability of community", are always based on the recognition and reality of our planet's ecological and natural resource limits.

f. **Degrowth, post-growth, and post-fossil fuels will all require national and global annual caps on the resource extraction of coal, cubic feet of gas, and barrels of oil.**

That cap number should decline each year until fossil fuel extraction is balanced with CO2 emission limits that keep us at net-zero carbon. This reduction in fossil fuel would have to guarantee fair access to the necessities of life *for everyone on the planet*. Essentially the concept of *sufficiency* for all and *overconsumption* for none. This would require a radical global movement and reorientation toward justice, self-reliance, and well-being that local, self-reliant "seed" communities could create as they network and trade for *sufficiency* needs with other self-reliant local communities.

g. **The Importance of Degrowth and Intentional Lifestyle Simplification**

Degrowth and intentional simplification are not just good ideas. They are essential if we are to create a sustainable future for humanity on this planet. The threats of neoliberal global capitalism as a dangerous force-multiplier on humanity's future extinction on this planet are becoming increasingly apparent and obvious. Quota rationing for fossil fuel energy, carbon caps, population limits, and extraction limits on a non-renewable resource is critical if we want a viable future for human life and human civilization on our planet.

Because degrowth and intentional lifestyle simplification directly confront the destructive myths of unlimited expansion and exponential growth, they help to awaken the collective human consciousness to the growing awareness of the harm neoliberal global capitalism is causing to nature and the planet.

h. **Climate change and storm intensification are rapidly driving the conflict between the "need" for change, and the primitive ego "fear" of change, toward some form of resolution.**

For those who accept the reality of global warming, climate change, and the need for humanity to embrace change and sustainability; the benefits of (a) self-reliant local communities, (b) increased sharing, (c) decreased consumption, (d) increased simplicity, (e) increased well-being, (f) increased focus on the common good, (g) less scarcity of needed critical natural resources, (h) a sense of well-being free from re-payment of debt, (i) the end of treadmill production for profit, and (j) the accumulation of individual wealth, are all becoming more apparent and appealing.

But the increasing tension, conflict, and stress created by our collective human primitive ego *fear* of change, and the growing recognition of the *need* to embrace change to save the world, is rapidly increasing. It increases anxiety and conflict individually, socially, politically, and internationally between those who accept the need for change and those in denial.

i. **We are at the fork in the road that leads toward the future. Humanity is rapidly approaching the point of no return.**

We need to make a choice *and soon*. Do we do nothing and simply wait for unlimited growth to collapse our planet's fragile ecosystems? Or do we embrace degrowth, intentional simplification of lifestyle, and powering down?

Unfortunately, as I pointed out earlier, *both choices* will lead to massive change and the likely collapse of human culture as we know it when the global economy collapses. The option is not which path is least painful. The real choice is *which path will give humanity the best chance of avoiding extinction.* And my concern is whether we will make that choice in time to prepare for resilience and survival. I see no viable future for humanity, human culture, or human civilization if we continue on the path of unlimited, exponential growth and profit.

I do see the possible extinction of our species on this planet.

The Sobering Reality That Supports the Creation of Local Communities, Degrowth, and Intentional Simplification

Renewable green wind and solar energy will *not* support continued global growth. As we discussed in the previous chapter, some believe that "renewable" wind and solar energy could support unlimited growth and profits if we could invest soon enough in that renewable, green infrastructure. As we saw in that conversation, science and reality do not support that claim for several reasons that we will look at below. Scientists warn that the belief that green renewable energy could support continued global *growth* is dangerous. This Tinker Bell assumption only creates indecision and confusion on the actions we *need* to take *now* to successfully prepare for the coming changes. Renewable green electric energy will *not* support continued growth or preserve our current global economy because:

a. Space and land acquisitions required to build solar and wind at the scale that would be needed would require massive economic and financial commitments by the world's governments. Solar infrastructure and wind turbines would require roughly 50 acres per megawatt for wind, and solar would require approximately 2.5 acres per megawatt.

b. The massive amount of fossil energy that would be required to extract the natural resources and then manufacture the renewable energy systems at the scale that would be needed would *alone* radically exceed the CO_2 emission limits required to keep the planet heating below 1.5° to 2°C.

c.   Making the massive social and economic changes that would be needed to finance the transition to "green" renewables would include:

- A global *reduction in the current level of consumption* that would result when fossil fuels are retired.

- The *massive resistance* from the fossil fuel industry itself.

- The opposition from the manufacturing industries.

- The end of fossil fuel shipping and transportation.

- A significant reduction in human populations globally.

- The *vast social lifestyle changes* that would be required when *intermittent renewable energy* stored in batteries would be used to energize the global economy, heat our homes, transport food, manufacture "stuff" for consumption, and cook the food for a global population that is expected to reach 10 billion in the next few decades.

d.   Renewable energy cannot supply the energy needs of large manufacturing machinery, airliners, cargo ships, and industrial processes that require liquid carbon fuels as raw material to produce steel, plastics, and fertilizers. Even if powering these industries were possible, the technical challenges to overcome the limitations of renewable energy would be massive. The current commitments to finance the development and construction of a renewable energy industry is roughly $50 billion. Experts estimate that a successful transition to renewable energy at scale would exceed $14 trillion by 2030. *But the physical and energy limitations listed above would still apply!*

e.   Wind and solar currently represented roughly 1.5% of the total energy production in 2018, and that figure represents *all the growth in renewable energy since approximately 1975.*

f.   Too often the information on renewable energy is (1) based on percentage numbers of very small numbers, (2) tends to be focused on achievements, (3) does not include failures, and most importantly,

4) much of the information is focused on *future objectives,* not actual accomplishments, and the current investment in renewables represent only 10% of the assets required.

g. Resistance to renewable energy include "not in my back yard", resistance to change in electrical consumption habits of individuals and corporations, resistance to the massive land use that would be required, the intermittency of green power, the limitations of battery storage, and the massive financial investments that would be required (estimated to be over $14T in the next ten years).

h. All of the above reasons why renewable green electric energy will not support continued *growth* or our current global economy *ignore the realities* of (1) the inevitable powering down from fossil fuels that is coming (energy that will not be available to produce the massive green energy systems and infrastructures required), and (2) the enormous financial and social impacts that global climate change, storm intensification, flooding, droughts, ocean level increases, food shortages, and the lack of freshwater availability, will inflict on international cultures, and national and local economies, in the near future.

Local green energy might be possible for small local communities that have intentionally adopted a simplified, sustainable, self-reliant local lifestyle. But it would not support our current neoliberal global capitalist economy or any Tinker Bell concept of *global growth.*

Why degrowth? Because the future of humanity is at a critical fork in the road, and unlimited economic growth is acting as a planetary-level cancer.

Our only realistic future is degrowth, powering down from fossil fuel energy, significant voluntary simplification of lifestyle, and the creation of sustainable, energy self-reliant, local communities. And we are running out of time to (a) prepare for the changes needed to respond to the existential force multiplier threats of Part 2, and the massive changes that will be created by those threats that are coming; and (b) the *existential* impacts that those force multiplier threats and massive changes are going to inflict on human civilization *whether or not we are prepared.*

Why degrowth? Everything in the lifestyle we are accustomed to in the western, developed world has to change soon and change radically.

Social sufficiency, self-reliant local communities, cooperation with others, unnecessary consumption, and respect for the natural world are *all needed to replace our current unsustainable and destructive addiction to growth and profit.*

Economic contraction of the current global economy, powering down from fossil energy, degrowth, and intentional simplification of lifestyle, *will* create social and civil collapse and life as we know it *whether or not we are prepared.*

Local self-reliant communities and local economies that do not need growth to survive are a viable and realistic path forward, but it will require significant preparation and an intentionally tamed *collective* primitive ego consciousness for long-term survival and success. We will need to get people on board with the *urgent need* for these self-reliant local communities, their life-affirming focus on well-being, and actively support their creation as a compelling and realistic post-growth alternative to replace the current destructive global addiction to growth and profit.

This will be a challenging and difficult task, given humanity's resistance to change.

Why degrowth? Degrowth is the post-growth reality of self-reliant local communities, the path to a self-reliant future that people worldwide are increasingly eager to embrace.

Self-reliant local communities and degrowth embrace a simplification of lifestyle based on increased sharing, repairing, the repurposing of already existing resources and infrastructures, library-principle resource centers for tools and machinery, common workshop space, domestic appliances, shared/co-housing to save energy (e.g., wood heat in winter), shared transportation, community gardens, community-supported agriculture, and increased support for members of the community including the caring and help for one another based on the compassion and mutuality of disaster collectivism. Local communities and local economies will evolve, mature, and evolve over time, *but they are not compatible with capitalism in that they don't "grow."* Growth in a local self-reliant community is based entirely on growth in well-being, growth in quality of life, growth in resilience, growth in sustainability, and growth in social equality.

Why Degrowth? Powering down from fossil energy, intentional simplification of lifestyle, and the collapse of neoliberal global capitalism are all inevitable.

We have already baked in 2°C, and that's assuming we reduce CO_2 emissions by 75% by 2025! As of this writing, in 2020, CO_2 emissions are *growing*!

Even at 2°C, many areas of our planet will be uninhabitable. Given the reality that inevitable tipping points and irreversible cascading feedback systems are *already* beginning to kick in, scientists are urgently warning that we are currently on course to reach 4°C well before the end of the century. *We need to wake up as species! Now!*

Why degrowth? Denial of global warming is "intentional ignorance."

This is not a time for debate or the suffering of fools. We are looking at the end of human civilization as we know it, and we need to prepare *now* if we want to create the resilience we will need to survive. And we need to intentionally tame and evolve our collective primitive-ego human consciousness, or we *will* quickly re-create the very greed-based thinking and economic systems that are currently destroying our ability to survive on a small and limited planet. The primitive thinking of early childhood, its need to be right, and its narcissistic hyper-individualism cannot cooperate, embrace limits, embrace systemic thinking, or live sustainability on a limited planet. We are out of time for debate. It's time for action.

Why degrowth? Act Now or Face Inevitable Consequences in the Near Future: Our Choice

The above analysis is essentially an obituary for fossil fuels *and* global capitalism. All of the above represent nails in the coffin of economic growth as we know it. When powering down from fossil fuels and the end of global capitalism become socially accepted realities, I see no way we can or will avoid global social and civil collapse. When people recognize the validity of the changes that are coming, and how unprepared we are to survive those changes, people will panic. When people are desperate, they will take to the streets. They will panic. They will be angry.

Why degrowth? The time for debate is over. We need to act.

And we need to avoid dangerous Tinker Bell thinking. There are no simple solutions that will "fix" the complex systemic challenges that are coming.

a.   The massive financial and energy investments required to make a successful transition to "renewable" green energy would bankrupt most nations and create a radical increase in CO_2 emissions.

b.   The significant lifestyle changes required for a country to go "green" would quickly create aggressive and destabilizing social unrest and the likely collapse of social and civil structures.

c.   The increasing depletion of oil and gas resources, the growing negative energy return on investment (EROI), and the rising social and economic impacts of climate change *will* eventually mandate a powering down from fossil energy. That mandate is coming soon, well before people will be prepared to deal with powering down, socially or economically.

d.   The inevitable reduction in consumption that will result from all of the above, including the resulting collapse of the global financial markets, will make *the collapse of neoliberal global capitalism and the social and civil collapse of human culture an inevitable certainty.*

As I have noted in this book, neoliberal global capitalism is based on *unlimited* expansion, *unlimited* growth, and *unlimited* profit. When those criteria are not met, neoliberal global capitalism ends. Period. COVID-19 is already illuminating the fragility and vulnerable cracks built into neoliberal global capitalism.

Why degrowth? We need to create new, post-growth structures and systems that promote degrowth and create the intentional simplification of life that local communities are designed to embrace and support.

However, the changes we need will never emerge until we have a social culture that demands them.

The ideology of unlimited growth and wealth accumulation has a firm grip on our collective human consciousness. But as Einstein warned, attempting to use the same thinking process to solve a problem, that was initially used in creating that problem, *will not work.*

To successfully create the post-growth changes needed, the first *and most important preparation for the future that's coming* is an intentional revolution in human consciousness that would include the taming, evolution, and maturation of humanity's collective primitive ego and its early childhood conditioning (described in Chapters 1 and 2).

Until a sufficient number of people embrace the taming and maturation of their human consciousness, humanity's collective use of primitive, early childhood conditioning in the adult, modern world will continue to be ***the*** primary existential force-multiplier threatening the future survival of humanity. Stated simply, the primitive early childhood conditioning of our collective human consciousness needs to be *intentionally* tamed, evolved, and matured for us to be successful in creating post-growth social and economic structures and systems that avoid the dangers of unlimited growth and profit.

The second preparation that will be needed is the cultural embrace of degrowth, and the intentional simplification of lifestyle, in the collective cultures of humanity. Degrowth and the creation of local, self-reliant communities is the most logical and realistic framework for understanding the global crisis we are in, and it is the only credible way forward with the ability to include a just redistribution of the financial resources that are currently held by the top 10%.

The future survival of every person on the planet will depend on how successful we are in (a) creating a global simplification of lifestyle, (b) creating sustainable, self-reliant local communities, and (c) a just access and redistribution of the planet's financial resources to every person.

When the massive changes arrive, obscene levels of wealth will not ensure anyone's long-term survival. Whether we are a multimillionaire or a poor peasant working hand to mouth to survive, we will all need food, oxygen, a supportive community, a climate that supports the growth of food, clean water to drink, and a healthy planetary ecosystem.

The days of wealth accumulation are coming to an end. Economic growth will become meaningless.

The wealth that will be important in a viable post-carbon degrowth future will be the wealth of security and well-being in a supportive, cooperative community grounded in the human values of equality, care, empathy, and compassion.

Some Final Thoughts and Conclusion of Chapter 8

We are consuming petroleum—a finite, non-renewable, irreplaceable natural resource—at a rate estimated at over 100 million barrels a day. And that *demand* is expected to continue growing for the next 10 to 15 years in our business-as-usual economy. But that assumption is Tinker Bell thinking that ignores the sobering reality and uncomfortable facts we talked about above; the truth that existing oil fields are producing less oil, and the hunt for new oil reserves are not producing enough new oil to cover that declining production. Stated simply, our entire global economy is based on a future, non-renewable fossil fuel energy resource *that's in decline.*

This sobering reality raises the questions:

a. What will happen as fossil energy becomes less available, as the energy return on investment (EROI) continues to go negative, and the price of this dwindling fossil energy begins to climb? The answer, of course, is the inevitable and unavoidable collapse of neoliberal global capitalism, increased social unrest and insecurity, and the inevitable social and civil collapse that will result when people become desperate.

b. How far can we kick the can down the road before this collapse become a reality? *Not much further.* Global warming and climate change, storm intensification, forest fires, droughts, polar ice melt, and flooding are already becoming difficult to ignore.

c. How long can we avoid the reality that the energy resources of our planet are limited? *Not much longer.*

d. How long can we ignore the reality that powering down, degrowth, the simplification of lifestyle, and the creation of self-reliant local communities are our human future. *Not long. The global local community movement is growing.*

e. Do we passively wait for social collapse? Or will we find the courage to accept the obvious reality that intentional degrowth *that begins now* is the only realistic preparation for the future that's available for humanity? *We will know soon.*

Waiting to prepare for a future that isn't what it used to be is "not" an option. Nor is waiting for our leaders and politicians to lead.

Until the commons aggressively address the reality of global warming and climate change, *politicians will be unwilling to act.* Without strong and aggressive public support, the likelihood of politicians actively supporting legislation to aggressively reduce CO2 emissions, global warming, and climate change would quickly end their political careers. It won't happen.

The only realist path forward that has the potential to create a viable future for human culture and human civilization is the creation of self-reliant local communities. And even that path has to begin now.

Conclusion

Reality: Widespread global acceptance of degrowth, and intentional simplification will not be possible for most people in the current growth-based neoliberal global economy until there is a significant threat of social and civil collapse and the threatened collapse of human civilization as we know it. When that realization arrives, it will be too late to prepare.

Reality: On the other hand, I see no way we can *intentionally* slow down the global economy of 7 to 10 billion people without also creating that social and civil collapse of our global social structures and the foundations of human civilization as we know it.

Reality: *The collapse is coming.* Reality is telling us that we cannot continue business as usual much longer.

Reality: The important question is not *when* will collapse happen. It's will we have prepared for that day? Will we have created the resilience to survive that transition from global growth to local self-reliance and well-being?

Reality: Resilience requires preparation before the crisis arrives. Not after.

Reality: We are devouring and destroying the planet just to keep people employed, create profit, create wealth for the top 10%, and keep the Tinker Bell myth of *unlimited growth on a limited planet* alive and growing. Until there is a significant social movement for change, intentionally killing the neoliberal global goose that's laying the eggs of gold *will not an option for corporations, the elite, or politicians!*

Reality: Decoupling global growth from destructive increases in the consumption of our planet's natural resources and continued growth in energy use is currently impossible to achieve without also creating economic, social, and civil collapse.

Reality: We need planned economic degrowth, but that would end neoliberal global capitalism, and that collapse would also create a social and civil collapse.

Reality: We are running out of inexpensive oil, which will eventually collapse neoliberal global capitalism and create a social and civil collapse.

Reality: We are emitting far too much CO2 and heating the planet. We need to reduce the burning of carbon fuels to zero net emissions. But that would also collapse neoliberal capitalism and create a social and civil collapse.

Reality: We need to end neoliberal global capitalism, but the end of neoliberal global capitalism will create the social and civil collapse of human cultures and human civilization as we know it.

Bottom line: I see no path forward that avoids the social and civil collapse of human cultures and human civilization as we know it. And that collapse is not only unavoidable, it is coming in the very near future. Beginning aggressive preparation *now* and creating self-reliant local communities and is the only realistic path forward I can envision in which we might survive that sobering reality.

We need to make the difficult decision to begin *intentionally* preparing *now* for a dangerous and challenging future. Our survival *will* depend on it individually and collectively.

Moving on to the Secondary Force-Multipliers

This is the last chapter on the *primary* existential force multiplier threats and economic triggers that *will* eventually end life as we know it, create social and civil collapse, and create the possible extinction of our species on this planet.

But before we move on to Localization and the creation of self-reliant local communities and a realistic hope for humanity in Chapter 10, we need to take a look in Chapter 9 at the *secondary force-multipliers* that will *actively support* the primary existential force multipliers we have been discussing when they begin to threaten life as we know it, the future survival of our human cultures, human civilization, and our survival as a viable species on our planet.

CHAPTER 9:

Secondary Force Multiplier Threats

We are the problem. We need to tame and evolve the immature and dangerous primitive ego childhood thinking and conditioning that created the secondary force-multipliers in this chapter. Each of the aspects of unconscious, unevolved early childhood primitive ego thinking listed below systemically reinforce and support the secondary force multiplier threats in this chapter.

✳ ✳

Primitive ego early childhood conditioning:

a. "What's in it for me?" greed.

b. Need to be "right" (aggressive arrogance, extreme cognitive dissonance/confirmation bias).

c. Inability to replace "me" thinking with "we" thinking (compassion, mutuality, cooperation).

d. I want what I want when I want it.

e. Blaming others for our feelings (inability to own our own feelings).

f. Ignorance regarding the danger of exponential growth (e.g., COVID-19).

g. A lack of interconnected, interdependent systemic thinking.

h. Survival-of-the-fittest thinking.

i. black versus white, zero-sum thinking ("You can't have that, it's mine!").

j. An exaggerated aggressive, narcissistic self-focused sense of entitlement.

k. An inability to connect short-term choices with long-term consequences.

l. The fear of change (uncertainty, not knowing).

m. The unending, obsessive desired for "more."

n. The need for power "over" rather than power "with."

o. The inability to embrace long-term thinking.

✳ ✳

Introduction to Chapter 9

In this chapter, we will take a look at the *secondary* primitive-ego force-multipliers. Unlike the *primary* force-multipliers, these *secondary* force-multipliers are *less likely* to be a major existential threat to our future. But each of them *will* prevent efforts to increase preparation for the impacts and massive changes of the *primary* existential force-multiplier threats, as they continue to grow in strength and aggressively threaten the increasingly fragile social and civil structures of human culture, human civilization, and life as we know it.

These *secondary* force-multipliers are best described as *destabilizers* that will increase the vulnerability of human culture and human civilization's social and civil structural foundations. They will significantly weaken our ability to survive when the primary existential force-multiplier threats inevitably reach critical, irreversible environmental tipping points.

Each of the *secondary* force-multipliers listed in this chapter will significantly limit our ability to:

a. Acknowledge and embrace the existential changes and threats that are coming.

b. Cope with unexpected black swan events such as COVID-19.

c. Decrease the destructive impact of the *primary* force-multiplier threats and our future ability to survive as a species when they arrive.

d. Undermine our ability to take effective action, enact effective political policies, and create effective social responses as the *primary* force-multiplier threats continue to increase in severity.

e. Significantly increase, intensify, and accelerate the *primary* force-multipliers' destructive impacts as they continue to grow in severity.

Each secondary force multipliers in this chapter is an important threat that needs to be intentionally included in the taming and evolution of our collective primitive ego human consciousness and its early childhood conditioning.

Wisdom Teachers and Intentional Growth in Self-Awareness

Awakening the unconscious mind through intentional growth in self-awareness has been the primary wisdom teaching of spiritual teachers throughout human history. It has been taught as *the* primary path to happiness. Some have described the journey to an awakened, self-aware consciousness as the journey to the top of a mountain. In other words, awakening and growth in self-awareness take intentional effort.

They taught their students that until the unconscious mind is intentionally awakened and evolved, our unconscious ego will attempt to "push the river" and resist reality and create unhappiness, conflict, stress, anxiety, and never-ending angst for *ourselves* and those around us.

Given that our ultimate goal is the survival of our species on this planet, there is no task more essential or important for us to undertake and master than the intentional evolution and maturing of our collective human consciousness.

In Chapters 1 and 2 of this book, I referred to this ancient awakening process as *intentional* growth in self-awareness, and the *intentional* taming of our unconscious primitive ego, and its unconscious early childhood conditioning.

Keeping in Mind the Goals of an Evolved and Matured Collective Human Consciousness

As we review the secondary force-multipliers in this chapter, and the distortions of reality that our immature unconscious primitive ego and its early childhood conditioning collectively and unintentionally created, we need to keep in mind the essential goals of this book:

a. The need to embrace our collective imagination and create social systems and structures that are more sustainable and work more cooperatively and systemically *with* the natural world.

b. The need to focus our attention on those primitive ego concepts, beliefs, and ways of thinking that each of us *personally* uses in *our own* thinking so we can more intentionally tame *our own* unconscious early childhood primitive ego thinking, grow in self-awareness, and begin awakening, evolving and maturing *our own primitive ego-consciousness*.

c. And most importantly, the need to remember that all of the secondary force-multipliers that follow in this chapter directly support and strengthen the potential for social and civil collapse as the *primary* force-multipliers continue to intensify in their ability to threaten our future.

Secondary Force-Multiplier #1: The Primitive Ego's Need to be "Right"

The collective human primitive ego's need to be "right" is one of the most powerful and destructive behavioral beliefs currently attacking civility in the modern world. I consider it one of *the most dangerous and common primitive ego beliefs embedded in our collective human consciousness*. It creates aggressive and rigid ideologies, and the inability to compromise or embrace the middle-path truths that are always found in the ideological positions on both sides of every issue. Ideologically rigid tribal thinking significantly increases *cognitive dissonance*, the inability to look for, or take in any information that conflicts with our own beliefs. Cognitive dissonance judgmentally impacts our ability to *process critical information* on pandemics, global heating, climate change, and all of the existential primary and secondary force-multipliers included in this book. We will explore the impacts of cognitive dissonance in more detail below.

The need to be "right" creates aggressive tribal division, extreme polarization, aggressive disrespect for the ideas and opinions of others, extreme partisanship, and zero-sum thinking; the idea that to "win" means the other person has to "lose." Zero-sum thinking rejects a "win-win" or "compromise" goal of negotiation.

The need to be "right" also tends to create single-party autocratic political governments, and it encourages the fascist tendency to deflect by creating false narratives that demonize *others* as *the evil enemy.*

The primitive ego's need to be "right" aggressively destroys the primary goal of a healthy human civilization: the goal to become a just, evolved, mature, intelligent, self-aware species. Our global ability to engage in essential debate on the causes, consequences, and responses required to deal with climate change issues, global warming, wealth inequality, and social justice are essentially trapped in a need to be "right" political and legislative gridlock, nationally and globally.

The need to be "right" works to undermine attempts to create national or global cultures in which people feel as if they belong and have a voice… regardless of the color of their skin, their political ideologies, their religion, their country of origin, or their sex. The aggressive need to be "right" quite literally creates all of the "ism's" that plague our world, including sexism, racism, capitalism, terrorism, Judaism, Buddhism, nationalism, realism, feminism, activism, Catholicism, individualism, socialism, conservatism, and liberalism.

The need to be "right" feeds the growth of animosity and hate, destroys the ability for cooperative interactions with others, and dangerously undermines both community and nations' social stability and resilience.

Resilience requires the intentional creation of social cohesion, tolerance, and acceptance that can only be created by communities and culture's that have intentionally awakened and tamed their collective primitive ego-consciousness and their childhood conditioned and immature knee-jerk need to be "right."

The Need to be Right Plucks the Chicken One Feather at a Time

When "tribal" political leaders begin to undermine the public's trust in the press, the judicial system, Congress, the Federal Government, or the Supreme Court, the public stops paying attention. They know their vote doesn't count anyway, so they disengage. Mussolini said it best when he said, "If you pluck a chicken one feather at a time, no one will notice." The foundational principles of our global democracies are currently being plucked one feather at a time, and the public is not paying attention.

The political need to be "right" is creating global chaos and blinding the global "commons" in nations around the world to the reality that their rights are being removed one feather at a time by the growing power of autocratic leaders; leaders who are using the fascist playbook to create enemy "others" as a way to distract.

During a national or global crisis, polarized ideological political thinking based on the need to be "right" is extremely dangerous. The total focus of global politicians and our social media should be focused on protecting the people. When autocratically inclined national leaders disseminate disinformation or fake news, it shuts down the public's ability to cope effectively and intelligently with national issues and global threats.

This reality was evident in the early stages of the COVID-19 pandemic, when the political need to be "right" in many nations seriously hampered our global ability to deal with the power of a coronavirus pandemic that propagated exponentially. And the need to be "right" continued to impede our global ability to limit the exponential contagion of COVID-19 when it continued to spread exponentially in mid-2020. Global deaths crossed the one million figure and the need to be "right" still had humanity unable to effectively implement the guidelines that could reverse the spread of COVID-19.

The primitive ego's need to be "right" has shut down our ability as a species to cope with the significant threat of COVID-19. Seeing the world through a red or blue, either/or need to be politically "right" thinking, simply creates an existentially dangerous lack of cooperation and an inability to embrace a middlepath thinking process that intentionally searches for the truths on both sides of every issue.

Threats like COVID-19 are not a culture war; they are a planetary war on humanity. And the need to be "right" has humanity currently losing that war.

Fake News and the Need to be "Right": The Decline and Erosion of Global Democracies

Political leaders and media that *intentionally* propagate fake news or disinformation in a national emergency are a significant and serious threat to national security. During a crisis, fake news and disinformation are tools of war. They create confusion and shut down the collective decision-making ability of a nation as they propagate by social media through the consciousness of a nation's thinking like an aggressive chemical weapon. Fake news and disinformation quietly pluck the ability to think clearly and make the critical decisions that are needed—*one fake feather at a time!*

When the *primary* force-multipliers discussed in this book create the conditions for social and civil collapse, that "collapse" will encourage those in power to further exploit the social trauma and increase their political power by turning people against one another to rally support for their self-serving agendas. Fascism, and autocratic politicians, use the collective primitive ego's need to be "right" playbook of *us versus them* politics to accrue power.[45] And we are seeing this dangerous and growing reality around the world and in the developed nations.

When national and state governments are financially stressed, ideologically rigid political and multinational corporate forces quietly work to deregulate, open public lands, ignore legal protections, exploit labor and

---

45 How Fascism Works: The Politics of Us vs. Them. Amy Goodman, www.democracynow.org.

natural resources, privatize critical natural resources, and replace cooperative globalization efforts with nationalist authoritarian leaders and governments that *promise* to restore their country to prosperity and greatness by expelling immigrants, ignoring the disastrous costs of fossil energy impacts on the climate, and increase military spending.

These fascist-leaning *promises* only tend to make the problems worse, since the financial benefits of those "promises" are intentionally designed to flow to the wealthy elite, not the commons. Autocratic leaders exploit the polarized political chaos created by the rigid political need to be "right" thinking. It provides them with a host of ready-made dangerous "others" on their journey toward power…one dangerous "other" feather at a time.

Autocratic leaders create a new crisis every day to distract. They blame the dangerous "others" for creating the problems that everyone should be focused on! They use the fascist playbook of polarized political ideologies to delegitimize elections, the media, and the press. They call honest errors a conspiracy. They intentionally distort information as a "systemic conspiracy" to distract people's attention from *their own* performance/problems. Stated simply, they *deliberately* use the need to be "right" to increase ideologically rigid political chaos. When political leaders use a need to be "right" thinking to critique and blame the media, it is the first step toward a state-controlled press. One distracting feather at a time.

The Need to Be "Right" Fans the Flame of Social and Civil Collapse

Insecurity and the need to be "right" make people susceptible to the false narratives of governments and autocratic leaders that attempt to blame "others" for the problems. Insecure and disempowered people can easily be turned toward anger and extremism, populism, polarized ideological tribal thinking, lack of compassion, increased "What's in it for me?" competition, and irrational fear of immigrants, and they are easily manipulated by false narratives designed to increase their sense of fear and insecurity. All of these dangerous emotions are created and supported by our collective, unevolved, immature, primitive ego's human need to be "right." Anything we see or hear long enough, including lies and distortions, eventually become "normal" one feather at a time. The plucking quietly continues one feather at a time, and nobody notices or pays attention. They are too distracted by the angst created by their ideological-political need to be right. And that angst includes the growing sense of social and civil collapse.

As I said at the beginning of this chapter, I consider the immature, unevolved, primitive ego's need to be "right" to be the most destructive, the most dangerous, and the most common, primitive ego belief embedded in our collective human consciousness. It needs to be tamed and evolved intentionally "now." Waiting is no longer an option. The longer we wait, the stronger the global autocratic leaders will become, and the weaker our multinational democracies will become. Humanity is not on a sustainable or viable path. And the future we are headed toward is not the future "it used to be."

The Need to Be "Right" Creates Dangerous Cognitive Dissonance... Another Tool of Autocratic Leaders

A primary danger embedded in the primitive ego's need to be "right" is its ability to create cognitive dissonance or "confirmation bias." Cognitive dissonance is the inability of a person to take in or look for information that might conflict with their personal beliefs, or the collective beliefs of their ideological "tribe." When their ideological tribe supports a person's need to be "right," it gives that person permission to be more aggressive and rigid when defending their beliefs.

When autocratically inclined leaders promote intentionally distorted information or promote ideologically extreme polarizing tribal beliefs, cognitive dissonance will quickly shut down the ability of people in that national or political tribe to search for or believe any information, or any source of information, that might conflict with their beliefs or the collective beliefs of their tribe.

The cognitive dissonance created by the collective primitive ego's need to be "right" gives autocratic leaders and governments an immense and dangerous power. They can pluck the feathers of their followers by the handful without anyone noticing or caring. This is especially true when autocratic leaders begin promoting conspiracy claims designed to intentionally target "others" as dangerous deep-state threats to the nation and the members of the leader's ideological tribe.

We see this dangerous trend increasing around the world. When social and civil unrest and collapse arrive, the power of autocratic leaders will increase dramatically.

Conspiracy theory threats are currently threatening the November 2020 national election results in the U.S. The latest conspiracy theory being promoted by the U.S. president, and adopted by his follower base, is the belief that mail-in ballots intended to protect low-income and disadvantaged voters during a pandemic would be hacked and threaten the validity of the election. Cognitive dissonance in his base will make refuting this dangerous conspiracy claim challenging despite the reality that undermining an election's validity is extremely dangerous to a democracy. It existentially undermines the electorate's trust in its government, "the" core foundational resilience and fundamental norm of democracy. Unproven conspiracy theories, and the failure to effectively contain the COVID-19 pandemic, has democracy in America walking a very precarious and uncertain path.

The loss of trust in governments around the globe is growing.

Social and civil unrest is growing globally.

The primary force multipliers we examined in the chapters above are (a) dramatically increasing the potential for social and civil collapse and (b) they are growing in strength rapidly.

Each of these warning signs are created and supported by humanity's collective primitive ego-consciousness, and it's need to be "right."

The need to be "right" is the most destructive childhood belief and conditioning unconsciously embedded in primitive-ego thinking and humanity's collective consciousness. It could be included as a primary force-multiplier in this book. The reason it's not, is because all of the *primary* force multipliers in this book are inevitable. They *will* eventually happen.

The need to be "right," however, is a choice in that it *can* be intentionally tamed. Unfortunately, it's highly likely it will continue to be an existentially dangerous and powerful secondary force-multiplier given the reality that not many persons will choose to awaken their consciousness and intentionally tame their immature primitive ego. But it's not inevitable.

Like the choice we have to awaken and avoid the extinction of humanity, it's a personal choice we *can* make.

The future is always a choice, not a given...until we run out of time.

Don't Push the River: The Water Always Wins

One of my favorite quotes is from the unique and gifted writer Richard Stine, who wrote, "My experiment right now is to attempt to lessen the emotional complications by communicating as simply as I can. To try not to feel that I have to attack or be defensive when I have to deal with a tough situation or a situation that challenges my beliefs. To just express the truth as I see it, and then let things develop the way they will, without trying to force them one way or another."[46]

Psychologist Jordon Peterson offers similar advice when he says, "Always speak your truth. Not *the* truth. *Your* truth. And when people stop listening, stop talking."[47]

The wisdom contained these quotes is the warning to pay attention to our own "need to be right." In other words, don't aggressively defend your beliefs. When you do, your aggressive energy and attitude will trigger the other

---

46   The Art World of Richard Stine, Welcome Enterprises, Inc. New York, 1994.

47   12 Rules for Life: An Antidote for Chaos. Psychologist Jordan Peterson, Random House Canada, 2018.

person's defensive need to be right. Our words and our attitude matter. Use science, data, and facts as a tool to direct attention, *not a weapon.*

And listen to Stine and Peterson. Their advice will protect you from the tendency to create aggressive "tribal cognitive dissonance" in those you are talking with. They will help you avoid the stressful angst that you will create for *yourself and the person you are talking with* if you attempt to push the river and convince them that you are right, and they and their tribe are wrong. The temptation to slide into a need-to-be right behavior and emotional attitude is deeply embedded in our unconscious primitive ego and its early-child-hood conditioning.

Like the teachings of wisdom teachers throughout history, both of these quotes encourage us to tame our primitive ego's unconscious early-childhood conditioning. When we feel ourselves getting angry or defensive when someone disagrees with us, simply pay attention. Remind ourselves it's only our child-hood primitive ego's need to be right that's getting triggered. Quietly remind yourself, "There is always truth on both sides of every subject, and no one is smart enough, or dumb enough to be right or wrong 100% of the time." And that includes *you* and *me.*

The intentional ignorance created by cognitive dissonance is always *dangerous,* and it's *never* helpful. Be a middlepath thinker who actively searches for the truths always found on both sides of every issue. Life will be a lot less stressful when we stop pushing the river.

People will be who they *are.* So just flow with that reality. When you attempt to push the river, you will only create conflict and defensive anger. Data matters. Facts matter. And truth matters. And they will always be the last realities standing when the dust settles. So don't push the river. Simply state your position, and when others stop listening, stop talking.

And keep in mind whenever we wrestle with the rightness or wrongness of a belief that *the other person or we hold,* remember to *focus on the "why" of the belief.* Why do I believe my belief to be true? Why does the other person think their belief is true? Don't focus on the rightness or wrongness of the belief itself.

The "why" of the belief will shift the conversation from the need to be "right" to a deeper and more gentle understanding of how we each came to hold our different beliefs. Knowing the "why" of a belief will help us sort through the consequences the belief is creating or will create in our life...and our future decisions.

Remind yourself of the reality that a river *always* finds its way around an obstacle, focusing on the "why" of our beliefs will give us new paths around the rocks of conflict that our primitive ego's need to be "right" creates when it takes over the conversation.

Conflict is simply another way to describe the reality we create when we attempt to push the river and insist on being right.

The need to be "*right*" and cognitive dissonance (a) *always* create intentional ignorance and (b) they *always* "push the river".

Secondary Force-Multiplier #2:
The Illusion of Separateness Shuts Down our Ability
to Embrace Systemic Thinking

The primary primitive ego belief that interferes with our collective human ability to intuitively embrace the concept of systemic thinking is our ego's illusion from early childhood that we are a *unique self* that is totally *separate* from the rest of creation or reality; the illusion that we are a separate *me,* and everything else in the created universe is *other* or *"not me."* Stated simply, the illusion of separateness turns everything in the universe into *"other".*

This dangerous, primitive ego illusion of *separateness* from the rest of reality shuts down our ability to both emotionally and logically embrace the concept of *"we-ness."* We understand that unlimited growth on a limited planet makes sense logically. It just doesn't apply to us emotionally. To understand how this contradiction is even possible, we have to understand the power of childhood conditioning.

Early Childhood Conditioning

The primary task of our young childhood ego was our focus on developing a strong sense of *self*...and then protecting that fragile sense of self from anything that would in any way threaten our sense of self. An excellent example of a defense from a threat to our sense of self is the primitive ego's need to be "right" as a way to avoid criticism. The need to be right also created our childhood ego's tendency to "split" the world into the simple categories of either/or, good/bad, and right/wrong. This primitive ego tendency for "either/or" splitting" was emotionally reinforced and supported by the primitive ego illusion that "me" was totally separate from the rest of the *"not me"* reality. Stated simply, the illusion of separateness and the need to be *"right"* worked together to create a view of reality that protected our childhood ego's fragile sense of self.

From childhood on, the illusion of separateness became a primary focus of our primitive ego. It created our narcissistic sense of entitlement and our obsessive focus *me, mine,* how *I* feel, what *I* want, when *I* want it, what *I* like, what *I* dislike, getting *more* than someone else, getting *better* than someone else, and being *first*. As we grew older, this sense of narcissistic entitlement turned into a focus on "immediate gratification" and a total disregard for the "not- me-ness" of nature, the planet, the planet's ecosystems, other life forms, and future generations.

As adults, we claim to care about others and the planet. However, our unconscious primitive ego, and its narcissistic childhood conditioning, are still in control of most people's actions and behaviors. The reality of this claim is seen clearly in the fact that very few people are willing to embrace the *changes* and *sacrifices* that would be required to actively care for *"other"*...the planet, future generations, the needs of others who live someplace else, those who believe differently, those who talk a different language, those who practice a different religion, those whose color of skin is different from ours...the narcissistic list of *"other"* is endless.

Until enough of us *intentionally* tame our primitive ego and embrace *systemic thinking* and evolve our thinking to include the "we-ness" of social justice, the well-being of others, and emotionally recognize that we are all interconnected and interdependent on one another...*our immature and unevolved collective human primitive ego will continue to be the most dangerous, narcissistically self-focused, entitled, need-to-be-right, secondary force-multiplier threat on the planet.*

When we empathically care for others, we acknowledge the simple reality that caring reveals our interconnected, mutual belonging. It is impossible to empathically care for another that we do not feel mutually connected with. And we can't fake that empathy because our "me-ness" sense of entitlement and actions will quickly reveal our narcissistic illusion of separateness and our emotional lack of interconnection, interdependence, and a "we-ness" sense of systemic belonging with "other."

Empathic caring and compassion for others reveal the presence of an internal, relational self that is authentically interdependent and systemically interconnected with the reality of the world that surrounds us.

Without a sense of systemic interconnectedness and an intimate understanding of belonging *with* nature, our collective primitive ego illusion of separateness will continue to treat the world we live on and its life-supporting gifts as objects or "its" to be mindlessly used and discarded.

The primitive ego illusion of *separateness* and the primitive ego's need to be right are destroying our planet and our future survival as a species.

A golden arch of this book is my belief that if the human species does not begin the task of collectively and *intentionally taming and evolving our narcissistic, self-focused, entitled, immature, primitive ego thinking,* and starting that work *now,* the extinction of humanity in the near future is all but certain.

We are an invasive species devouring and consuming the life-supporting gifts that nature has provided us. We treat nature as an *it* or *other* that we are not connected with or an integral part of. The biological world would define us as a dangerous and malignant cancer. Nature has a long history of eliminating invasive species, and she is beginning to show us her anger. If we fail to embrace systemic thinking, understand that we are an integral part of this planet's ecosystem, and learn to work sustainably with nature, she *will* win the war.

Denial of this obvious reality is existentially dangerous, intentionally ignorant, Tinker Bell thinking.

Population growth, declining biodiversity, climate change, global heating, unsustainable marine fisheries, ocean dead zones, declining aquifers, declining freshwater availability, ice cap melting, ocean water levels increasing, increasing storm intensification, droughts, flooding, forest fires, rising heat waves, irreversible tipping points—climate scientist warnings have me wondering how many examples will it take for humanity to pay attention and recognize how systemically interconnected and interdependent we are with our planet, with others, and with reality?

Unpacking the Concept of Systemic Thinking: The Butterfly Metaphor

To ensure our future as a species means we have to change how we live and learn to embrace systemic thinking. That includes the reality that *everything* in the created universe is interconnected and interdependent on everything else in the universe. It also includes the reality that human cultures and human civilization are examples of extremely complex and systemically interconnected global social and economic systems. A human system comprised of complex environmental, economic, social, geopolitical, cultural, and civilizational interconnections that all feed into and interact with one another. Systemic thinking means embracing the reality that every action, and every impact we make on this planet as an invasive species, *will* directly impact every other part of this complex life support system we casually refer to as nature. *And that includes recognizing that every change and impact we are currently creating in the complex system called nature will eventually and directly impact our ability to continue as a viable species on this planet.*

When complex global systemic social and economic structures are over-stressed, those systemically interconnected and interdependent structures will be vulnerable to the likelihood of self-reinforcing cascading collapse. And when those complex, interconnected and interdependent systems begin to collapse, that collapse will be virtually impossible to stop. We need to acknowledge that reality and begin now to prepare for what scientist Jem Bendell refers to as "deep adaptation." Preparation and deep adaptation for the massive changes that are coming will help humanity, especially younger generations, begin building the resilience they will need to survive those changes.

Systemic thinking embraces the concept that the wings of a butterfly flapping on the other side of the planet could eventually impact the entire planet's weather.[48] This butterfly metaphor is a helpful way to think about the concept of complex global systemic thinking.

Our global social, civil, and economic systems are a complex collection of interconnected, infinitely complex, butterflies interacting together in a way that produces something more significant than the sum of its parts. And no part of a complex system ever stands alone.

For example, when we begin the transition to a post-growth or powered-down economy, *every* aspect of our global human civilization, and *every* aspect of our global human culture, will be impacted and a part of that transition.

Systemic thinking requires critical thinking and the ability to look seven or more generations into the future; the ability to think and imagine the impact our actions will have on the yet to be born and unborn, the human and the non-human, and look below the surface of things to understand how things work.[49] Stated simply, *it is impossible to address a crisis in one part of a complex system without including **all** of the other parts.* Complex systems require complex solutions when a crisis or problem emerges. Simplistic, one-dimensional strategies are incapable of solving complex systemic crises, and they can significantly aggravate them.

---

48   https://copyblogger.com/butterfly-effect-environment/.

49   Article: Systems Thinking and How It Can Help Build a Sustainable World, Megan Seibert, resilience.org, 7/12/18.

When we tip into social and civil collapse, it won't be a single black swan COVID-19 coronavirus that creates that collapse. The black swan event will simply be *"the"* triggering shock that overstressed the global economy and sped up the collapse of the *already* fragile systems and *unstable* conditions we created over decades of immature, unevolved primitive ego thinking; including the Tinker Bell illusion that we were somehow separate from all of those life-supporting resources that we were polluting and over-consuming in our pursuit of unlimited growth...on a separate, "not *me*," limited planet.

The longer we put off dealing with the inevitable social and civil collapse that is coming, the steeper the descent will be for human civilization. The sooner we recognize our systemic interdependence with the rest of reality and do the work of maturing and evolving our collective primitive ego human consciousness, the more likely we will be able to prepare for and survive that now-inevitable collapse.

We need to develop better a more holistic and systemic understanding of the interconnected, unpredictable, and uncontrollable butterfly complexity of the world we live in. We need to tame our primitive ego-consciousness from its narcissistic focus on "me and mine" and evolve a more mature and collective focus on "we" and "us." And we need to do it *now*, because we are rapidly running out of time. And waiting is no longer an option.

Secondary Force Multiplier #3:
The Illusion of Separateness Shuts Down our Ability to Understand Nature as Systemically Embedded Spirit

The primitive ego illusion of separateness virtually ignores what quantum physicists have discovered on the quantum level. Current scientific research shows us that every aspect of creation, down to the smallest energy particle, actively communicates and continuously shares information with every other part of creation *regardless of the distance between them!*

Nature is simply chemistry, biology, and physics that function systemically inside the laws of the physical universe. Nature does whatever chemistry, biology, and physics dictate. Her response will be determined by how much we pollute our planet and how much we heat the planet by the carbon emissions we pump into the atmosphere. But most importantly, we need to continually remind ourselves that nature always gets to bat last, and because she always bats a thousand, *she* will win, not humanity. It is also essential to remember that nature has several billion years of experience dealing with invasive species.

We need to reimagine a sustainable global economy based on the enlightened wisdom of ancient indigenous cultures: Their ability see "spirit" embedded in all of creation; the wisdom to embrace systemic thinking, and intentionally protect the well-being and health of all living systems for seven generations into the future.

I talked briefly about this subject in the chapter on neoliberal capitalism. Still, I will expand on the concept here since it is relevant to secondary force-multiplier impacts and the primitive ego illusion of separateness that we are talking about.

The collective primitive ego illusion of separateness and our current obsessive, greed-based accumulation of wealth and power called business-as-usual has our species on the fast track to extinction. We need to recover that ancient indigenous wisdom and the ability of those ancient indigenous cultures to promote the common good and maintain their cultural integrity for thousands of years. To those indigenous cultures, nature was a "thou" that contained the essence of "spirit" in every aspect of reality. *They embraced nature as an ecologically sustainable and interconnected living network of interdependent systemic relationships.*

The indigenous embrace of "spirit" in all of reality was not "religious." It was systemic thinking. Those ancient indigenous cultures simply recognized, honored, and protected the systemic interdependence and interconnected "thou" embedded and present in all of reality for seven generations into the future.

We need to reclaim that wisdom and intentionally tame our primitive ego's illusion of separateness. We need to acknowledge the reality that we, too, are an integral part of the interconnected planetary web of life. The future survival of our species is existentially dependent on a vibrant and healthy planet, and a "well-being" quality of life for *all* living systems.

For example, poisoning our pollinating honeybees into extinction (which we are currently doing) is not a problem. It is an existential crisis that could critically impact global food supplies, create global hunger, create social and civil collapse, rapidly end life as we know it, and threaten the possible extinction of our species on this planet.

Creating Our Future

When we talk about wholeness or systemic thinking, it's helpful to remind ourselves that we are a co-creative conscious species that can plan and think and dream about possibilities. We can create the things we think about. We can imagine and then create what we imagine. And we *are* capable of *creating* the futures we can imagine. We have been given that amazing and incredible gift. Stated simply, we are co-creators with the spirit of the Creator that began this universe; a universe comprised of trillions of stars and galaxies. A universe grounded in the incredible reality of *never-ending change, evolution, and endless becoming.*

And we have been given all those co-creative gifts. It's time we began to embrace our collective ability to create a future that embraces an evolved and tamed primitive ego consciousness. I know of no better definition of hope than the possibility that we could actually achieve that future if enough of us rolled up our sleeves and began the intentional awakening and growth in self-awareness work that needs to be done. The creator of this universe has already given us the incredible tools and ability to do this work. I have to imagine the Creator might be getting impatient that it's taken us so long to recognize that simple reality.

**Our planet is not merely a "thing" that needs protecting.
It is a living "ecosystem" that needs protecting.**

It is a living organism, not unlike our human body. Our planet and our human body are both comprised of an almost infinite number of pieces and parts that all have to co-exist and work together cooperatively to stay healthy and functioning. Like our human body, our planet is a *whole* that systemically connects a virtually infinite number of pieces and parts that all have to be healthy and cooperatively co-exist for it to survive.

People say that living organisms cooperate, but they also compete with one another for survival. So how does that fit with our body metaphor?

The answer is every part competes for the resources it needs to survive, *but it does not use more than it needs*. It does not hoard the body's resources. It does not prevent other parts of the body from accessing the resources they too require to survive. In other words, the pieces and parts of our body all work and co-exist cooperatively together. The same is true for our planet.

And this metaphor also holds a sobering reality for both our planet and our human body. When any organ or part of our body begins to hoard or devour resources needed by other organs, we refer to that as cancer. When we relate that to our planet's ecosystem, humanity has become an invasive form of cancer inside our planet's ecosystem that is hoarding and devouring resources required by our planet's ecosystems in order to survive.

We have become an invasive species!

And like our human body, that cancer has to be removed, or the planet dies. If our species is to survive, we must intentionally embrace the concept that we are only part of the larger living organism or ecosystem we call nature. And every part of that living organism called nature has to survive and thrive to ensure the health and survival of our human species.

Why Is This Indigenous Way of Thinking So Important?

So why am I spending so much time talking about the primitive ego's illusion of *separateness* and our primitive ego's *need to be right*? Why is the indigenous belief that spirit is systemically embedded in all of nature so important?

I am convinced that the *primitive ego illusion of separateness* is the primary belief in the collective human consciousness that is shutting down our ability as a species to embrace the indigenous wisdom that our planet is a complex, systemically interconnected, and interdependent living system. And our primitive ego's need to be "right" is the primary belief in the collective human consciousness that shuts down our ability as a species to creatively dialog together and cooperate when we are confronted with a crisis that requires cooperation.

I am convinced that unless we tame and evolve and mature these two primary primitive ego beliefs from our early childhood conditioning, *and do that taming soon*, the extinction of our species is all but certain. Our planet is not merely a "thing" that needs protecting. It is a living ecosystem that needs protecting. It is a living organism.

Our planetary life support system's collapse is accelerating rapidly due to humanity's invasive inability to think systemically. We are *not* a separate, stand-alone, self-reliant part of our planetary living ecosystem, and we are not always "right." It's time we grew up and became a more evolved species. We have the power to co-create using our brains, but unless we intentionally tame those two *existentially dangerous* primitive ego beliefs, we will become an extinct footnote in the history of our planet.

We are a species that no longer honors the systemic interconnectedness of reality.

We believe we can continue to massively overexploit our planet's fragile ecosystems and continue to pollute the planet's critical air and water life-support systems, the very systems that support human life on this planet. How we move forward as a species is *our decision* to make.

The choice is ours, but we are rapidly running out of time to act. Waiting is no longer an option.

I will leave this subject with one of my favorite comments on systemic thinking and the interconnected and interdependent unity of all of creation by Thich Nhat Hanh.

Be One With The Leaf

I asked the leaf whether it was frightened because it was autumn and the other leaves were falling.

The leaf told me, "No. During the whole spring and summer I was completely alive. I worked hard to help nourish the tree, and now much of me is in the tree. I am not limited by this form. I am also the whole tree, and when I go back to the soil, I will continue nourish the tree. So I don't worry at all. As I leave this branch and float to the ground, I will wave to the tree and tell her, 'I will see you again very soon.'

That day there was a wind blowing and, after a while, I saw the leaf leave the branch and float down to the soil, dancing joyfully, because as it floated it saw itself already there in the tree. It was so happy. I bowed my head, knowing that I have a lot to learn from the leaf."

"… So please continue to look back and you will see that you have always been here. Let us look together and penetrate into the life of a leaf, so we may be one with the leaf. Let us penetrate and be one with the cloud or with the wave, to realize our own nature as water and be free from our fear. If we look very deeply, we will transcend birth and death.

Tomorrow, I will continue to be. But you will have to be very attentive to see me. I will be a flower, or a leaf. I will be in these forms and I will say hello to you. If you are attentive enough, you will recognize me, and you may greet me. I will be very happy. Thich Nhat Hanh

Secondary Force-Multiplier #4:
Exponential Growth and the Unevolved Primitive Ego's Inability to Embrace Limits

The massive inability of humanity to embrace the reality of *"limits"* and internalize the dangers of *exponential growth* even when exceeding those limits is existentially life-threatening to the future of our species, is directly supported by (a) the unevolved primitive ego illusion of "separateness" and (b) the cognitive dissonance created by the collective primitive ego's need to be "right" that we discussed above.

We understand it logically, but we can't emotionally embrace it because we are trapped by cognitive dissonance in the greed-based "What's in it for me?" narrative" and the lifetime conditioning of unlimited economic growth. That's the economic "religion" that we have been brainwashed into believing. Economists have convinced us that economic growth can and *will* continue forever.

Unfortunately, as we saw in Chapter 3, our complex neoliberal global economy is extremely vulnerable to the Seneca collapse; the Seneca Curve concept that things go up slowly but collapse rapidly cannot be embraced *emotionally* because of cognitive dissonance. The notion of systemic economic collapse violates the primitive ego belief that economic growth will grow forever *despite the fact that "forever growth" is, by definition, exponential growth.*

Keep in mind the exponential growth teaching story I included in the introduction about a very large "stadium" where the ancients gathered for festivals. It illustrates very clearly the danger of exponential growth. One of the ancients was bound for a seat at the top of the stadium. Then a magic water dropper put one drop of water on the floor of the stadium. A minute later, it put two drops of water on the floor. At minute three, it put four drops of water. At minute four, it put eight drops. At minute five, it put 16 drops. This process *continued to exponentially double the number of drops each minute.* At minute 45, the stadium was still 97% free of water. The man at the top of the stadium drowned at minute 50. If you use a hand calculator to multiply one by two, then two by two, then four by two, then eight by two, then sixteen by two, and so on, most small calculators can't do this accurately past about the twentieth time you multiply by two! That's exponential growth.

The reason I include this story is that most people shake their heads when I share this story. Or they remind me that there is no such thing as a magic water dropper. Others reach for a hand calculator to see if my information is credible. And this story is only about a doubling fifty times.

COVID-19 is a coronavirus that grows exponentially. But despite warning after warning by the health professionals about the incredible danger of exponential growth, most people still refused to wear masks. As I write this chapter, the contagion of COVID-19 is growing exponentially in most areas of the world.

As we take a realistic look in the following material about what *limits* and *exponential growth* would mean for our future, keep in mind what we've discussed regarding the existential threats posed by primary and secondary force-multipliers.

Concrete and Practical Examples of the Need for Limits and the Costs of Exponential, Never-Ending Growth

Reality A: Anything that grows at two percent a year, doubles in size in 35 years. Two-percent growth was considered anemic before COVID-19 arrived. Five percent was considered *normal* and is the goal that *business-as-usual* would like to get back to as soon as possible.

Reality B: If two-percent growth doubles our current economy in 35 years, that would mean

doubling the current level of oil extraction in the next three decades, current agricultural output, current manufacturing, and present CO_2 emissions pollution. And then doubling again to four times the size of *today's* economy in the next 35 years!

Reality C: Three percent growth = doubling the current economy in 24 years, 4.2% growth = doubling the current economy in 17 years, and 5%

growth = doubling the current economy in 14 years (and quadrupling our current economy in 28 years).

Reality D: We need a 50% reduction in CO2 emissions in the next ten years, that is, by 2030, to hold global warming to 2°C. (2°C is currently considered to be existentially threatening and is considered by many scientists to be an extremely conservative estimate of severity. Many scientists believe we are already committed to 3°C or higher, and that's not including unavoidable, non-reversible tipping points.)

Reality E: Sixty percent of mammals, birds, fish, and reptiles have been eradicated since 1970.

Reality F: Unlimited growth represents a gross and total rejection of climate science and systemic thinking.

Reality G: Unlimited growth is the narcissistic primitive ego greed-based drug addiction to never-ending *more.*

Reality H: Scientists are alarmed and are warning that the natural world is crumbling under the *current* and *growing* weight of unlimited economic expansion.

Reality I: We need to *relearn* how to keep ourselves alive and healthy ***without:***

a. The *never-ending growth* embedded in neoliberal capitalism.

b. The *unlimited extraction* of non-renewable natural resources.

c. Without a *never-ending increase* in the consumption of atmospheric-polluting fossil fuel energy.

It's hard to believe our collective species could ignore the dangers and threats we are creating for the future survival of our species as we continue to embrace the concept of *unlimited economic expansion on a limited planet.*

Those exploring that sobering reality tend to assume that we are somehow overwhelming people with facts instead of making the dangers more personal, that is, more likely to directly impact them personally in the near future. But that assumption doesn't seem to support the human behavior observed in COVID-19 and the overwhelming resistance to wearing a mask even though *not* wearing a mask and COVID-19 is about as personal and *personally threatening* in the near future as you can get. And yet the resistance to wearing a mask has grown, not diminished in the last few months as I write this material in September 2020.

The inability of our collective human consciousness to internalize the dangers of unlimited exponential growth on a limited planet and its refusal to limit the extraction of non-renewable resources to support that unlimited profit and wealth are not limits easily embraced in the human consciousness. They are the results of humanity's untamed, immature, and unevolved childhood conditioning illusion of separateness, the need to be *"right,"* the inability to understand systemic thinking, and the inability to accept exponential growth or the reality of limits on a limited planet.

To understand how this resistance to the dangers and threats we are creating to the future survival of our species is possible, we have to revisit cognitive dissonance. In other words, it's not an inherent human inability. *It's simply an unwillingness to entertain any thoughts or ideas, including beliefs that would conflict with the primitive ego's "What's in it for me?" entitlement and greed.* They are simply ideas that, if consciously embraced, would directly conflict with our primitive ego's childhood belief that happiness in life is getting *more.* More of *everything...even if that denial of unlimited growth is destroying our planet.* In the case of resistance to masks, it is the belief that a mask is a threat to *their entitled* "personal freedoms and rights."

The resistance to logic and limits does not have to be reasonable or logical. It only has to conflict with a firmly held belief—and when it does, cognitive dissonance and the need to be "right" takes over even when the consequences are the destruction of the planet, possible extinction, or catching a coronavirus in the middle of a global pandemic.

I have included these primitive ego beliefs in the *secondary* force-multiplier list to illustrate how powerful these immature, unevolved primitive-ego childhood beliefs are in their ability to ignore reality, even when that reality is life-threatening.

Cognitive dissonance, the inability to embrace the concept of limits, the inability to embrace systemic thinking, and the inability to internalize the dangers of unlimited exponential growth on a limited planet are excellent examples of intentional ignorance embraced by humanity's unevolved, immature primitive ego consciousness.

The only viable awakened path forward that does not threaten humanity's future survival needs to include the *intentional* taming and evolution of our collective primitive ego-consciousness and preparing for the existential changes that are coming by creating the self-reliant local communities of Part 3. Even in a local community, however, the members of those local communities would need to have *intentionally* tamed their *collective* primitive ego-consciousness for those self-reliant local communities to survive long term.

A self-reliant local community could likely survive the social and civil collapse of our human culture as we know it, but an unevolved collective primitive-ego thinking in the community would eventually destroy the community's ability to embrace the consensus decision-making that would be required to collectively and successfully solve the life-threatening challenges they would be facing to survive for more than a few years into the future.

Immature primitive ego "What's in it for me?" greed, the illusion of separateness, the need be "right," and the fear of "other" would eventually destroy the community's ability to work cooperatively with one another.

Secondary Force Multiplier #5:
Food Shortages, Population Growth, Wealth Inequality, and the Lack of Social Justice

The secondary force-multipliers listed above could easily be included in the list of *primary* force-multipliers. The only reason I have them in the *secondary* force-multiplier list is the fact that food shortages, population growth, wealth inequality, and lack of social justice are the primary vulnerabilities and embedded fractures in the social and civil structures and institutions of humanity that *will* ultimately ensure the inevitable social and civil collapse of human culture and human civilization as we know it when the *primary* existential force-multipliers reach their critical irreversible tipping points.

When the Commons Get Desperate and Hungry, They *"Will"* Take to the Streets

We have used the immature thinking of our childhood conditioning to create our modern human civilization. We assume we are separate from the rest of reality. We have used greed to construct our global economic systems. The primitive ego's need to be "right" creates aggressive ideological polarization and shuts down our ability to negotiate and cooperate with others. Most importantly, we have disenfranchised and exploited 90% of the human population as we have created massive wealth inequality for the 1% elite.

Here are some examples.

- Even before COVID-19 arrived, nearly 40% of Americans would struggle to cover an unexpected $400 expense, according to a new report by the Federal Reserve—a stark reminder of many people's anxiety and financial insecurity even during average pre-COVID-19 economic growth.

- Nearly three in ten (28%) of U.S. adults **have no emergency savings**, according to Bankrate's latest Financial Security Index. One in four **have** a rainy-day **fund**, but not enough money to cover three months' worth of living expenses.

- One-third of homeowners have less than $500 in savings, and nothing set aside for an emergency home repair, according to a report released Wednesday, and that includes 50% of homeowners with an annual household income of less than $50,000.

- There's growing concern and anxiety among many Americans that the economy won't restart from COVID-19 in time to save them from delinquent rent or mortgage payments or going hungry.

- Some 38% of Americans could not come up with $500 in cash without selling something or taking out a loan, and one in ten are planning to withdraw from their emergency (retirement) savings to pay bills during the COVID-19 economic impact.

- Nearly 25% of all Americans had no emergency savings and 16% have taken on more debt, and nearly one-third of American households report significantly lower income since the start of the pandemic.

- Income inequality is at its highest level in 50 years, and COVID-19 is just getting started.

- Today, fewer than 1% of the world's population owns more than 50% of "all" wealth. And that 1% number is continuing to grow smaller.

- Wealth inequality and poverty increase food shortages, crop failures, mass starvation, and mass migrations. As of this writing, in 2020, 130 million people are lacking adequate food, access to clean water, and facing death from starvation.

Given that many of these statistics reflect life in the richest nation on the planet, the future collapse of our global social and civil institutions are all but certain. Our immature primitive ego thinking has created international economic, political, and social structures that are too fragile to survive the primary and secondary force-multipliers that are coming. They are already significantly stressed due to COVID-19.

As the impacts of climate change continue to increase, global food shortages are going to increase. Life is going to get significantly more challenging as food supplies decline and fossil energy reductions increase. Food shortages will be a significant secondary force multiplier on the fragile global structures that humanity depends on for survival.

When food shortages become severe enough, they will increase the potential for mass migration and the likelihood of major social unrest. These realities are already being experienced in many nations around the world as COVID-19 creates increased unemployment, reduced income, and increased debt. And again, COVID-19 and the social unrest it is already creating *is just getting started*. A post-CPVID-19 world is months or even years in the future. Economic recovery from COVID-19 is expected to take years, not months.

The social and civil impacts of global climate change, global population growth, and the global lack of social justice are already here. They just aren't distributed equally *yet*.

When the commons get desperate and hungry, they *will* take to the streets to survive.

Summary of Secondary Force-Multipliers #1 to #5

To summarize these *secondary* force multipliers, we need to remind ourselves how dangerous cognitive dissonance, the illusion of separateness, the need to be "right," unlimited exponential economic growth, and ignoring the reality of limits on the extraction of non-renewable resources on a limited planet *that is already beginning to show clear signs of financial stress created by increased global warming and climate change, planetary heating created by increasing CO2 emissions, growing storm intensification, floods, forest fires and droughts, global food shortages, global population growth, global wealth inequality, and the global lack of social justice.*

Were it not for (a) climate changes due to CO2 emissions; (b) massive debt that is already stressing local, state, and national economies; (c) the inevitable powering down from fossil fuel energy, and (d) the growing fragility of global capitalism, these secondary force-multipliers would not, by themselves, create a social and civil collapse in the near future.

But given the sobering realities of the *primary* existential force multiplier threats that *are* coming, these *secondary* force multipliers *will* dramatically increase the likelihood of social and civil institutional collapse as *neoliberal global capitalism* weakens and collapses from *dĕgrowth*, the *intentional simplification* of lifestyle, *reduced consumption*, and the inevitable global *powering down* from fossil fuel energy.

Life as we know it *is* going to change. And our survival will depend directly on how well we are prepared to survive those changes *when* they arrive. And these force-multipliers are not coming one at a time. They are all systemically interconnected and increasing at the same time.

They are all one massive systemic butterfly flapping its wings, and we are pretending it's fake news or alarmist rantings of the scientists as we continue the Tinker Bell business-as-usual life we call "normal."

The Future Is a Choice, Not a Given

We have significant challenges to meet, but we have the ability to choose our response to determine the future we would like to create.

Given the threats to our future, is hope realistic?

Is it even possible in the face of the almost certain collapse of human civilization as we know it?

Is hope only a feel-good Tinker Bell world view to avoid the emotional suffering that scientists are increasingly warning us is coming if we allow climate change and global warming continue to intensify?

Governmental polarization created by the collective primitive ego's need to be "right" has the world arguing about who's right and who's wrong when the real conversation needs to focus on preparation...just in case the scientists are right. And so far, the climate intensification evidence is overwhelmingly in their favor.

In simple terms, the power of cognitive dissonance and confirmation bias is in a life-and-death battle with scientific facts, data, and evidence. The need to be right is a powerful supporter of "intentional ignorance" and the failure to embrace middlepath thinking and *intentionally* search for the truths on both sides of every issue.

Given the Threats to Our Future, Is Hope Realistic?

I offer this quote as one of the best responses I've seen regarding that question.

"As one more white man who isn't getting any younger, I want to put my faith somewhere else. If there is any hope worth having, in a time when we are rightly haunted by the thought of an 'uninhabitable Earth,' then I don't believe it lies in the triumph of reason, nor the recovery of an imagined past. If I have any clue where it lies, I'd say it's in the difficult work of learning to feel and think together again; to come down off the high and lonely horses that some of us were taught to ride, to recognize how much has been missing from our maps, how much has gone unseen in our worldviews." (Dougald Hine, "Is There Hope?" resilience.org 2/21/2020.)

If We Live in Constant Fear, We Will Eventually Disconnect from Reality

If we live in constant fear, the likelihood is high that we will either totally give up or begin to embrace Tinker Bell thinking and disconnect from the realities that are coming, and continue living life *as if everything is normal.* This defensive disconnect from reality is already affecting much of our human population. Accepting the arguments of those who deny the destructive power of the force-multipliers I have discussed in this book is far more comforting than dealing with reality. So, most people don't. Irrational hope and false optimism are far less stressful.

Embracing a more rational version of hope allows us to accept that the future isn't what it used to be. Massive change is coming and far sooner than most believe. Unfortunately, as we have been exploring, the solutions available to deal with the growing climate crisis and global warming, such as CO_2 emission reduction, degrowth, intentional simplification, powering down from fossil energy, all lead to the same social collapse of human culture and human civilization that would be created by doing nothing.

So, what would a rational, realistic hope look like?

I believe we have to embrace challenging but achievable solutions. Solutions such as intentionally taming our collective human primitive ego-consciousness and creating the self-reliant local communities we will explore in the final chapter of this book; local communities and local economies designed to intentionally build self-resilience by preparing now for the massive changes that are coming.

Final Thoughts, Conclusion of Part 2, and Other Systemic Vulnerabilities

The future is not a given.

- Things won't work out by themselves while we sit back and passively watch!!

- Democracy is not a given!!

- A sustainable global economy is not a given.

- Bringing global warming to an end is not a given!!

- World peace is not a given.

- Unlimited economic expansion and unlimited consumption on a limited planet is an existentially dangerous myth.

- The creation of a global economic system that is sustainable and cooperates with nature is not a given.

- Creating a sustainable future is a choice, not a given.

- Embracing simplicity and inconvenience is a choice, not a given.

- If we continue to ignore the challenges and massive changes that are coming, and continue to assume the survival of humanity, climate change, and the threats that climate change *will* bring us will all *somehow* be magically solved by *somebody* using Tinker Bell thinking, *is* an excellent example of *intentional ignorance* and reflects the likely extinction of life on our planet—but fortunately it's not a given...*yet!*

- Protecting the Constitution and the balance of power in Washington is a choice, not a given.

- Protecting the many democracies around the world is not a given.

- Removing the wealth of the 1% out of politics and political elections is not a given.

- Wealthy corporations are not considered individual citizens as defined by the constitutional phrase "We the People."

- Protecting our constitution's integrity and getting corporate money out of politics and political elections is not a given.

- Replacing wealthy, old white men and the good old boys club with smart young women and young men of color in American politics is not a given.

- Ending wealth inequality of the 1% and shifting wealth and political power back into the hands of the American middle class and an economy that works for the middle class is not a given.

- Preparation for climate change and its financial attack on humanity and human civilization is not a given.

- The survival of humanity from global warming and storm intensification is not a given. IPCC scientists are telling us that time is running out! The statistical possibility of reversing global warming and ensuring the future survival of humanity is dropping rapidly.

- Wealth inequality, massive debt, unfunded pensions, increased storm intensification, increased droughts, increased flooding, increased coastal flooding, and increased forest fires are all massive financial drains on insurance costs and local governments, but they are not a given.

- These are all choices and actions and possibilities that we need to both imagine and then actively embrace. A goal that would be best accomplished by undertaking an intentional taming of our collective unevolved and immature human primitive ego consciousness and its childhood conditioning.

Other Secondary Systemic Vulnerabilities That Will Increase the Chaos When the Primary and Secondary Force Multiplier Impacts Above Begin to Intensify

As we review the secondary systemic vulnerabilities below, we need to:

a. Focus on the consequences of *"what if?" possibilities*, not on the *ideological beliefs* behind them.

b. What primitive ego beliefs need to be confronted and tamed.

c. What preparations might mitigate the impacts of the coming force-multipliers if those "what if?" possibilities became realities.

d. Because life as we know it *is* going to change, paying attention to *"what if?"* future *possibilities* will become increasingly important; especially attention to the growing scientific warnings of our climate scientists.

Vulnerability #1: Overpopulation

Overpopulation is a significant problem. Scientists are warning us that the sustainable human footprint on our planet is roughly one billion humans. And we are currently over 7 billion headed for 10 billion in the next few decades. **Our current human footprint is unsustainable.** A significant part of the underlying problem in overpopulation is the developed nation's lifestyle of overconsumption. Overproduction. Overuse of fossil energy. Our primitive ego lack of systemic thinking. Our primitive ego illusion of separateness. And our primitive ego entitlement and need to be "right." Reducing the number of humans on the planet, reducing the over-consumption of our planets' non-renewable life-sustaining resources, and intentionally taming and evolving humanity's collective primitive ego-consciousness are all critical for humanity to survive.

If the human population lived in right relationship with nature, embraced intentional simplicity, consumed what they *need* instead of what they *want*, and lived sustainably within a self-reliant local community, there would be far fewer people living on our planet. And their footprint on the planet would be significantly smaller and less invasive on the ecosystem than the footprint and impact of our current human culture. And yes, that would mean a return to human cultures and a human civilization as it existed two hundred years ago when the community's well-being and those who lived in the community were a top priority. The climate crisis will result in the social collapse of human culture. As we discussed above, the climate crisis is a primary force-multiplier on the institutional and economic vulnerabilities of our human civilization. Avoiding social collapse might have been possible if we had started reducing carbon emissions and aggressively preparing for climate change three decades ago, but it's not possible today. We are not even preparing for the massive changes we *know* are coming. Without the resilience that comes from aggressive preparation, the extinction of human civilization as we know it, and even the possible extinction of humanity itself, is growing more and more likely.

We need to reduce our human footprint to a sustainable level. An expanding population creates an ever-rising demand in consumption, and the current global growth rate is about 1.1%. In other words, we are adding roughly 1 billion more people on the planet every 12 years! Stabilizing the human population is considered by scientists to be a "critical" goal toward protecting the future viability of the human species. Future generations will require a global population that allows for ecological stability and a "sufficiency" level of consumption of our planet's natural resources. In other words, an economic system that meets their basic "needs," not their "wants." Encouraging small-family norms globally would be a step in the right direction, as would ensuring and increasing women's voice in reproductive decisions and increasing the availability of family planning services *globally*.

It is time for humanity to evolve its collective consciousness, begin dealing realistically with the destructive realities we have created, and start living sustainably on our planet. Given the current growth rate in population, the use of immature primitive ego thinking, our current *want*-based lifestyles, and our current rate of planetary consumption, we are on a very short road toward extinction.

Vulnerability #2: Not Taking the Reality of Social and Civil Collapse Seriously

A significant threat to humanity's complex global economic, social, and civil systems is much like the "angle of repose" in a sand pile. Like a sand pile, our global human civilization is a complex, interconnected, interdependent collection of individual grains or entities. And like a sand pile, it can grow in size and continue to look stable, but that's an illusion. There are many hidden cracks in a sand pile that can cause instability. And small cracks add up. Eventually, one of the cracks *will* trigger the inherent instability of the sand pile and create an avalanche.

In the same way, small cracks add up in our complex global human civilization. It's only a matter of time until one of the many cracks or vulnerabilities in the global human culture that we have been exploring gets triggered by a primary or secondary force multiplier and exposes our global civilization's inherent instability. And when it does, human culture will experience a systemic "avalanche" or collapse in human society's social and civil foundations.

Reduced consumption, intentional simplification, powering down from fossil energy are only three of the many primary and secondary force multipliers that will eventually create social collapse. As we saw in Chapter 3, global capitalism is itself extremely vulnerable to collapse.

Stated simply, complex systems tend to collapse. They don't slowly "decline." And everything in the universe is impermanent and subject to change. Everything in the universe is evolving and becoming something new. Because change is a fundamental reality in our universe, we need to begin preparing "now" for the life-altering changes that are coming; changes that include aggressive reductions in CO_2 emissions, degrowth, intentional simplification, powering down from fossil energy, climate change, storm intensification, flooding, droughts, heatwaves, forest fires, ice melt, ocean heating, and ocean water level increases all have the ability and potential to create social collapse and life as we know it.

Social and civil collapse is common when:

a. The commons lose the ability to prepare for existential threats.

b. The natural resource that initially allowed the culture/empire/nation to grow is exhausted or disappears.

c. The wealthy elite benefit from the dysfunctional economic and social systems and create a massive wealth inequality that undermines the healthier economic structures that initially created the empire/nation; *the future of our global human civilization is grim unless business-as-usual comes to an end **soon.***

Most scientists are skeptical we can reduce CO_2 emissions and stay below the 2° to 3°C target they recommend. They warn that we have at best a 12-year window to limit the climate catastrophe. And that 12-year assumption does not (a) include the high probability of environmental tipping points that could make things far worse far sooner, or (b) assume a current business-as-usual economy that has global GDP more than doubling by 2050!

Exponential growth is no longer realistic or possible if we want to avoid the extinction of humanity. The health and sustainability of all life and all living systems on the planet, taming the collective primitive ego-consciousness of humanity, and a massive transformation of our values as a species *must become humanity's primary goals!*

A fundamental focus on a systemic human interconnectedness with the web of life on our planet must become a fundamental concept in the foundation of our human civilization and culture, and waiting to embrace that systemic interconnectedness is *not* an option!

The political systems of Western-style democracies globally are manifesting the emergence of oligarchies in which a small number of people have massive power and control over the politics of a nation. As a result of this growing global movement toward oligarchies, we are witnessing the *intentional* dismantling of green-energy initiatives, loss of control over democratic decision-making, increase in extreme wealth inequality, and a dangerous loss of faith in people of the commons in their ability to impact the political and economic decisions that affect their own lives—that is, their ability to collectively imagine and create the future they would like to create. When that happens, the commons stop paying attention, and they become susceptible to strong autocratic leaders who promise to save their lives from threatening "others."

As we see clearly in this book, we are not headed in the right direction.

The lifeblood of creativity is possibility and imagination.

When the commons lose the encouragement and inspiration to imagine, they get angry, but they also shut down and give up caring. The most significant near-term threat to social collapse is the increasing feelings of hopelessness, fear, powerlessness, the feeling of not mattering, not being visible, not being heard, feelings of desperation, hunger, bankruptcy, unemployment, debt, and loss of expected income from pensions when retired. These reflect and multiply the potential for social anger, social unrest and violence, social upheaval, and ultimately, social and civil collapse.

The sobering reality I mentioned in the introduction to this book is that almost all of the actions required to reverse climate change and deal with the social structures vulnerable to the force-multiplier effects of climate change will themselves increase the threat of social collapse. And that includes continuing to do nothing to address the rapidly growing existential force-multiplier threats.

We are trapped between a rock and a hard place. We're damned if we do and damned if we don't. But doing nothing will lead to *certain* extinction. We should do what we can even if that means simply preparing the best we can to build some resilience into our lives and our future. *Any preparation for resilience is better than no preparation and no resilience. It's time to embrace our imaginations and create possibilities.*

I believe joining or creating an awakened, tamed primitive ego, localization community that I will discuss in Part 3 of this book is the most realistic place to begin.

The signs of global social and civil collapse are already growing.

The rural backlash of anger against the metropolitan urban elite is already creating political unrest in the United States and nations worldwide. People are feeling left out and invisible, and they are increasingly angry. It is creating extreme ideological and angry divisions between the political left and the political right globally. The tendency to intentionally blame *"others"* for the problems we are experiencing creates convenient targets for social anger. Social violence is increasing in many nations worldwide as people increasingly act out their anger, frustration, and sense of powerlessness.

Good anger clarifies issues, gets conversations moving, and helps build a social consensus. Destructive anger creates rage, zero-sum black-and-white ideological thinking, indifference, and a lack of compassion and empathy for the pain and suffering that others experience.

That indifference creates a level of social violence that is self-generating. Truth is ignored. and lies and distortions are increasingly accepted as facts.

This is how democracy dies in the 21st century: in a musty courtroom. There are no power grabs in the dead of night, no tanks rolling down the streets, no uniformed officers taking over TV stations. Just the steady drip, drip, drip of the erosion of democratic norms, the corruption of institutions, and the cowardly compromises of decision-makers in courts and congresses.[50]

---

50   Sheila Coronel, the *Atlantic*, June 16, 2020.

The plucking of feathers, one feather at a time.

Human civilization is headed in the wrong direction. Empires require imperial thinking. Empires are unstable. Empires grow until they are defeated or go bankrupt. And they *always* collapse.

Humanity is no longer dealing with individual local crises. Our global sand pile is deteriorating into a worldwide systemic emergency involving all of the planet's most critical global systems designed to form a unified whole but is now facing pressing, interdependent, interconnected, systemic global challenges and likely collapse.

We are a planetary species employing Tinker Bell thinking in the hopes that the existential challenges and threats will somehow magically all go away.

Climate change is the symptom of a toxic human way of life created by the collective primitive ego-consciousness of humanity and our unevolved childhood conditioning and beliefs. *All of our lives are going to change radically.* We are not going to stop the momentum of climate change or climate intensification. That moment has passed. And if we do act soon enough to bring CO2 emissions to the IPCC levels required to avoid the worst impacts of climate intensification, the primary force-multipliers that we have been exploring in this book *will* be triggered, and will *themselves* ensure the social collapse we are trying to avoid.

Our decades of collective denial have positioned us between a rock and a hard place.

Vulnerability #3: Wealth Inequality

The wealthiest 1% holds roughly 80% of global wealth. Wealth is essentially the power to *influence* and *control*. An estimated 50% of humanity lives on income less than $2 to $10/day as corporations ship their manufacturing costs and pollution to Third-World countries and low-income workers.

Wealth inequality is a significant historical factor leading to the collapse of empires.

Wealth inequality increases the probability of autocratic governments, autocratic leaders, the erosion of personal rights, and the growth of fascism. It creates mass human poverty, political instability, erodes social cohesion, interferes, and undermines decision-making structures. Too many people have no voice, which leaves political decision making in the hands of a numerically small number of very wealthy people.

Wealth inequality locks in rigid patterns of conflict, oppression, ecological destruction, lack of sustainability, and pollution; puts small businesses out of business; creates poverty zones in cities; destroys the ability of small independent farmers to survive; and keeps wages lower than needed to ensure a viable quality of life and the well-being of Third-World workers.

To deal with the 2008 recession and the underfunded banking industry, the U.S. Federal Government printed and manufactured "phantom money" in the hopes that it would incentivize banks to lend to corporations so they could invest in their future and their workers. It has been described as trickle-down on steroids.

Unfortunately, most of that money trickled up to the top and exacerbated the already significant wealth inequality in America. It also massively increased the national debt and allowed corporations to drive up their stocks' price by repurchasing their own stocks. The wealthier stockholders (the top 10% of Americans own 84% of the stock market), corporate CEOs, and upper management who held stock options and often got paid in shares of their stocks, ended up significantly wealthier. It also inflated financial assets more than the real economy and created the current economic "bubble" poised to collapse *before* COVID-19 arrived on the scene. The bottom line, like most of the rest of the world, the average American recognizes once again that the system is stacked against them.

Even more sobering is that not only did we miss the lesson from the attempts to "fix" the 2008 recession, we just had another rate cut in March 2020. The U.S. Federal Reserve just added insult to injury by printing another $1.5T of manufactured phantom money to the national debt to deal with the coronavirus threat, a clear sign that the Fed is concerned about the dangers a global pandemic could inflict on a globalized economy and its systemically interconnected banking systems.

More importantly, it will help Wall Street and the global stock markets, but it will leave real people behind again. A financial cycle that will once again increase wealth inequality until the coronavirus or one of the other 12 force-multipliers/global stressors creates the perfect storm that collapses the profoundly interconnected and fragile global financial systems, including human civilization as we know it. As I write these words in mid-2020, the global financial market is concerned that the global economy is all but certain to experience a 1929-level of collapse *or worse.* The hole we are digging is getting deeper by the day.

As a friend of mine said recently, if you trip over a rock once, it's an accident. If you trip over the same rock a second time, it's a sign of ignorance and a serious inability to pay attention.

Vulnerability #4: Reoccurring Pandemic Threats

As we continue to stress our planet's natural ecosystems, increase human populations, and continue the movement of people traveling around the planet, the probability of viruses jumping from animal hosts to human hosts will continue to grow. Scientists and health experts have been warning us of this reality for decades. We *know* more lethal viruses *will* appear again in the future. And some of them will be more lethal than COVID-19. And when they do, as a secondary force-multiplier, they will also impact our vulnerable global economy and our global financial systems.

We see the economic impact of this COVID-19 pandemic on the global economy as it has spread exponentially around the planet. Our planet is engaged in a no-win battle between saving the global economy and saving people from rapidly rising human death tolls. Schools in the United States and around the world are struggling with how best to reopen. Washington is in gridlock as Congress struggles to pass financial legislation that will protect those most vulnerable to our national and global economy's slowing and increase the national debt.

The more our human civilization attempts to globalize, the more pandemic risk will increase. The urgency and need to increase resilience in our existing global systems is becoming more difficult and challenging. As global stability weakens under the pressure of the force-multipliers in Part 2, it increases our collective human tendency for short-term thinking. And a short-term focus on immediate threats threatens our adaptive capacity to avoid the conditions that will create even more catastrophic financial and social system failures in the future.

The likelihood of destabilization and catastrophic system failure is growing, and we are not preparing to deal with those sobering realities. The need to create social and economic resilience will require the political courage and social will to take aggressive action and begin facing these rapidly growing threats. Until we change the *never-ending-growth narrative*, the primary and secondary force-multiplier threats in Part 2 will continue to rise in severity *outside most people's awareness*.

COVID-19 is having a massive impact on global and national economies. But this economic impact was not created by COVID-19 alone. The global economy was already in a giant financial bubble vulnerable to force-multipliers and a pandemic. It was only a matter of time until one of those existential threats would inevitably lead to the collapse of a global economy that was struggling to grow at roughly 2% over the previous decade.

To summarize, we are altering the climate on our planet. Environmental breakdown is contributing to a rise in infectious diseases. The World Health Organization (WHO) warns that there is an apparent increase in many infectious diseases caused by environmental, social, and other changes in our ways of living. They affirmed the reality that climate change will also continue to affect contagious disease occurrences. One team of scientists recently found 28 novel viral groups in 15,000-year-old melting ice, all of which were entirely new to science.

Pandemic outbreaks will happen more often, and they *will* continue to be a critical force-multiplier on the stability of our global economic system, the fragility of neoliberal capitalism, and its grow-or-die global stranglehold on our systemically interconnected and interdependent global financial system and its carbon-based energy-intensive global supply chains.

We have created a global economic system poised to oscillate between growth and collapse, not a system based on financial stability. All of the force multipliers in Part 2 have the potential to destabilize it without warning. We have created an increasingly fragile debt-fueled and crash-prone economy based on fossil fuel-supported global supply chains.

COVID-19 has exposed the vulnerable underbelly and vulnerable financial circulatory system of our global economy and the dangerously complex systemic supply lines required to keep the system alive and healthy. It has dramatically reduced the global flow of goods, money, and people. The impact of this one black swan force multiplier has exposed the liabilities embedded in our complex global neoliberal capitalist economic system and its need for uninterrupted profit and growth to survive. It has exposed the critical lack of resilience in our complex global economy. When complex systems collapse, simple solutions will not fix it. Complex systems require equally complex solutions if they are to be effective.

A pandemic virus is only one of the force-multipliers that I've listed in Part 2 of this book. One more example of how the future isn't what it used to be. Massive change is coming. It's just waiting for the next black swan force-multiplier challenge. Climate change. Massive debt. Wealth inequality. Rising political populism. Mass migration. Droughts. Floods. Powering down from fossil energy. Heatwaves. Storm intensification. International dysfunction is prevalent and widespread and growing. You get the point. All of them have the potential to collapse the complex interconnected and interdependent systemic structures that support our critical social networks; our complex global economic systems; and human civilization as we know it.

There *will* be more pandemics. Modern globalization was made possible by modern medicine. The only question is, will we be socially and economically capable of successfully coping with the next force-multiplier threat, the one that *"is"* coming?

We have lost control of the vital life-supporting resources we need to survive. We urgently need to re-localize those resources. I will expand on this concept in Chapter 10 on Localization.

Embracing Hope in a Dark Future

The future path is indeed dark, but we are a self-aware, conscious species that can plan and imagine and dream about possibilities. And we are capable of *creating* that future that we can imagine. Stated simply, we are *co-creators* with the "spirit" of the Creator that began this universe; a universe comprised of trillions of stars and galaxies all embedded and grounded in the reality of never-ending change, evolution, and "becoming." It's time we began to *more intentionally* embrace our ability to create what we can imagine, and *more intentionally* create our human future; a future that embraces a more evolved, more mature, and a more *intentionally* tamed collective primitive ego consciousness.

I know of no better definition of hope for our future as a species than the possibility that we could achieve a more enlightened and viable human future if enough of us rolled up our sleeves and began *intentionally* taming our collective primitive ego and its immature early childhood conditioning. Awakening our collective human consciousness and *intentionally* embracing our collective growth in self-awareness is the most critical challenge humanity has ever faced. How well we meet that challenge will, more than anything else, determine our future survival as a species on this planet. Waiting and praying for God to magically create this enlightened future for us is hazardous Tinker Bell thinking. The Creator of this universe has already given us the tools and ability to do this work. We are co-creators of reality. We can create what we can imagine in our minds. And I have to imagine that the Creator might be getting impatient that it's taking us so long to wake up and recognize that simple reality.

On that note, we will move onto Chapter 10 in Part 3 and explore creating a future that is both realistic and achievable, a future based on community *well-being* rather than individual financial *profit and never-ending growth.*

As we end Part 2 and this closing summary, I will leave you with this quote from Richard Heinberg, Post Carbon Institute Senior Fellow, 4/22/2020:

> *The coronavirus pandemic reminds us that we are vulnerable biological organisms, strands in Earth's web of life. Due to our special human gifts…notably, our linguistic and tool-making abilities… we have come to think of ourselves as special and apart, more gods than critters. We have used our unique powers to kill off the macro-predators that once threatened us…the lions, tigers, and bears. But a micro-predator, far too small to be seen even with a powerful optical microscope, has shown up unexpectedly to remind us that we are still links in the food chain. If something good is to come from the terrifying experience we are all sharing as we cope with covid19, perhaps it will be the reminder that our survival depends not on defeating nature (something we can never really do because we are nature), but instead on learning to live in a state of intelligent, dynamic balance within Earth's nourishing yet fragile and perilous complexity.*

– Richard Heinberg

PART 3:
LOCALIZATION: THE CREATION OF SUSTAINABLE, SELF-RELIANT, SELF-SUFFICIENT, LOCAL COMMUNITIES AND LOCAL ECONOMIES

Creating an Awakened, Sustainable, Self-Reliant, Self-Sufficient, Local Community and Local Economy

Our resistance to evolve our thinking keeps us blind to the changes that need to be made.

"We" are the problem. We need to tame and evolve the immature and dangerous primitive ego childhood thinking and conditioning that will interfere with our ability to successfully create viable, long term successful self-reliant local communities and economies.

The list below contains all of the unconscious, immature, and unevolved thinking and conditioning of early childhood that needs to be intentionally tamed and matured in the collective consciousness of humanity.

* *

Primitive ego early childhood conditioning:

a. "What's in it for me" greed.

b. Need to be "right" (aggressive arrogance, extreme cognitive dissonance/confirmation bias).

c. Inability to replace "me" thinking with "we" thinking (compassion, mutuality, cooperation).

d. I want what I want when I want it.

e. Blaming others for our feelings (inability to own our own feelings).

f.   Ignorance regarding the danger of exponential growth (e.g., COVID-19).

g.   A lack of interconnected, interdependent systemic thinking.

h.   Survival-of-the-fittest thinking.

i.   Black or white, zero-sum thinking ("You can't have that, it's mine!").

j.   An exaggerated aggressive, narcissistic self-focused sense of entitlement.

k.   An inability to connect short-term choices with long-term consequences.

l.   The fear of change (uncertainty, not knowing).

m.   The unending, obsessive desired for "more."

n.   The need for power "over" rather than power "with."

o.   The inability to embrace long-term thinking.

* *

Introduction to Chapter 10: Localization.
The Golden Arch of the Book

As I said in the Introduction to the book, I wrote this book to offer those in the younger generations a realistic and hopeful vision of a future that could help them prepare for and survive the massive changes that are coming.

a.   The ability to *pay attention* to the realities happening in the world. In other words, staying focused on the big picture existential-force multipliers of Part 2. Don't get caught up in the day-to-day media news details.

b.   *Understanding the long-term impacts, consequences,* and systemic interconnections of those big-picture Part 2 existential-force multiplier realities.

c.   *Assessing* the primary and secondary force-multipliers in Part 2, and *their ability to impact the vulnerable social and economic systems* we have created in human civilization.

d.   Realistically *assessing the self-reliant skills and resources that will be required* to survive a future far more challenging and dangerous than few in the developed world have experienced in generations.

e.   Most importantly, *find ways to survive the massive changes* that are coming as human cultures and human civilization as we know it begins to collapse; when the primary and secondary force-multipliers, and the existential threats they represent, work together systemically to ensure that collapse.

I wrote Part 2 to illustrate that it is OK to be an alarmist when the threats that are coming are genuinely alarming. And yes, I understand that many readers will assume that I have gone off the deep end. However, I did not write this book for them.

I wrote it for the younger generations, and those who already recognize they are inheriting a precarious, unstable, and challenging future. A future that will present existential challenges and threats that will threaten *their* survival and the future survival of their children.

I wrote it for anyone who recognizes the need for change in a world that has demonstrated little to no social or political will to deal with the existential challenges discussed in Part 2.

I wrote Chapter 10 to offer them a lifeline blueprint on how to create a successful, self-reliant local community and local economy. I believe the creation of self-reliant local communities is the best realistic hope they will have for survival *when life as we know it* comes to an end.

And lastly, I wrote it for parents and grandparents who want to support and encourage their children and grandchildren as they prepare for the coming changes.

The social movements toward localization and the creation of self-reliant local communities will increase when the changes and existential threats in Part 2 begin to more personally and negatively impact people in the commons. The need for greater self-reliance will grow rapidly when (a) they recognize and accept the reality that humanity's competitive quest for wealth accumulation and unlimited growth is suicidal, and (b) the recognize a more self-reliant, frugal, and simplistic lifestyle needs to be intentionally embraced by themselves and the rest of human civilization.

When that day arrives, the movement toward creating self-reliant, sustainable, local communities and economies will begin in earnest. People will recognize the need for a collective control of their local community and begin creating local community gardens and orchards for food, drilling wells for access to local water, and constructing green wind and solar energy for access to local energy.

My Concern

My concern in writing this book is that most people will begin creating self-reliant local communities too late to create the level of survival resiliency that will be needed. Waiting to prepare for the massive changes and challenges that are coming will seriously limit their ability to avoid the pain and suffering those changes and challenges will create.

The golden arch of this book and my deep concern is that preparation for those changes and challenges begins in time to support our species' future survival on this planet. Those who start creating self-reliant, sustainable, local communities *now* will have the time they'll need to acquire the knowledge, skills, resources, and experience to develop viable and resilient local communities *before* the inevitable impacts of the force-multipliers in Part 2 arrive. Those *who wait too long to begin* creating a self-reliant local community will face overwhelming challenges as they struggle to access the resources required for success and long-term survival.

Creating a Self-Reliant Local Community: The Cracks and Fragility of Capitalism Are Becoming Visible

Our consumer-based, capitalistic society is showing its fragility. COVID-19 is helping the cracks in global capitalism to become visible. The neoliberal global obsession with unlimited growth, endless profit, and affluence is already showing signs of stress. When global capitalism begins to experience collapse, the primary and secondary force- multipliers in Part 2 will systemically support that collapse and rapidly turn it into a cascading avalanche of unavoidable social and civil collapse. Because that day is coming far sooner than most people are preparing for, or even believe will happen, waiting to create resilient, self-reliant local communities and local communities is *not* an option.

In a world of social collapse and severe scarcity, only an established sustainable and self-reliant local community would have the ability to provide its members with the necessary life-supporting resources and local food they would need to survive. Access to startup capital, acquiring critical physical resources such as shovels, rakes, a hand-pumped well, wood stoves for heat and cooking, access to wood, and learning fundamental survival skills to preserve and process food are just a few examples of the resources a self-reliant local community will need to acquire to be successful.

Once established, a self-reliant local community would enable community members to create a local economy through trade and barter services. In other words, a local economy that's not based on money, interest, or debt. The over-arching focus of the community would be on the long-term security and well-being of all community members.

A local exchange trading system (LETS) would create "money" in a self-reliant local community by exchanging trade and barter IOUs *inside* the community. Regulations, and disputes that arise in the community would be resolved through community consensus decision-making. The primary focus of consensus decisions would be made based on their support of, and impact on, the community's long-term success and survival.

No capital would be "lent" or "borrowed" from outside of the community. Loans would only be created for good causes *inside* the community. Members could offer personal savings without interest or dividends, but *the community would own all resources, equipment, and assets*. There would be no *"private ownership"* in the community. One hour of work by anyone in the community would be equal to one hour of work by any other individual in the community. In other words, one hour of work would be valued as one hour of work regardless of who in the community provided it.

Everyone in the community would have a secure livelihood as full use of labor and contributed personal talent would ensure that there would be no unemployment. A self-reliant local community would embrace the economic principles of zero growth and no poverty. Essentially, a self-reliant local community would be structured as a locally owned cooperative focused on the human well-being of every member of the community, and environmental sustainability.

Waiting Is Not an Option

The primary focus and golden arch of this book is the encouragement to begin creating these sustainable, self-reliant local communities *now*. The resilience and likelihood of survival, both individually and as a species, will be significantly improved the sooner we begin to prepare for the reality of the coming threats and changes we covered in Part 2. Waiting is *not* an option. *The sooner a self-reliant community begins to form, the more likely it will survive the changes that are coming.* And the more successful the members of the community are in their ability to intentionally tame and evolve their collective primitive ego-consciousness and its early childhood conditioning, the more likely it will survive as a viable community long-term and become an integral part of the future foundation of human culture.

Why Social and Civil Collapse Is Inevitable

The primary and secondary force-multiplier threats we examined in Part 2 *will* create the coming social and civil collapse of human civilization. And that collapse *will* include the collapse of economic globalism. Neoliberal global capitalism and the ideology of unlimited growth were both created by inexpensive energy-dense fossil fuels. And both have been actively supported for generations by the use of energy-dense fossil fuels. Fossil fuels have been described as a contract with the devil, because no other energy source has the energy density to replace the energy density of petroleum fuels in a world that is:

a. Already experiencing a significant depletion in petroleum reserves, and a growing decline in petroleum production and quality of energy in a business-as-usual, unlimited growth economy.

b. Continuing to increase its human population.

c. Experiencing the rapidly growing social impacts and mounting costs of global warming, flooding, forest fires, droughts, and storm intensification.

d. Recognizing that neoliberal global capitalism *is all but certain to* continue to weaken and move toward likely collapse sooner than most believe possible.

When the unlimited use of energy-dense petroleum fuel is no longer possible because of global climate change and declining reserves, globalism and our neoliberal *global* economic system of unlimited growth and unlimited economic expansion will no longer be possible. When that day arrives, social and civil collapse will be inevitable. When social and civil collapse begin, the survival of our human species on this planet will depend on the long-term success of sustainable and self-reliant local communities that were created *before* the inevitable economic and social collapse in the global foundations of human culture and human civilization.

These self-reliant local communities will likely create small local *networks of trade* with other self-reliant local communities that have also embraced the concept of a tamed and evolved collective human consciousness and way of thinking, *but long-distance food production and manufacturing products for global trade will be both extremely limited, and unrealistically expensive, without fossil fuel energy.*

The Need to Assume More Responsibility

We need to assume significantly more responsibility preparing ourselves *before* the financial and social impacts of natural disasters, and the force-multipliers of Part 2, arrive. And most importantly, we need to begin *now* to create sustainable and self-reliant local food production for the day our current global food chains are no longer functional. I believe food shortages will be *the first* and the most critical and primary crises to threaten humanity's future. Food shortages will also likely be the primary crisis that will create social and civil collapse.

Business-as-usual on a limited planet is not only Tinker Bell thinking; it's simply not possible. As a result, business-as-usual and its embrace of unlimited growth is currently on course to ensure that our human species becomes no more than a dusty footnote in the history of our planet.

Until humanity is willing to assume more responsibility by aggressively, and

a. *Intentionally* taming, evolving, and maturing its collective immature primitive ego's what's in it for *"me"* greed-based thinking process, and humanity's collective greed-based addictive focus on unlimited growth and unlimited economic expansion on a finite planet and it's non-renewable natural resources, and

b. *Intentionally* embracing the creation of self-reliant *local communities and economies* that are *"we"* focused on sustainability and well-being; our future extinction as a species on this planet is all but certain.

We Are Caught Between a Rock and a Hard Place

The global economy and our planet's environmental systems have systemically co-evolved. The global economy *is* capitalism, and capitalism *is* systemically dependent on non-renewable, energy-dense petroleum fuels, the natural environment, and our planet's natural resources. When the natural resources that fuel capitalism are no longer available, global growth and profit will end. When that happens, capitalism as an economic system will die, and business-as-usual will end. And its death *will* create social and civil collapse. So, we need a sustainable economic system that replaces neoliberal global capitalism *before* that natural death happens.

When neoliberal global capitalism dies, the replacement for neoliberal global capitalism needs to *already* be in place, fully operational, and fully functional in providing a secure future for those who survive the coming social and civil collapse. To fix the systemic problems embedded in neoliberal global capitalism that are currently devouring our planet, the creation of a new *global* economic system would need to embrace a more *socially just* economy based on long-term *sustainable growth;* the *well-being* of all of humanity, not only the 1%; the well-being of all of our planet's fragile *ecosystems;* and the well-being of all of the *other life forms* that share the planet with us. Because the new *"replacement"* economic system would essentially be designed to end neoliberal capitalism as we know it, there is no way we could create that global replacement system without triggering the very social and civil collapse we are trying to avoid.

That puts us back between a rock and a hard place. We can't continue on the path we're on, and we can't create a new *global* economic system to replace neoliberal global capitalism without creating the social and civil collapse we are trying to avoid.

In other words, we need to fundamentally change the structural economic forces at the *root* of capitalism. The only realistic and viable path forward is to accept the unavoidable reality that the collapse of global capitalism *is* inevitable, and it *will"* create social and civil collapse in the near future; a reality I see no way to avoid. And we need to begin preparing *now* for that collapse by creating the self-reliant, highly self-sufficient, sustainable, local communities we will explore below.

When the global economy collapses and self-destructs, the supermarket shelves will be empty very quickly, given the reality that most of the food and products we purchase are shipped to us from around the world. We got a taste of that reality when COVID-19 arrived. Critical food and supplies were picked clean from store shelves within a few hours.

Survival after social and civil collapse will depend entirely on how well we have created self-reliant and highly self-sufficient local communities capable of managing a self-reliant and self-sufficient local economy that depends on local resources such as local food, simple technologies, a well-stocked pantry, heritage seeds for the next year's garden, chickens, a goat or two, a well-mulched garden, some fruit trees, beehives, a reliable source of drinking and irrigation water, and access to wood and a wood stove for heat and cooking.

The greed-based neoliberal global economy, and its ideology of unlimited growth and profit, is not sustainable, and it needs to end. But when it does, we need to have prepared for that day by creating an economy that doesn't need growth to survive. If we continue on the business-as-usual path we are on, social and civil collapse is inevitable. When rationing begins due to that social collapse, people will panic, and social unrest will take to the streets. The world will get dangerous very quickly.

We need to create a post-growth narrative of local stability, self-sufficiency, and self-reliant local communities, not growth. That means embracing degrowth, consumption contraction, intentional simplification of lifestyle, and increased self-sufficiency. And we need to begin creating that resilience *now.*

Resilience: Surviving the Social and Civil Collapse of Life as We Know It

Resilience is the capacity of a system or local community to survive significant disruption and maintain its basic structure and ability to function as a viable community. In the likely collapse of human civilization as we know it, including human social culture and life as we know it, there is a high probability that the internet and the power grid could become intermittent, or even collapse.

Because this would likely destroy access to knowledge, wisdom, music, instruction manuals, science, math, history, manufacturing experience, and survival skill knowledge, we need to prepare now to protect, collect, and preserve as much of this knowledge as possible. Local community resilience will increase significantly if this required knowledge is collected *now* and shared with other self-reliant local communities.

Resilience for survival requires preparation before the crises arrive, not afterward. And the creation of self-reliant local communities and local economies could become a movement that offers future generations a viable social model based on cooperation and well-being rather than the current social model that embraces zero-sum competition, greed, and profit.

Without the *intentional* taming and maturation of humanity's collective primitive ego thinking and early childhood conditioning, immature primitive ego thinking will always threaten to regain control of the collective human consciousness.

To create long-term resilience and survivability, self-reliant local communities, and the future generations of those local communities will need to:

a. Have the structures in place to *intentionally* tame their immature, collective primitive ego and its early childhood conditioning.

b. Teach the children of those self-reliant local communities the dangers embedded in this kind of immature, unevolved, primitive ego thinking, and help them understand how close that kind of immature thinking came to destroying the planet and the future of our human species.

For long-term resilience and the survival of local communities, this early childhood educational process would need to include the intentional taming of their children's primitive ego and be a fundamental part of every local community's early childhood educational system.

Looking Forward: The Power of Local Communities to Create Resilience

I believe creating self-reliant local communities is the best option for a viable future as we move forward. We are running out of time to access the assets and resources that self-reliant, local communities will need to be sustainable and successful. I wrote this book to illustrate why waiting to begin creating these local communities is not an option. I will do all I can to help create and support the local self-reliant community movement in the days and years ahead.

We need to prepare now for a broad-scale societal disruption or collapse. You are not irrational or an alarmist when the massive changes and existential threats that are coming are alarming. The force-multipliers in Part 2 are coming.

As I illustrated in Part 2, the fragile political and financial systems we have created are all far too fragile to survive when those existential threats arrive.

The threatened collapse of our global economic system will create far broader impacts in the future than those created by war, famine, pandemics, or financial crisis. But economic collapse will likely include the impacts of all of those events; and more.

Scientists warn that increased storm intensification, droughts, flooding, forest fires, ocean level increases, melting polar ice, global heating, and conflicts due to population migration will increase economic pressure on our already financially stressed international governments and local municipalities.

After the COVID-19 pandemic, the world will likely be insecure and unstable far longer than most people will be prepared for, and that's assuming we can avoid a more extensive and irreversible cascading systemic collapse that could result if any of the other force-multiplier threats in Part 2 increased their destructive black-swan pressure on our already fragile global economic system.

Time will tell us how we managed those impacts, but frankly, I'm not optimistic. As I stated above, I believe social and civil collapse is unavoidable because (a) business-as-usual, neoliberal global capitalism, and unlimited economic expansion *are* coming to an end; (b) the inevitable powering down from fossil fuel energy *is also* coming; and (c) massive global debt, global hunger, and global heatwaves are all increasing destructive pressure on our fragile social systems.

As a result, I believe creating self-reliant local communities and local economies will be the most realistic creators of the resilience that humanity will need for survival when the changes that are coming create social and civil collapse.

Resilient, Self-Reliant Local Communities: The Future That's Coming

History shows us that societies and empires begin to unravel and collapse rapidly under the pressure of climate change, environmental degradation, extreme wealth inequality, out-of-control debt, and societal complexity escalation begins to reach critical levels. And all of those conditions are currently confronting us on a global scale. The systemic changes necessary as business-as-usual comes to an end *will* be difficult and frightening and will likely lead to social and civil collapse. And the sacrifices that we will need to make going forward as life as we know it comes to an end...*will* be a challenge.

But life is not linear. Life *is* change. And that change doesn't happen *to us*. Change just *happens*. Sometimes the change is significant; sometimes it's small; sometimes it's pleasant; sometimes it's unpleasant. Sometimes we get to choose the change. Often, we don't. But change doesn't define who we *are*. Who we *are* is determined by how we cope and adapt to the reality of change when it *happens*.

What I have attempted to illustrate in this book is the certainty that *life as we know it is coming to an end*. Sustainability, survival, self-reliance, water availability, wood for heating and cooking, and local food sources (personal and community gardens) *will* become the primary focus of life moving forward. And localization communities will be the seeds that create a new human economy. The members of those self-reliant local community *will* need to be grounded in the collective and *intentional* taming and evolution of their primitive ego-consciousness, and the the maturation of their early childhood conditioning.

Some will see the challenges that are coming as "the end of the world." I prefer to see them as an opportunity to learn new skills; to be a more integral part of a local community; to surround ourselves with people who care; to take action; to protect the ecosystems in our "place"; and work to maximize our long term sustainability as a species. We need to begin creating the self-reliant local communities we have been exploring in this book, and waiting to intentionally start that undertaking is *not* an option.

Ignoring the massive threats and changes that are coming is merely adding to the growing momentum pushing humanity and human civilization toward the abyss of extinction. Without preparation, and the resilience that intentional preparation offers, survival is unlikely for much of humanity. Don't be a part of those who fail to pay attention. The more you pay attention and connect the dots, the more likely you will survive the future that's coming.

I encourage readers to stay focused on creating a moral and ethical world based on wealth equality, an intentionally evolved collective human consciousness, reducing poverty, and increasing the security and well-being of all persons. Happiness, life satisfaction, a sense of security, justice, cooperation, community, family, more equal distribution of wealth, and greater economic self-sufficiency are the ways we need to evaluate economic performance in the future. Not greed, profit, and unlimited growth.

These are the values and principles that most people want to see when we talk about the meaning and purpose of "progress," *not* GDP.

When well-being for all is missing, the social fabric is weakened.

When groups of people are disenfranchised for generations, the social fabric is weakened.

When people in the commons live with extreme wealth inequality, the social fabric is weakened.

Historically, these attacks on the social fabric inevitably lead to cynicism, disillusionment, and loss of belief in a positive future. The loss of hope in the disenfranchised people of the commons has been the cancer responsible for the collapse of every empire and civilization in human history. Once the vision of the future begins to decay in the commons, for whatever reason, the culture will not long survive.

The commons are the inherited guide to the meaning of well-being and hope. We need to teach sustainability as a way of life. The commons are not a thing. They're a vision; a collective intelligence and wisdom. The commons worldwide are losing faith in their leaders, capitalism, never-ending wars, famine, the future, and hope. We *know* we have lost confidence in the ability to live sustainably. Most people don't know the sobering reality that civilization is far more fragile than most people believe.[51]

So How Do We Move Forward?
A Brief Summary.

a. Localization and the creation of self-reliant local communities is a realistic viable path forward.

b. The success of that path toward a future of well-being and hope will be based primarily on whether we have the wisdom and courage to begin preparing *now* for the changes and challenges that are coming because once social collapse has started, it will be too late to create successful, local, sustainable communities.

c. We are running out of time to awaken and tame our collective primitive ego consciousness and create sustainable, self-reliant local communities capable of surviving the massive changes that are coming. And this work to co-create these dreams, visions, and possibilities of a viable, sustainable, self-reliant local community into tangible form and reality needs to happen now, before social, civil, and economic collapse happens. We need to wake up as a species and recognize that our competitive quest for wealth and unlimited growth is suicidal. These self-reliant, local communities will be the foundation of the regenerative, sustainable social culture we will need post-capitalism and post-social collapse.

d. My goal in writing this book is not a focus on who deserves to survive social collapse, but rather what we can do to give those who *want* to survive a fighting chance. What will be required? How can we begin to prepare now so they can create the resilience they will need to successfully deal with the massive changes coming, the tools and the

---

51 **The Unraveling of America**, Wade Davis, 8/6/2020 (https://www.rollingstone.com/politics/political-commentary/COVID-19-end-of-american-era-wade-davis-1038206/). This is one of the better articles I've read supporting the concepts that a self-reliant local community would need to embrace, and why they are needed.

skills to survive in a low-energy world; skills that include hunting, carpentry, gardening, preserving food, living with less, creating social structures that build well-being values, what it means to be human, basic principles, empathy, compassion, cooperation, mutuality, listening skills, consensus decision-making, middlepath thinking, skills to work interdependently and effectively in a diverse community, and most importantly, a sustainable connection with the land and "place."

Reconnecting with Place, Reconnecting with the Land

We have lost our bond with the land. And "place." Reconnecting with the spirit embedded in nature is the most important work we need to be doing. Embracing the spirit of the land means embracing the concept of systemic interconnection and interdependence with the land, the people in our community, the *place* we call home, and putting down roots into the soil in a place we call home.

We've lost that bond and connection with "place." And home is not a house we live in. Home is the farming community we are bonded and connected with, in a particular *place* called home. A place where resources, information, tools, seeds, and food are shared, a place where the community shares "ownership."[52]

Business, corporations, social movements, and politicians will not bring about the voluntary structural economic changes we need to redesign and replace capitalism. It won't happen. They know that giving voice to the coming realities would lead to massive social disruption and likely social and civil collapse. Capitalism will not, and never has, prioritized people's health, eco-systems, or life before profits. It can't. If it does, it will die.

In other words, a social movement will never replace neoliberal, market capitalism. Only tangible preparation by real people of courage and vision;

---

52   The Unsettling of America: Culture and Agriculture, by Wendel Berry. Far and away the best book I've ever read. Don't miss it. It embraces the concepts that a self-reliant local community would need to embrace...and why.

people who begin creating self-reliant local communities *before* the inevitable coming social collapse; will have the ability to create a viable future and hope that humanity will need to survive.

The History of Local Communities

History has shown that local communities that embrace the morality of shared responsibility, cooperation, and interdependence increase the ability to survive when confronted by a crisis. Unfortunately, over time, immature and unevolved primitive ego thinking has increased the human tendency for domination, individuality, competition, selfishness, aggression, hierarchical dominance, patriarchal-dominated societies, vertical power domination systems, and zero-sum thinking.

The concept of local, self-reliant communities discussed in this book is based on the assumption that all members in the community would have *intentionally* embraced a tamed, adult, evolved, mature collective thinking process to ensure that those immature human tendencies would not be allowed to return.

This would involve educating the children of the community from early childhood to adulthood in the concepts of:

a. Systemic thinking.

b. The interconnectedness of all aspects of reality.

c. Individual training in the taming of their primitive ego consciousness and its early childhood conditioning.

d. Embracing the wisdom of all the great spiritual teachers to awaken and grow in self-awareness.

e. Teaching the indigenous cultural wisdom that *"spirit"* is embedded in all of the natural world.

f. Education in the systemic, interconnected unity of all life and the deep interdependence and interconnectedness of all aspects of reality, would be the best way of ensuring that the destructive regression to an immature collective primitive ego-consciousness does not happen again.

This early childhood teaching would include

a. The importance of cooperative relationships, interdependent responsibility, reciprocity, and redistribution.

b. Valuing the well-being of all our relationships with family and nature.

c. The community obligation to nurture and care for everyone in the community.

d. The cyclical commitment to balance what is given and taken.

e. The commitment to share what one possesses, including material wealth, one's skills, time, and energy.

Stated simply, children would be taught that quality of life is based on well-being, not the accumulation of wealth and power.

They would learn the promise of unlimited energy from fossil fuels was an amazing gift, but it created a critical collapse in regional and local self-reliance, and the CO_2 pollution it has created is now threatening the long-term survival of life on our planet.

They would grow up knowing that humanity is now faced with the challenge of returning human culture to its roots of rural self-reliance and creating a future that is once again rural, self-reliant, and sustainable.

They would grow up knowing that taming the primitive ego needs to be a foundational aspect of human thinking and human consciousness in creating these self-reliant local communities if our goal is to avoid the extinction of our species and life this planet.

Their education would incorporate these principles of traditional wisdom into an integrated system of values that are needed to create and protect the survival of humanity in the face of massive change. They would grow into adulthood knowing that hope is not based on the certainty of outcome. It's based on the imagination of what's possible if we all worked together to create a world of cooperative, sustainable, and self-reliant local communities.

A world of cooperative preparation for resiliency and survival rather than hyper-individualism.

A world that affirms life rather than material wealth.

A world based on degrowth, simplification of lifestyle, and the intentional powering down from fossil fuel energy; the core values needed to create and protect humanity's survival in the face of massive change.

A world that intentionally creates a mature collective human consciousness, a humanity that uses a tamed primitive ego-consciousness that embraces the simple principle that every generation, everywhere, has an equal right to the enjoyment of the natural wealth.

Access to Land: A Critical Obstacle to Creating a Self-Reliant Local Community

Creating sustainable, local, self-reliant communities will depend mainly on access to land. It will be one of the more critical obstacles that will need to be overcome if the localization movement is to be successful. It will be more important than climate intensification, ecosystem collapse, overconsumption, or overpopulation. All of those force-multipliers will collapse of their own weight when we experience social and civil collapse. But the ability to begin creating self-reliant local communities will depend almost entirely on acquiring affordable land *before* the inevitable social and civil collapse has happened. In other words, the land will need to be purchased *before* acquiring the many resources a self-reliant local community will need to survive.

In the words of Henry David Thoreau, "I am convinced, both by faith and experience, that to maintain one's self on this earth is not a hardship but a pastime, if we will live simply and wisely." Preparing *now*, and purchasing land *now* to get started, are important goals if we are to make Henry David Thoreau's vision of voluntary simplicity a reality.

As a generation of pioneers moving into a post-growth, low-impact, low energy "local" future that's focused on well-being, the goal of creating a sustainable local community will depend mainly on access to land, and that access will be a prime barrier to people living simply and moving successfully beyond the consumer culture of modern capitalism.

A post-growth future will not be what it used to be, but it could be a future that has the potential to be an essential evolutionary step upward in the collective consciousness of humanity, a consciousness that embraces sustainability and well-being as a way of life.

In the words of Buckminster Fuller, "You never change things by fighting against the existing reality. To change something, build a new model that makes the old model obsolete."

I believe sustainable, self-reliant local *communities* are that new model. When I read Wendell Berry's book, *The Unsettling of America: Culture and Agriculture* many years ago, it changed my life. I joined the back-to-the-land movement and began homesteading on 30 acres in the early 1970s. This picture is of me standing in front of the rough-cut oak barn we built, on the fieldstone foundation my son and I constructed using the stone wall building techniques used by New England settlers in the 1800s.

"The land has nothing to do with the left and the right. The land—the given world—is of ultimate value, and the caretaking of it is a matter of paramount importance. If you eat, you are involved in agriculture," is one of my favorite Berry quotes.

Caution: Going It Alone Is Not an Option

I see no way individuals "going it alone on the land" will survive the future that is coming. The existential threats and force-multiplier challenges will be far too overwhelming for any individual to survive independently. The only way I see humanity surviving is in the creation of small, sustainable, self-reliant local communities and local economies based on the *well-being* of every member in the community, the land, and its ecosystems. A community grounded in the values of compassion, empathy, mutuality, cooperation, teamwork, and the well-being and care for everyone in the community.

The need for "a sense of purpose" and "emotional connection with others" is critically important when life as we know it is threatened. And the threats listed in Part 2 *will* increasingly threaten the foundations of the social and civil structures that support human culture, life as we know it, and even the very survival of our species. Only localization and the creation of small, local, self-reliant "seed" communities we have been discussing offer the possibility of true hope, not Tinker Bell thinking.

Now is the time to think outside the box and engage our collective imagination to create a vision of hope and what might be possible. I believe localization and the creation of small local "seed" communities is a post-growth vision and narrative of hope. These local "seed" communities could interact and trade with other local "seed" communities to preserve human knowledge, human history, and create a viable *post-growth, local community* future for human civilization.

Reclaiming Hope: Our Focus on the Big Picture, Strategic Action, Resilience, and Preparation

Hope is always based on shared values and achieving the best possible outcomes when change arrives, and it *will*. Everything in the lifestyle we are accustomed to as Westerners will experience change in our lives, our diets, our jobs, our sense of self, how we relate to others, how we co-exist with others, our respect for the natural world, and embracing voluntary simplicity. Stated simply, the status quo will not work!

The inevitable contraction of civilization and social collapse will be a disaster unless we are prepared for it. We will need self-reliant local communities and local economies that embrace a debt-free currency, local health, and social services, focused on well-being and quality of life, not wealth, profit, or unlimited growth.

Shifting our attention from economic growth to sustainable local communities in Part 3 will require embracing new ideas of what it means to live within the limits of our planet and letting go of the deep social conditioning of growth, profit, and wealth that primitive ego greed has unconsciously embedded in our human social consciousness. If we fail to tame our primitive ego and evolve our human thinking, it will only be a matter of time before we revert to the destructive, greed-based thinking that is currently encouraging nature to remove humanity as a species from this planet.

Stated simply, localization and the creation of a self-reliant local community that works sustainably with nature, not against nature, is a post-growth narrative of hope. I encourage readers to use *localfutures.org* to self-educate on the importance of local community. In the material below, we will take an in-depth look at the importance of creating these sustainable and self-reliant local communities, including the specific moral and social concepts they embrace to develop and build the resilience that will be needed as the world begins to experience the massive changes that are coming.

Self-reliant local communities will need to embrace the concepts that:

a. We experience all of life through "relationships."

b. Happiness happens when we learn to focus on what our soul "needs," not what our ego "wants."

c. Things *just happen;* they don't happen *to us!*

As I pointed out above, life *is* change. Change alone does not have the ability to define who we are. How we cope with and adapt to that change *will* ultimately determine who we are.

Preparation for the coming changes is best achieved when we keep in mind the simple reality that everything in the universe is continually changing, becoming something new, and evolving. The more we embrace and accept these realities, the better prepared we will be when they simply "happen."

Self-Reliant Local Communities as the "Commons"

A self-reliant local community is essentially the intentional creation of a "commons." A "commons" is defined as a concept of shared resources in which each stakeholder has an equal interest in the *cultural and natural* resources that are accessible to all members of a community or society, including natural resources such as air, water, and a habitable earth. These resources are held in common, *not owned privately*.

The concept of the commons is also defined as a social practice of governing a resource not by state or market, but by a community of users that self-governs the resource through *consensus decision-making* and the social institutions that those decisions create.

A commons is essentially about *creating, strengthening,* and *maintaining* equitable relationships between people, of past, present, and future generations based on justice, well-being, and sustainable lives for everyone in the commons or local community...socially, economically, and institutionally (politically). In other words, each sphere of the local community or commons is not separate or distinct; each sphere is systemically interdependent and interconnected with all of the others, and each sphere simply provides a different perspective for looking at any given issue.

In other words, all spheres of the community work together organically as a "living" system or organism.

Each sphere or part of a "commons" is peer-governed and focused on the moral and ethical interconnection, interdependence, and well-being of all of nature and reality. As we have discussed above, a critical aspect of a self-reliant local community is the ethical or philosophical concept that each member of the local community would be expected to have intentionally embraced the taming, maturation, and evolution of their immature primitive ego and its early childhood conditioning. A simple way to describe this concept is each person in the community has adopted a tamed and evolved, middlepath consciousness that has given up the need to be "right" and has adopted an evolved middlepath consciousness that assumes that truth is always found *on both sides of every issue.* Decisions in a self-reliant local community are made using a consensus decision-making process that assumes that:

a. Nobody is smart enough to be right or wrong 100% of the time.

b. The goal is always the well-being of all members in the community.

c. Everything in the self-reliant local community is *systemically intercon-nected* with everything else in the self-reliant local community.

d. All decisions made by the community are based on the concept that *we are all in this journey together,* not on immature "what's in it for me?" thinking. In consensus decision-making, each person speaks "their" truth, not "THE" truth.

The primary, core value of a self-reliant local community or "commons" is the principle that everyone in the community has intentionally tamed, evolved, enlightened, and awakened their primitive ego and its immature early childhood conditioning, and has become *self-aware* of the beams in their own eye. In other words, each member of the local community has achieved the ability to come together and work cooperatively with an open heart and an open mind to embrace change while focusing on the long-term well-being, welfare, and survival of every *"we" in* their self-reliant local community.

The Benefits and Importance of Creating and Living in a Self-Reliant, Highly Self-Sufficient Local Community

A self-reliant local community is a engaged in the production of new knowledge, a place of "home" *with* one another that practices the principles of reciprocity, cooperation, interdependence, and respect…a *community* way of life that gives its members the ability to live at walking speed, reconnect with their surroundings and the natural world, the ability to pay attention to the passing clouds, the passing time, and enjoy all of the things that petroleum has made us less aware of as we zip at high speed between here and there; in other words, no relationship, awareness, or understanding of the reality between here and there.

A self-reliant local community offers new ways of living on our limited planet. But we need to acknowledge that the existing social, civil, and economic systems can't be directly replaced when creating a local community. We need to develop new self-reliant and sustainable local financial systems—economic systems that function locally at the community level.

Successful self-reliant local communities will need to build relationships based on the concepts and principles of an interdependent and interconnected natural ecosystem way of thinking that uses our human bodies as a template. A system where every part of the whole shares the life-giving resources needed to survive. Where the well-being of every cell in our body shares equally. A holistic approach that recognizes that any part of the body that hogs the resources, or attempts to grow independently of the community's larger *wholeness,* is identified as a form of cancer that needs to be removed from the community.

Like the human body, human civilization is a community. Humans discovered eons ago that resilience for survival was best achieved when they lived and cooperated with others in a local community. The more the local community embraced the concepts of cooperation, social responsibility, teamwork, interdependence, generosity, networking with other local communities, and the well-being of all community members, the more resilient they had when their survival was challenged.

Sadly, education in our modern schools is currently geared towards the needs of corporations rather than the diverse needs of a self-reliant local community that include place-based knowledge, the skills required to survive off the land, the generational wisdom of regional agriculture, decentralized production of food, local investing, local banking, local currencies, local business alliances, local networking, mechanical and farming equipment expertise, permaculture farming, regenerative agriculture, and intentional biodiversity *(growing food in human-designed ecosystems that mimic the diversity and resilience of natural ecosystems).*

In other words, all of the skill development that will be required for self-reliant local communities to survive the massive upheavals and challenges that are coming. Challenges that will include powering down from fossil energy, social and civil collapse, the collapse of human culture and life as we know it, the collapse of our modern financial systems, collapse of our underfunded human social structures such as water, electricity, health care, droughts, and food disruption, flooding, toxic pollution of air and water, climate migration, or the growing social anger created by fear and insecurity and the other destabilizing force multipliers we discussed in Part 2.

Stated simply, our modern world is woefully unprepared to cope with the challenges and force-multiplier threats and economic triggers in Part 2 that our unevolved, immature, self-focused collective primitive ego consciousness has created on its journey toward success in the corporate world, wealth accumulation, and the accumulation of "stuff" that was supposed to make us happy.

List of the Basic Concepts Embedded in a Self-Reliant Local Community

Rather than attempting to describe all of the details and concepts embedded in a self-reliant local community as a wordy narrative, I believe it will be more useful for the creation of a self-reliant local community, and members of a local community, if the basic concepts, values, principles, morals, foundational structures, and detailed aspects of a self-reliant local community are presented as a numbered list for easier reference.[53]

When using this list to create a self-reliant local community, it will be essential to keep in mind:

a. The Part 2 primary and secondary existential force-multipliers and economic triggers that are coming sooner than most believe.

b. The likely and all but certain reality that social and civil collapse will arrive far sooner than most people think possible.

c. Most importantly, when social and civil collapse happens, it *will severely limit* access to the critically needed resources, tools, and equipment a local community will need to be successful; resources we take for granted today.

Self-Reliant Local Communities' Need to Stay Remote and Invisible

As I'm sure you are well aware by now, an essential concern and focus of this book is the urgency to begin preparing for social and civil collapse *"now."* The sooner we start to prepare for that collapse of life as we know it, the more successful we will be in creating sustainable, self-reliant local communities.

Because the social unrest during economic, social, and civil collapse will be significant and potentially violent, locating self-reliant local communities in more remote locations away from cities and high population centers will significantly increase the ability to protect the self-reliant local communities from people who are desperate. Not a pleasant thought, but an inevitable reality to prepare for as you choose location and access to freshwater and a source of wood for heating and cooking.

It will be essential to keep in mind that greed, "What's in it for me?" thinking, the survival of the fittest, power over others, fear of others, the need to be right, the illusion of separateness, and narcissistic self-entitlement, will

---

53   See Bibliography for references used.

be controlling the behaviors of desperate and hungry people when social and civil collapse happens.

Stated simply, they will be dangerous.

And the best defense for a local community will be invisibility. Be prepared to keep a low profile for as long as possible. Self-reliant local communities will need to be carefully located well away from urban population centers and be intentionally designed to look impoverished. The more "invisible" they are, and the more they are located off the beaten track, the safer they will be.

Another basic cautionary concept to keep in mind is the golden arch of this book, the reality that *we are the problem*. For much of human history, our cultures, traditions, personalities, and even our bodies have evolved in connection with community and nature. But the modern, neoliberal global economy has severed these connections with false promises that include the belief that economic growth is the key to progress, more stuff and more money will make us happy, and technology will solve all of our problems.

Transitioning the community consciousness from that mindset of greed and exploitation to a philosophy of collaboration, abundance, and happiness will be a significant challenge to overcome.

Taming the local community's collective primitive ego-consciousness will be critical to its long-term success as a viable self-reliant local community. We all participated in the modern world, "What's in it for me?" greed-based capitalism, neoliberal global economies, the creation of global warming, storm intensification, and the force-multipliers of Part 2. We consciously and unconsciously bought into the addictive message that profit and wealth create happiness and the deeply embedded and conditioned belief that *lack of wealth means a lack of success and happiness*.

Because this life-long conditioning will be a significant challenge to overcome, it will be necessary to:

a. Always keep in mind the primary goal of a self-reliant community is viable, long-term survival.

b. Always be prepared to deal with individuals in the local community who struggle or resist taming their primitive ego thinking.

They will be easy to identify; an aggressive need to be "right," a lack of empathy and compassion for others, a self-focused "What's in it for me?" greed, and a need for private ownership of resources, to name only a few of the untamed primitive ego behaviors that will threaten the long-term survival of a local community. They will be a challenge, but these people *will* exist, and they *will* be a dangerous social cancer in the community.

Because we have been conditioned, indoctrinated, brainwashed, encouraged, and addicted by human culture for generations to believe that wealth, greed, profit, private ownership, and power over others is normal and necessary for happiness, not everyone in our self-reliant local communities will be able to tame their narcissism, addiction, entitlement, and greed-based "What's in it for me?" thinking.

Be ready to deal with that cancer when it shows up.

The long-term success and survival of your community will depend on how well you deal with that threat. Like any cancer, it will take over the long-term life support structures of your community very quickly.

In other words, sometimes tough decisions *will* be required.

As discussed above, a self-reliant local community's long-term success will depend on educating the children in the community from kindergarten to adulthood on the critical need to *intentionally* tame, evolve, and mature their collective primitive ego-consciousness.

Because all members of the community may not achieve this self-awareness and "inner change," it will be essential to remember that the positive changes a community creates to create security and well-being for all members of the community *will always be vulnerable to being co-opted by members of the community who hide their regressive, immature, untamed collective primitive ego-consciousness conditioning of greed and profit.* Over time they could use those positive changes in the local community to subtly re-create the greed-based systems of the current economic system as they attempt to subtly shift the focus of the community back to "growth" and "profit."

Adapting to life in a self-reliant local community focused on well-being and cooperation is simply re-learning what ancient indigenous cultures *knew: the reality that the "inner" and the "outer," and the human and the non-human, are inextricably intertwined.* Over time, self-reliant local community living will help us reconnect and once again experience the interdependent world; the world we have known and survived in throughout human history; a world that reflects and honors the interdependent web of life. The living web of which we are, and always have been, an interdependent and interconnective part of since the birth of our species.[54]

But evolving the community's consciousness from an unconscious, top-down concept of competition, scarcity, and exploitation mindset to a mindset of collaboration, abundance, and happiness will be a significant challenge, and a potential threat, to the long-term survival of a self-reliant local community for generations.

Always keep in mind the long-term goal of the local community is that of survival. And there *will* be times when tough decisions will be required.

How to Use the List as You Create a Self-Reliant Local Community

When you use the list below, keep in mind that it's not any single item on the list that defines a self-reliant local community. A self-reliant local community requires the truths and essence of *all* of the concepts included in the list. The self-reliant local communities we create will be "communities in process" for as long as they exist. Change and adaptation to that change are how our universe evolves. There is no perfect long-term blueprint for a successful self-reliant local community. That long-term blueprint will *always* be a work in process. But it bears repeating, the only item in the list that will be *essential* for a self-reliant

---

54 Concepts embedded in: *Localization: Essential steps to an economics of Happiness*, Helena Norberg-Hodge, Local Futures, www.localfutures.org, 2016.

local community's long-term viability is the *intentional* taming of the community's collective primitive ego.

Without that intentional awakening in self-awareness and taming, the members of a local community "will" eventually revert to the same immature greed-based "What's in it for me?" primitive ego thinking and destructive behaviors that created the force-multipliers in Part 2; the "self-focused," greed-based, collective human consciousness and thinking process that could quickly re-emerge and re-create the same behaviors and force-multipliers that are currently devouring our planet and threatening the future extinction of our human species.

The collective taming, maturing, and awakening of human consciousness is a goal that humanity needs to embrace. The failure to achieve this collective matured level of consciousness, and then maintain that level of evolved consciousness, will ultimately condemn humanity to extinction.

The List: Basic Concepts That Define the Values, Principles, and Beliefs of a Self-Reliant Local Community

1. **Self-reliant Local communities protect local ecosystems** as they build more localized, place-based economic structures. Transition Towns, Local Futures, and Global Ecovillage Network are internet resources that can be helpful.

2. **A well-being focus of a localization community will include** economic equality of basic needs, a reduction in financial hardship for all people, increased time for parents to focus on children, meaningful work, shared governance, and consensus decision-making.

3. **Self-reliant local community resources**: hand pump (or solar pump) well for water, robust compost systems, cold cellars for storage, smoking and salting for preservation, canning, solar panels for local energy, farm tools, blacksmithing skills, community gardening, community beekeeping, community fruit trees, use of restorative farming

techniques and local plants when possible, use and recycle heritage seeds whenever available.

4. **Self-reliance in the local community** will require creating self-reliant **local renewable energy systems** and **community-owned energy installations**. When power is produced within the community, there is no need to expand expensive transmission infrastructures. Residents also have greater control over their energy costs and are not dependent on distant energy companies. Local power would be used primarily for lighting, health equipment, charging portable tools, and equipment such as a community radio station. This local green energy system would not be designed to provide energy for heating or air conditioner cooling.

5. **Sustainable prosperity** for all members.

6. **Consensus** decision-making.

7. **No private ownership**.

8. **Intentionally tamed collective primitive ego consciousness** (evolved and matured collective consciousness) to (a) avoid re-creating the same crises that we are currently facing *and* (b) ensure the social longevity and protect the deeply ingrained values and evolved levels of consciousness that will be needed by future local self-reliant "seed" communities ("seed" communities = creating a sustainable future human culture on our planet).

9. **Firmly grounded** in objective science and natures laws.

10. **Willingness** to teach skills to others.

11. **People** in a local community can talk and deal directly with other members of the community versus anonymous bureaucrats.

12. **Everyone** in a local community depends on family, friends, and neighbors.

13. **Mutual well-being** of all members and an equal voice in all consensus decision-making.

14. **A basic worldview** of partnering with nature.

15. **Networking** with other "local" communities that also (a) value these concepts and (b) have done the work of intentionally taming/evolving their own collective community consciousness.

16. **Local community** = **real people** working and playing together versus powerlessness and insecurity when capitalism encourages people to feel inadequate, self-conscious, inhibited, and not "successful" because they don't have *"more"* or live up to "social" standards when "more" defines one's "adequacy as a person" and "successful" is defined by capitalism, consumerism, and modernization.

17. **Women and the work they do** is valued versus capitalism/consumerism, where women become invisible, don't earn money for their work, are defined as non-workers, earn less than more successful "men," are considered inferior than men, inadequate, and so on.

18. **Children stay connected** to the wisdom of their grandparents/elders versus intolerance between young and old, where children leave home to be "successful" and move from rural areas into large urban centers where power and decision-making are in the hands of a few.

19. **Each person is an "individual"** free to be themselves versus the need to conform, pressured to live up to the idealized images of *success,* that is, to become a *somebody.*

20. **Self-reliant local communities** more fundamentally respect human needs, natural limits, and reclaim the concept of love, not as an abstract, all-embracing fantasy but accountability and responsibility in the implementation of a clear set of ethics, principles, values, and behaviors.

21. **All members** of the local community would be required to intentionally tame and evolve their collective primitive ego-conscious and its childhood conditioning and embrace the concepts that love and compassion are justice in action, and the simple reality that love and compassion are behaviors, not feelings.

22. **Conserving and reusing** non-renewable resources.

23. **The ability for every member** of the local community to ask for help without judgment, shame, sense of lack, sense of failure, fear of rejection, fear of vulnerability, or prejudice.

24. **Every member** of the local community is seen, heard, and cared for; including the ability of every member to embrace a spiritual worldview that honors the "spirit" or "thou-ness" embedded in others, in nature, and all of reality. Stated simply, the ability to embrace the systemic interconnectedness and interdependence of all aspects of reality in our thinking.

25. **Local self-reliant communities** manifest conversation and trust, empathy, compassion, cooperation, middlepath thinking, social justice, and most importantly, the ability to avoid cognitive dissonance when information and data and facts disagree with previously held beliefs.

26. **Divisive narratives** based on the primitive ego need to be "right" disappear.

27. **Use renewable resources** only up to their regrowth rates.

28. **Conserve** and honor biodiversity.

29. **Eliminate** the gap between the rich and the poor.

30. **Reduced** energy use and pollution (uses community-based local green solar and wind energy).

31. **Increased accountability** and transparency in local governance through consensus decision-making.

32. **Do no harm** and create benefit for all members.

33. **Affirm and support** individual callings.

34. **Value** leisure time.

35. **Reduce** consumption.

36. **Focus** on needs, not wants.

37. **Focus** on quality of life.

38. **Recognize and honor** that nature and our planet has limits.

39. **Value** sustainability over growth.

40. **Create** local banking, and a local currency, and develop a local barter system. People will list the services or goods they have to offer and the amount they expect in return. Their account is credited for goods or services they provide to other members, and they can use those credits to purchase goods or services from anyone else in the local system. Thus, even people with little or no "real" money can participate in, and benefit from, the circulation of credit within the local economy.

41. **Require members** of the local community to have embraced an *intentional* taming of their immature primitive ego thinking, and its early childhood conditioning, so as to successfully create a viable, long-term, successful local community.

42. **Embrace a "we" focus** on community well-being, not profit.

43. **Self-reliant local communities** are designed to support local businesses.

44. **Self-reliant local communities** are designed to support intentional simplification and reduced consumption.

45. **Small diversified farming.** Localization shortens the distance between producers and consumers and eliminates fragile global supply chains that put food availability at risk. A handful of corporations now control a growing proportion of the world's food supply, but the large-scale monocultures they create are less productive per acre than smaller, more diversified farming. Diversity and systemic thinking are ignored by globalization and monoculture farming. The diversity embraced by systemic thinking is essential for life. Erasing diversity and systemic thinking in monoculture farming is simply incompatible with life.

46. **Local self-reliant communities** have significantly more control over their own affairs, their agricultural diversity, and most importantly, their food production. Cities and urban populations and communities are separated from their most basic human needs. Their survival

resilience in times of crises (that will be created by the existential threats of the coming force-multipliers in Part 2) is dangerously low. Globalizing monocultures drive people from the land and disconnect them from one another and nature.

47. **Localization isn't about returning to the past.** But it does mean acknowledging what older cultures did well: they relied on local resources and local knowledge to meet people's material needs, and as a result, they did so with a minimum of environmental impact; and they put a high value on community ties, which enabled them to meet people's psychological need for connection and security.[55] These are lessons we need to keep in mind as we create self-reliant local communities to cope with the existential challenges, threats, and changes of Part 2 that are coming.

48. **Self-reliant local self-reliant communities** help younger-generation members build critical survival skills required to create sustainability and resilience and increase their local wisdom and local knowledge and ability to work sustainably with their local ecosystems.

49. **Self-reliant local community schooling.** In the modern world, schooling is increasingly geared towards the needs of corporations, which are presumed to be the future employers of today's children. Training in skills relevant to the export economy rather than the local or regional economy. **A primary goal of schooling** in self-reliant local communities will need to focus on alternative place-based learning, homeschooling, regional agriculture, natural healing methods, learning about local plant and fungi identification, wilderness self-reliance, and basic survival skills; the skills and learning required to deal with a condition many describe as a debilitating "nature-deficit disorder" embedded in current modern education.

55   Localization: Essential steps to an economics of Happiness. Helena Norberg-Hodge, Local Futures, www.localfutures.org, 2016.

50. **Self-reliant Local communities** create and support sustainable use of resources for seven generations.

51. **Nature** is not a machine.

52. **Self-reliant local communities** recognize that "Life isn't fair, it just is, and it's always changing and becoming something new."

53. **Self-reliant local communities** change the dominant economy and the pressures that separate us from one another, the natural world, and our deeper human needs. "At the most fundamental level, localization is the economics of happiness" (Helena Norberg-Hodge).

54. **Two significant threats to localization** and the creation of a viable, self-reliant local community will be (a) the psychological pressure to modernize (created by capitalism and the belief that *more* is needed for happiness), and (b) avoiding the need to tame our collective human primitive ego consciousness (the false belief that we can't grow and evolve our collective human consciousness and its early childhood conditioning).

55. **Local community** is a more straightforward way of life. A home economy focused on gardening, preserving, repairing, fixing, looking after animals, making furniture, toys, chicken pens, keeping bikes going, recycling, composting, cutting firewood, maintaining machinery, engaging in hobbies, arts and crafts. Respect and reputation will depend mainly on how capable you are at doing many varied useful things. Being as self-sufficient as is reasonably possible—that is, a simple way of life, especially at the household and community level; a community's resilience will be a function of the number of people who can make and grow and do and fix many things.

56. **Local community** is a collaborative economy based on well-being, security for all members of the community. A community that is built on the taming/evolution/maturation of its collective primitive ego-consciousness and **with an "us" focus** versus concentration of wealth in the hands of a few.

57. **Local community** embraces the concept that to love your neighbor, you need to know your neighbor…not judge or dislike! People come first, not ideas and beliefs!

58. **Relationships in a local, self-reliant community** tend to be mutually reinforcing and encourage harmony and stability. The bonds and responsibilities in a local community offer a profound sense of security, a prerequisite for inner peace, contentedness, and a sense of well-being.

59. **Resiliency is created by preparation**. If/when the global economy self-destructs, the supermarket shelves will be bare within a few days, but a local community will have skilled, productive people capable of running a highly self-sufficient local economy that depends mostly on simple technologies.

60. **Self-reliant local communities** are based on the concept that living frugally and self-sufficiently is a benefit. Not a sacrifice!! This includes avoiding waste, recycling, and using the resources you have; producing some of your own food and entertainment; making repairs, not using much, not having to buy much; being able to make it, not buy it; focus on what's good enough, what will do the job well enough; focus on needs, not wants; care of self and neighbor; no debt; everyone contributes what they can.

61. **Self-reliant local communities** encourage relearning how to keep ourselves alive without capitalism and its blind and growing extraction of natural resources.

62. **Self-reliant local communities** are based on the creation of an economy of trust, well-being, loyalty, and local diversity. A focus on non-monetary economies, culture, community, spare time, well-being, communal bonding, local cooperation, support, solidarity, increased time for friends rather than money, and less fear about the future.

63. **Self-reliant local communities** embrace living more in the presence of *now*, a place of simple observing consciousness where one can better experience the present moment, the only place that is reality.

64. **Self-reliant local communities** believe that every outcome we experience in life is created by a choice we *made,* or *failed to make*, whether consciously or unconsciously.

65. **Self-reliant local communities** create strength and resiliency when people come together to build a connection with place, the natural world, and each other—an identity of who they are and where they "belong," that is, where their roots are as they create a place-based relationship with others, the land, with nature, a real economy, genuine interdependence, and a community.

66. **Localization** is nature's most generous friend and supporter as self-reliant local communities tame the dangers of economic globalization and the unlimited power of corporations!

67. **Collapse of social and civil structures** is a very real threat. When it happens, humanity's best shot at survival will be adopting the principles of localization (local communities) and the intentional taming of our collective primitive ego consciousness.

68. **In a self-reliant local community,** decision-making itself is transformed; we create systems that are small enough for us to influence, but we also embed ourselves within a web of relationships that informs our actions and perspectives at a deep level; that is, our situational "experiential awareness" in general is increased. Our ability to prepare for the future is enhanced.

69. **Self-reliant local communities are cooperatives,** that is, local networks versus global supply chains. They can shift from outsourced global corporate supply chains to locally produced items that are needed to sustain their lives. COVID-19 reminds us that *we should never outsource and lose control of critical resources that sustain and support our lives any more than is absolutely necessary.* Cooperatives focus on the needs of their members, and they function on the concept of cooperation and the creation of the "well-being" of its members.

Cooperatives are essentially local communities that honor labor's sovereignty and the cooperative interdependence and autonomy of local labor. They believe the purpose of work is to improve the community. Like cooperatives, self-reliant local communities are based on cooperation, compassion, solidarity, and generosity as the primary underlying principles of life and community. Every person contributes, however they can, to the well-being of the community. Every person is cared for regardless of their contribution. They take care of one another.

A self-reliant local community is a cooperative that understands the need to intentionally tame and evolve their collective consciousness. They understand that cooperation and consensus decision-making is hard work, not a Tinker Bell utopia. Members have rights, but they also recognize that with those rights come responsibilities. A self-reliant local community is a cooperative that is best defined as *"a way of life."*

70. **The concepts in localization and self-reliant local communities are** about slowing down, scaling back, and fostering deep connection to restore the social and economic structures essential for meeting our material and deeper human needs in ways that nurture the only planet we have. The business-as-usual path that humanity is currently on, is leading us relentlessly towards fast-paced, large-scale, monocultural, techno-development. It's a path that separates us from each other and the natural world and accelerates our downward social and ecological decline.

71. **Self-reliant local communities** do not depend on long-supply-line exports when it comes to the necessities of our own lives!

72. **Self-reliant local communities understand systemic thinking** involves adaptation to, and acceptance of, diversity. Systemic thinking embraces the fundamental premise to never put poisons in your water. Always assume "change." And don't do anything when you have no idea what the effects will be. (Wendell Berry)

73. **Localization and self-reliant local communities** are a revival of the **neighborhood principle** to help each other and embrace active interdependence. Agribusiness is focused on profit. Putting small farmers out of business increases the profits of agribusiness monoculture farming. So, they quietly support the concept that rural is backward. In other words, they actively promote a breakdown of genuine local economies connected to the land, all in the name of progress and efficiency. We need to start a journey back to the land. (Wendell Berry).

(I have written this book in the belief that creating self-reliant local communities would create and support that important journey back to the land, hopefully in time to build resilience for the massive changes that are coming to human civilization as we know it.)

74. **Self-reliant local communities** embrace Wendell Berry's Precautionary Principle which states that when there is a threat of severe and irreversible damage, we don't need to wait for "all" the evidence to come in before acting; we are justified in acting to "protect" because it might well be too late by the time "full evidence" is available.

75. **Globalism** *is* capitalism.

76. **Localization and self-reliant local "seed" communities** could help us prepare for the massive changes that are coming and help us build resilience before social and civil collapse happens, a growing and likely reality! We are recipients of a great gift: We have the opportunity (which subsequent generations may not have) to begin now to move towards a more sustainable future. We have the opportunity *and* the responsibility.

77. **Local, self-reliant communities** need to embrace the concept of **reducing inequality**. It needs to be at the core and heart of all post-growth, powering down, degrowth, and intentional simplification of life actions—that is, equality and justice need to be embedded as core issues and objectives.

78. **Self-reliant local communities** embrace the economics of both **justice and sustainability** because they dramatically shrink the gap between rich and poor while reducing energy use and pollution. At the personal level, localization is the economics of happiness because it reconnects us with community and nature.

79. **Self-reliant local communities** are the **opposite of globalization.** "I saw how ideas about progress, education, individualism, and democracy were transformed into blind support for economic growth and development; how idealism and goodwill ended up in the service of mindless waste, consumerism, unemployment, and insecurity" (Helena Norberg-Dodge).

80. **Self-reliant local communities** recognize the debate between mitigation and adaptation has been amplified by the UN IPCC report that is warning that little more than a decade remains before it will be impossible to prevent "irreversible" damage to the climate. **Job One for Humanity** is supporting both. They say we have to do what we can to mitigate to minimize global warming impacts *and begin preparing for adaptation (localization) to ensure that humanity avoids extinction in the coming decades. They say both are urgent!* Adaptation assumes that we have created change in our institutions, practices, and policies. In other words, we have done everything we can to end business as usual, that is, *not* preserving the present world!

81. **Self-reliant local communities recognize** that a primary goal of both adaptation and mitigation for the changes that are coming will need to include the creation of healthy, sustainable local economies. Effective adaptation or mitigation efforts would need to be based on building and supporting local communities and their cooperative interdependence networks. *"Well-being"* and *low-impact sustainable living* **would have to replace** *"profit."* Without the taming, evolution, and maturation of their collective primitive ego-consciousness, self-reliant local communities would eventually regress to our current aggressive

and competitive business-as-usual economic system. The local community's ability to embrace cooperation would weaken, resulting in the likely extinction of both the community and the individuals in the community. Stated simply, avoiding the extinction of humanity will depend on humanity's ability to tame their collective primitive ego-consciousness and create resilient, cooperative communities that place *all* of its members' well-being as their primary goal.

82. **Self-reliant local communities will require purchasing land *away* from cities.** Enough acreage to support a community of people that might want to join your community. A localization *community* would be necessary to build a base of skills and knowledge large enough to be successful long term. *The future will not be what it used to be. **Going it alone will not be an option** when climate change begins to collapse the social structures that support human civilization as we know it. **You will need people of all ages and backgrounds and experience to be successful.***

83. **Localization preparation:** Begin now to obtain the long-term survival gear, tools, and equipment that will be needed. (The local hardware stores may no longer be available.) For example, wood stoves for heating and cooking, good hand saws for gathering wood (fossil fuels for chain saws and wood splitting equipment may not be available to power modern tools), axe's, matches, batteries, a well for water (hand-pumped, or solar pumped, but not grid electric pumps), good wood availability on or near the property, animals for food (chickens, pigs, goats for milk and meat, turkeys, horses and/or mules, including how to butcher and feed those animals, composting systems large enough for all of the gardens, fruit trees, bees for honey and pollination, solar panels, wind generators, food preparation and storage (cold cellars), rain collection systems for irrigation water, firearms for hunting and community protection from desperate people who failed to prepare— these are just *some* of the systems and equipment that will be needed.

Preparing your community for long-term survival will take the better part of 10 years, so waiting to start is not an option!

And there are two more critical preparations that will also be required to ensure your community's long-term survivability (a) the intentional taming, evolution, maturing, and awakening of your collective childhood primitive ego-conditioning, and (b) letting go of your collective adult conditioning of capitalism's myth and belief that happiness, well-being, and life purpose are achieved only through the acquisition of unlimited growth, expansion, consumption, and the need to have *"more"* .....the life-long adult conditioning embedded in neoliberal global capitalism that taught *"more"* is required for success, well-being, and happiness.

84. **Self-reliant local communities versus false hope and the death of true hope.** False hope blinds us to reality and the real *possibilities* that just might save our future from the likely extinction of humanity. Things are already not OK. And they are getting worse rapidly. The future is *not* going to be OK. Grounding "hope" in Tinker Bell thinking is a form of intentional ignorance and insanity. False hope leads us away from the present, away from where we are right now, and toward some Tinker Bell imaginary future. Giving up false hope means you cease relying on someone or something else to solve your problems, and you just begin doing whatever it takes to solve those problems yourself. True hope is always grounded in reality.

I will close this section of the book with the following quote on hope. It is one of the better quotes I've read on the "the death of false hope" and a great way to close the book. I believe Derrick Jensen wrote it on his *Orion* magazine column called "Upping the Stakes," but I'm not positive. (Sorry, Mr. Jensen, if I misquoted you. However, it's a great quote if you want to claim it.)

"You come to realize that when "hope" died, the "you" who died with the hope was not "you," but was the you who depended on those who exploit you, the you who believed that those who exploited

you would somehow stop on their own, the you who believed in the mythologies propagated by those who exploit you in order to facilitate that exploitation.

The socially constructed you died.

The civilized you died.

The manufactured, fabricated, stamped, molded you died.

The victim died!!!!"

And who is left when that "you" dies?

The "you" who thinks not what the culture taught you to think but what **"you" think!**

The you who feels not what the culture taught you to feel but what **"you" feel.**

The you who is not who the culture taught you to be, but who **you are**.

The you who can say yes, the you who can say no.

The you who is a part of the land where you live.

The you who will fight (or not) to defend your family.

The you who will fight (or not) to defend those you love…to defend the land upon which your life and the lives of those you love depends.

When you give up on false Tinker Bell hope you have taken the first step toward being really alive. You are no longer vulnerable to those who would exploit you. You begin to actually "see" the world you live in. The exploiter/victim relationship is broken. When you give up on false hope, you turn away from fear.

And when you quit relying on false hope, and instead begin to protect the people, things, and places you love, you become very dangerous indeed to those in power…and that's a very good thing."

A Summary of My Thoughts on Hope and the Importance of Self-Reliant Local Communities for Our Future

- **Behind every thought** is a conscious or unconscious mental belief, assumption, expectation, prejudice, certainty, a core value, illusion, fantasy, habit, or bias.

- **When we distort or deny reality,** it makes us weak, sad, powerless, unhappy, stressed, anxious, helpless, overwhelmed, angry, aggressive, and depressed.

- **When we feel weak**, we tend to be self-absorbed, narcissistic, and tend to move even deeper into our reality-distorting beliefs.

- **In other words,** rather than questioning our beliefs, we harden them and move deeper into our false self and away from our true, essential, authentic self. We become rigid and inflexible and *lose our ability to be compassionate, flexible, middlepath, integral, civil, just, affirming, loving, and caring.*

- **We become obsessively "we" focused,** the essential ingredient required to create greed.

- **"What's in it for me?" greed and the need to be "right"** are the two most dangerous beliefs of our collective primitive ego human consciousness.

- **They create aggressive ideological tribalism that vilifies others**, and effectively destroys the ability to manifest compassion, kindness, "we-ness," cooperation, compromise, and middlepath thinking. *These two aspects of primitive ego thinking are the most dangerous threats to the long-term creation of successful self-reliant local communities.*

- **Embracing the concepts of wholeness requires non-duality, middlepath thinking**, and the ability to embrace all of reality: the pain, the suffering, the joy, the grace, and resisting the temptation to dualistically align with only one side or aspect of reality.

- **The dark night for humanity is coming. Simplify.** Simplify your life. See where your garden is. See what is real. Get prepared. See what is truly important in life. Get real about things that will stretch who you are.

- **Embrace the truths that are coming.** Economic collapse, debt crisis, political gridlock, global instability, environmental challenges, excess consumption, and the inevitable energy crisis are only a sample of what is coming because we have disassociated so severely from reality.

- **We have denied the dark side of reality.** We have obsessively been grasping for only the positive side of reality. We have attempted to deny and avoid the wisdom of the dark side of reality. Unless we begin to embrace and acknowledge both sides of reality, we will not react appropriately until we are in the midst of crisis.

- **We need to begin transforming and preparing our lives** *now* to survive what our scientists and our instincts are telling us is coming. Unfortunately, the future is not *coming,* it is already here. We are destroying trees, creating massive species loss, global hunger, global economic crisis, population growth, warming our oceans, melting our polar ice cap—the list is almost endless.

- **We are in the painful process of having attempted to live into only the positive side of reality.** Because we lacked a clear vision of what we wanted as a species, we tried to ignore the negative side of what we were creating. We attempted to ignore the reality that both sides of reality are real. Both sides need to be included in our thinking and our actions. We need to begin intentionally embracing that obvious reality.

- **If we continue to make ourselves unconscious through dualistic either/or thinking, we will continue on the path to crisis**. Our human future is threatened because of our unconscious denial of the dark side of evolution. We are now in the middle of the crisis—and the consequences will deepen and continue to unfold. We are now recognizing that we have to awaken and pay attention to what we have created.

- **And the sooner we embrace that reality and begin creating self-reliant local communities,** the greater our resilience will be to survive the growing dark side of reality; the side of reality that *we* have created…and attempted to ignore and deny. The side of reality that will threaten the future survival of humanity on this planet.

- **The most important and critical short-term actions we can undertake are** (a) taming the collective primitive ego-consciousness of humanity and its early childhood conditioning and (b) creating as many sustainable and self-reliant local communities as possible before economic, social, and civil collapse become unavoidable realities. No other actions will have as much short-term positive impact on our future as a species and the sustainability of our planet.

Chapter 11

Summary of Book and Concluding Thoughts

The Dark Side of Reality:
We Are Standing on the Edge of the Cliff

The force-multipliers that threaten our future include:

1. The lack of systemic thinking.

2. The lack of understanding regarding the dangers embedded in **exponential growth**.

3. **Unlimited growth** on a limited planet.

4. Unregulated neoliberal global capitalism.

5. The need for degrowth and a reduction in consumerism.

6. **Powering down** from fossil carbon energy.

7. The growing **climate crisis** and climate change/intensification.

8. The unwillingness in human culture to **embrace change.**

9. The insane growth in personal and governmental **global debt.**

10. The impact of underfunded pensions.

11. Continued population growth.

12. Wealth inequality.

13. The reality of reoccurring **pandemic threats.**

These thirteen fragile structures are all powerful force-multipliers and economic triggers that threaten humanity's self-destruction, as they increasingly interact systemically to exert a dangerous and rapidly growing pressure on the critical and vulnerable fracture points supporting human civilization. If ignored, I am convinced that they are all force multipliers that *will* collectively create the inevitable social and civil collapse of human civilization; a collapse that will happen in years, not decades; a collapse that could lead to the likely extinction of our human species.

If the coronavirus is showing us anything, it's that when preparation is inadequate, unforeseen factors can quickly crush a fragile and vulnerable market, the global economy, and most importantly, the global working class and families that are already struggling to survive financially. I fear that this coronavirus pandemic has the potential to threaten the economic stability of global capitalism and human civilization, or worse.

The questions I pose for humanity in this book are clear.

a. Do we ignore the warnings and take another step forward and continue business as usual?

b. Or do we turn around and begin the process of preparing for the resilience we will need?

A preparation that includes powering down from fossil energy, embracing intentional simplification, reducing consumption, and taming the immature collective childhood primitive ego-consciousness of humanity and its immature early childhood conditioning.

As of the writing of this book, the future does not look promising. There seems to be little social or political will to address the rapidly growing climate crisis, or any of the other twelve fragile foundations that support human civilization; *and waiting is no longer an option.* The time for choice is here. The time for action is *now.* We are at the "Y" in the road. Which fork in the road will we take? Will we choose action and step forward? Or will we choose "business as usual"? Or will we simply turn around and go home in defeat and wait for the end-times? We will know the answers to those questions in the next few years. Perhaps sooner.

When we focus on the *root causes* of global warming, climate change, capitalism, and the other force-multipliers/threats that existentially threaten our future, we will be intentionally facing an extremely challenging and uncomfortable reality: The sobering recognition that our primitive ego-consciousness resists and fears change. And that is especially true when it comes to changing our existing cherished beliefs and assumptions on how things "are" and "should be." In Part 1, we learned how the primitive ego's obsessive need to be "right" is one of the most influential and most destructive beliefs embedded in humanity's collective consciousness.

The black swan force multiplier challenges/threats and economic triggers we explored in Part 2 are *symptoms* that humanity created using the collective untamed immature primitive ego-consciousness and its immature and unevolved childhood beliefs, illusions, delusions, and assumptions.

We are clearly the problem!

We are an invasive, immature species on our planet that has accepted the insane belief that *unlimited* growth and *unlimited* economic expansion on a *limited* planet is even possible.

We are not a viable species.

Ignoring a reality as evident as this is best described as an *intentional, species-wide, collective embrace of ignorance*. Given the severity of the force-multiplier threats and economic triggers we have created, waiting to intentionally tame and mature the collective primitive ego-consciousness of humanity is not an option. We have run out of time. The world clock is now only seconds away from midnight.

One is not an alarmist when the facts are alarming.

Only Preparation Before a Crisis Will Create Hope and the Resilience Required to Survive.

Those who prepare for the changes and challenges that are coming by creating small, local, self-reliant "seed" communities; communities built on an evolved and awakened consciousness that intentionally embraces a tamed primitive ego, and its awakened, matured, self-aware, evolved, adult level of human thinking; will significantly increase the odds that they *might* survive to rebuild a new and more sustainable human civilization.

Preparation before a crisis is how we best create a sense of realistic hope. And we are running out of time to make the transition from unlimited, business-as-usual to long-term survival.

"Rugged individualists" who attempt to go-it-alone in the future that is coming, will *not* survive. Survival *will* require the efforts and consciousness of a well-prepared, self-aware, self-reliant, sustainable, awakened, and intentionally tamed primitive-ego "community" of people.

Wrapping Up The Three-Year Project Called "Writing This Book"

First: I did not write this book to convince the reader that the planet is warming or that warming has been created by humanity's burning of carbon-rich fossil fuels. As I said, those realities are already well established by scientific facts and evidence.

Second: Those who have been paying attention already know we are facing an existential crisis. Those who believe climate change is not real are trapped inside a dangerous subjective "opinion" based on cognitive dissonance or confirmation bias and are simply not paying attention to the facts. The untamed primitive ego uses this cognitive dissonance thinking to deny or distort reality and make it conform to its cherished beliefs. It's a process called intentional ignorance. We explored cognitive dissonance in Part 2.

Third: I wrote this book as a training manual on preparing for social and civil collapse and the massive changes that are coming. In Part

3, we looked at creating self-reliant, sustainable local communities that have the potential to become "seed" communities to rebuild human civilization for future generations. They offer what I believe is a realistic hope for a future that is not going to be, or look like, what it used to be.

As I began the writing, I looked for some quotes that would capture the essence of the book, and I settled on the words of three of humanity's better-known prophets. It was Mark Twain who said, *"It ain't what you don't know that gets you into trouble. It's what you know for sure that just ain't so."*

The denial of climate change and the fact that global warming is the result of humans burning fossil fuels are "denial beliefs" held by many, but those Tinker Bell denial beliefs are simply not supported by climate scientists and scientific facts…in other words, *"they just ain't so."*

The collective immature primitive ego-consciousness of humanity fears "change," so it aggressively ignores the reality of "change."

The second quote is from Alvin Toffler, who said, *"The illiterate of the 21st century will not be those who cannot read and write, but those who cannot learn, unlearn and relearn."*

Letting go of our cherished beliefs is a challenge for our immature primitive ego-consciousness.

And the final quote that captures the moment we find ourselves in: *"In times of change 'learners' inherit the earth, while the 'learned' find themselves beautifully equipped to deal with a world that no longer exists"* (Eric Hoffer).

As we discussed in the book, the collective primitive ego of human consciousness and its obsessive need to be *"right"* make letting go of what we *"know for sure"* very difficult. It makes unlearning and relearning an almost impossible challenge. And it has a significant percentage of humans on this planet unprepared for the future that's coming but well equipped to live in a world that is likely to cease to exist in their lifetime.

Intentionally awakening and taming our immature primitive ego-consciousness, and its early childhood conditioning to become more self-aware, is one of the most important collective tasks humanity needs to undertake, *and it needs to begin now!*

Fourth: I did not write this book as a novel or a Ph.D. thesis on the importance of climate change. I wrote it as a training manual on preparing for the massive changes coming and how to create self-reliant local communities for long-term survival.

Only through (a) the awakening, evolving, and taming of our collective primitive ego of humanity, and (b) intentional preparation for the massive changes that are coming, will we successfully create the resilience that will be needed to effectively cope with a future that won't be what it used to be. And waiting to begin that preparation is not an option.

This is especially true for the younger generations that will need the information contained in this book:

a. To improve the probability of their survival.

b. To support themselves as they struggle to redefine what it means to live a meaningful and dramatically simplified life of well-being inside a self-reliant, sustainable "local community" that will become their "family."

The COVID-19 pandemic is offering the world a powerful and essential preview of how quickly social collapse can happen, and how quickly social collapse can compromise the ability for individuals, communities, and nations to survive when collapse descends on those who have not prepared.

The massive changes created by the social collapse that's coming will require a level of resilience that only preparation can offer. COVID-19 is teaching us a critically important lesson on just how quickly social collapse can happen. We need to pay attention and begin now to prepare for the inevitable changes of Part 2 that are coming. Changes, not unlike COVID-19, that *will* threaten social collapse and the possible extinction of our species on this planet.

Fifth: I did not write this book to avoid the social collapse of human culture. As we explored in Part 2, I see no realistic way humanity can avoid social collapse. Collapse is inevitable. The foundations of human culture and human civilization are vulnerable to each of the force-multipliers and economic triggers covered in Part 2. Each of them individually has the ability and potential to create massive social collapse in the near future. Because they are systemically interconnected, interdependent, and self-reinforcing, a total cascading systemic collapse is all but inevitable. When that systemic collapse happens, the social collapse of human culture and human civilization as we know it *will* follow. Those working *now* to improve their ability to survive when that social collapse happens are already taking the need for preparation "*now*" seriously.

The stories and ideas in this book are thanks to the efforts of those in previous generations who wrote to pass on their wisdom and knowledge so we might learn and pass down some of that knowledge to future generations. This book is my attempt to embrace that concept. The younger generations will need all the wisdom, help, and support we as elders can offer them.

Sixth: I believe the two force-multipliers in part 2 that are most likely to lead to the creation of social collapse are:

a. Our collective primitive ego's inability to understand the power of **systemic thinking** and its potential to create social collapse. As we discussed in Chapter 1, our immature primitive ego-consciousness and its childhood conditioning believes that "*it*" is a "self" that's separate from everything else in the universe. As we discussed in Part 2, everything in the universe is interdependent and interconnected with *everything* else in the universe. When we change *anything*, that change is systemically connected to other things, and often in ways we don't realize. When we ignore that simple reality, we are in danger of creating existentially dangerous changes that threaten our very existence on this planet in ways we don't understand or realize. Until we learn to embrace systemic thinking, our immature primitive ego can be very narcissistically self-focused. And that self-focus can be very dangerous when we fail to see the larger long-term consequences of our short-term actions, decisions, choices, and behaviors.

b. The second force-multiplier in Part 2 most likely to lead to the creation of social collapse is our immature primitive ego's inability to understand the existential dangers embedded in the concept of **unlimited exponential growth.** This inability played a significant role in our failure to deal effectively with the COVID-19 pandemic. Our scientists tried to explain and teach us about **exponential growth** and its importance in fighting an epidemic, but most people did not fully comprehend its destructive power. That remains true even today as I write these words.

Here again I refer the ancient wisdom story for readers about the dangers embedded in the concept of **exponential growth** and the dangers embedded in growth that simply doubles over time. I offered this teaching story earlier in the book about a huge "stadium" where the ancients gathered for festivals. One of the ancients was bound to a seat at the top of the stadium. Then a magic water dropper put one drop of water on the floor of the stadium. A minute later, it put two drops of water on the floor. At minute three, it put four drops of water. At minute four, it put eight drops. At minute five, it put 16 drops. This process continued to exponentially double the number of drops each minute. At minute 45, the stadium was still 97% free of water. The man at the top of the stadium drowned at minute 50. If you use a hand calculator to multiply 1 by 2, 2 by 2, 4 by 2, 8 by 2, 16 by 2, and so on, most small calculators can't do this accurately past about the twentieth time you multiply by 2.

Seventh: I Don't Have a Crystal Ball. I do not have a crystal ball, so I can't predict "when" social collapse will begin, but I see no realistic way to avoid a social collapse that does not include dangerous and fatal Tinker Bell thinking. The primary focus of this book has been a focus on the big picture of inevitable social collapse, not its timing. The primary focus of the book has been on:

a. How we can identify and then tame or evolve our collective primitive ego human consciousness in Part 1.

b. Exploring how our collective childhood primitive ego human consciousness has created the dangerous force-multiplier threats in Part 2.

c. How we can work together to create the self-reliant, sustainable, local "seed" communities for long-term survival that we explored in Part 3—the local communities we *will* need to survive the massive changes and inevitable social collapse that the existential force-multipliers/threats and economic triggers in Part 2 *will* create.

d. Modern human civilization was created by energy-dense fossil fuels, and our entire global economy is based on that energy-dense fossil fuel. Climate scientists are warning us that we have to stop burning fossil fuels, and we have to accomplish this net-zero carbon powering down in less than twenty to thirty years. We have to begin achieving significant reductions in carbon emissions in the next five to ten years. Given how dependent our human culture and our global economy are on fossil energy, I see no realistic way this powering down from carbon energy can be accomplished without collapsing human civilization as we know it. Capitalism is based on growth and profit, and when growth and profit end, capitalism as an economic system dies. And as of this writing, I see no social or political will to address the problem. Fossil fuel consumption is continuing to increase.

e. Unless we embrace massive preparation for the changes coming, the existential force multiplier threats or economic triggers will individually or collectively create social and civil collapse. Their destructive impact on critically needed social structures *will* rapidly create a level of social panic, desperation, and anger that *will* lead to massive social collapse and the end life as we know it, and if we fail to prepare for that collapse, the possible extinction of the human species on our planet.

I know that I am offering a view of the future that is dark and hard to fathom or embrace and I know for some readers the initial response to the book's concepts will be to shake your head and mutter something about unrealistic or too fatalistic. Some will liken me to a bearded profit standing on the street corner with a sign that reads "Doom: Repent," or something of that nature. My only response is *one is not an alarmist when the threats are truly alarming.*

I encourage all my readers to check the science facts. They *are* alarming! Do not rely on media "spin," intentional denial, or deliberate unwillingness to embrace the actual severity of the crises coming because of the fear that it would "destabilize our economy." Remember the fundamental rule of capitalism: "*Money rules. Period!* Until it *doesn't!* When money flow ends, capitalism dies very quickly.

I do not have a crystal ball, but I have held to the values of honesty and the intention to name the immoral injustices and abuses of power that have put our planet and the future generations of children and grandchildren in peril by condemning them to live in a world in the future that no one of this generation would want to live in…all in the name of business-as-usual, collective greed, and our blind pursuit of personal power, profit, and unlimited wealth.

What if? Having read the book, I encourage you to ask a simple question: *What if?* What if I'm wrong? Have you wasted your time reading this book?

Three years of research have convinced me we are indeed headed for a dark future. But I *don't* have a crystal ball! I *could* be wrong. But even if I am wrong, what do you stand to lose if you assume I *might* be right? You would be living your life in a community focused on well-being and self-reliance. Or to ask the question another way, are you prepared to embrace the consequences if you dismiss the ideas in the book, and it turns out I *was* right? Remember Mark Twain's quote, "*It ain't what you know for sure that will create problems in your life, it's what you know for sure…that just ain't so.*"

Eighth: We Are Standing at a Fork in the Road and Both Paths Forward Are Dark! Our human civilization is facing an existential crisis, but our leaders are repeatedly demonstrating their inability to respond. The question is, why? I believe it's because the primary and secondary black swan force-multiplier challenges/threats, economic triggers, and existential threats that include climate crisis threats, the collapse of capitalism, the end of fossil energy, and intentional simplification of daily life *are all so massive and disruptive* that any *realistic* solutions our politicians might come up with, or recommend, would likely lead to a social panic that could collapse the already fragile social structures of human civilization.

Politicians may be susceptible to greed, but they are not dumb.

They know global capitalism embraces unlimited growth and profit, or it dies.

They know capitalism and the global economy were not only created by energy-dense fossil energy but are powered by energy-dense fossil energy.

They know the lack of social will to address the climate crisis and power down from carbon energy means they cannot advocate for the changes required to power down from fossil energy or deal with the existential force-multiplier threats of Part 2. To do so would very quickly end their political career, so they are unwilling to speak the truth. Telling the truth would end fossil energy, end capitalism, and it would kill the golden goose and its golden eggs of unregulated neoliberal global capitalism and unlimited fossil energy, the very systems that are making the privileged and those in power very, very wealthy. I resisted adding more "very's."

The only way we will embrace the radical changes that are needed to effectively reverse the course human civilization is currently headed toward; a future headed toward crisis and collapse; will be when we have massive global social movements that *demand* the existential changes scientists have been telling us for decades are critically needed. Until that happens, business as usual will continue. And we will continue to walk toward possible extinction.

Ninth: We need to remind ourselves that the future is a choice, not a given. We are at a fork in the road. We can choose to take the path of action or choose the path of no action. But we need to remind ourselves that neither way will guarantee that we avoid the social and civil collapse of human civilization as we know it. But the path of action *might* help some of our younger generation to survive. That is the hope that drove me to write this book.

We need to encourage and support the younger generations as they take on the challenge of building the sustainable, self-reliant local communities of Chapter 10; the local, self-reliant communities they will need to transition from unlimited growth to that of long-term survival. The younger generations will need wisdom, skills, and farming tools, and know how to preserve food, how to smoke, salt, or dry food, how to acquire blacksmithing knowledge and skills, how to build and use a cold cellar, and how to create energy-rich compost so they can efficiently grow the food they will need. Their future isn't what *our* future looked like when we were their age. And they *will* need our help, our support, and our encouragement.

Because (a) there will be very little social or political will to embrace the massive changes that are coming or (b) very little social or political will to support the creation of sustainable local communities, the younger generations will need all the encouragement, wisdom, bravery, strength, and support (both physically and emotionally) we can offer them. They, too, will be accused of doomsday thinking. They also will be ridiculed. People will tell them they are wasting their time. There will be times as they look at the "normal" world around them—a world that appears to be doing just fine, a world that is just hum-de-dumming along—that they will ask themselves, "Am I crazy? Am I dooms daying the future? Nobody else seems to be concerned."

Preparation for resilience in a world that doesn't see the future that's coming can indeed appear "radical and extreme." Those are the times the younger generations will need our support and encouragement to continue preparing for a future that isn't going to be or look like what it used to be or what it used to look like. Our support will be an acknowledgment that we, too,

400

are aware that we are leaving them a very unsustainable world, and a future that will *"not"* be what it used *to* be.

Tenth: A final Warning and Word of Caution The immature, unevolved, untamed primitive ego-consciousness of humanity and its unconscious early childhood conditioning has been defining and creating our human civilization for thousands of years. That immature, unevolved, primitive thinking process has created the world and the existential force-multiplier threats and economic triggers that are currently threatening the future of our human species. We need to acknowledge the reality that primitive ego thinking is not going to go away overnight. It's tenacious. It is firmly embedded in the collective consciousness of humanity. Without an *intentional* taming of our collective primitive ego-consciousness, our immature, unevolved primitive ego thinking will continue to influence our human consciousness and the immature decisions we make for generations. The sobering reality is the recognition that we will not survive as a species if that immature, unevolved thinking continues to reflect humanity's collective consciousness.

If the local communities discussed in Chapter 10 are to be successful and avoid returning to the current greed-based economic systems and the immature thinking of the past, they will need to intentionally teach the concepts of a tamed, evolved, awakened primitive ego consciousness to their children. And that evolution and maturing of their consciousness will need to begin in kindergarten; continue in all levels of their education; and stay awakened in human culture for the rest of their lives to become the bedrock of human thought and decision-making in the future.

Failure to embrace that kind of *intentional* evolution in their thinking process will significantly increase the danger of local communities returning to the dangerous consciousness of the unevolved greed-based "What's in it for me?" primitive ego consciousness that has been so historically and deeply embedded in the consciousness of humanity; the immature childhood conditioning and primitive ego thinking that humanity is using to devour and consume our planet in its quest for unlimited growth and profit.

And Most Importantly, Decisions Made Today Will Define Our Future for Centuries

Unfortunately, we are currently stuck between the impossible and the unthinkable. There is little social or political will to address the existential force multiplier threats of Part 2 that we have created as a species. Those in power are focused on never-ending growth and wealth accumulation, and most people either don't care or feel powerless to change things.

Many believe some kind of Tinker Bell technology will somehow come to the rescue and save us from the massive existential changes that are coming. In the meantime, we feel powerless to change the "system" called business-as-usual that is destroying our planet and our future. So we passively embrace the Tinker Bell drug called "hope" and wait for *something* or *somebody* to stop the coming disaster. *We need to let "hope" die and begin to take action.* We need to roll up our sleeves, start doing whatever it takes, and do whatever we *can* to change the system. Waiting is no longer an option. We need to prepare *now* for the massive changes that *are* coming if we want to create the resilience we will need to survive when those changes arrive.

I am convinced that the best and perhaps the *only* viable option we have is beginning *now* to create self-reliant, sustainable, local communities. To come together in local, place-based communities and segue from profit and unlimited growth to smaller-scale, less energy-intensive, more localized, self-reliant communities that focus on food growing, knowledge sharing, inclusiveness, cooperation, and consensus decision making.

We need to learn from the wisdom embedded in indigenous cultures, past and present, the understanding that living sustainability with nature and the natural world is not only possible, it is the only viable way we will survive the future that is coming. Many of history's indigenous cultures succumbed to the allure of capitalism and the myth of "more" not because there was a flaw in their culture they wanted to abandon. The psychological pressure of capitalism and "progress" and capitalism's sense of shame and inadequacy if one is not "successful" is like an addictive drug to the untamed primitive ego. We need to avoid that fate.

As humanity struggles to survive the future that's coming, it will be critically important for those living in a self-reliant local community to *intentionally* tame their collective primitive ego consciousness to maintain coherence, survive long-term, and become viable *seed* communities for the future of human civilization.

The primary golden arch or goal of this book is helping the younger generations understand the *fundamentally critical* and *necessary* need and importance of *intentionally* taming their collective primitive ego-consciousness and its early childhood conditioning for the long-term survival of their self-reliant local community.

Preparation *now* for that future is critical.

It's our collective responsibility to respond and participate in the creation of our collective future. When the disruptive impacts of the coming changes have arrived and changed life as we know it, our failure to act cannot be blamed on someone else. Blaming others won't hold water when it's *we* who have failed to step up to our responsibility and accept the challenge to join the human movement to prepare. *Claiming we didn't know* will not be an acceptable excuse for denying the overwhelming facts, data, and observable reality. Our lack of resilience will be its own reward.

We are the only evolved species on our planet with the ability to imagine, anticipate, or create its future. I am hopeful that we have the collective wisdom and courage to embrace that ability. Because we can only create what we can imagine, it's time to collectively imagine what a *sustainable* and *just* world might look like...and then roll up our collective sleeves and get to work creating that future.

Giving in to despair and hopelessness is not an option. We have to hang onto hope and begin working for the future and the quality of life we want to create for ourselves and future generations. This is our world. We can participate in actively creating its future, or we can sit passively, wringing our hands, waiting for the changes that are coming to impact our lives, the lives of our children, our grandchildren, and future generations. Like it or not, this is the only choice and decision the future is offering us.

I believe we are wise enough to embrace reality and work together collectively to change the future we have unconsciously created. Embracing and nurturing our imagination is our species greatest strength. Collectively we can create any reality we can imagine.

Lack of imagination will be our greatest failure.

I believe humanity's future on our planet will depend on the long-term success and viability of the self-reliant local "seed" communities discussed in this book. I see no other realistic or viable path forward for the long-term survival of humanity. I choose to avoid "Tinker Bell" false hope. I choose to look at reality and think about the long-term consequences of the choices we could, or need, to make today. I prefer to base my "hope" on facts and scientific evidence that verifies my "hopeful" premise.

Every choice we make or fail to make will create a consequence or outcome.

Every choice we make or fail to make will create incredibly significant outcomes for humanity's future.

And being unprepared for those consequences will make them far worse if we fail to prepare for them as best we can, *now.*

I am convinced that the two unavoidable realities that will define our future are:

a. The inevitability of social and civil collapse created by panic and economic instability that will be created by the existential force-multiplier threats of Part 2: the climate crisis, storm intensification, powering down from fossil energy, massive global debt, and the collapse of neoliberal global capitalism.

b. The need to create "seed" localization communities if humanity is to survive and avoid the suffering that will result when the massive changes that are coming inevitably arrive…far sooner than most people believe possible, or will be prepared to survive.

As I was wrapping the book up for publication, I read this Facebook quote from Daniel James Morrell and thought it was a good quote on which to end the book.

> *Why is it that everyone I meet, that expects a pending societal collapse, is focused on weapons? Do you have seeds? Do you have tools? Do you know how to filter water? Where are your crafters? Who can blacksmith, work leather, sew, do carpentry? Who knows medicine, herb lore, and can identify edible plants? We won't survive a collapse by killing each other. We will only survive with benevolent skilled communities working together. Get with it.*

– Daniel James Morrell

Thank You for Reading This Book

Please pass it on to someone in the younger generation and encourage *them* to read it. And if they accept the challenge to create a self-reliant local community, do all you can to support them financially, emotionally, and socially. They *will* need your support.

If you join or create a local self-reliant community, and it turns out I am wrong about the assumptions I have made in this book, you will get to reconnect with the land and live in a supportive community that embraces life as a journey toward increased security and well-being. If I am right about the assumptions I have made in this book, being part of a self-reliant local community could save your life, the lives of those you care about, and the lives of countless future generations, perhaps even the future of humanity and human civilization.

If you are uncertain about the assumptions I have made throughout this book, I strongly encourage you to do your own research. Get informed. Pay attention. If you do, you will likely tell me I significantly understated the urgency to begin preparing *now* for the existential force-multiplier threats, challenges, and changes that are coming.

The fundamental rule of life embraced in this book's writing is the concept that we have to *know* what we're talking about. Facts matter. Data matters. Science matters. And most importantly, truth matters. And we have to come to the table of dialogue and consensus-making with evidence. We all have to distinguish between knowledge and speculation, knowledge and wishful thinking, true knowledge and subjective personal beliefs/assumptions. And always keep in mind, *"It's not what you're certain about that will cause you harm, it's what you are certain about…that just ain't so."* (Mark Twain)

Walking the path between complacency, doubt, and denial, and the all but certain likelihood of extinction will be a severe challenge for us if most of those around us continue to ignore the existential challenges and threats that are coming. I recognize that I am being redundant but trust your instincts. Stay awake. And most importantly, *pay attention.* Keep focused on the big picture and connect the dots. And when in doubt, prepare for what your instincts are telling you. Resilience requires preparation. Most people won't prepare until it's too late.

When in doubt, remember:

- Waiting is not an option.
- Resilience requires preparation *before* the crisis
- The transition from unlimited growth to long-term survival needs to begin *now.* The day is coming. You will be thankful that you *did.*
- Pay attention to the world around you. Don't be unaware. The primary support of preparation is the ability to pay attention. The warning signs are always present and visible if you learn to pay attention to them.
- And always remember. Change is how the universe functions. It does not mean change is a crisis. Change is always going to be present; it's just called life! The key is paying attention to the changes that are coming and then preparing for those changes. Humans have been

dealing with change for tens of thousands of years. It's not an imposition designed to ruin *your* life. When you're prepared, *it's just called life.*

The energy of my hopes, dreams, and support for you will always be with you as you do the challenging work of creating a sustainable, self-reliant, local human civilization.

Your success will be your legacy in human history. Our future is in your hands.

Be well, dream big, and in the words of humanity's best-known futurist, "Live long and prosper." The future of humanity is counting on you.

I hope this book is helpful as you create your future.

BIBLIOGRAPHY

Chapter 1: Primitive Ego

- Book: Adult Spiritual Development: The Creation of an Authentic Spirituality for the 21st Century: The Journey from Unconscious Primitive Ego to a Spiritually Awakened Adult Consciousness, Dick Rauscher, Second Edition 2014, (www.amazon.com)
- Book: Primitive Ego Psychology for Life Coaches & Therapists: Taming the Primitive Ego—The Journey Toward Middlepath Thinking and Growth in Self-Awareness, Dick Rauscher, 2016, (www.amazon.com)

Chapter 2: Taming the Primitive Ego

- Book: Adult Spiritual Development: The Creation of an Authentic Spirituality for the 21st Century: The Journey from Unconscious Primitive Ego to a Spiritually Awakened Adult Consciousness, Dick Rauscher, Second Edition 2014, (www.amazon.com)
- Book: Primitive Ego Psychology for Life Coaches & Therapists: Taming the Primitive Ego—The Journey Toward Middlepath Thinking and Growth in Self-Awareness, Dick Rauscher, 2016, (www.amazon.com)

Chapter 3: Capitalism

- Book: Local is our Future, Steps to an Economics of Happiness, Helena Norberg-Hodge, Local Futures, 2019 (www.localfutures.org)

- Article: Worker Self-Directed Enterprises: The Cure for Capitalism, Kevin Gustafson, resilience.org, 3/12/2020

- Article: We Need to Talk About Catastrophic Global Risk, David Korowicz, resilience.org, 3/5 2020

- Article: The End of the Corporation, Marjorie Kelly, Resilience.org, 3/3/2020

- Article: Market Got Its Excuse to Crash, Daniel J. McLaughlin, 3/18/2020

- Article: Access to Land Plus a Participation Income Could Change the World, Samuel Alexander, resilience.org, 3/4/2020

- Article: The Promise of Ecological Economics, Aaron Karp, resilience.org, 3/3/2020

- Article: Here's what could really sink the global economy: $19 trillion in risky corporate debt, CNN, 3/14/2020

- Article: At our current pace it'll take 80 years to repair all the structurally deficient bridges in the US, a report finds, CNN, 3/14/2020

- Article: The Delusion of Boundless Economic Growth, Ian Christie, resilience.org, 10/15/2019

- Article: Catabolism: Capitalism's Frightening Future, Craig Collins, relisience.org, 12/3/2019

- Article: The Limits of Capitalism, Laurie Adkin, resilience.org, 1/14/2020

- Article: Capitalism: A Self Organizing Structure That Leads to Self Extinction, Norton Smith, resilience.org, 1/7/2020

- Article: Economic Globalization, Local Futures, https://www.localfutures.org/learn-take-action/learning-guides/learn-about-globalization, 1/3/2020

"Globalization is an economic process centered on deregulating trade and finance in order to enable businesses and banks to operate globally,

leading to the emergence of a single world market dominated by transnational companies. It is a continuation of the process of conquest and colonialism that began 500 years ago, when European powers spread an extractive economic system—one reliant on slavery, the destruction of local cultures and economies, and the imposition of monocultural ideas and practices—all across the world."

a. a) transnational corporations are unaccountable to voters or the governments.

b. b) transnational corporations displace local businesses and jobs.

c. c) transnational corporations have one focus, and that is profit. The ecological consequences of their decisions are irrelevant.

d. d) transnational corporations encourage countries to rely on imported goods to meet basic needs.

e. e) transnational corporations increase wealth inequality.

f. f) transnational corporations erode rural economies and create massive population shifts from rural areas to cities and put food security at risk worldwide. (Economic Globalization, Local Futures, https://www.localfutures.org/learn-take-action/learning-guides/learn-about-globalization/"

(I encourage readers to use localfutures.org to self-educate on the importance of local community. We take an in-depth look at creating sustainable and self-reliant local communities in Part 3.)

- Article: The Corruption of Capitalism by Guy Standing: Review, by Brian Davey, 11/20/2017

- Article: Climate Change and Capitalism: A Political Marxist View, Simon Mair, resilience.org, 5/15 2019

- Article: Human Predators, Human Prey; Human Predators, Human Prey Part 2; and Human Predators, Human Prey Part 3, Richard

Heinberg, resilience.org, 8/29/2018, 4/19/2019 (Humanity = Super-predators, Society as Ecosystem)

- Article: Dare to Declare Capitalism Dead—Before It Takes Us All Down With It, George Monbiot, 5/10/2019 ("The economic system is incompatible with the survival of life on Earth. It is time to design a new one. Capitalism is broken. It is like a gun pointed at the heart of the planet.")

- Article: Scientists Warn the UN of Capitalism's Imminent Demise, Nafeez Ahmet, resilience.org, 5/4/2019

- Article: The Race of Our Lives Revisited, Jeremy Grantham, 4/26/2013

- Article: Why and How Capitalism Needs to Be Reformed, Ray Dalio, April 5, 2019

- Article: The "Disintegration" of Global Capitalism Could Unleash World War 3, Warns Top EU Economist, Nafeez Ahmed, resilience.org, 2/26/2019

- Article: The Way of Exploitation—Can We Do Better? Rob Dietz, resilience.org, 9/3/2018

- Article: Growing Apart: A Political History of American Inequality, Colin Gordon, inequality.org, 3/14/2018

- Article: The Unacceptable Collateral Damage of Overconsumption, Daniel Christian Wahl

- Article: Reordering the Anthropocene, Matt Hern, resilience.org, 5/24/2018

- Article: COVID-19 and the Death of Market Fundamentalism, Paul Gilding, resilience.org, 4/17/2020

- Podcast: "The 10,000 Mile Cod and Insane Global Trade," by Crazy Town. Well worth the time to listen to this excellent podcast (https://www.postcarbon.org/crazytown) (As you listen to this podcast think about the force-multipliers/threats and economic triggers in this book, and their potential impact on supply chain disruptions)

- Article: The Black Death Killed Feudalism. What Does COVID-19 Mean for Capitalism? John Feffer, Resilience.Org, 5/15/2020

- Article: Averting Apocalypse, Daniel Pinchbeck, resilience.org, 8/23/2017, (https://www.resilience.org/stories/2017-08-23/averting-apocalypse/)

- Article:Tomgram: Nomi Prins, A Rendezvous with Destiny? TomDispatch, 5/28/2020 (A world of staggering inequality that the present coronaviral crash has left in ruins; the haunting has just begun.)

- Article: COVID-19: Neoliberalism Is not Going Down without a Fight, Daniel Vargas-Gomez, relilience.org, 5/27/2020

- Article: How We Broke the World, Thomas L. Friedman, May 2020

- Article: What Indigenous Wisdom Can Teach Us About Economics, Helena Norberg-Hodge, resilience.org, 9/9/2020

- *Article: Replacing rentier capitalism is one of the defining challenges of our age, Christine Berry, resilience.org, 11/9/2020

- *Article: Einstein's Take on Capitalism, Socialism, and a New Kind of Business, Eduardo Sasso, resilience.org, 11/3/2020

- Article: Money, Gods, and Taboos: Re-sacralizing the Commons, Ugo Bardi, resilience.org, 10/13/2020

- Growthism: Its Ecological, Economic and Ethical Limits, Herman Daly, resilience.org, 3/28/2019

Chapter 4: Climate Change / Global Warming

- Article: What will it REALLY take for our governments to end the global warning-caused extinction emergency? Job One For Humanity, 2020 (Telling people a painful and difficult truth is not an act of scaring them. It is an act of informing them of reality, so as adults, they can make better choices for their remaining options.)

- Article: Rising Tides, Troubled Waters: The Future of Our Ocean, Jeff Goodell, Rolling Stone, 4/3/2020 (Because we live on land, we often think of the climate crisis as a terrestrial event. But as the planet heats up, it's what happens in the ocean that will have the biggest impact on our future.)

- Article: US Megadrought 'already under way', Matt McGrath (Environment Correspondent), BBC News

- Article: The Parched West Is Heading into a Global Warming-Fueled Megadrought That Could Last for Centuries, Bob Berwyn, Insideclimate News, April 16, 2020

- Article: A Megadrought Has Started in the United States That Will Have Disastrous Global Consequences, Job One for Humanity, April 18, 2020

- Article: Q&A: Could Climate Change and Biodiversity Loss Raise the Risk of Pandemics? www.carbonbrief.org/Q-and-A

- Article/Book: Climate and Ecological Delusions and Contradictions That Will Rapidly End Humanity…Unless…Delusions and Contradictions. cloudfront.net

- Article: Tomgram: Naomi Oreskes, Why Science Failed to Stop Climate Change, TomDispatch, 11/12/2019

- Article: Don't Call Me a Pessimist on Climate Change. I am a Realist, William E. Rees, resilience.org, 11/13/2019

- Article: Atmospheric Rivers Fuel Most Flood Damage in the U.S. West. Climate Change Will Make Them Worse, Bob Berwyn, InsideClimate News, 12/5/2019

- Article: As Climate Change Worsens, A Cascade of Tipping Points Looms, Fred Pearce, Yale E360, 12/6/2019

- Article: What will it REALLY take for the governments of the world to end our global warming-caused extinction emergency? Job One for Humanity, 2/28/2020

- Article: The Climate Has Changed Before. But This Is Different—Look at the Archeological Record, Peter B. Campbell, 11/9/2017, www.theguardian.com/us

- Article: Averting Apocalypse, Daniel Pinchbeck, resilience.org, 8/23/2017, (https://www.resilience.org/stories/2017-08-23/averting-apocalypse/)

- Article: Why the "Anthropocene" Is Not "Climate Change," Julia Adeney Thomas, resilience.org, 2/28/2019

- Article: What We Should Really Do for the Climate, Samuel Miller McDonald, resilience.org, 3/20/2019

- Article: The Climate Emergency Continuum: from Bad to Cataclysmic, Jonathon Porritt, resilience.org, 6/7/2019

- Article: What Would It Mean to Deeply Accept That We're in Planetary Crisis? Dahr Jamail, resilience.org, 6/4/2019

- Article: Cheerleaders for Doom, Albert Bates, resilience.org, 2/4/2019 (Review of David Wallace Wells book The Uninhabitable Earth: Life After Warming)

- Article: The Reality of Climate Change: Jody Tishmack, resilience.org

- Article: A Postmortem for Survival: on Science, Failure and Action on Climate Change, Julia Steinberger, resilience.org, 4/26/2019

- Article: Climate Crisis Forces Us to Ask: To What Do We Devote Ourselves? Dahr Jamail, resilience.org, 5/19/2019

- Article: Climate Change Puts U.S. Economy and Lives at Risk, and Costs Are Rising, Federal Agencies Warn, Bob Berwyn, InsideClimate News, Nov 23, 2018

- Article: The Big Picture, Richard Heinberg, resilience.org, 12/17/2018

- Book: This Changes Everything, Naomi Klein

- Article: What Makes 2025 the most dangerous global warming fossil fuel reduction deadline that we must not miss? Lawrence Wollershein, Job One For Humanity, 5/30/2019

- Article: Dancing with Grief, Dahr Jamail, resilience.org, 7/15/19 ("When you are in doubt, be still, and wait; when doubt no longer exists for you, then go forward with courage." Chief White Eagle)

- Article: Job One Part 1: Get Yourself, Family and Business Prepared for More and Bigger Global Warming Disasters, Job One for Humanity

- Article: The Four Most Critical Global Warming Deadlines and Tipping Points We Must NEVER Forget or, We Go Extinct, Lawrence Wollershein, Job One for Humanity, 4/23/2019

- Article: Why Global Warming is now irreversible or at least 50 more years and what this means to your future (Localization is realistic future/sustainable culture), Job One for Humanity, 9/28/2018

- Article: Take Unprecedented Action or Bear the Consequences, David Spratt, resilience.org, 8/22/2018 ("Less emphasis on climate models and more on scenario planning," Hans Joachim Schellnhuber, Potsdam Institute for Climate Impact Research)

- Article: The 20 Worst Consequences of Global Warming, Job One for Humanity, 8/3/2018

- Article: Global Warming Is Now Irreversible, Job One for Humanity

- (https://www.joboneforhumanity.org/global_warming_is_now_irreversible)

- Article: Shell Knew Fossil Fuels Created Climate Change Risks Back in 1980s, Internal Documents Show, John H. Cushman Jr., InsideClimateNews, April 5, 2018

- Article: Of Warnings and their ripple effects, Albert Bates, resilience.org, 11/12/2019 (Good material re: list of systemic impacts of global warming)

- Article: Why the New "Adapt to Global Warming Extinction" Slogan for 2020, Lawrence Wollersheim, Job One for Humanity, 1/10/2020 (Excellent links to other articles on Job One for Humanity website.)

- Article: What Are the Seven Greatest Global Adaptive Challenges Facing Millennials, Younger Generations, and Humanity as a Whole? David Pike, Job One for Humanity, 10/1/2018 (Good Material for Climate Change)

- Article: Our Last Chance, 2015 Global Fossil Fuel Reduction Targets for Individuals, Businesses and Nations, Job One for Humanity, 9/20/2019

- Article: Analysis: Why Scientists Think 100% of Global Warming is Due to Humans, Zeke Hausfather,

- Article: Impact of Warming Seas Felt by Northeastern Fisheries, David Pike, 2/26/20018

- Article: Today's Fossil Fuel Infrastructure Already Locks in 1.5 Degrees C Warming, Study Warns, InsideClimate News, 7/3/2019

- Article: Global Warming Is Pushing Arctic Toward 'Unprecedented Sate,' Research Shows, Bob Berwyn, InsideClimate News, 4/8/2019

- Article: IPCC: Radical Energy Transformation Needed to Avoid 1.5 Degrees Global Warming, Bob Berwyn, InsideClimate News, 10/8/2018

- Article: These Are the Toughest Emissions to Cut, and a Big Chunk of the Climate Problem, InsideClimate News, 6/28/2018 (Without improvements in shipping, cement and steel, major sources of greenhouse gas pollution will be locked in for generations, new research shows)

- Article: Welcome to the End of the 'Human Climate Niche,' David Wallace-Wells, 5/19/2020

- Article: What are the Most Critical Global Challenges Facing Generations Z,Y, and X?, Job One for Humanity, Lawrence Wollersheim, May 26, 2020

- Article: Cascading Apocalypses Now Coming, Part 2, Behind the COVID-19 Pandemic, Job One for Humanity, Posted by Lawrence Wollersheim, May 26, 2020 (Human survival means that far fewer of us must take far, far, far less from our Real Mother, Mother Earth)

- Article: Tomgram: Nomi Prins, A Rendezvous with Destiny? TomDispatch, 5/28/2020 (A world of staggering inequality that the present coronaviral crash has left in ruins, the haunting has just begun.)

- Article: New Study Shows Global Warming Intensifying Extreme Rainstorms over North America, Bob Berwyn, InsideClimate New, 6/2/2020

- Article: It Will Get Darker Before the Dawn, Paul Gilding, resilience. org, June 2020

- Article: At this rate, it's going to take nearly 400 years to transform the energy system, James Temple, 3/14/2018 (https://www.technologyreview.com/2018/03/14/67154/at-this-rate-its-going-to-take-nearly-400-years-to-transform-the-energy-system/)

- Article: Estimates of Present and Future Flood Risk in the Conterminous United States. (Environmental Research Letters), (https://www.researchgate.net/publication/323500717_Estimates_of_present_and_future_flood_risk_in_the_conterminous_United_States)

- Book: The Great Work: Our Way into the Future, Thomas Berry, 12/13//15

- Article: The Climate Cliff does not occur in 2025. We already went over it in 2015, Job One for Humanity8/14/2020

Chapter 6: Debt

- Article: Great Reset Update: $50 Trillion Debt Coming, John Mauldin, September 26, 2020

- Article: A debt reckoning is unavoidable- will activists seize the moment?, Aaron Karp, 10/29/20

- *Article: We Need to End Growth Dependency, but How?, Mark Burton,

Chapter 7: Powering Down

- Article: Oil Majors Face up to Plunging Asset Values, Financial Times, 7/4/2020

- Article: Manifesto for the Future, Sam J. Knights, Resislience.org, 1/26/2020

- Article: A simple way to understand what's happening… and what to do. Richard Heinberg, resilience.org, 10/21/2020

- Article: Has Oil peaked? Richard Heinberg, resilience.org, 10/10/2020

- Article: The Fracking Industry is Hurting. Its Future Should Be an Election Issue, Andrew Nikiforuk, resilience.org, 10/19/2020

   (Powering Down Statistic/Energy: A single barrel of oil, costing roughly $40 in today's market, contains energy that's equivalent to roughly five years of hard physical work.)

- Article: The Fracking Industry is Hurting. Its Future Should Be an Election Issue, Andrew Nikiforuk, resilience.org, 10/19/2020

- Article: Has Oil Peaked?, Richard Heinberg, resilience.org, 10/10/2020

- Article: A Simple Way to understand what's happening….and what to do, Richard Heinberg, resilience.org, 10/21/2020

Chapter 8: Degrowth and Simplicity

- Article: Unlearning: From Degrowth to Decolonization, Jamie Tyberg, Rosa Luxemburg Stiftung, New York Office, 2020 (Degrowth is more than a critique of the current growth society, but a full-fledged alternative to it. In short, degrowth tells us to care for the earth's systems, to care for the people, and to redistribute any surpluses back to the land and the people.)

- Article: The Limits of Renewable Energy and the Case for Degrowth, Philippe Gauthier, resistance.org,

- Article: Unlearning: From Degrowth to Decolonization, Jamie Tyberg

- Article: Pandemic Response Requires Post-Growth Economic Thinking, Richard Heinberg, resilience.org, 4/14/20

- Article: How to Get Off Fossil Fuels Quickly—and Fairly, Robert Jensen, resilience.org, 6/29/20

- Article: Life in a "degrowth" economy, and why you might actually enjoy it, Samuel Alexander, Local Futures, 5/18, 2017

- Article: The Case for Degrowth: Review, Brian Davey, resilience.org, 9/23/2020

Chapter 9: Systemic Thinking, Secondary Force Multipliers

- Article: Global Boom, Pandemic, Crash: Is History Just Repeating Itself? Andrew Nikiforuk, resilience.org, 5/2020

- Article: Pandemics: A Story of Life Versus Growth, Julia Steinberger, resilience.org, 5/5/2020

- Article: How Does Pandemic Change the Big Picture? Richard Heinberg, resilience.org, 3/31/2020

- Article: Pandemic Response Requires Post-Growth Economic Thinking, Richard Heinberg, resilience.org, 4/14/2020

- Article: Sleepwalking Is a Death Sentence for Humanity, John Foran, (https://www.resilience.org/stories/2017-10-02/sleepwalking-is-a-death-sentence-for-humanity/)

- Article: Look and See; Listen and Hear: Wendell Berry and the Contradictions of our Climate, Erik Lindberg resilience.org, 7/23/18 (Based on Berry's book The Unsettling of America; Culture and Agriculture—one of most important books I've ever read.)

- Article: Systems Thinking, Critical Thinking, and Personal Resilience, Richard Heinberg, Resilience.org, 5/25/18

- Article: After Juneteenth, a reminder that millions of African Americans have NO access to affordable health care or quality education. MarketWatch, 7/22/2020

- Article: How our future will be controlled or destroyed over the next 10-20 years by these 13 critical global challenges! Lawrence Wollersheim, Job One for Humanity, 7/21/20

- Article: Modern Civilization and Its People Without Spirit, Victor M. Toledo, resilience.org, 11/9/2020

- Article: We're Dumb About Exponential Growth. That's Proving Lethal, Andrew Nikiforuk, resilience.org, 8/14/2020

Part 3: Localization

- Article: Pandemics: A Story of Life Versus Growth, Julia Steinberger, resilience.org, 5/5/2020

- Article: Unlearning: From Degrowth to Decolonization, Jamie Tyberg, Rosa Luxemburg Stiftung, New York Office, 2020 (Degrowth is more than a critique of the current growth society, but a full-fledged alternative to it. In short, degrowth tells us to care for the earth's systems, to care for the people, and to redistribute any surpluses back to the land and the people.)

- Article: Our Conversation with a Coronavirus, Kurt Cobb, resilience. org, 6/29/2020

- Article: The Search for a New Community, John McLeod, resilience. org, 4/19/2020 (An excellent article on the importance of a collective tamed primitive ego consciousness.)

- Excellent website on Local Community. (https://www.localfutures.org)

- The Transitions Handbook (https://www.amazon.com/dp/B00ENOIM5O/ref=dp-kindle-redirect?_encoding=UTF8&btkr=1)

- Local Is Our Future: Steps to an Economics of Happiness, by Helena Norberg-Hodge,

- Ancient Futures: Learning from Ladakh, by Helena Norberg-Hodge.

- Post-Growth Localisation, by Helena Norberg-Hodge and Rupert Read. (https://www.localfutures.org/wp-content/uploads/Post-growth-Localisation.pdf)

- Localization: Essential Steps to an Economics of Happiness, Helena Norberg-Hodge, (https://www.localfutures.org/learn-take-action/learning-guides/learn-about-globalization/)

- Article: The Unraveling of America, Wade Davis, 8/6/2020 (https://www.rollingstone.com/politics/political-commentary/COVID-19-end-of-american-era-wade-davis-1038206/)

- Article: Disaster Localization: A Constructive Response to Climate Chaos, Kristen Steele, resilience.org, 10/31/2019

- Article: The Age of Collapse, Umair Haque, resilience.org, 8/8/19

- Article: The Pressure to Modernize, The Helena Norberg-Hodge, local futures, 12/9/19 (Excellent material re: threats to localization by capitalism and consumerism that have conditioned our thinking)

- Article: Love in Action: A Force for Social Justice, Sophia Parker, resilience.org, 12/6/2019

- • Article: Hope and Fellowship, Derrick Jensen (his *Orion* magazine column is called "Upping the Stakes")

- • See Derrick Jensen articles on hope. https://orionmagazine.org/article/beyond-hope/

- • Article: 2018-06-2020, SHN#299: Insights from the Wilderness, "What If"…the Two Most Important Words of Our Time, Dick Rauscher Nuggets

- • Article: The Patterning Instinct: A Cultural History of Humanity's Search for Meaning, Jeremy Lent

- • Article: What Indigenous Wisdom Can Teach Us about Economics, by Helena Norberg-Hodge, resilience.org, 9/11/2020

- • Article: Localization: A Strategic Alternative to Globalized Authoritarianism, Helena Norberg-Hodge, Local Futures, 11/10/2020

- • Article: Caring and Thriving: The Social Security Engendered by Commoning, David Bollier, resilience.org, 10/20/2020

Conclusion

- Article: Fareed: The Pandemic Should Be a Great Equalizer. It Isn't. October 16, 2020

  Covid-19 "is ushering in the greatest rise in economic inequality in decades, both globally and in the United States." The World Bank estimates 100 million people will fall back into extreme poverty worldwide. In the US, between 6 and 8 million have been pushed into poverty, by one estimate—and while the top 25% of earners has largely recovered, the bottom 25% "has cratered." Still, Congress can't agree on another economic relief package.

- Article: Manifesto for the Future, Sam J. Knights, Resislience.org, 1/26/2020

- Article: What If? There was a daily imagination lesson?, Rob Hopkins, resilience.org, 11/13/2020

- *Article: Preparing for the end of the world as we know it, resilience.org, 9/1/2020

- Article: Who is "we"?, Robert Jensen, resilience.org, 10/13/2020

- *Article: Manifesto for the Future, Sam J. Knights, resilience.org, 1/26/2020

- Article: The Unraveling of America, Wade Davis, Rolling Stone, 8/8/2020

- Article: The Five People Shaping My Worldview, John Mauldin, Mauldin Economics, 2018

- Article: Four Reasons Civilization Won't Decline: It Will Collapse, Craig Collins, resilience.org, 8/1/2020

ADDENDUM 1:

*PRIMITIVE EGO: A SUMMARY OF BELIEFS
AND BEHAVIORS OF THE PRIMITIVE EGO*

1) The Primitive Ego Uses Black-and-White Thinking

- To keep the world safe and manageable, the primitive ego splits the world into right and wrong and believes that it is right, and it alone possesses "the truth" on all matters.

- The only outcome possible from this primitive way of thinking is the creation of categories of "otherness" and conflict.

- Generosity is possible, but only when it is in the interest of the primitive ego achieving more power and control.

- Sustained intimacy and vulnerability are not possible for the primitive ego.

- The primitive ego is comfortable only when others are in total agreement with its beliefs and opinions.

- Criticism is not allowed, and groupthink is mandatory.

- Anyone who disagrees with a primitive ego is immediately labeled as them, enemy, wrong, perverted, or evil.

- The primitive ego often hides its aggression, violence, and judgment under a veneer of moral righteousness.

- It is unable to perceive complexities, accept diversity, deal with ambiguity, or embrace inclusiveness. The primitive ego sees the world in either/or terms.

- The primitive ego tends to think in black-and-white, always/never terms that lead to extreme over-generalizations or labeling of both self and others.

- Its primary goal is to be right.

- Driven to be "right" rather than "wrong," the primitive ego tends to strive for perfection. This belief leads to exhaustion, depression, despair, self-criticism, and hopelessness. Since perfection and failure are mental illusions and not real, the primitive ego tends to have low self-esteem.

- The primitive ego is always a victim.

2) The Goal of the Primitive Ego Is Survival: A Survival-of-the-Fittest Thinking Process

- The primary focus of the primitive ego is safety and survival, not seeking truth, not seeking peace, not seeking cooperation, not seeking compassion.

- The primary thinking process of the primitive thinking process is known as vertical power or survival of the fittest (an early evolutionary imperative for the human species).

- The power and control that come with vertical power thinking are the primitive ego's primary goal.

- When overwhelmed, the primitive ego will often run away and hide in a safe place, such as a bedroom or basement. The way to run away psychologically is by disassociation, avoidance, repression, and denial.

3) The Primitive Ego Is Unable to Own Its Own Feelings

- The primitive ego is unable to own its own feelings.

- The primitive ego believes that all happiness and unhappiness comes from the world.

- This belief leads to projection and blaming others for whatever it's feeling, the desire for revenge, and the inability to forgive.

- The primitive ego uses thoughts to create feelings and emotions

- The primitive ego has very little ability to disconnect feelings from thoughts and very little ability to perceive the relativity of one's feelings and beliefs.

- The primitive ego uses frozen, stuck, distorted thoughts and beliefs from childhood to create its feeling responses to the environment.

- Assumptions, jumping to conclusions, and mind reading are three primary generators of primitive ego feelings.

- All feelings are assumed to be factual reality. "I feel. Therefore, it's true."

- All conflict is personalized. Anyone who disagrees with the primitive ego is labeled as stupid or ignorant, and all difference of opinion is considered a personal attack.

4) The Primitive Ego Is the Narcissistic Center of the Universe

- The primitive ego believes that it is the center of the universe, and it takes everything personally.

- This belief leads to high levels of defensive reactivity.

- This belief results in very low empathy and compassion for others. In psychological language, this is known as narcissism.

- The primitive ego is defensively reactive to criticism or any perceived threat to its many narcissistic beliefs, opinions, or assumptions.

- The primitive ego wants what it wants.....now!

- The primitive ego is very impatient. It gets angry when its narcissistic needs and wants are not immediately satisfied. It has virtually no ability to see the long-range picture, develop long-range goals, or delay gratification.

- The primitive ego is narcissistically always right. Therefore, it is emotionally impulsive and thinks concretely. Responses tend to be simple, concrete, unconscious emotional knee-jerk responses to outside stimuli.

- The primitive ego uses magical thinking and grandiosity. Magical thinking often drives the narcissism of the primitive ego. "I should get what I want, because I want it." Or, "If others really loved me, they would know what I want and need without my having to ask."

- The primitive ego is very concerned with what others think about it.

- The primitive ego is very concerned with the greedy acquisition of money, prestige, and worldly possessions. In Buddhist terms, this is called attachment.

- The pathological narcissism of the primitive ego leads to cut off and poor differentiation. There is very little ability to separate me from not me.

- The primitive ego has very little ability to tolerate or affirm the autonomy of another person and still remain a differentiated self.

- The primitive ego does not understand or have the ability for reciprocity, empathy, or mutuality (the ability to actively listen and appropriately respond to the cognitive and affective world of another and assume that others have the same rights to get their needs met as we do).

- The narcissism of the primitive ego leads to strong feelings of entitlement and the need to always be in the spotlight, getting the attention of others.

- The narcissism of the primitive ego does not allow for sustained intimacy or mutuality with others, that is, the differentiation of self in relationships.

- The "reasonable, coherent wholeness" assumed by other developmental theorists is not sustainable by the primitive ego when under stress.

5) The Primitive Ego of the Inner Child Is Stuck in the Past and Unable to Embrace Change

- Since the primitive ego is about eight years old and is the operating system of the unconscious inner-child, it sees the world through the eyes of the child it once was. It passionately resists change in order to keep things safe and protect its power, control, possessions, beliefs, and self-identity.

- The primary tools to accomplish these goals are called *bent-nickel* beliefs and survival skills.

- Change is experienced as a form of death to the primitive ego. Homeostasis is safety.

6) The Primitive Ego Believes Its "Self" to be a Totally Separate and Unique Being

- The primitive ego ("me") insists that it is a separate being. One object out of a universe filled with objects. This belief makes cooperation and teamwork virtually impossible for the primitive ego to either understand or achieve.

- The primitive ego does not experience itself as a systemic part of a living, conscious universe.

- This leads to loneliness and a deep sense of disconnection from the world and others.

- The primitive ego can only think alone; it is not capable of the creative process of collective thought.

7) The Primitive Ego Is Only Capable of a Conditional Love That Always Loves Based on a "Because"

- The primitive ego is unable to love unconditionally. It always loves conditionally, based on a "because" or internal belief.

- The primitive ego can love only if it is not threatened by the loss of items 1 to 6 above.

- When items 1 to 6 above are threatened or challenged, the primitive ego becomes defensive and aggressive; emotionally angry, judgmental, critical, blaming, or shaming.

8) The Primitive Ego Is Taught to Be Respectful, Submissive, and Obedient to Authority

- The child is trained to be obedient during the culturalization process, which teaches children that they are the property of their parents. When they are "bad" and disobey the rules of the powerful parents, they expect to be punished.

- Most children do not understand the concept that all choices will result in an outcome or consequence that is only helpful or unhelpful. A common survival skill of the primitive ego is oppositional behavior.

SUMMARY

The primitive ego can appear to have the same abilities and consciousness as the adult "observing ego," but it is unable to sustain the matured ego responses and abilities of the observing ego when it is emotionally challenged. Because of this, very few people manifest the ability to sustain Piaget's formal operational stage of cognitive development under emotional stress. The world has very few enlightened spiritual mystics and virtually no enlightened politicians.

The evolution of human consciousness from the primitive ego of early childhood to higher levels of an enlightened adult consciousness is the most imperative human challenge of the twenty-first century.

* *

Addendum 2: Aspects
of Primitive Ego Thinking Presented as a List

Our resistance to evolve our thinking keeps us blind to the changes that need to be made.

We are the problem. We need to tame and evolve the immature and dangerous primitive ego childhood thinking and conditioning that created the force-multiplier threats of Part 2.

We are the problem, because of aspects of unconscious unevolved early childhood primitive ego thinking that systemically reinforce and support each other.

Primitive ego early childhood conditioning:

a. "What's in it for me?" **greed.**

b. Need to be **right** (aggressive arrogance, extreme cognitive dissonance/confirmation bias).

c. Inability to replace *me* thinking with *we* thinking (compassion, mutuality, cooperation).

d. I want what I want when I want it.

e. **Blaming** others for *our* feelings (inability to own our own feelings).

f. Ignorance regarding the **danger of exponential growth** (e.g., COVID-19).

g. A lack of interconnected, interdependent **systemic thinking**.

h. Survival-of-the-fittest thinking.

i. Black versus white, **zero-sum thinking** ("You can't have that, it's mine!").

j. An exaggerated aggressive narcissistic self-focused sense of **entitlement**.

k. An inability to connect short-term choices with long-term consequences.

l. The fear of change (uncertainty, not knowing).

m. The unending, obsessive desired for **more.**

n. The need for power "over" rather than power "with."

o. The inability to embrace long-term thinking.

p. A lack of interconnected, interdependent **systemic thinking.**